Daily
Guideposts, 1997

A
JANET
THOMA
BOOK

THOMAS NELSON PUBLISHERS
Nashville • Atlanta • London • Vancouver

Published in Nashville, Tennessee, by Thomas Nelson, Inc., and distributed in Canada by Word Communications, Ltd., Richmond, British Columbia, and in the United Kingdom by Word (UK), Ltd., Milton Keynes, England.

ACKNOWLEDGMENTS

All Scripture quotations, unless otherwise noted, are from *The King James Version of the Bible.*

Scripture quotations marked (NIV) are from the *Holy Bible, New International Version.* Copyright © 1973, 1978, 1984 International Bible Society. Used by permission of Zondervan Bible Publishers.

Scripture quotations marked (RSV) are from the *Revised Standard Version of the Bible.* Copyright © 1946, 1952, 1971 by the Division of Christian Education of the National Council of Churches of Christ in the U.S.A. and are used by permission.

Scripture quotations marked (NAS) are from the *New American Standard Bible,* © 1960, 1962, 1963, 1968, 1971, 1972, 1973, 1975, 1977 by The Lockman Foundation. Used by permission.

Scripture quotations marked (TLB) are from *The Living Bible,* © 1971. Used by permission of Tyndale House Publishers, Inc., Wheaton, IL 60189. All rights reserved.

"Love Is . . ." series was written by Elizabeth Sherrill.

"Letters to Wally" series was written by Mary Lou Carney.

"Closer to the Cross" series was written by Marilyn Morgan Helleberg.

"Jehovah Jireh: God Will Provide" series was written by Carol Kuykendall.

"The Candles of Christmas" series was written by Eric Fellman.

"Barter" excerpt by Sara Teasdale, reprinted with the permission of Simon & Schuster from *THE COLLECTED POEMS OF SARA TEASDALE* (New York: Macmillan, 1937).

"I Will Not Hurry" by Ralph Spaulding Cushman is from *I Have a Stewardship,* by Abingdon Press, © 1939. Used by kind permission of Elizabeth Stiles.

"Thank you . . ." excerpt by Michel Quoist from *Prayers.* Reprinted by permission of Sheed & Ward, Kansas City, MO 64111.

Designed by Holly Johnson
Artwork by Ron Bucalo
Indexed by Patricia Woodruff
Typeset by Com Com, an RR Donnelley & Sons Company
Printed in the United States of America

ISBN 0-7852-7558-4

3 4 5 6 — 00 99 98 97 96

Table of Contents

Introduction   5

JANUARY   7
    Love Is . . .   8
    Words of Wonder   18
    Everyday Wonders   32

FEBRUARY   35
    Love Is . . .   36
    Letters to Wally   37
    Words of Wonder   48
    Everyday Wonders   60

MARCH   63
    Love Is . . .   64
    Words of Wonder   75
    Closer to the Cross   82
    Everyday Wonders   92

APRIL   95
    Love Is . . .   96
    Words of Wonder   108
    Everyday Wonders   120

MAY   123
    Love Is . . .   124
    Words of Wonder   134
    Everyday Wonders   148

JUNE   151
    Love Is . . .   152
    Words of Wonder   164
    Everyday Wonders   176

TABLE OF CONTENTS

JULY 179
 Love Is . . . 180
 Words of Wonder 191
 Everyday Wonders 204

AUGUST 207
 Love Is . . . 208
 Words of Wonder 221
 Everyday Wonders 234

SEPTEMBER 237
 Love Is . . . 238
 Jehovah Jireh: God Will Provide 243
 Words of Wonder 251
 Everyday Wonders 264

OCTOBER 267
 Love Is . . . 268
 Words of Wonder 279
 Everyday Wonders 292

NOVEMBER 295
 Love Is . . . 296
 Words of Wonder 308
 The Candles of Christmas 320
 Everyday Wonders 322

DECEMBER 325
 Love Is . . . 326
 Words of Wonder 338
 Everyday Wonders 352

Fellowship Corner (Authors) 355

Authors, Titles and Subjects Index 373

Introduction

The dictionary defines a "wonder" as "a cause of astonishment or admiration; a miracle." Sometimes God astonishes us by acting with unmistakable power, as He did in the life of ancient Israel or in the early days of the church. But more often, God shows Himself to us in little things, in the situations and relationships that make up the fabric of our everyday lives. Through a friend, a spouse, a child or grandchild, a colleague at work, an acquaintance at church or a stranger with a word of encouragement, God amazes us with a glimpse of His loving presence.

Since it began, *Daily Guideposts* has combined Scripture, prayer and first-person stories to help readers recognize the wonderful presence of God in their own lives. So it's fitting that the theme in this our twenty-first volume is "The Wonder of God's Love." We've asked our *Daily Guideposts* family to share the many, sometimes mysterious and hidden ways that God's love has surrounded and sustained them in their life's journey.

Every month, in "Love Is . . . ," Elizabeth Sherrill will introduce you to the remarkable people who have taught her the meaning of Paul's great hymn to love in I Corinthians 13. During Holy Week, join Marilyn Morgan Helleberg as she follows Jesus through the streets of Jerusalem in search of healing and draws "Closer to the Cross." At Advent and Christmastime, Eric Fellman illumines the holidays with the wonderful light of "The Candles of Christmas." In February, Mary Lou Carney, editor of *Guideposts for Kids,* finds her own life transformed as she answers the letters that come in to the popular "Dear Wally, I've Got This Problem . . ." column. In September, journey to Mount Moriah with Carol Kuykendall as her faith is tested by her daughter's illness in "Jehovah Jireh." And throughout the year, Marion Bond West shares the transforming peace that God's love brought to her mother's struggle with cancer.

Among our forty-six contributors are many other old and precious friends, including Fred Bauer, Marjorie Holmes, Oscar Greene, Ruth Stafford Peale and Arthur Gordon. And, as in every year's *Daily Guideposts,* some new voices are on hand to join in our chorus of praise: Kjerstin Easton, a student spending a year in Germany; Mark Collins, a young father from Pittsburgh, Pennsylvania; Roberta

Rogers, a wife, mother and amateur radio enthusiast; Karen Barber, a contributing editor of *Guideposts* magazine; Julia Attaway, a wife and new mother from Brooklyn, New York; and her husband Andrew, the new *Daily Guideposts* editor at Guideposts Books.

But "new" this year is not confined to our writers; *Daily Guideposts* has crossed the frontier into cyberspace. If you have a computer and access to the Internet, you can visit our Guideposts site on the World Wide Web at http://www.guideposts.org. There you will find each day's devotional and our Fellowship Corner, as well as selections from our books and magazines: *Guideposts, Angels on Earth, Guideposts for Kids* and *Positive Living.* And you'll have instant access to the spiritual heart of our work at Guideposts, Prayer Fellowship, where we join together in petition, thanksgiving and intercession for the daily needs of all the members of our Guideposts family.

So welcome to *Daily Guideposts, 1997.* Whether you've let us walk with you many times before or you're a new friend, we hope that *Daily Guideposts, 1997* will help you to experience the wonder of God's love in all the joys and sorrows, all the busy days and quiet times of the coming year. —*The Editors*

*Blessed be the Lord God, the God
of Israel, who only doeth wondrous things.* —PSALM 72:18

January

S	M	T	W	T	F	S
			1	2	3	4
5	6	7	8	9	10	11
12	13	14	15	16	17	18
19	20	21	22	23	24	25
26	27	28	29	30	31	

LOVE IS . . .

When Elizabeth (Tib) Sherrill's nephew Doug and his fiancée were plan-
ning their wedding, they asked her to read from the Bible. The passage
Doug and Anna had chosen was St. Paul's magnificent ode to love in
I Corinthians. "Love is patient. Love is kind. . . . Love . . . keeps no record
of wrongs." Why, *Tib thought,* more than a picture of human affection, this is a description of the way God loves. This is how Jesus
loved. *"Love is never selfish." "Love bears all things."*

   I Corinthians 13 gives us a portrait of divine love, and every time we
see one of these qualities in a human being, we are seeing a bit more of God.
Family, friends, people we work with—they come into every life, these men
and women who mirror the love of God. Throughout the year, we'd like
you to meet some of those who've come into Tib's life; in reading her en-
counters you may be able to find the moments of divine love in your own.
Record your "Everyday Wonders" on the diary pages of each month.

                                                                    —The Editors

1

WED

[Love] keeps no record of wrongs.
                              —I Corinthians 13:5 (NIV)

Her name was synonymous with forgiveness. Corrie ten Boom, imprisoned in a German concentration camp for aiding Jews during the
Nazi occupation of Holland, returned after the war with a message
of God's love. "Jesus' death writes 'Paid in Full' to our sins," she told
her former enemies. "And His heavenly Father throws away the list."

   "How hard that must have been!" I said to her as my husband and
I sat before the cheery coal fire in her home. "To forgive those who've
harmed you."

   "It was very hard," Corrie agreed. "But there's something still
harder—forgiving those you thought were your friends."

   Clearly glad to unburden herself to visitors who didn't know the
people involved, she plunged into the story of a group who'd spon-
sored a speaking tour, then kept the offerings intended for her work.

   "Later they did release part of it. But it wasn't a quarter of what they took. I can show you!" She went to a drawer and, stooping down, drew out a folder of papers. "I have it all down in black and white!"

She straightened slowly, a stricken look on her face. "O Lord Jesus," she whispered so softly we could barely hear, "when You've canceled all my debt and thrown the list away. . . ."

And for the next few minutes, the three of us fed a pile of papers into the fire.

God of love, let me carry no burden of the past year—no hurt, no bitterness, no unforgiveness—into the year that begins today.
—Elizabeth Sherrill

2
THU
And, lo, I am with you always, even unto the end of the world. . . . —Matthew 28:20

"Time to put away all the Christmas decorations," I told my husband Roland. "How about giving me a hand?"

The tree went into the car trunk to be taken to the recycling lot where it would be shredded into mulch. Wreaths, strings of lights, baubles and a fat snowman made of cotton were packed into boxes. So were the carved camels, sheep and donkeys. And the crèche.

I hesitated at the figure of the baby Jesus. It didn't seem right for Him to be stuck beneath the eaves with all the rest of the holiday paraphernalia. *Besides, a brand-new year is facing us,* I thought. *It will probably contain as many trials as the preceding ones. War, strife, disease, crime and cruelty seem to go on forever. Where's the Lord in all this mess?*

I stood there thinking for a while. Then I put the Babe back on the mantel.

Roland came back down from the attic for another load of decorations. "Haven't you finished packing up the manger?" he asked.

"I think we'll just leave it out this year," I answered. "Sometimes the world seems out of control and Christmas seems very far away. When it does, we can look at the mantel and remember that God is with us and that He'll make good on His promise of peace."

Lord, give me the faith to see Your presence in the signs of the times, all year round. —Isabel Wolseley

3
FRI

As commissioned by God, in the sight of God we speak in
Christ.   —II Corinthians 2:17 (RSV)

Growing up in a Presbyterian minister's household, I often saw my
father reading from his Bible with its blue leather cover. Early on, I
learned that he'd selected a "life's verse"—one that he especially re-
lied on and tried to live by. It was Philippians 4:13: "I can do all
things through Christ which strengtheneth me." In time I chose my
own life's verse, Proverbs 4:18 (RSV): "But the path of the righteous
is like the light of dawn, which shines brighter and brighter until full
day."

Then one January morning in 1980, I found what I called my
"commission verse" in Isaiah 50:4 (RSV): "The Lord God has given
me the tongue of those who are taught, that I may know how to sustain with a word him that is weary." When I read it, I knew I had
found my particular place in God's work.

I've since had the privilege of being a "word encourager." Last
spring, just after my friend's husband took his life, she cried to me
in anguish, "I lost. I fought so hard for him and he gave up."

The sustaining word, the one that restored her confidence and
hope, tumbled from my lips: "You didn't lose, you won. You gave
him eleven years—years that he would not have had if you hadn't
tried so hard."

A life's verse rallies us, personally, in our walk by faith in Christ;
a commission verse is almost like the pulse of God, reaching from
inside us to rally others. Have you selected yours? You'll recognize
them when you come across them; it will feel like coming home.

Open Your Word to me, Lord, verse by verse, until I find my particular
promise to live by and purpose to work for.   —Carol Knapp

4
SAT

Open thou mine eyes, that I may behold wondrous
things. . . .   —Psalm 119:18

Today, I imagined I was eighty years old. Then I wrote a letter of
advice to myself on how to live my remaining years. I've tacked it
above my desk to remind me of what's important to my soul. If you
decide to try this, your list will be different, but a few items from mine
may help you get started.

• Begin and end each day with your best-loved form of prayer.

• Value your senses while they're still acute, by listening to birds, to lovely music, to the sounds of children playing and the whisper of wind in the pines. Drink in mountain views, flaming autumn leaves, the slant of moonlight, the sky at dawn.

- Challenge your mind daily. Read the great masters, the truth-tellers. Ponder unanswerable questions, for the joy of it.

- Express love daily, especially to family. Feed and water your garden of friends. Touch the suffering (including yourself) with love and mercy.

- When relationship tangles arise, ask yourself: What is *my* part in this? Where is *my* comb?

- Do something silly every day.

- Continue to discover your spiritual path, a moment at a time. Keep it authentic to your soul.

- Try to live from your *heart,* grateful for *all* that is. Trust God. Trust yourself. Hold to the heart.

Here in the shortness of my life, Lord, help me to treasure-hunt moments of wonder.   —Marilyn Morgan Helleberg

5
SUN

Saith the Lord: for I will forgive their iniquity, and I will remember their sin no more.   —Jeremiah 31:34

"Oh, no!"

I came fully awake with the words I'd just spoken echoing in my ears.

"Hit by another bad memory?" Larry murmured. My husband had been through this with me before.

"Yeah."

"Go back to sleep," he advised.

But I couldn't. Instead, I lay there reliving my embarrassment two months before when I had missed a speaking engagement because I'd written down the wrong day on my calendar. Just one more item in a fifty-year accumulation of goof-ups and embarrassing moments that sometimes stumbled out of my subconscious to wake me in the middle of the night. What to do? I couldn't go on losing sleep like this.

Then our minister preached a sermon about Lot's wife, who looked back at the destruction of Sodom and Gomorrah and turned into a pillar of salt. "If you keep focusing on the mistakes of the past, you'll freeze up and not be able to move ahead," he said. "Quit looking back at the things you can't change. Forgive yourself, and focus on the future."

So now, whenever one of those bad memories pads up behind me, I don't turn to dwell upon it. Instead, I pray, "God, I know You've forgiven my foolishness. Help me to forget it." And then I turn over and go back to sleep.

Father, please walk with me today, away from the past and into the future.
—Madge Harrah

6   *For the Lord will give you insight. . . .*
MON   —II Timothy 2:7 (NIV)

Does one word in the dictionary ever lead you to another? That happened to me with the word *epiphany.* Besides its religious meaning, I learned, it also means "a sudden insight into the significance of something."

I remembered the moment I realized for the first time that I was in love with my husband, the time I just "knew" that the job I was offered was the right one for me. *Wouldn't it be nice,* I thought, *if all of life were like that? A series of questions with easily discovered answers?*

Unfortunately, life more frequently hands us what could be called "puzzlers": long, involved questions with no easy answers. Should I take this job? Spend time with this person? Call my friend Kim, after not having seen her for ten years? When talking over this lack of answers with a friend, she laughed. "What's slow to you may be just the right time to God. Sit and meditate and pray. Perhaps God will lead you to what I call a 'slow epiphany.' "

I smiled. I liked that term. And over a course of morning meditation and prayer, the answer did come: The job was not for me; this person might be; I should phone my friend Kim. No, they weren't answers surrounded by lights or "aha!" but they came with a quiet certainty. And as I enjoy my renewed friendship with Kim, and continue to search for the "right" job, I've decided to be thankful for these "slow epiphanies."

God, let me consider the questions of my life today and come—through Your grace—to a slow epiphany.
—Linda Neukrug

7

If we claim to be without sin, we deceive ourselves and the truth is not in us.   —I John 1:8 (NIV)

My wife Rosie, my son Ryan and I were on our way home from New Orleans and decided to stop at a restaurant for breakfast. At the breakfast table, Rosie was busy trying to keep eight-year-old Ryan from getting dirty. When I noticed that he was eating too fast, I reached across the table, caught his arm, squeezed it and said, "Not so fast." Then I continued eating my breakfast. Suddenly, I looked up and saw Ryan rubbing his arm, tears rolling down his cheeks. I had inflicted pain on my son's arm and there was hurt and disappointment in his eyes. I knew I had to apologize to Ryan, but I was afraid to admit I had made a mistake.

As we got into our van about fifteen minutes later, I reached over and drew Ryan close to me. Quietly, I said to him, "Daddy made a mistake. I shouldn't have hurt your arm. I am sorry. Will you please forgive me?"

A big smile swept across his face as he said, "Yes, Daddy, I forgive you because I love you and I know that you love me, too."

As Ryan's father, I could have acted as if everything were okay and I hadn't done anything wrong. But I knew that even in my role as a father that it was better for my son to hear me say, "I'm sorry." For me, it was a special moment. *I was wrong, I made a mistake, I'm sorry* and *Please forgive me* are hard words for some men to say. As a man, a husband and a father, I want these phrases to come to my lips whenever they're appropriate.

Lord, I thank You for the reminding me that it's okay to say, "I'm sorry."
                          —Dolphus Weary

8

My purpose is that they may be encouraged in heart and united in love . . . in order that they may know the mystery of God. . . .   —Colossians 2:2 (NIV)

"Everything in life," a famous film director was quoted as saying recently, "conspires to take away our sense of wonder." I can't believe there is such a conspiracy. It seems to me, rather, that life offers endless invitations to wonder, from a rainbow to a falling star. It's our own indifference that keeps us from responding to them.

Not long ago I read about a little boy whose mother asked him why he seemed to derive so much enjoyment from dropping pebbles into a pond. "Because when I do," he said, "the water smiles at me."

Surely, there is wonder in that scene and in those words. Indeed, when I contemplate that small boy and his spreading ripples, much larger ideas come to mind. For instance, when pebbles of prayer are dropped into the universe, does eternity smile back?

Who can say that it doesn't?

Father, awaken us to the magic and mystery of the gifts You offer us.
                                                —Arthur Gordon

Editor's Note: Arthur Gordon has been sharing his experiences with wonder for many years. His classic *A Touch of Wonder* (available from Fleming H. Revell at your local bookstore) was published more than twenty years ago and continues to delight readers with its beautiful prose and Arthur's unique appreciation of the wonder all around us. This year, we asked Arthur to write a book especially for us, looking at wonder anew from the vantage point of his eighty years. If you are interested in ordering a copy of this inspiring book, *Return to Wonder,* please write: *Return to Wonder* (200501435), Guideposts, PO Box 569, Brewster, New York 10509. The cost per book is $12.95, plus postage and handling. No need to send payment now; we will bill you later. Allow 4–6 weeks for delivery.

9
THU   *Pleasant words are as a honeycomb, sweet to the soul, and health to the bones.*   —Proverbs 16:24

My mother had an extraordinary way with words. She knew how to use them to heal instead of hurt, to build up instead of tear down, and she had the knack of taking a negative situation and, through a few well-chosen words, turning it into something positive and uplifting. In my mother's vocabulary, no one was ever "nasty"; they merely had a most "unfortunate disposition," in need of help and encouragement.

As a little girl, I was prone to pout when things didn't go my way. Mother didn't scold. Instead, she raised her eyebrows, shrugged her shoulders and said, "Feeling a bit *out of sorts?*" When I was misbehaving, Mum didn't use words like *naughty* or *bad.* Rather, she would look me in the eye and in her crisp British accent say, "Come along now, stop being *awkward!*" *Awkward,* an excellent word!

Recently, after a series of financial reversals, a young friend of mine had to give up her cozy little apartment and move back home with her parents. "I feel such a failure," she moaned over tea in my kitchen.

"Not at all," I replied, praying for the right words with which to encourage her. "We all go through times when we need to . . . to *regroup* our lives."

Her eyes lit up, "Hey, that's exactly what I'm doing. I'm *regrouping* my life!"

Yup, there are words that work.

Help me to choose my words carefully, Lord, to heal instead of hurt.
—Fay Angus

10

I was sick, and ye visited me. . . .   —Matthew 25:36

I have a friend who is fond of boasting, "I never get sick!" She says it with such rectitude that I feel like a moral failure whenever I reveal my own dreary health woes. When I informed her I'd just had my flu shot, she looked at me with a mixture of pity and mild disdain. So the other day when I checked in with her, I was more than a little surprised to hear her moan, "I'm sick."

I could hardly accept what I was hearing. Katherine sick?

"The doctor says it's the flu," she wheezed piteously. "I haven't any idea what to do with myself. I don't know how to be sick!"

"Stay in bed, rest, drink fluids, let yourself heal," I said, rattling off the list most of us know by heart. "You'll be better before you know it." It felt good to be able to comfort Katherine for once. Being sick, after all, is something you learn how to do. Katherine would need help.

Over the next week, a procession of friends tromped through her apartment, cooking, cleaning, cheering her up, but keeping her down when she tried to do too much. "Angels" we designated ourselves, though really we were just friends of the girl who never gets sick showing her how to get better. The hardest part for Katherine was letting herself depend on us. "I feel so bad putting you all to so much trouble," she kept saying. But we insisted and by the end Katherine got used to being cared for. "I'll have to get sick more often," she joked. "I didn't know how many real friends I had!" I suspect she spent an extra day in bed just because she was enjoying all the attention.

We got Katherine back on her feet soon enough. She was grateful to us, and a little more understanding of other people's ills, I think. But I was grateful to her, too, for letting me help and for reminding me, in the middle of the flu season, that loving friends are the best medicine, always—God's own miracle drug.

Lord, keep me in good health. And when I am ill, keep my friends close.
                                                      —Edward Grinnan

11
We have different gifts, according to the grace given us.
                                         —Romans 12:6 (NIV)

Not long after bringing our tiny newborn Maria home from the hospital, I was holding her close to me, trying to soothe her fussiness. Soon she was relaxed and happy, dozing in my arms.

"She should be wrapped in a blanket," I told my husband Paul, with all the easy authority of a second-time mother, "the way she was in the hospital." Paul took her from me, and she immediately started crying. The blanket only made things worse; she began to bellow, and neither of us could console her.

"Well, that was a quick lesson," Paul said. "She was happy the way she was, and if she's happy, don't change anything!"

That's a tough lesson to learn. Too often I frustrate myself and those I love by deciding what *should* make them happy. For instance, a friend of mine told me she was thinking of taking a part-time job at a fast-food restaurant.

"Oh, you need something a little more glamorous than that," I responded.

"But the hours are perfect for me, and the money's not bad. . . ." Her voice trailed off, and I could hear her disappointment in my negative reaction. Later, I had to ask myself, *Am I thinking of what she wants or what I want?*

Of course, I want the best for my family and friends, so it's hard to keep from wanting to choose for them. But when my friend took the job and enjoyed it, I discovered that while I always *want* what's best for those I love, I don't always *know* what's best. Now I think back on Maria and the blanket, and recognize that the best choice I can make is to let her be when she's happy, even if she has chosen differently than I would have. After all, those differences are God's way of recreating His world and challenging me to see it always in a new way.

Open my eyes, Lord, to see the people in my life not as mismatched parts of a patchwork quilt, but as unique fibers in Your human tapestry.
                                                      —Gina Bridgeman

12
SUN

He hath made every thing beautiful in his time. . . .
—Ecclesiastes 3:11

When we were teenagers, my brother Bobby wanted to help me look like a TV star. "Come on, Susan," he said to me one day. "Let me give you a treatment and straighten your hair. Then you can wear it in a flip. You'll look just like Mary Tyler Moore. You'll be cool!"

We had both inherited curly hair, and we were self-conscious in a world in which the people who we thought were "in" had fashionably straight hair.

"Oh, all right," I said reluctantly. "I hope you know what you're doing."

He applied the treatment, and when it was finished, the curl was gone, but so was the body of my hair. It was limp and dead, like moss from the creek. I retreated to my room in tears and stayed there for the rest of the day. On Monday, I skipped school and went to the lady who cut my hair. "Milly," I moaned, "I'm ruined."

She ran her fingers through my hair. "Yep," she said matter-of-factly, "it's dead, that's for sure. You had the most beautiful hair. Why did you do it?"

"I don't know," I cried. "I wanted to be beautiful."

"But, Susan, you *are* beautiful, just the way God made you. Don't ever think you can improve on God's handiwork. He knows what He's doing."

Milly put her arms around me and gave me a squeeze. "When you get a little older, you'll understand that being true to yourself is what's beautiful. Now don't you fret anymore," she ordered. "I can give you a style that will tide you over till your hair grows." And she did.

Father, keep me true to the beauty with which You created me.
—Susan Schefflein

13
MON

I can do all things through Christ which strengtheneth me.
—Philippians 4:13

Why, I wondered, *did I pick up this particular book?* The story of a radio reporter, paralyzed from the chest down, wheeling around the world with a tape recorder reporting on leaders, wars and erupting volcanoes seemed pretty far away from my daily life. It was called *Moving Violations,* written by John Hockenberry, now a TV reporter for ABC. His tales of his life since he was paralyzed in an accident as a nineteen-year-old college student are raw with pain, angry with life, but full of excitement, laughter and triumph.

He's an accomplished pianist—but how to use the pedals when he can't feel his legs? He finds a way. A wheelchair in the desert sand? Get fatter tires. Suddenly, as the pages turned and, against all odds, his career prospered, I found myself propelling an armless wheelchair—armrests for paraplegics are for wimps, Hockenberry tells us—up and down the narrow, perilous streets of old Jerusalem.

The next day I was walking to the office, back in New York City, after my fantasy wheelchair journey. A young woman in a wheelchair across the street from me negotiated the steep curb without a second of hesitation. She forced the front wheels of her chair up and over the obstacle, chatting over her shoulder with a companion struggling to keep up with her briskly moving wheelchair. There was a ramp on the opposite corner. She rolled right up onto the sidewalk without breaking her conversation.

Thank God for sidewalk ramps, I thought, *and for all the other handicapped-accessible parts of daily life.* I had known they were there, of course. Now, thanks to a writer who was gutsy and talented enough to share his victories and frustrations, and to a woman who personified courage, I understood how it felt to need them.

Help us, Lord, to think of the difficulties of others and to honor quiet courage.   —Brigitte Weeks

---

WORDS OF WONDER

Praise to the Holiest in the height
And in the depth be praise;
In all his works most wonderful,
Most sure in all his ways.
—JOHN HENRY NEWMAN

14

In His arm he will gather the lambs. . . .

TUE   —Isaiah 40:11 (NAS)

The call we'd been waiting for came at seven on a May evening while I sat on my mother's front porch with my husband Gene. Out of earshot of my mother, I answered the portable phone.

"Marion . . ." The doctor's voice seemed heavy—determined. Cars passed by Mother's house. Neighbors talked in the yard. A bird sang a late afternoon song. I wanted to throw the phone into the bushes. "Your mother's scan shows what I suspected. The breast cancer from ten years ago has returned in her spine."

Gene and I sat motionless and silent for a few moments as though the call hadn't come. Then I made myself go inside and tell my mother. She didn't seem surprised or terribly alarmed.

We were spending the night, and we all got ready for bed routinely. But once I was in bed, the "what ifs" that had tormented me twelve years ago, when my first husband Jerry had brain surgery for cancer, struck without warning. The night was unbelievably long and sleep never came. The sky was becoming light when I realized that I hadn't talked with God about this news.

I'm not angry, Lord. It's just that I didn't expect to have to do it again. I don't know if I can. I feel very far away from You.

Sleep came for perhaps fifteen minutes. In a vivid dream, someone approached me from behind and lifted me as though I were a child. *What powerful arms,* I thought. At first, I believed it was Gene. But this person was incredibly strong and so tall I couldn't even see his face as I rested my head against him. He carried me effortlessly.

Oh, Father, I forgot how strong Your arms are! Amen.

—Marion Bond West

15

In a dream, in a vision of the night . . . then he openeth

WED *the ears of men, and sealeth their instruction.*

—Job 33:15–16

On Martin Luther King Day, at the dinner table, our son Timothy quoted a line he'd learned by rote at nursery school. "I have a dream that we shall walk together hand in hand."

"Very good!" we applauded. His older brother William, not to be outdone, gave us a brief summary of Dr. King's achievements: the marches; the protests; the "I Have A Dream" speech; the insistence on peaceful means of change. "And he was thirty-nine years old when he died," he concluded.

Only thirty-nine? I thought. I had never realized how young he was when he died. My age, in fact. He accomplished so much. What would he have done had he lived longer?

Lower lip quivering, Timothy stared at us in amazement and asked, "He's dead?" William, all too willing to correct his younger brother, reiterated the facts.

"But, but," Timothy said on the verge of tears, "he must miss his family!"

"He's in heaven," I said, trying to calm Timo, "where his family will join him someday. I'm sure he's happy there."

Mollified, Timo went back to his quote: "We shall walk together hand in hand."

Then I thought of all the children in nursery schools learning the dream, and the second-graders discovering what it meant to give yourself to a noble cause, and the adults like me who were still moved to tears by the man's vision of a better world. *As with all great dreamers,* I realized, *his dream lives on.*

Thank You, Lord, for the inspiring example of Your greatest dreamers.
—Rick Hamlin

16
THU

Praise the Lord from the earth . . . lightning and hail, snow and clouds, stormy winds that do his bidding.
—Psalm 148:7–8 (NIV)

Sleet rattled the windows. It poked holes into a thick layer of snow covering the ground. Looking out between stabs of icicles, I was battling my own inner storm. My daughter Wendy was teaching in Japan. My daughter Laura and son Jonathan were away at school. Their recent independence filled me with fear and loneliness that whipped and rattled like the storm outside.

Through the sleet-driven window, my head turned to a flicker in the corner of my eye. A tiny sparrow danced around like a windup toy on a bent, icy limb, its feathers shrugging off the sleet. *Optimistic little cuss.*

I put on my waterproof gear and stepped outside. The sleet went *rat-tat-tat* on my hood, while tree branches swayed, keeping time in the wind. A musical score of animal prints graced the crusted snow.

The weeds cracked in spindles of ice. The brook sang around frozen shapes of glass slippers. The music of a storm, just as I'd heard it as a child, full of questions: *Why doesn't the grass blow away? Why don't the trees break in half? Why doesn't the sparrow need a coat?* And the simple profound answer I was given: *Because God takes care of them.*

And He still does, I thought, as a gust of wind hurled an icy blast under my hood. God has uniquely dressed His creation for life's storms. As I slid back up the icy path to my porch, I was still lonely for my children. But the fear was gone. My heart had found comfort and resilience in the music of the storm.

Father, may we find the song You have put within us, because our praise pleases You most. Amen.   —Shari Smyth

17
FRI

Our Father . . . hath given us . . . good hope. . . .
—II Thessalonians 2:16

Within a year after David and I were married, I became pregnant with our first child, but life-threatening complications ended the pregnancy. Serious surgery followed, and while I was all alone in recovery, an unthinking doctor told me I would never have children. The doctor's words shattered my hopes, and a terrible depression fell on me in the next months. I felt useless, abandoned. I had fallen in a dark hole and climbing out was pointless.

And then, on a cold January day, my father said, looking me square in the eyes, "Today, you are going to start living again. You are going to do this because no matter what's happened, life still has a lot of good to offer."

Then, he handed me a little book, *Please Don't Feel Blue.* Its message was brief. "Even though things sometimes do look dark . . . the first star still comes out each night at dusk . . . snow is still soft and white and deep . . . shells still sing songs if you listen."

A few years later, despite the doctor's prognosis, I gave birth to Brock and then to Keri. My mother-career wasn't always easy, but Daddy's gift of hope kept renewing itself in night skies, new snow and spring rain.

Father, no less sure than the moon and the star, You are here. You are my hope.   —Pam Kidd

18
SAT

We know that all things work together for good to them that love God, to them who are the called according to his purpose.
—Romans 8:28

Every time I buy a novel or check one out of the library, I think of my Grandmother Smith, who lived with us awhile when I was in my early teens.

Grandmother was a tall woman who wore long dresses and piled her waist-length hair into a bun on top of her head. She loved to read, and I kept her supplied with books from the library. In my mind's eye, I can see her in her rocking chair, glasses, which she bought at the dimestore, perched on her nose, completely absorbed in a book.

Grandmother Smith had one very annoying habit: Whenever I brought her a new novel, she would turn to the last chapter and read it first. Although I didn't say anything, my annoyance must have shown, because one day she said to me, "Kenneth, I know it bothers you for me to read the last chapter first. But at my age, I don't want to invest a lot of time and energy in reading a book if I don't like the way it ends."

Over the years, I've had to make many decisions without knowing exactly how things would work out. And I've often wished that, like Grandmother Smith, I could skip ahead and know the outcome in advance. I can't, of course. But I can find guidance. Some of it comes as I think through the choices I face or discuss them with friends whose judgment I respect. And I can pray for help in interpreting what I already know. After all, the One Who wrote the Book knows the end of the story.

Father, let me face life's decisions with confidence in Your providential care.
—Kenneth Chafin

19
SUN

For the kingdom of God is not food and drink but righteousness and peace and joy in the Holy Spirit.
—Romans 14:17 (RSV)

It was Sunday, and my church, Hillsboro Presbyterian, with its mostly white suburban congregation, was having its semiannual exchange with Spruce Street Baptist, an inner-city church with a predominantly black membership.

I was pretty young when our two churches started getting together this way. It goes like this: On one Sunday, we close Hillsboro, and the entire congregation travels over to Spruce Street. Our minister, my dad David Kidd, preaches, our choir sings, and Spruce Street feeds us a great supper at noon. The next week the process is reversed, with Spruce Street's congregation, minister and choir traveling to Hillsboro, and it's our turn to put on the feed.

I can remember a few times when visitors to Hillsboro got up and walked out when they discovered the nature of the service. I guess they didn't feel comfortable worshiping with African Americans. Or perhaps the visitors were uncomfortable with the forty-plus adults with disabilities, members of our weekly Friendship Class, who love this particular service.

I can't say for sure what makes the occasional visitor walk away from our exchange Sundays, but I can say for sure that they've missed something wonderful. This "sisterhood of churches" has really come to mean something special to me and to all of us over the years. Something happens on those Sundays that's hard for me to explain. But on this particular Sunday, when Reverend Bowman stepped into Hillsboro's pulpit, he put my feelings into perfect words.

"As I stand here before all of you," he said, "and I look around, I think I've got a glimpse of what heaven is going to look like."

A host of Presbyterians and Baptists—the lame, the weak, the whole and healthy, black and white, rich and poor and in-between—answer back in one clear voice: "Amen."

Father, help me to say Amen to the signs of Your kingdom.
                                                        —Brock Kidd

20

MON   *Be strong and of a good courage. . . .*   —Joshua 1:6

Even for a New England winter, the winter of 1934 was memorable. The temperature dipped to twenty-seven degrees below zero; many days it hovered at ten below. Our furnace was silent because there was no money for coal. Father couldn't find work, and we had to squeeze by on what Mother made doing housework for wealthy families.

Our house was a refrigerator, except for our kitchen. The kitchen was kept warm with scrounged wood for our stove and foraged kerosene for our space heater. Many mornings I got up early to build the fire and light the heater. In a few hours, the kitchen was warm and cozy, ready for the family to wash and dress in. And my homework was done!

My parents never complained about hardship. They never blamed others for our plight. Instead, they moved forward day after day. Despite the Great Depression, the endless worry about money and the crippling cold, they spoke of hope. "Work hard, study and dream" was their message. Their hope warmed me more than the kitchen's heat.

The kitchen was the heart of our home. It showed me how I could build a room of faith, a room that would be cozy and warm against life's frigid blasts.

Gracious Father, thank You for filling the rooms of my life with Your love and Your encouragement.   —Oscar Greene

21
TUE

And this I pray, that your love may abound still more and more in real knowledge and all discernment.
—Philippians 1:9 (NAS)

It was a hard day. Elizabeth woke up out of sorts, with her normally large vocabulary reduced to a single word: *No.* Nothing made her happy for long. I patiently tried painting, modeling clay, singing songs, playing hide-and-seek, building block towers—just about everything I could think of to do with a seventeen-month-old on a cold winter day. But she didn't even want to cuddle or read books. My sweet little girl seemed to have evaporated overnight, replaced by a fussy child I barely knew.

Once my entertainment repertoire was exhausted, it was hard not to feel Elizabeth was being obstinate. On top of everything else, she wouldn't eat or drink. Still patient on the outside, I channeled my pent-up frustrations into a grim determination to get something into her tummy. When all else failed, I resorted to frozen blueberries, her favorite food. Elizabeth ate a grand total of seven. Little as it was, I counted it a success. That night I collapsed into bed, utterly drained.

At midnight I was awakened by her plaintive cries. Sensing something was wrong, I turned on the light in Elizabeth's room before picking her up. What a sight! The poor little thing had thrown up in her sleep; a deep purple mess covered her hair, sheets, blankets, pajamas and stuffed animals.

As I stripped off Elizabeth's soaked pajamas and consoled her, the day's events started to make sense. She was cranky because she didn't feel well. She wouldn't eat because her stomach was upset. And I, obstinately trying to make her happy, missed the point of all the messages she was sending me. My one success of the day—the blueberries—was really a sign of my failure to see what was going on. And the stubbornness I had disguised as patience was as plain as the purple stains on her bedclothes.

Father in heaven, You call me to help others in the way they need to be helped. Help me to serve them according to Your wishes, not mine.

—Julia Attaway

22
WED

So God created man in his own image . . . male and female created he them.   —Genesis 1:27

Let's face it—husbands and wives just don't see things alike. Take TV remote controls, for example. I'm a channel-grazer. When I watch the news, I flip back and forth through four different networks.

"It drives me crazy when you do that," my wife Sharon complains. I don't understand why she has no interest in other channels. After all, this is a curious woman I married, one who wants to know everything going on in the neighborhood and church and among all the relatives. Just one button away might be a program on *How to Lose Fifty Pounds by Eating Chocolate Sundaes* or *How to Understand Weird Husbands.* But, no, she won't change channels, not even if she dislikes the program she's watching.

"This talk show host makes me so angry!"

"Then why don't you change the channel?" I ask.

"Because I can't stand people who are always changing channels."

Differences. No right or wrong, just differences.

"The first law of civilization," said an old philosopher, "is to let people be different." I don't need to convert Sharon to my ways, and she doesn't try to make me be like her. We simply take turns monitoring the remote control.

Lord of Creation, help me to appreciate the variety in all the people I love.

—Daniel Schantz

23
THU

Give thanks in all circumstances; for this is the will of God in Christ Jesus for you.   —I Thessalonians 5:18 (RSV)

I had a stroke in October. It wasn't life-threatening, thank God, but it certainly put a crimp in my style of living. After a week or two, there was the matter of rehabilitation to straighten out. The therapy unit that was said to be the best agreed to take me, but by the time they had space for me, they didn't want me because I was too well.

So a month had disappeared, and I had to find some kind person who would agree to be a twenty-four-hour watcher of a fairly impatient patient. I found two: the first was Douglas, who stayed with me until Eddie appeared to see me through.

It's been three months now, and Eddie has gone home and I am alone. I take therapy at the hospital three times a week for speech and the return of power in my right side. They say it will take time. I'm a pretty lucky old fellow, and I know it.

How do I know it? Suppose you had been there in the hospital and seen the number of friends who came, and came again. You'd think I was a movie star, the floral display was so immense. The cards and letters that arrived, from the office, from those of you who knew, from people in my apartment building I only had nodded to—they made me feel valuable, and indebted.

It's a question of time. I don't know when, but I know in the meanwhile, if you want to see a grateful man, look no further.

Father, I thank You for friends and loved ones and for life.

—Van Varner

24
FRI

Encourage the fainthearted, help the weak, be patient with them all.   —I Thessalonians 5:14 (RSV)

Years ago, when I was in high school, I tried hard to become an athlete, but I never made it. It seemed to me that everyone else could play softball, tennis and volleyball, or jump over horses in gym. I couldn't catch a ball, much less throw one. Tennis balls whizzed past me. I bounced off gym horses and came away bruised.

My biggest failure was ice skating, my friends' favorite winter sport. They would take me along with them and leave me shivering on the sidelines while they skated away, waving to me as they raced and spun by. When I tried to skate, my ankles caved in, and down I went.

I especially admired a girl named Harriet Schmidt. She was new in my class, and she excelled at everything athletic. On ice, she was dazzling. I used to enjoy watching her, but I never dared to say hello.

One bitterly cold afternoon, while I stood at the edge of the pond,

Harriet glided over to me. "Hi," she said with a warm smile. "Why don't you come and skate with us?"

"I can't stay on my feet," I explained, embarrassed.

"Sure you can," Harriet said, reaching for my hand. "I'll help you."

With some reluctance, I let her steer me toward a group of my friends. My ankles were starting to bend inward, but Harriet's grip was strong, and I stayed on my feet. She asked another girl to take my other hand, and off we went across the pond. We didn't do anything fast or fancy. We simply skated slowly until my ankles straightened and held me up. I was thrilled and asked my two friends to let go so I could try to skate on my own. I did it . . . with a few wobbles and some hands reaching in to steady me.

"You see? You really *can* skate!" Harriet said.

I'm still not an athlete. But Harriet taught me that we don't have to excel at something we want to do. We can do it just because we enjoy it. And because somebody cares enough to hold us up until we learn how to stand on our own.

Dearest Lord Jesus, we know that Your hand is always in ours and You will not let us fall. Amen.   —Phyllis Hobe

25   *God had made them rejoice with great joy. . . .*
SAT   —Nehemiah 12:43

"What person, place or thing brings you joy?" asked a friend of mine who was doing research for his doctoral thesis.

I pondered his question before answering, replying first that joy has many faces. He agreed, but pressed me to give him some examples.

"Oh, when I see a beautiful sunset shimmer across the waves in front of our Florida cottage," I began. "Or when one of my grandchildren snuggles up and plants a wet kiss on my cheek. Or the joyful satisfaction I feel when my E.L. (Ever Lovin') Shirley and I make up after a tiff. Or when God answers my prayers and frees me from some sleep-robbing worry."

My answers revealed a lot about my priorities. Sometimes, I fear, I miss many of life's felicities—those daily hugs that God gives us—because I'm consumed by the hustle and bustle. I wonder how many gifts of grace have I failed to acknowledge today? How about you? The secret, I believe, is to keep our eyes peeled for His caring hand.

Joy may be elusive when we're carrying heavy burdens, anxieties, loneliness, guilt, illness, grief—but His love is certain and constant.

David provided an everlasting promise for God's people when he wrote in the Thirtieth Psalm that "weeping may endure for a night, but joy cometh in the morning." When we're hurting, it's good to know that His joy is just around the corner.

Teach me, dear Lord, that life's sweetest joys
Often come whispered far from crowd noise.

—Fred Bauer

26

SUN

Serve wholeheartedly, as if you were serving the Lord, not men.
—Ephesians 6:7 (NIV)

It was the typical pre-Super Bowl shopping flurry at the grocery that cold January Friday. A man juggling a tray of cold cuts, two bags of chips and a case of soda cut ahead of me in the express lane, growling, "Service isn't what it used to be."

"I just had a root canal, and I'd like to get home," I mumbled as the cashier chattered endlessly about his new big-screen TV.

That night I fell, hitting my mouth right where I'd had the root canal. By Sunday evening, my mouth was bruised and swollen and throbbing in pain. "I'll never reach my dentist on a Sunday," I groaned to my husband, "let alone Super Bowl Sunday. But I can't stand it until Monday." Reluctantly, I dialed Dr. Hildebrand's number and left a message on his answering machine. Then I packed my face in ice, took another pain pill and went back to bed.

Within thirty minutes, the telephone rang. It was Dr. Hildebrand. "Can you meet me at the office, Roberta?" he asked. "We need to get some X-rays and check you out right away."

Dr. Hildebrand took plenty of time to examine me and explain everything. I couldn't resist asking why he had changed his plans, on today of all days, to help me. He just smiled shyly and said, "Oh, I looked forward to the game, but my patients come first. I couldn't let you wait. I can always catch it later on video."

On that Super Bowl Sunday, I was blessed to discover that service is sometimes even better than it used to be.

Thank You, Lord, for people in all lines of work who serve You in serving others.
—Roberta Messner

27   *Thou shalt be called by a new name, which the mouth of*
MON   *the Lord shall name.*   —Isaiah 62:2

One day, shortly after Julia and I got engaged, I came upon an article in the newspaper about marriage and names. It seemed that "nineties couples" were no longer satisfied with hyphenating his and her last names. No, the trend now was to make up entirely new last names. If Mr. Redding was marrying Miss Blue, they'd put their names together and call themselves Mr. and Mrs. Purple. Or they might take part of her name and part of his, and become Mr. and Mrs. Bledding.

Julia and I teased each other about the article for a while, but our names (Johnson and Attaway) posed difficulties. We didn't have any colors to mix, and most syllable combinations, like Johnaway or Attajohn, sounded funny. Then we came up with a winner: Sonatta. We both loved music, and the possibilities were endless. We could name our first child Moonlight if she were a girl, while a boy could get Kreuzer or Hammerklavier.

In the end, though, good sense prevailed over good humor. And when we did get married, we discovered that there was a lot more to becoming a couple than taking a name. After a few years of wearing the rough edges off of each other, we're still working at it.

So everyone in our house is named Attaway: Julia and Andrew and Elizabeth. Everyone except our cat—she'll always be Kitty Cotta Sonatta.

Lord, give all married couples the grace to be one flesh, one spirit in You.
     —Andrew Attaway

28   *The Lord your God carried you, as a father carries his*
TUE   *son. . . .*   —Deuteronomy 1:31 (NIV)

Bill and I were having an out-of-sorts day, the kind that all marriages know, when one says something that hits the other the wrong way and soon each is hiding behind wounded pride and the shine has gone out of life. I wanted a way back to the flow of love, and I knew he did, too. I just didn't know how to get there without making the situation worse. I sat at the dining room table, my fingers wrapped around a cup of coffee, my heart hurting, anger and forgiveness struggling within me.

Then I remembered Tommy, our oldest son, at three and a half. Although his F's got tangled up with his S's, his ideas still came across clearly. Like the day I peered out the back door and saw him on the steps, broken fire truck in one hand, his child's tools clutched in the other. I realized that he had tried to fix the toy himself but didn't know how. Now he headed for the driveway where Bill was tinkering with the car.

"Where are you going, Tommy?" I called through the screen.

"My sire truck broken." He turned to look at me from the bottom step. His face was full of consternation, but the words rang out in absolute certainty: "My daddy will six it!"

Now, years later, I knew Tommy's childlike response was still the correct one. I bowed my head at the kitchen table and prayed, "Father, I don't know how to 'six' this break in communication between Bill and me. Please, fix it for us."

Within minutes, my anger gave way to peace. With it came phrases to say to Bill that would bridge the gap between us. Leaving the coffee to cool, I went to find him.

Lord, let me never lack the confidence to come to You, no matter what the problem. You will never fail to respond.   —Roberta Rogers

29

WED   *So we are ambassadors for Christ, God making His appeal through us. . . .*   —II Corinthians 5:20 (RSV)

I received a phone call yesterday from a dear friend in North Carolina. In the midst of our conversation, Carol said, "Do you remember a letter you wrote to my son Mark when his dog was lost?" Embarrassed, I couldn't recall writing the letter. But Carol's question brought back a flood of memories.

Mark was a ten-year-old boy, and I was his pastor. When my golden retriever had puppies, Mark got the pick of the litter. Boy and pup quickly bonded and became best of friends. But one day the dog did not come home. After days of searching, it was apparent that the dog had been stolen. Mark was shattered by his first brush with grief.

Carol tells me that I wrote a letter to comfort Mark; words about life and love and loss. Mark saved the letter, and years later he took it with him when he went to college. Recently, he told his mother that from time to time he pulls out the yellowed pages and rereads my words.

The contribution I make in the life of another is often in the simplest of ways and quickly forgotten. Every smile can be important, every word significant, every action helpful for someone. There is no wasted kindness in God's kingdom; no letter of love unanswered.

Dear God, may You touch someone through me this day. Amen.

—Scott Walker

30
THU *The gift of God is eternal life through Jesus Christ our Lord.*   —Romans 6:23

When the invitation arrived in the mail, my children knew immediately that it was for them. David threw down his favorite blue ball; Jamie let her doll slip from her arms. On the envelope were pictures of balloons, streamers and confetti: Someone was having a birthday party!

"The party's for Moriah," I read while the children became giddy with anticipation. "It'll be held in another three weeks."

The long-awaited day finally arrived. While I wrapped the birthday gift, David, my five-and-a-half-year old, announced, "I want to give Moriah a present."

"You *are*," I responded. "I'm wrapping it now." He disappeared.

As I pulled a shiny purple ribbon over the box, David walked into the room holding what looked like rumpled yellow paper. "This is for Moriah," he told me. I looked down at the awkwardly folded thing in his hands. It wasn't wrapping paper; it didn't say "Happy Birthday" on it anywhere. But inside it was David's blue ball.

Father, help me to remember Your example, which shows that true giving is always from the heart and reflects the love that's found there.

—Robin White Goode

31
FRI *In you I trust, O my God. . . .*   —Psalm 25:2 (NIV)

Switzerland was always a favorite vacation place for my husband Norman Vincent Peale and me. And one of our favorite spots was St. Moritz, situated on a beautiful lake and surrounded by mountains.

One winter we went to St. Moritz with our three children, all in their early teens. About mid-morning on a beautiful day we decided to take the mountain railroad to the top of the highest peak in the area. We had been looking at the snow-covered mountain each day, and when we discovered that a cog-railroad train went to the top, we decided it would be a great experience.

All went well. The view at the top was spectacular. We followed the path to a lookout spot where a metal map on a pedestal pointed to and named all the surrounding mountains. After a light lunch, we decided it was time to return to our hotel. Our older daughter Margaret got on the train with us, but our son John and our daughter Elizabeth said they would return on the next train.

I was hesitant, but Norman said, "You must learn to trust them, Ruth, and let them go."

Well, they didn't come down on the next train—or the next. Norman said, "Ruth, put them in the Lord's hands and trust Him."

Norman's confidence was catching. I surrendered my anxiety to the Lord and went off for an afternoon siesta. And, of course, Elizabeth and John came down in time to wake me for dinner. They had simply become enthralled with the view down another walking path.

Thank You, Father, for reminding me every day that I can trust in Your promises. Amen.
                                                    —Ruth Stafford Peale

Everyday Wonders

1 _____

2 _____

3 _____

4 _____

5 _____

6 _____

7 _____

8 _____

9 _____

10 _____

11 _____

12 _____

13 _____

14 _____

15 _____

16 _____

17 _____

18 _____

19 _____

20 _____

21 _____

22 _____

23 _____

24 _____

25 _____

26 _____

27 _____

28 _____

29 _____

30 _____

31 _____

Herein is love, not that we loved
God, but that he loved us, and
sent his Son to be the propitia-
tion for our sins.   —*I JOHN 4:10*

February

S	M	T	W	T	F	S
						1
2	3	4	5	6	7	8
9	10	11	12	13	14	15
16	17	18	19	20	21	22
23	24	25	26	27	28	

1

SAT   **LOVE IS . . .**

Love . . . does not envy. . . .   —I Corinthians 13:4 (NIV)

Her room is closet-sized, barely big enough for a bed and a small desk
and chair. Four hangers hold her entire wardrobe. The floor is rug-
less, the single window uncurtained. The other three nuns with
whom Sister Irene shares the apartment in Boston's Dorchester sec-
tion are elderly now; much of Sister Irene's time is spent doing the
shopping, cooking and cleaning for all four.

The rest of the day she strolls the neighborhood as she has for more
than twenty years, talking to the beggars, the homeless, the school
dropouts, the addicts, the abused children. Sometimes she puts people in touch with a private or government agency; sometimes she in-
vites them to her weekly Bible study; sometimes she simply stops to
talk. "They add so much to my life," she says. How *much* she has,
not how little, is the emphasis of everything she says.

The reason Sister Irene makes such a personal impact on me is that
I've known her family ever since her sister and I took dance lessons
together at age eleven. They lived in the same New York suburb we
did—in a far larger house than ours. They took vacations in Europe
and had a box at the Metropolitan Opera. Her four brothers and sisters all married. The sister I danced with has a magnificent home on
Long Island; one of the brothers is an ambassador.

Sister Irene, who took her religious vows forty years ago, has never
owned a house or a car. Far from envying me my eight grandchildren, or her siblings their wealth, she's sure that she's the privileged
one. "Why should I have all this?" she asked me once. Her arm
swept the tiny room, the dingy neighborhood beyond. "Why should
God love me so much?"

God of love, help me to know that in possessing You, I possess all there is.
                                                    —Elizabeth Sherrill

2

SUN   *And he . . . encouraged them to the service of the house of*
       the Lord.   —II Chronicles 35:2

"Please don't forget to lower the song!" my twelve-year-old daughter Rebecca pleaded. "You know I can't reach that high E!"

Earlier in the year, Rebecca had won "Top Blue" on a solo at

County 4-H Days. Now, she'd worked up the courage to sing the lovely hymn "Let Us Break Bread Together" for our church worship service. I gave her a reassuring hug before I sat down at the organ to begin the prelude. "Honey, I'll play in a lower key," I promised.

But I forgot, and Rebecca strained to reach the high notes. Her voice was clear and true, but painfully thin. She finished the song, but she cried all the way home. "I was awful!" she sobbed. "I'll never sing again." My apologies didn't help a bit. "Of course you thought I was okay! You're my mother!"

Then Mrs. Marine called. "Rebecca, it was wonderful to hear you sing!" she exclaimed. The next day she received a note of appreciation from Mrs. Unruh. And Mrs. Stude asked her to sing for a club meeting the next week.

Because they encouraged her early efforts, Rebecca's mature and lovely voice now praises the Lord during worship, adds a grace note to weddings and provides comfort at funerals. Each time I hear her sing, I'm grateful for the unexpected heartfelt encouragement these gracious women gave Rebecca. Thank you, Mrs. Unruh! Thank you, Mrs. Marine! Thank you, Mrs. Stude!

Thank You, Lord, for the "encouragers" who bring out the best in all of us.
—Penney Schwab

LETTERS TO WALLY

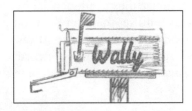

In addition to being a longtime Daily Guideposts *contributor, Mary Lou Carney also edits our children's magazine* Guideposts for Kids. *As part of that endeavor, she often assumes the persona of Wally the Turtle—a wise, human-size creature who answers hundreds of letters from children each month. Wally even has his own video series* Guideposts Junction, *which features his answers to kids' letters. But Mary Lou is quick to admit that she, as much as the children, is helped by this advice-giving process. Mary Lou and Wally have invited us to share some of the letters from their "Dear Wally" mailbag—and gather a little advice for our own use along the way.*
—The Editors

3
Day 1: Expect an Answer

Morning by morning, O Lord, you hear my voice; morning by morning I lay my requests before you and wait in expectation.
—Psalm 5:3 (NIV)

I opened my eyes to the predawn shadows on my wall. Immediately, I thought of the letters. So many letters! My mailbox—Wally the Turtle's mailbox—was stuffed daily with letters from kids asking for his help and advice. My e-mail, too, had become a way for kids from around the world to tell Wally their problems.

And those problems were all too real: teasing; family fights; divorce; death; disappointment. What could Wally possibly say to help? How could one person—one turtle—make a difference? As always, I prayed for the boys and girls who would find their way into my life.

I climbed out of bed and raised the shade, watching the first rays of morning sun appear. At the end of the driveway, I saw my mailbox. But I saw something else, too. I saw the kids who would check their own mailboxes today, certain of a letter. Sure that help was on its way.

Expectation. These kids believed in Wally's wisdom, believed that his answer was coming. And their faith had strengthened my own faith. God knew all about these children and their problems. He knew just what advice they needed, what nudge of self-esteem or gentle reassurance could set them on the right path.

And God knew, too, that soon I would be at my computer—surrounded by my Bibles and concordances and mail—working and waiting, expecting His help, listening for these answers that always come.

You, O God, are the Source of all wisdom and truth. How glad I am that You choose to share those treasures with us!   —Mary Lou Carney

4
Day 2: Walk the Talk

". . . Showing yourselves to be my disciples."   —John 15:8 (NIV)

The line to check in at the gate was long, and my luggage was getting heavier by the minute. It looked like it would be a full flight.

Then, when I was almost at the front of the line, a lady appeared out of nowhere and pushed her way up to the desk. She waved her ticket at the attendant and began talking in a loud voice about seat assignments and connections.

I was furious! Who did she think she was, butting in like that? What gave her the right when I had been standing in line for fifteen minutes? I set down my load and reached out to tap her on the shoulder, determined to tell her as much. Then I saw the letter I had just been reading sticking out of my briefcase.

Dear Wally,
I've come to know the Lord. The problem, though, is that I don't show it.

Jessica

I dropped my arm, smitten with the reality that I, like Jessica, was hardly demonstrating Christlikeness. I tried to imagine Christ angry at a line-jumper, and I smiled at how silly that picture was. What was the advice I had given Jessica?

Dear Jessica,
Begin by praying about the behaviors you want to change. Then work each day to make those changes. Repent when you need to; don't get discouraged. Becoming like Christ is a lifetime job!

Wally

"Oh, Lord," I prayed as the lady continued her animated discussion, "I find myself short on gentleness and patience these days. Give me opportunities to practice both."

A few minutes later, the culprit blocked the aisle of the airplane, struggling to get her luggage into the overhead bin. "Here," I said, "let me help."

It was a start.

Dear God, You created us in Your likeness. Help me to act like it!
—Mary Lou Carney

5
WED   **Day 3: Small Steps Count**

Walk in the footsteps of the faith. . . .   —Romans 4:12 (NIV)

BOY, 11, MURDERED UNDER OVERPASS. The headline glared out at me, and I tried to imagine the mother of that child. Not only had her son been killed by gang members, he himself was suspected of killing a fourteen-year-old girl earlier that week. The rest of the paper seemed no better. Our local school district's standardized reading scores were down again. The Florida panther was in danger of extinction. Landfills were filling up. And cuts in government funding threatened numerous senior-care programs in our county. I thought about Bijan's letter I'd received recently:

I've got this problem. I want the world to be right.

Me, too, I thought as I tossed the newspaper into the recycling pile. But what could I do? What could anyone do? *Well, you're recycling,* an inner voice seemed to say. *That's good.* I thought about the advice I'd given Bijan:

Be responsible for your own corner of the world. Treat others the way you want to be treated. Love God, the earth and your fellow creatures.

Simple advice, but was I following it? Maybe I could check into "adopting" an elephant at the zoo. Or becoming a storyteller for the elementary school in my neighborhood. I could use fewer paper plates. Support groups working with troubled teens. Maybe read the newspaper to an elderly neighbor.

"Every small act of kindness is a step toward making the world right," I'd written Bijan. I determined to make it a week of many "steps."

Dear God, keep me from the paralysis of pessimism. Help me to take daily steps down the path to a better future.   —Mary Lou Carney

6

THU   **Day 4: Help Is Close By**

What time I am afraid, I will trust in thee.   —Psalm 56:3

The house was strangely quiet. Not even our pesky water pump was kicking on and off in its customary fashion. It was midnight, and I was alone. A rare occurrence. My son Brett was staying overnight with a friend, and my husband Gary was making his yearly trip to Florida for heavy equipment auctions. I found myself tensing as the minutes passed. I was afraid . . . but of what? We lived in a sheltered rural community, and I had two watchdogs outside. But the fear refused to go away. That day I'd received a letter from Michelle:

I love God. And I know He is with me all the time. But I'm still scared.

What had been my answer?

Michelle,
   Everybody is scared of something. Talk about your fears with someone you trust.

Well, it was midnight. Whom could I talk to? I considered close friends. Maybe Gary at his motel. But then I remembered my second piece of advice to Michelle: "Pray about it." Who could be better to talk to than the One in charge?

And so I began. Soon I found my fears were about more than squeaky stairs. They were about my daughter Amy Jo alone in a big town; my mother's deteriorating health; our own approaching retirement years. It was a long conversation, but when at last I slipped toward sleep, I knew that there was nothing to be afraid of. Ever.

I'd add that to my letter to Michelle . . . first thing in the morning.

O God, You are our Protector and Benefactor—day and night. Thank You!
                                                          —Mary Lou Carney

7
Day 5: Give Somebody Something

"Treat others as you want them to treat you."
                                              —Luke 6:31 (TLB)

Robin began her letter the way so many of the kids do: *I've got this problem.* She went on to say:

My little brother is mean! I used to be able to beat him up but now he is so mean. I think he got it from me.

I smiled, thinking that Robin was probably right. I'd found that in families, behaviors were often caught rather than taught. When I hear my daughter Amy Jo's impatient tone, I remember my own impatience. When I see my son Brett's cheerfulness as he works, I know he learned it from his dad. Amy Jo's attention to detail, Brett's finicky eating habits—all are behaviors my husband Gary and I modeled for them. I wrote:

> *Dear Robin,*
>   *Why not give your little brother some other behavior to "get" from you? Something positive and happy, something helpful and unselfish.*
>   *Wally*

That was advice I'd remember in dealing with my own family, too. Maybe I could become "contagious" with the kind of behaviors I'd like to see in them. It was certainly worth a try!

Forgive me, Father, when I infect others with meanness of spirit. Let me be a goodwill "carrier" for You.   —Mary Lou Carney

8

Day 6: Grieving Is Okay

[God] comforts us . . . so that we can comfort those in any trouble with the comfort we ourselves have received from God.
                                                      —II Corinthians 1:4 (NIV)

It was the wrong day to open Mandy's letter. The anniversary of my grandmother's death always makes me sad, and now Mandy's letter seemed to pick at the scab that had been forming for more than a dozen years.

> *Dear Wally,*
>   *My grandma died. I'm angry, sad and upset. Everyone feels sorry for me, but I want to be a normal kid again. Should I forget about her or act as if she's alive? Help!*

First grief, in all its shattering enormity—that's what Mandy was feeling. I remembered that feeling well. Grandma had always lived with us, had been as much a part of my childhood as my own mother had. Then, suddenly, she was gone. *Dear Mandy,* I wrote,

> *I'm sorry about your grandma. Even though God will help ease the hurt, in some ways you will miss her all of your life. Store up the memories of her; they will become one of your most cherished possessions.*
>   *Wally*

Downstairs, I heard my daughter Amy Jo playing the piano. The strains of "Shall We Gather at the River" floated into my office. It was Grandma's favorite song.

But don't spend all your time thinking, I continued. *Play with your friends, read your favorite books. And be assured that you are a normal kid . . . just a wiser kid.*

I found myself humming as I addressed Mandy's envelope in green ink—Wally the Turtle's trademark.

Oh, God, thank You for the comfort You give in times of grief. Whatever our ages, we remain children in need of You.   —Mary Lou Carney

9
SUN

Direct me in the path of your commands, for there I find delight.   —Psalm 119:35 (NIV)

The Sunday before our family was to leave for six months in New Zealand, we had planned to skip church and pack, but instead we felt compelled to go. As the service began, my mind churned with distractions: *When will I finish all the errands? With our suitcases already too full, what can I possibly leave home?* Struggling to pry my mind free, I reached for a service book. Inside, I found a bookmark that read, "How to Worship: BEFORE the service, speak to God. DURING the service, let God speak to you. AFTER the service, speak to one another."

"Speak to God." Quickly I confided my anxieties to God, asking His help.

"Let God speak to you." With my mind quieted, I listened to the sermon about Peter walking on the water to Jesus. I heard, *Keep your eyes on Me, not on the wind and waves. Amid the packing and pressures these next days, look to Me for guidance.*

"Speak to one another." I had planned to rush home and skip coffee hour, but this phrase drew me downstairs, where I received encouragement and offers of help.

Countless Sundays later, that little card continues to help me. When distracted, "Speak to God" reminds me to commit my cares to Him. "Let God speak to you" helps me to listen for God's message today. "Speak to one another" encourages me to take the ini-

tiative with people and form new friendships. And every Sunday—
and on all the days in between—God has new gifts to give me.

*Father, thank You for reminding me to confide in You, listen to You and
deepen my bond with Your family.*   —Mary Brown

10

Pray in the spirit on all occasions. . . .
—Ephesians 6:18 (NIV)

When we arrived at the Japanese restaurant for my sixteenth-birthday
dinner, my brother, my grandparents, my parents and I were led to
a *teppan* table opposite another family, a mother with two daughters.
I smiled across at them and then turned to my brother. "And when
the right-hand mirror bumped the cone," I said, "I thought I would
cry! But the examiner didn't say anything, so now . . ." I dangled the
family car keys on my new key ring, which my mother had given me,
in front of his nose.

My mother leaned over to the waitress and whispered loudly, "It's
her sixteenth birthday!"

The woman across the table nodded knowingly at my mother.
"They grow up quickly, don't they? The way your daughter was
smiling, I knew today must be special."

Mom needed no more encouragement to fall into the inevitable
mother-to-mother talk of SAT scores, grades and colleges. When the
salad was served, they stopped chatting long enough for Mom to ask
me to hand her my keychain, which read, *"Instructions:* 1. Insert key.
2. Turn right. 3. Pray to God!" My friends had laughed apprecia-
tively, saying that if my own mother didn't feel safe driving with me,
they'd rather walk to the movies on Saturday.

Mom handed the key chain to the woman, who turned it over in
her hands slowly. Finally, she looked up at me, beamed and said,
"That *is* a good reminder now, isn't it? Nowadays, it's easy to forget
how important prayer is until you really need it."

It took me a moment to understand what she was saying. She
hadn't seen the dark humor in the gift; she hadn't thought it funny
at all. Taking the instructions as they were, she had seen what
was truly important. As she handed the keys back to me, I knew
this chance acquaintance had given me something priceless for my
birthday.

Dear Lord, help me to call upon You faithfully not only in times of trouble,
but in thanks, praise and joy.   —Kjerstin Easton

11
TUE   *The Lord is full of compassion and is merciful.*
                                           —James 5:11 (NAS)

It was one of those awful days when nothing seemed to turn out right.
A project at work I had been planning for weeks was summarily rejected. My son had been accepted at a college, but that day we were
turned down for financial aid, and we couldn't afford the out-of-state
tuition. A long-anticipated vacation had to be canceled because I had
forgotten to turn in frequent flyer miles before they expired. And now
I was waiting at church to see our new pastor about a committee assignment—not exactly my favorite pastime.

While I waited, I looked into the church's preschool classroom just
as a fine-looking four-year-old burst into tears and wailed, "It's ugly!
It's ugly! I worked and worked, and it's ugly!"

Before him was a large sheet of paper on which he had been finger painting. Coming up behind him, the teacher whisked the "ugly"
page away, placed another in front of him and said, "It's okay, Kevin.
Here's a new paper. Just try to do better next time."

Maybe it was because I was in church, but through her words I
heard God speaking to me. With one hand, He swept the awful day
away and said, "It's all right, Eric. Tomorrow I'll give you a new day.
Just try to do better next time."

Lord, help me to turn the page on yesterday and look to tomorrow with hope.
                                           —Eric Fellman

12
WED   *Present your bodies a living sacrifice, holy, acceptable*
           unto God. . . .   —Romans 12:1

Sometime in late February or early March, at Sunday school, we were
given little boxes in the shape of a church with a cardboard steeple
and a slit in the top, perfect for receiving our dimes and nickels. Starting with Ash Wednesday, we put our coins in them, shaking the boxes
each time, hearing the jangle of change, as satisfying as money in our
piggy banks. And just in case we wondered what we could do with

all that copper and silver, the Sunday school bulletin board was filled with vivid displays of maps and photos: one dollar would feed a family in Africa; a few dollars would buy a household's rice for a month in Asia.

Once a week in our house we'd have macaroni and cheese or spaghetti without meat so my mom could put some change in our little boxes—symbolic seed money, it was. But we were supposed to find our own ways of going without, too—skipping the weekly trip to the candy store or going without a comic book. Then on Easter Sunday, we gathered those little churches, weighty with coins, and delivered them up as our offering.

Years later I learned more formally about Lenten fasts, and I met people who gave up all sorts of things for the forty days, from sweets to roast beef. I myself have practiced forgoing a certain favored food, but I have never done it without remembering cardboard churches at Lent and the lesson they held. For if you take a little less for yourself, simplifying your life, you can turn it into a lot more for someone else.

Lord, help me to give up what I can, so I can have more of my life to give.
                                                                    —Rick Hamlin

13
THU *Inasmuch as ye have done it unto one of the least of these my brethren, ye have done it unto me.*   —Matthew 25:40

During a recent snowstorm in our area, cars were backed up for miles and miles and hours and hours on Interstate 80, most of the occupants without food or water. Later I talked with one of these travelers, a woman who had picked up a few bananas at a grocery store before heading home to Kearney from Grand Island.

She was eating a banana and thanking God for providing for her needs, when a windblown young man knocked on her car window. Did she have any food to share? She thought quickly and then said, "No." After all, she couldn't feed everyone on the highway. Besides, she had no idea how long she'd be stranded. So she watched as the young man went from car to car, collecting what he could, while she got more and more upset that he'd take advantage of people that way. Then she saw him cross the median, and there, in the eastbound lane, was a schoolbus full of hungry children.

The woman pulled up the hood of her coat, grabbed the bananas and began her trek toward the bus. On the way, she again met the young man. "I'm so sorry," she said, and then handed him the bananas.

He accepted her apology, thanked her and then added, "Inasmuch as you have done it unto one of the least of these. . . ."

"When I got back to my car," said the woman, "I found I had something more than food to be thankful for. I was thankful for having a second chance."

Lord, we know You are the God of second chances . . . and third . . . and more. Thank You, Father, that as long as we live, it's never too late to serve You by serving others.   —Marilyn Morgan Helleberg

14
FRI

"I have loved you with an everlasting love; I have drawn you with loving-kindness. I will build you up again. . . ."
—Jeremiah 31:3–4 (NIV)

My heart was aching, and the last thing I was in the mood for was sending valentines. But I'd promised my friend who works as a therapist at a Native American residential school that I'd get them in the mail that night. We'd hit upon the idea months before, and I'd excitedly made arrangements with the Loveland, Colorado, post office to cancel them with their special Valentine's Day postmark.

Many of the girls who would be receiving the valentines had a history of abuse or abandonment and needed to know they were really loved. But tonight, so did I. I had been deeply wounded by a trusted friend. Dutifully, I sat at my kitchen table and opened the school's yearbook. As I carefully wrote each name, I studied the beautiful, round faces of my faraway friends, each one unique in the universe. Their smiles soothed my hurting heart.

Fifty times I prayed as I wrote the same anonymous message: "From someone who thinks you are very special." And each time I wrote the words on the embossed, Victorian-style cards, they echoed in my heart. *She is very special to Me . . . I have loved her with an everlasting love.* By card number fifty, the message grew clear: Like those fifty hurting girls, I am special. Because to Jesus, we all are.

Precious Jesus, thank You for Your loving words of life, which gladden our hearts each time we hear them.   —Roberta Messner

---

— W O R D S   O F   W O N D E R —

He Giveth More

His love has no limit, His
    grace has no measure,
His power no boundary
    known unto men;
For out of his infinite riches
    in Jesus
He giveth and giveth and
    giveth again.

—ANNIE JOHNSON FLINT

15

SAT

As soon as Jesus heard the word that was spoken, he saith
... Be not afraid, only believe.   —Mark 5:36

"What are you doing, honey?" I once asked my little girl, who was crouched, head down, on a small throw rug.

She looked up, eyes shining. "Playing magic carpet. It's wonderful. I know you won't believe this, but it really works! It goes places, it lifts right up and flies, wherever you want."

"Where? What places?"

"I've mostly gone to easy places like Grandma's. But I've been to Oz and Fairyland! And when I get my Dutch doll, I think we'll go to Holland." Beaming, she hopped up. "Try it! But you've got to *scrooch* down and hang on tight, or you might fall off."

"Okay, I'll be careful," I promised.

"And you've got to *believe!*" she added. "That's the most important of all."

Gingerly, I followed her directions, suddenly aware of the limited confines of this craft. You could fall off, at that! And if you got scared and didn't believe, it was no use. . . .

That little girl has children of her own now; she has learned there is no magic carpet that will fly us to the lands of our dreams. But she knows that God has given us something better: the Bible. And if we do our best, and believe what it tells us, there is no limit to the wonderful places we can go with Him.

Dear Lord, You know how often I've had to scrooch *down and hang on hard in my journey of faith. But please help me spread the word that Your Word has never failed me!*   —Marjorie Holmes

16
SUN

Thy word is a lamp unto my feet, and a light unto my path.   —Psalm 119:105

Even though I don't do a lot of cooking, I'm in the kitchen a few hours every day, usually at the counter, reading mail, paying bills, writing letters, talking on the phone or watching the news. Ever since we moved into this house, I've wished that the kitchen ceiling light was brighter. The fixture would only allow sixty-watt bulbs, and as my fiftieth birthday and a new eyeglass prescription loomed, I decided it was time to "light up my life."

I brought home a huge light fixture that held four four-foot-long fluorescent bulbs. After my dad installed the thing, we had our first ceremonial "turn on." Light bounced off the walls, from window to door, ceiling to floor. There was light everywhere! It made me so happy that I couldn't wait to get up in the morning to turn it on.

At the same time, another area of my life was as dreary as my kitchen had been: my faith. Oh, I went to church every Sunday, said my daily prayers and even taught Sunday school to high school sophomores. But my faith wasn't growing.

Then I read in our church bulletin that Father Ron was starting an adult Bible study class. I decided to go. As we made our way through the Gospel of John, I felt my faith grow brighter and stronger as I gained new knowledge of God's Word.

I only wish I'd done this earlier! Now I can't wait to get up each morning and turn on my faith, too.

Lord, help me to light up my own faith and spirituality by continuing to learn about Your Word.   —Patricia Lorenz

17
MON

First of all, then, I urge that entreaties and prayer, petitions and thanksgivings, be made on behalf of all men, for kings and all who are in authority. . . .
—I Timothy 2:1–2 (NAS)

When my wife Beth and I were dating, she was an intern for Gov. Jimmy Carter of Georgia. Later, after we were married, Governor Carter became President Carter. I had a proud and excited wife!

Soon after the election, Beth and I were invited to a dinner where I met the President-elect. I was amazed at how "human" he was: physically small, with a soft voice and shy smile, twinkling eyes and a sense of humor. I related to his accent because we are from the same region of Georgia. He seemed so much like the folks I had known all my life, he could have been my neighbor.

On that night, more than twenty years ago, the President of the United States became for me not a TV luminary but a real human being, flesh and blood, with needs like my own. I realized the awesome weight and responsibility that were on his frail shoulders. I began to pray daily that God would guide and encourage him.

Every Presidents' Day, I renew my resolve to support the President with my prayers. Whether I agree or disagree with his policies, he needs guidance from God that only prayer can impart.

Dear God, be with the President of the United States this day. Give him Your strength and wisdom. Amen.   —Scott Walker

18
TUE   *Put on a heart of compassion. . . .*
                              —Colossians 3:12 (NAS)

I left my mother in the car while I hurried into the drugstore to get a prescription filled for her. We'd just learned she had cancer of the spine, and she was now living with us. A conversation I'd had with a nurse at the doctor's office still rang in my ears.

I'd called with a question about my mother, and I thought the nurse had been rude to me. Probably I'd overreacted, but I couldn't shake off my hurt feelings. Neither could I handle anyone talking sharply to me. Maybe it was just that my feelings were so fragile now. Cancer often makes the caregiver feel like a child—helpless and not too smart. I was desperate for encouragement of any kind.

The druggist looked gruff, as though he weren't having a very good day. Looking way up at him in his ivory tower behind the high counter and feeling even more unstable, I handed him Mother's prescription. *Would he ask difficult questions about Mother's insurance? Maybe he would be out of the pain medication. Would I have to wait forever?*

"Here you are, miss," he said, interrupting my wandering thoughts. As I reached for the bag, he opened it and dropped two pieces of peppermint candy in with the prescription. If he'd dropped two gold nuggets into the bag, I wouldn't have been happier or more encouraged. I was still smiling when I got back to the car.

Dear Father, teach me how to share Your kindness with everyone I meet. Amen.   —Marion Bond West

19
WED

He gathers the lambs in his arms and carries them close to his heart; he gently leads those that have young.
—Isaiah 40:11 (NIV)

I work in the main office of MOPS (Mothers of Preschoolers) International, an outreach ministry that nurtures and encourages mothers during that demanding, fatiguing season of life when they are raising young children. Most of our one thousand groups meet in churches, and each has a "Titus Woman," an older mom like me who mentors the younger moms. So part of my job is to talk to young moms and ask them how older moms can help them.

"I need understanding," a mom told me recently. "I need someone to acknowledge my feelings, not try to talk me out of them. Like yesterday in the grocery store. There I was, zooming up and down the aisles with three little kids jumping in and out of my shopping cart. I finally got to the checkout stand, where I felt like an octopus, trying to keep six eager little hands from grabbing gum off the candy rack in that narrow aisle. I was about to lose it.

"Just then, an older woman wheeled her cart in behind me, smiled sweetly and said the words I often hear from moms who have already raised their children. 'Honey, enjoy these years,' she told me. 'They pass so quickly.' I know she meant to encourage me, but suddenly I felt guilty, because at that moment I didn't enjoy being a mom at all. I needed someone to understand my feelings and let me know that I'm not a bad mom if I sometimes feel that way."

As I listened to her, I knew that I make the same mistake. I quickly give out advice or reflections from my nice and neat "empty nest" before giving out some compassion. I tell others how they *should* feel, before acknowledging how they *do* feel. So as I finished my conversation with this young mom, I wrote myself a reminder in the form of this prayer:

Jesus, You taught us how to show genuine compassion and understanding to others. Help me follow Your example.   —Carol Kuykendall

20

THU

"Be strong, and of good courage. Fear not. . . ."
                         —I Chronicles 22:13 (RSV)

I saw the notice in our daily newspaper. The Phoenix Suns basketball team was holding auditions for singers to perform the National Anthem at home games.

I've sung all my life, even sung the anthem a few times, and being a big Suns fan, this sounded like fun. But almost immediately the doubting voices inside me weighed in. *There must be lots of singers better than you. Your performing days are over. You should stay in church choir where you belong.* Soon any thought I'd entertained of taking a chance had been frightened away.

Then I ran across a quote by playwright Neil Simon that first made me laugh, then think. Simon wrote, "If no one ever took risks, Michelangelo would have painted the Sistine floor." How right! After all, what did I have to gain by not trying?

So I drove down to the arena and auditioned with about two hundred other hopefuls for only thirty singing spots. The place seemed cavernous, empty but for a microphone at center court and a few people, other auditioners and our judges, sprinkled throughout the courtside seats. It was nerve-wracking, but it felt good to stretch my risk-taking muscles, to feel the adrenaline pumping, the nervous excitement, to use the gift God had given me.

I wasn't chosen, but I have to say it was worth the gamble. Even though I didn't succeed in reaching my ultimate goal, I felt success in trying. Enough, at least, that I'm ready to give it another try next year. I'll let you know how it goes.

Lord, give me the courage to stretch past my safe boundaries, so I don't paint the floor but reach for the sky.   —Gina Bridgeman

21

FRI

If we are to share his glory, we must also share his suffering.
                         —Romans 8:17 (TLB)

From the very beginning, Andrew was certain we should get married. I sure wasn't! I was the paragon of caution: We'd been seeing each other regularly for months before I'd even concede that we were dating. I warned him repeatedly that he shouldn't hope too much, and that he certainly shouldn't expect me to be ready too soon.

Then New Year's Eve rolled around. After I'd cooked a special dinner, Andrew leaned back and said, "I don't know what I'm going to do if you don't marry me."

I smiled at him in the candlelight and replied, "Well, you haven't asked me lately." Surprised, he asked. I said yes.

As sometimes happens, however, there were a few seeds of worry left in my heart. After the excitement of sharing the happy news of our engagement wore off, my worries slowly took new root. Unbeknownst to Andrew, within a few months they were in full blossom. And so it was that one evening after we'd had a minor spat, I burst into copious and unexpected tears.

"I don't know if we should get married!" I wailed. "What if we don't get along? What if ten years down the road we get on each other's nerves? What if? . . ." My voice trailed off as anxiety about the future tightened my throat.

Andrew was quiet for a minute. Then he took my hand. "Julia," he said slowly, "there's one thing you can be sure of. If we are meant to walk this road together, there must be a cross on it somewhere."

I married him. It was the best decision of my life.

Lord Jesus, only by walking with You on the road to Calvary can we arrive at Easter Day. Help me to remember that every trouble can bring me closer to You, if only I let it.   —Julia Attaway

22
SAT

For God . . . made his light shine in our hearts to give us the light of the knowledge of the glory of God in the face of Christ.   —II Corinthians 4:6 (NIV)

Once when our granddaughter Jessica, about twelve at the time, came to visit my wife Shirley and me in Princeton, New Jersey, we made an excursion to some of the area's historical sites. Jessica's class had been studying the Revolutionary War, and she suddenly became aware of the fact that her grandparents live in the middle of some significant American landmarks.

Among the places we visited were Washington's Crossing, Pennsylvania, where General Washington crossed the Delaware; Trenton, where the Continentals surprised the Hessians on Christmas Eve, 1776; Princeton Battlefield, marked by an old oak under which Gen.

Hugh Mercer was mortally wounded; and Nassau Hall, the first building of Princeton University, which was hit by cannon fire during the battle. We also followed roads that were traveled by General Washington and his troops, and crossed over some bridges that are silent sentinels of history.

Jessica was impressed. "Just think," she said, running her hands over the old stones of Kingston bridge, "George Washington was right here!"

Now her history lessons about some of the events that shaped our country will take on new meaning. Rather than just reading names and dates in a book, she will have concrete images to go with them. Amazing what firsthand experience can do for our understanding and appreciation of things.

It's certainly true in matters of faith. The famous painting of George Washington kneeling in prayer in the snow at Valley Forge is a powerful reminder that we all have Someone to Whom we can turn when troubles mount, that we don't have to fight our battles alone. I doubt it was either the first or the last time the "father of our country" called upon his heavenly Father for strength and sustenance.

For once we feel His abiding presence, once we see the breadth of His grace, once we personally know the depth of His love, we are changed forever. Like Jessica's history lessons, faith in our Creator becomes real when we experience it firsthand.

> *When perplexed and troubled by life's mystery,*
> *Help us discern, O God, Your hand in history.*
>
> —Fred Bauer

23
SUN   *My mouth is filled with thy praise. . . . Do not cast me off in the time of old age. . . .*   —Psalm 71:8–9 (RSV)

"Don't get old!"

That's advice I hear every Sunday from the ladies I pick up for church as they struggle to get into the car. One turned ninety last year, and the others are all in their eighties.

"Don't get old," they repeat, and we all laugh ruefully. Because we know there's no help for it—we *are* getting old. And as I see them slowing down, unable to do all the things they used to do, I know that eventually the same thing will happen to me.

Yet in the things that count, my friends aren't getting old. They come to church faithfully every Sunday. Several of them are faithful members of our Thursday evening prayer meeting. Martha and Julia bake cakes and goodies for our church coffee hours, and Vera always makes the coffee. Agnes crochets lap robes to be given away. Viola makes hundreds of craft items for our semiannual flea markets at which all of them help out. Their spirits have stayed young.

Then tonight I read Psalm 71. "An old man's prayer" is the title given to it in *The Jerusalem Bible.* I was surprised to find that the Psalmist didn't protest his getting old. He just asked for God's continued presence and blessing so he could go on praising God for all His wonderful deeds, "even to old age and gray hairs" (Psalm 71:18, RSV).

As I get older, I want to follow my friends' examples: to keep busy for the Lord. But even more, I want to follow the Psalmist's example: "O God. . . . My mouth will tell of thy righteous acts, of thy deeds of salvation all the day long" (Psalm 71:12, 15, RSV).

Lord, keep me youthful in spirit, and always praising You.
—Mary Ruth Howes

24
MON   *Confess your faults one to another. . . .*   —James 5:16

"All right, *I'll* put them to bed!" I grumbled. Frightened little faces glanced around the dinner table through the field of hostile energy that surrounded their scowling parents.

Later, alone in the dark, I sat on the edge of my daughter's bed and tucked her in. "All right," I said sternly, "let's say our prayers."

Silence. So I began, "Dear Lord, bless Mommy, Daddy, sisters, Aunt Nan and our doggy."

Silence, then a miniature echo of my words.

With a start, I realized that I never had prayed about what was really going on in my life when I prayed with the kids. I had been teaching them about prayer, but I wasn't praying. I thought about the fuss I had had with their mother and how my anger had frightened them.

Confess, a voice in my head said firmly.

"Maybe she won't respect me if I confess," I said silently.

Well, at least you'll have told the truth.

So I began again, "Dear Lord, forgive me for being controlling and trying to boss Mommy around at the dinner table. Help me not to do that anymore."

Silence. Then a tiny voice in the dark, very hesitant: "Dear Lord, forgive me for tinkling under the big tree in the backyard last summer."

My daughter is grown up now, and she prays with her own children. I hope that she remembers my honest confession the way I remember hers.

When I come to You in prayer today, dear God, may it be with simple and honest words, and an open and listening heart.   —Keith Miller

25
TUE   *Give to him that asketh thee, and from him that would borrow of thee turn not thou away.*   —Matthew 5:42

In the 1930s, when the Great Depression was strangling the country, our family always had well-stocked pantry shelves. My father was a wholesale grocer, and he was able to buy us canned meats and vegetables at a very low cost. But not all our neighbors were as fortunate.

Mrs. Richardson often visited in our kitchen while Mother was preparing lunch. She would stand where her glance could take in the pantry and silently inventory its holdings. A few minutes after she left, her little boy would appear at our back door.

"Mama wants to borrow a can of green beans until Saturday," he would say.

Mother would put a can of beans into a slightly rumpled brown paper bag. Sometimes she'd add a can of something else, like corn or peas.

"Tell your mother I'd appreciate her trying this corn and giving me her honest opinion of it," she'd say.

I was grown before I fully understood what those "borrowings" had meant. My mother knew that she was blessed to have all of that good food. She also knew that Mrs. Richardson probably had nothing in her house to make a proper meal and, most likely, no money to buy anything. So Mother, in her genteel way, shared even more than she was asked.

Lord, when I meet anyone who might be hungry, remind me to "add a little bit of meat to the stew."   —Drue Duke

26
"What she has done will also be told, in memory of her."
—Matthew 26:13 (NIV)

In February 1993, I received a letter from a woman in Chili, Wisconsin, named Linda Roehl. She was trying to get a pen pal named Linda in every one of the fifty states and had seen my name in a magazine. Would I be interested in corresponding?

How ridiculous! I thought at first. *What on earth would we correspond about?* But on the spur of the moment I decided to write to her.

The "other Linda" and I corresponded for over a year. On the surface, we had nothing in common: She was a Wisconsin native, while I grew up in bustling New York City and now live in California. She had children; I had none. Our hobbies—hers were needlework and corresponding with pen pals; mine were moviegoing, walking and studying sign language—were very different. Yet when I shared my worries about a friend's surgery, Linda comforted me in her next letter. When I told her that my husband's new job required traveling and I missed him, she told me how she coped with her truck-driver husband's absences. And she told me that she was sick, though she didn't dwell on her pain.

Two months ago, I got a letter written in an unfamiliar handwriting from a now very familiar address in Wisconsin. Linda Roehl had died.

I was heartbroken. Through Linda's letters, I had grown to know her and to treasure her as a friend. And I had come to see that she had ministered a rare gift of comfort, thanks to her whimsical idea of a "Linda" pen pal club. So I decided to continue the club. Anyone named Linda could join by writing to me and I'd match them up with a Linda in another state. The idea seemed almost ridiculous. But what could be more of a tribute to my pen pal than to carry on her work of connecting people?

Dear God, help me to remember my departed friends by carrying on their good work in my actions today.   —Linda Neukrug

27
Jesus Christ is the same yesterday and today and for ever.
—Hebrews 13:8 (RSV)

A few years ago, my sister's family underwent major changes when her little girls were three and five years old. One day the five-year-old was particularly cross. When she and her mother got into a rousing shouting match, my sister decided a time-out was necessary for both of them. A few minutes later little Erica came down the stairs. "Mother," she said matter-of-factly, "you must know that's not what I'm *really* mad about. I'm really mad about something else."

"Well, then," said Tresa, smiling, "have you figured out what it is you're *really* mad about?"

"I'm mad," declared Erica, crossing her arms over her chest and emphatically stomping one foot, "because there's so much change around here! *And I don't like change!*"

Tresa thought for a moment. "Erica," she said, "let's think of things that *are* the same, while everything else changes. I'll start. We still sleep in the same house. Now your turn."

"It's still my birthday next week!"

"You still go to the same school."

"I still like gummy bears!"

Tresa's children have survived their family upheaval. And now, whenever the changes in my own life—children growing up and the years passing by—begin to upset me, I remember Tresa's wisdom and make my own list:

I still have two of my three children at home.

I still have my friends.

I still *don't* like gummy bears.

And I still have One Who will never leave me.

In the midst of change, You, Lord, are my abiding constant.

—Brenda Wilbee

28   *I cry to you for help, O Lord; in the morning my prayer*
FRI   *comes before you.*   —Psalm 88:13 (NIV)

"Is she there?" I asked Sherry, when my call bounced from my mother's room to the front desk. Sherry is one of the supervisors at the group home in Michigan where my mother, stricken with Alzheimer's, lives.

"She's praying with some of the other ladies," Sherry replied. It was a new Friday activity for the unit, along with shopping at a nearby mall and lunch at a popular restaurant.

Later, I got through to Mom in her room. "I called this morning," I said by way of reassuring small talk.

"Well, I must have been busy praying," Mom replied.

Strange, I mused, *that she should say that. Sherry must have just reminded her about those morning prayers.* Mom's illness forces her to live very much in the moment. She rarely remembers having spoken to me even fifteen minutes after the fact. When I call, she reacts with spontaneous joy, as if I am her long-lost prodigal son. Every conversation is a kind of reunion.

The next time I called on a Friday afternoon she said the same thing: "I was busy all morning praying."

Mom hadn't remembered the mall or the restaurant, so I asked Sherry about this mnemonic oddity. "Oh, yes," Sherry assured me. "The one thing your mom never forgets is her prayers. We never have to remind her."

What can be crueler than a disease that steals our memories? My mother's mind is irreversibly eroding, like a sandy strip of beach being swept off by the charging surf, grain by grain. But prayer is a practice of the soul, an ongoing reunion with God. Mom has been in conversation with heaven for a long time. It helps me to know that her conversation continues, uninterrupted.

God, I will remember that prayer is a reunion with You.

—Edward Grinnan

Everyday Wonders

1 _____

2 _____

3 _____

4 _____

5 _____

6 _____

7 _____

8 _____

9 _____

10 _____

11 _____

12 _____

13 _____

14 _____

15 _____

16 _____

17 _____

18 _____

19 _____

20 _____

21 _____

22 _____

23 _____

24 _____

25 _____

26 _____

27 _____

28 _____

For God so loved the world, that
he gave his only begotten Son,
that whosoever believeth in him
should not perish, but have ever-
lasting life.   *—JOHN 3:16*

March

S	M	T	W	T	F	S
						1
2	3	4	5	6	7	8
9	10	11	12	13	14	15
16	17	18	19	20	21	22
23	24	25	26	27	28	29
30	31					

1

LOVE IS . . .

Love bears all things. . . .   —I Corinthians 13:7 (RSV)

She greeted me at the door of her tidy mobile home in Eureka, California, its walls hung with pictures of grandchildren, a sixty-something woman with a radiant smile. "And that's my husband Ken." She pointed to a photo of a man in his mid-fifties.

It was in order to have more time together that eight years earlier Ken and Clyda Holbrook had quit their separate jobs and taken on the management of a 158-unit motel in Los Angeles. Ken had set the coffeemaker late one night—Ken always woke Clyda with coffee for their morning prayer time—when the night bell rang. When Ken opened the door, two men entered. At knifepoint they made Ken and Clyda open the wall safe, then lie face down on the floor. As the couple lay prone, the departing thieves stabbed both of them in the back.

Ken was dead before the ambulance arrived, Clyda in the hospital for months of surgery on her punctured lungs and kidneys. Released, but still in constant pain, Clyda had other blows to bear. Friends avoided her; the motel owners refused her calls; prospective new employers turned her down.

How could this be? She was the victim, not the criminal! It was in her prayer time one morning—Clyda makes the coffee herself now—that God helped her understand. *Seeing you reminds people that violence could happen to them, too.*

It was to find work that Clyda had moved up here to the opposite end of the state. And it was here during that daily rendezvous with God that He spoke again. *When the world keeps handing you blows, keep handing back love.*

Love in response to violence, love in answer to fear. "When I asked God for opportunities to love, they came right to my trailer door." Lonely old people, tired young mothers, the sick, the discouraged. "And each in turn passes the love along. We've started a 'love wave' here instead of a crime wave." Only in this case, she said, "it's more like a tidal wave. Because it's not our own love we hand on. It's His."

God of love, Who endured the worst the world could do, give me the love that turns every loss into gain.
                                —Elizabeth Sherrill

2

Continue in prayer, and watch. . . .   —Colossians 4:2

It began as a simple comment in our Sunday morning "Prayer Can Change Your Life" class.

"Why don't we try recording our answered prayers?" Steve, a young businessman, suggested some months ago. "We'll all fill out cards with each class member's prayer request, then pray for these specific needs throughout the week. If any of the prayers we say for each other are being answered, shouldn't we acknowledge it?"

We agreed to try Steve's idea. In anticipation of our next meeting, someone rummaged through the Sunday school supply closet and came up with a large sketch pad and a fancy box of new magic markers. "With such creative materials, shouldn't our resident artist Karinne officially transcribe our answered prayers?" someone asked.

A light mood danced across the morning, but inside I worried: *We're going out on a limb here. With no answered prayers, will our class dwindle away?*

The next Sunday Karinne opened the pad. The first empty page didn't seem to intimidate her. *Are we putting our faith to an unfair test?* I fretted.

Jim, who calls himself our prayer-class skeptic, spoke up first. "Okay, so last week, I was only about half-serious when I asked you to pray for my sick computer. Well, not only did it work when I got home, it's worked great all week! For me, that's an answered prayer. Write it in the book!"

"I asked you to pray that my girls got home safely from their weekend trip," Cindy added. "They arrived safe and sound."

"The gossip at work really does seem to be leveling off," another member admitted.

Nothing earthshaking, I thought. But that was before the pages of our "answered prayer book" started filling with healings of hurt feelings *and* incurable cancer, of changed hearts, job promotions and solutions to financial problems. Now, following the lead of these faithful friends, I continually see prayers being answered; sometimes exactly as asked, other times with a cleverness that only God can manage.

Father, offering my prayers to You, I watch for Your answers with thanksgiving.
                                                                    —Pam Kidd

3   *And even the very hairs of your head are all numbered.*

MON   —Matthew 10:30 (NIV)

Some years back, I was scheduled for major surgery to remove a large recurring tumor inside my head. All of my hair would have to be shaved off. A friend, sensing my sadness at losing the long, layered, frosted shag I'd worked so hard to acquire, treated me to an appointment with her beautician.

"I think we should trim it a little," Gary recommended after he shampooed and conditioned my hair. He pointed to a picture on the wall featuring a snazzy style slightly shorter than mine.

What's the use? I thought. *In a couple of days it will just end up in a paper sack by my hospital bed. I've been through this twice before.* Nevertheless, I agreed reluctantly and left my curls behind in a plastic dustpan on the black-checkered linoleum floor.

Three weeks later, Gary telephoned out of the blue to tell me he had a gift for me. Without my suspecting it, he'd saved a snippet of my hair so he could surprise me with a wig in precisely the right color. It was so becoming that I sometimes wore it even after my hair grew back just to bask in the compliments.

Today, that act of kindness is tucked away in my memory. But I treasure it all the more for the spiritual lesson it taught me: In the darkest hours of life, when we least suspect it, our Heavenly Father is making provision for our every need.

Lord, help me to remember that You love me so much, You even know the number of hairs on my head.   —Roberta Messner

4   *You shall open wide your hand to your brother. . . .*

TUE   —Deuteronomy 15:11 (RSV)

When you're away at college, there's something wildly lavish about ordering pizza. My friend Rob Hoskins and I had been cramming for a huge marketing test half the night, and we were starving.

"Kidd, you got any money?" Hoskins asked. "I'm thinking pizza."

I went through my pockets. One dollar bill. Two quarters. About enough for two colas. I went over to the desk and riffled through the drawer. Seven pennies. In the meantime, Hoskins had come up with another dollar and fifteen cents.

"Oh, man," I said, "I wish you hadn't mentioned pizza."

A little loopy from studying, we went to the living room of the fraternity house where we lived. We lifted the cushions on the couch and looked under all the furniture. Another nickel, a dime and another quarter.

"Hey, what about our coat pockets!" I said, heading back toward the room. I was now a man with a mission.

On the way, something told me to stop at the mail table in the hall. I was surprised to see a letter addressed to me in my sister Keri's handwriting. I ripped open the letter, and a ten dollar bill fluttered to the floor. "Have a pizza on your sister," I read in amazement. Keri was in the ninth grade at the time. I knew that this was money she had earned baby-sitting.

Before the hour was over, Rob and I were eating the best pizza of our lives.

Now I smile to myself, remembering those empty-pocket days. I think there will never be another pizza quite like the one Rob and I shared that night.

Or maybe there will be, I think as I slip a twenty into an envelope addressed to my sister at Birmingham Southern College. "Have a pizza on your brother," I write at the end of my note. I feel rich beyond description.

God, help me to remember how rich it makes me when I give freely to others. —Brock Kidd

5

WED   *Hide me under the shadow of thy wings.*   —Psalm 17:8

Roland and I had met a decade before, and several years after his wife's death we renewed our acquaintance. Now we decided to marry. So on this March day, I found myself sitting in an airplane, bound for Syracuse, New York, and a new life.

I already feel alone, and we're not even close to Syracuse yet. I don't know a soul there except Roland. He has scores of colleagues at the university and friends he's known for years. Will they accept me? Will I ever fit in?

Suddenly, my thoughts were interrupted by a voice from the cabin's loudspeaker. "This is your captain. If you'll look out the windows on the left side of the aircraft, you'll see a circular rainbow with our plane's shadow in the center of the bull's eye. Pilots often call this corona 'the glory.' It occurs when atmospheric conditions are perfect—as they are now—and when sun, plane and shadow are in a straight line."

All of us passengers were awestruck. *Well, if God can put a heavenly halo around a whole plane full of passengers flying at thirty-five thousand feet, His loving presence can go with me anywhere! So why should I ever feel alone? Or afraid?*

I tilted my seat back and relaxed.

Thank You, Lord, for hiding me under the shadow of Your wings. I know I'm always safe there.   —Isabel Wolseley

---

6   *Behold, I have graven you on the palms of my hands. . . .*
THU   —Isaiah 49:16 (RSV)

It was a one-in-a-million happenstance. A nice-looking, dark-haired man approached my sister-in-law at an elementary school picnic in western Washington. The man, who'd learned her name was Carol Shirk, paused to scrutinize her. "No, you're not Carol. I thought you might be the Carol Shirk I once knew back in sixth grade."

My sister-in-law asked where he had attended elementary school. When he replied, "Loma Vista in Spokane, Washington," she burst out, "My husband's sister went to that school, and her name was Carol Shirk!" The man confessed, in a voice laden with nostalgia, that I had been his "first love."

When Carol told me the story, I could picture Tom clearly. He sat in the middle of the back row in our classroom. His slicked-down hair was always neatly parted on the left. His family had moved to California without my ever suspecting that he'd worn my name engraved on a chain around his neck for two years!

On a recent visit to my brother and his wife, I had the opportunity to meet Tom, but I chickened out. I didn't want to disappoint him. Thirty years is a big bubble to burst. The fear of "not measuring up" packed enough power to keep me away from a potentially enjoyable reunion.

It has blocked me in other places as well, sometimes even keeping me from drawing near to God. I need to remember Romans 5:8

(RSV): "But God shows his love for us in that while we were yet sinners Christ died for us." God accepts the whole package, my failures and imperfections included.

When I next visit my brother and his family, I'm taking something I left behind the last time: self-confidence born of the certainty that I am loved and accepted by God. And if Tom's still in town, I'll look him up. How else am I going to learn if he's still got that chain with my name engraved on it?

Dear God, with Your acceptance I can meet the world! —Carol Knapp

---

7
FRI

But you, O God, do see trouble and grief; you consider it to take it in hand. . . .   —Psalm 10:14 (NIV)

My mother died in a car accident when I was in the eighth grade and my brother Kelly was in the sixth. Since Mother's death, my father and I had made regular visits to her grave, but Kelly had always been reluctant to accompany us. He never seemed to want to talk about Mother. He seemed content to forget her completely, and that made me angry.

Then one sunny day toward the end of my sophomore year in college, I was driving home and decided to stop at the cemetery on my way. As I cleaned up the ground around Mom's grave, I saw something bright on the headstone. I took a closer look, and saw that it was a high school graduation tassel—and Kelly had graduated only a few days before.

I couldn't believe my eyes. After all those years of acting like he didn't care, Kelly had wanted to share this milestone in his life with Mother, in the only way he could think of. I had had no idea of the pain he carried with him. Just because I couldn't see it, I assumed it didn't exist.

Today, Lord, I pray for all those in my life with hidden hurts.
                                                        —Hollie Davis

---

8
SAT

For he shall give his angels charge over thee. . . .
                                                        —Psalm 91:11

I was talking to my poet friend Paula about my apartment, which has been home for some twenty-three years. They have been, on the whole, good years in a place where I've always felt a sense of security.

"You probably have had a good angel looking after you," said Paula.

"Angels," I scoffed. "Don't talk to me about angels."

"You don't believe in them?"

"It's just that everybody is seeing them these days. It's like an epidemic. Okay, I know what the Bible says—they're real—but never having seen one myself, it's hard for me to believe in them."

"Oh," she said, "is it like your faith? You need evidence of something 'seen'?"

"Don't be smart," I said.

Not too long after that conversation, I had an appointment and crossed the street to my bus stop. As I stood there waiting, my eyes roamed over the facade of my apartment building. It's a large, pre-war structure with some fanciful towers and a generous amount of ornate decoration. I found the windows of my apartment and the air conditioner for my bedroom and . . .

For the first time in twenty-three years, I noticed a head peering over the air conditioner, its wings looming neatly behind it, a figure carved in stone—an angel.

Father, You are full of surprises, but I'm going to read Your Word more carefully to minimize them.   —Van Varner

9
SUN

I have called daily upon thee, I have stretched out my hands unto thee.   —Psalm 88:9

One Sunday morning—at a time when I was finding God peculiarly silent in answering a prayer—our church music director was frustrated by our choir's rehearsal of a difficult anthem. The piece divided into eight parts, two singers to a part, and as we split, the harmony dissolved into cacophony. It wasn't that we weren't hitting all the right notes; it was that we were hitting them at the wrong time, colliding into a musical logjam, our director flailing his arms like a traffic cop until he turned red in the face.

"I have an idea," he finally said. "Let me stop conducting you."

"No!" we protested. How could we manage without his high-flying hands? We would be lost.

"Let's try it," he insisted.

So we did. And an amazing thing happened. Instead of looking to the director for our cues, we looked at each other, listening carefully on those passages when we doubled each other, coming together for the occasional passages of unison, making perfect harmony. "It worked!" we said triumphantly.

And at that moment, it occurred to me that here was a key to my prayer problem. A spiritually astute friend once said, "Sometimes, Rick, God seems slow in answering prayer because He wants us to look around us for an answer that's already there." Sometimes He wants us to listen more closely to one another, finding guidance in family and friends instead of gazing at the heavens for some celestial cue.

"We need to listen to each other," I whispered to my fellow tenor.

"Amen," he said.

Lord, You have never not answered a prayer. Help me to see Your answer today.   —Rick Hamlin

10
MON

Moses was a hundred and twenty years old when he died: his eye was not dim, nor his natural force abated.
—Deuteronomy 34:7

"You owe a lot to Norman Vincent Peale, don't you?" a friend suggested recently.

"Yes, I do," I replied. "He gave me my first writing job (when as a young man I came from our mutual birthplace, Ohio, to New York), and he was always full of encouragement." I have a folder full of uplifting letters he wrote me over our thirty-year friendship. Of course, that was his stock in the trade: encouragement.

He was never too busy to pen a spirit-raising note to someone he felt needed a boost. Once I asked how he found time to answer so many letters. "I take the time to build people up," he replied, "because we've already got too many people in the demolition business."

One of my last meetings with him took place at his farm home, a few months before he died in 1994 at age ninety-five. Though his step had slowed and his once-powerful voice lacked its trademark timbre, there was nothing diminished about his spirit. It was, to use a favorite Dr. Peale word, *indomitable.* I remember asking him about one of his last speeches, a commencement address made at his alma mater, Ohio Wesleyan, on the seventy-second anniversary of his own graduation.

"What did you tell the graduation class?" I queried.

With eyes twinkling, he reported, "Shoot for the moon, and even if you miss, you may fall among the stars."

No wonder the whole country mourned his death.

Inspire us, God to use our utmost for Your glory,
To dare, to risk, to give our all—and not be sorry.

—Fred Bauer

11
TUE

"Let the little children come to me, and do not hinder them, for the kingdom of God belongs to such as these."
—Mark 10:14 (NIV)

My wife Rosie generally takes our children to see the doctor when they are ill. It was no different one Tuesday afternoon when she took our seven-year-old son Ryan to the doctor. While they were waiting to see him, Ryan went over to a bookshelf full of kids' books. He chose one, sat down and began to read aloud, not at all concerned about the opinions of the others who were waiting. He finished the book, went back for another one and continued reading.

By the third or fourth book, the people in the waiting room were amazed at Ryan's reading ability and asked Rosie how old he was and where he went to school. Without waiting for Rosie to answer, Ryan, with a gleam in his eye, responded, "I attend Genesis One Christian School in Mendenhall."

From the mouth of a babe came a testimony for our Christian school. On this day, our seven-year-old was a witness to everyone who heard him.

As Rosie shared what had happened with me, I thought, *Lord, take away my fear of witnessing and help me to speak out rather than be concerned about what people might think.* As parents, it's our responsibility to instruct our children, but isn't it wonderful to know that God can use them to teach us as well?

Lord Jesus, help me to have childlike faith and the boldness to witness to You.   —Dolphus Weary

12

He that speaketh truth showeth forth righteousness. . . .
—Proverbs 12:17

I read some of my stories to a second-grade class at one of our local schools. After I had finished reading, a little girl went to the closet and brought out a tray of frosted cupcakes her mother had made. I held on to the cupcake, intending to eat it later. Then I noticed that the children were staring at me. After a few moments, one of the students got my attention. She dropped her eyes and said, "Mr. Greene, we can't begin eating until you do." *Of course*—I was the guest, so it was up to me to begin.

A few days later, I went to my favorite bakery to buy some apricot fills for my daughter-in-law. As the clerk took down a large box for the cookies, a co-worker said, "Don't use that. Use the smaller box."

The clerk was slipping in the last of my cookies when the store owner happened by. "What are you doing?" she said to the clerk. "Don't pack those cookies in such a small box! By the time that man gets home, all he'll have is crumbs. Use the large box!" The owner grabbed the large box the clerk had been told not to use and as she packed the cookies, the clerk's embarrassment grew. The clerk didn't defend herself; she remained quiet, and so did I.

Then I remembered the little girl in that second-grade class who was uneasy about speaking up but felt she had to do so because it was right. I looked at the store owner and said, "In all fairness to the young lady, a co-worker told her to use the smaller box."

"Who told you to use the smaller box?" the owner asked.

When the clerk answered, the owner smiled, shook her head and patted the young lady's arm. Instantly, the tension and embarrassment vanished. As the clerk handed me my change, her smile filled the bakery.

Lord, when we see a wrong around us, give us the courage to speak up for what is right.   —Oscar Greene

13

God commanded me to make haste. . . .
—II Chronicles 35:21

"Have you finished your letter to your friend Phoebe?" my husband Paul asked me.

"I'll do it tomorrow," I said. "I'll write an extra line or two to make up for the fact that it's late."

The next day: "You asked me to remind you that you owe a letter to Phoebe," commented Paul.

"I'll double the length of the letter and make it extra interesting," I replied.

Day number three: "That letter?"

"I'm going to buy the Walnut Creek newspaper and cut out some clippings she'd be interested in. She'll see that it was worth waiting for."

Paul lifted an eyebrow. "Remember the booties?" he said, reminding me of the time several years earlier when a friend of mine was having a baby.

"I'll knit you a pair of booties," I had promised her. Those booties would have taken an hour or so for me to knit, if I had just sat down and knitted them. A few months later, when I saw her, I fibbed, "Oh, I decided to make you a crib blanket instead." But I put that off, too. The following year, I said, "I thought a three-piece sweater set would be nicer."

"Linda," she said, "My little girl is about to start nursery school!" I confessed the truth, and the two of us had a good laugh at how my procrastination had turned a pair of booties into an entire layette— both nonexistent.

I sat down with one piece of stationery and began. "Dear Phoebe. This letter may be short, but it will be prompt."

Today, God, push me a little to get started on that easy task I need to complete.
                                                        —Linda Neukrug

14

FRI

Do you not realize that Christ Jesus is in you?
                                        —II Corinthians 13:5

Early in Mother's illness, just after she'd come to live with us, Barbara Wright, a new friend of mine, came to the house to meet her. "What a pleasure to meet you, Mrs. Grogan," Barbara said, giving Mother an impromptu hug.

Mother beamed. "I'm really just fine. Of course, I have this . . . little c. It's not a big deal. It's just a tiny thing. It's not the Big C!"

Barbara got very close to Mother and said in a hushed voice, "Oh, but you do have the Big C. I can see that you do!" Barbara looked ecstatic.

Mother leaned forward, waiting for an explanation.

"You have Jesus Christ—He's the Big C. He's so much bigger than that 'little c' you have." The happiness on Barbara's face seemed to leap over to Mother's face, and they both beamed with delight.

Mother adored the idea. She told her doctors about "the Big C and the little c." She explained it to strangers in doctors' waiting rooms. She told her friends, the women in the beauty shop where she had her hair done and people waiting in line at the cafeteria where we often eat. She never tired of sharing that wonderful truth.

Lord Jesus, thank You for being bigger than any of my problems.

—Marion Bond West

WORDS OF WONDER

What wondrous love is this, O my soul, O my soul,
What wondrous love is this, O my soul!
What wondrous love is this that caused the Lord of
    bliss
To bear the dreadful curse for my soul, for my soul,
To bear the dreadful curse for my soul!

—AMERICAN FOLK HYMN

15

SAT   *Jesus wept.*   —John 11:35

I saw my father cry only once. I was nine. It was a Saturday night at dinner. He was sitting at the head of our table talking quietly and distractedly about the terrible ordeal our family was undergoing. Bobby, my mentally retarded twelve-year-old brother, had been missing for several weeks; police feared the worst. In a few days, they would be proved right when the winter ice gave way to spring thaw and they found his body in a nearby lake.

But now my father still clung to some strand of hope. Suddenly, he stood up, almost toppling his chair. I think he wanted to get away from us. Instead, he smothered his face in his napkin and his whole body convulsed; then deep, speechless sobs filled the silence. I sat at the far end of the table, rigid. Tears dripped from my father's chin. Finally, I heard my mother whisper, "Oh, Joe . . ." and soon my father was silent. I tried to finish my dinner. For the first time in my life, my father seemed destructible, and it frightened me more terribly than my brother's disappearance.

A week later, at my brother's funeral, my father didn't cry. I had decided that I wouldn't either. All through the service I sat stiffly in the pew trying not to look at Bobby's casket at the foot of the altar, trying not to listen to what was being said, trying not to cry. At the cemetery, a chill Michigan wind snapped at the priest's robes as he sprinkled holy water on the descending coffin. When we got to the restaurant where thirty or forty of us gathered afterward, I was relieved to be in out of the numbing spring cold, relieved it was over.

I looked around at the adults. They were hugging and crying, even the ones who like me had remained stoic throughout the long morning. Here they all were, their hearts overflowing, relieving their grief.

I found my big sister in the crowd. She was talking to an uncle. I wrapped my arms around her waist. I don't think she noticed as her wool skirt soaked up my tears.

Jesus wept, and in so doing proclaimed His humanness. Thank You, Father, for the gift of tears.
—Edward Grinnan

16

SUN   *Harden not your hearts. . . .*   —Psalm 95:8 (RSV)

I hadn't talked to my friend Geoffrey in quite awhile, although there was no particular reason for our lack of communication. Knowing that he was in the middle of an increasingly messy custody dispute, one Sunday after church I finally made it my business to track him down.

"How are you?" I asked. Over the years we'd talked a lot about prayer, so Geoffrey knew I was asking about both his emotional and spiritual state.

"Actually," he said, "I'm doing quite well. It's been really hard these past few months, but my prayer life is amazingly strong. I sort of stumbled onto a technique that has helped me enormously."

I asked him what it was.

"Well, whenever I find myself getting really angry or bitter, I bring myself to the foot of the Cross and kneel there. And then I mentally bring my former wife to kneel at my side."

"Wow," I said, "that sounds really hard."

"It can be," he replied. "Sometimes it takes a long time to let go enough to bring her there. But the way I look at it, if I can't kneel with someone in front of Jesus, my problems are much bigger than the problems I face in this world. So whenever I recognize an obstacle in my heart to that kind of union, I just pick it up and hang it on the Cross."

It takes courage to use Geoffrey's technique, as I discover every time I try it. It's the kind of courage I need more of.

Jesus, help me to realize that nothing is as hard as the wood of the Cross.
—Julia Attaway

17
MON

And so we shall always be with the Lord. Therefore comfort one another with these words.
—I Thessalonians 4:17–18 (RSV)

My Sunday school class was having fun celebrating St. Patrick's Day. We had found Ireland on the map and learned how St. Patrick introduced the people there to Christianity. As we cut out bright green shamrocks, we talked about the plant with its three leaves being like Father, Son and Holy Spirit, all one God.

But before we could have our shamrock cookies and green punch, the mood turned somber. Several children offered tearful prayers for grandparents. Lori's grandma had died the previous week, Ann's grandpa was battling cancer, and Christopher still missed his grandpa who had died four years ago.

I sympathized with the children. On St. Patrick's Day, I keenly missed my own dad, for he had exulted in this holiday. He had us all wear green, exclaiming, "For today, our name is O'Hohenstein!"

At the coffee hour after class, I found the social hall gaily decorated for the holiday. At the entrance was a papier-mâché Blarney stone to "kiss if you wish." On the walls were large green shamrocks with photos glued in the center. *Ah,* there was Christopher's grandpa with his arm around his wife. I studied the other faces smiling out from the emerald leaves—some parishioners already departed to their heavenly home, but others still serving here on earth.

I thought of how I missed Dad. Yet those photos in the center of each shamrock pointed to the invisible reality: Encircled in the eternal love of our Triune God, we are still together, with the arms of God around us, holding us close.

When we yearn for those who have gone ahead of us, Lord, help us draw near to You.   —Mary Brown

18
TUE   *My son . . . do not forsake your mother's teaching.*
                                              —Proverbs 6:20 (NIV)

I had just settled comfortably into my seat, ready to fly out of Chicago, when a tall man skidded breathlessly in beside me. With his numbered, red-and-blue satin jacket, he looked like a basketball player.

"Whew!" he gasped. "This is the third airplane I nearly missed today."

"How's that?" I asked.

"You know how it is. I got to watching the Lakers with my buddies in the bar and didn't hear the boarding call."

"Twice? Two flights?" I was incredulous.

"Yeah, pretty bad, huh?" He stretched his long legs out into the aisle, "Where've you been?"

I told him that I was on my way home to California after speaking at a Christian women's conference in the Chicago area.

"You're a church lady!" He nodded knowingly. "My mother, she's a church lady." Then he chuckled. "Come Sunday she made us kids get to Sunday school, and we better have known that Bible verse. Oh, yeah!"

We spent the next hour talking about his childhood and his mother's many good works in South Central Los Angeles. He had drifted away from his family and his faith. He hadn't seen his mother for more than a year.

When the flight attendant came to offer us drinks, he pulled out two dollars for a beer, then suddenly shoved it back in his pocket. "Hey, I'll have coffee."

When dinner was served I asked, "Did you say grace as a kid?"

"Oh, yeah," he said, "at every meal."

"On behalf of your church lady mother," I said, "could I say grace for us right now?"

"Sure, I'd like that."

"For what we are about to receive, dear Lord," I prayed, "we are truly thankful. . . . And bless this young man, his dear mother and all his family, wherever they may be. Amen."

A resounding "Amen" came from the flight attendant and many of the passengers in the seats around us.

"I'm gonna call my momma," he said. "Soon as I get off this plane, for sure, I'm gonna call."

After we had landed and I was trundling my suitcase through the bustle of the airport, I saw him hunched over a phone. He waved and gave me the high sign.

Little miracles are around us for the grasping. This one came from two missed airplanes and the blessed remembrance of a "church lady" mother.

Watch over our children who have slipped out of touch, dear Lord, and bring them safely home.   —Fay Angus

19
WED
Out of the mouth of babes and sucklings hast thou ordained strength. . . .   —Psalm 8:2

My dear granddaughter Hannah,

You are only two, and yet you have already mastered attitudes that have eluded me for half a century.

You react to life. You laugh or cry outright. You squeal or sing, jump up and down and shout. You seem to reach out and touch life, extracting joy from thin air. I act at life, trying hard to hide my true feelings. I am calm, controlled, dignified. No one would ever know how sad and lonely I can be. Or how excited!

You see opportunities everywhere; I see problems. You want to climb the attic stairs. You see steps; I see danger. You want to paint. I see mess; you see colors.

You love to learn. With wild abandon you tackle new words, new skills. You find laughter in mistakes; I find embarrassment. You want to know everything. *Book* is your favorite word. Questions are your favorite tools. I struggle to learn, hoping to master the computer in one easy lesson or not at all. I've forgotten how to laugh at blunders.

You live in the moment, your life a series of thrilling "nows." I languish in nostalgia or stew about a frightening future.

You are trusting. I could easily overtax your energies, but you trust my love completely, and with good reason. I am cautious. Disillusioned by people so many times, I've come to expect disappointment.

You are courageous. You walk right up to a stranger and smile. At lunch you boldly bite into broccoli, and though you dislike it, tomorrow you will tackle cauliflower with the same exuberance; I stick with the familiar favorites.

I love you for who you are!

Grandpa Dan

Dear Lord, if it's not too late, help me to grow up and become just like Hannah.   —Daniel Schantz

20
THU   *And ye shall know the truth, and the truth shall make you free.*   —John 8:32

"Your stepfather has the beginning of Alzheimer's disease," the neurologist told me. "That's why he has memory lapses."

I felt numb with dread. Besides forgetting things that had happened five minutes earlier, my dad was also getting his words mixed up. He'd say "clock" when he meant "telephone," or "book" when he meant "door." He realized it, too. He was embarrassed, frightened and very confused.

"Do we have to tell him?" I asked.

"I do," the doctor said. "I always tell my patients the truth. They have a right to know what to expect." Reluctantly, I went along with his decision, although I didn't agree with him. I wanted to spare my stepfather the pain of knowing he had an incurable disease.

As the doctor and I rejoined my stepfather in the examining room, I had all I could do to keep from crying. The doctor was direct but compassionate, and my dad listened carefully to every word. "Ray," he began, "you have a disease called Alzheimer's. A lot of people have it, and so far there isn't a cure. In your case, since you're eighty-five, it will progress slowly. You've had to remember so many things in your lifetime, so if you forget a few now and then, it's okay."

My dad took the news better than I had. He actually seemed relieved to know that his memory lapses weren't his fault. And now, several months later, he seems less confused than he had been. For instance, when he can't remember something, he simply says, "I forget," and we let it go at that. When he can't think of a word, he stops, starts his thought over and takes his time. Usually, he finds the right word.

Day by day, I'm understanding a little more of what Jesus meant when He said, "The truth shall make you free." For my stepfather, it means freedom from embarrassment and fear. He knows he isn't going to get better, but he also knows it's okay to grow old. For me, it means freedom from trying to carry a loved one's burden all by myself.

Lord, may we always love the truth and have the courage to live in it.
—Phyllis Hobe

21
FRI

Keep sound wisdom and discretion . . . and they will be life for your soul. . . . —Proverbs 3:21–22 (RSV)

Last Saturday, we had to put our cat Mookie Wilson to sleep. Mookie was a great mouser, but not too accurate with the litter box. Then, last week, she decided to hide behind the washer and wait for death.

I cried when I left Mookie at the vet's for the last time, but not only for the expected reasons. It was something the vet had said: "An outdoor cat like Mookie—well, twelve years is a ripe old age."

"You mean they usually die of feline leukemia or something?" I asked.

"Well, things like that, of course," the vet replied. "But mostly, it's cars."

I don't frighten easily; I've shot the rapids and climbed rocks. But two tons of metal spinning out of control is not a game or a thrill. It's blood and broken bones and funerals and regret.

So I was crying, not because of what I'd lost, but because of what I could lose, because I was scared. I was thinking of my kids, who won't be driving until the year 2007. I was thinking of all that I needed to tell them. I was thinking of how invincible I felt when I was sixteen, and drove like it. How the grace of God and good brakes had saved my life at least a dozen times.

And I was crying because I knew that someday I would let my daughters leave, keys in hand. They'll get into the car, and they'll drive safely until they're out of sight, and I'll wave to them, trying desperately to breathe around the heart lodged in my throat, wondering if I've told them enough, wondering if they'll learn the way I learned, wondering if it's too late.

Lord, don't let me waste the wisdom You and the years have taught me. And watch over everyone driving—today and always. —Mark Collins

CLOSER TO
THE CROSS

22
SAT   **Saturday before Palm Sunday**

And Jesus went about . . . healing all manner of sickness . . .
among the people.   —Matthew 4:23

In early January, I had a back-twisting fall that left me with a pinched
sciatic nerve, causing murderous pain that shot from back to hip, leg,
ankle and foot. I stood and walked bent over, and even sitting and
lying down hurt. I couldn't get away from the pain. After trying
every possible medical remedy, two doctors recommended surgery.
But I held off for months, praying almost constantly, hoping for a
miracle.

Yet God seemed far away, unreal. I truly believed that Jesus healed
many during His earthly life, but I began to question: Does He still
heal? Could He, would He actually heal *me?*

Then one evening, after "storming heaven" with prayer, I sat in
the stillness and listened. An idea began to form in my mind. Perhaps I could imagine that I was one of those among the crowd of sick,
deaf, blind and lame who came to Jesus for healing. Perhaps Jesus'
healing presence might come alive in my life now, so I could truly
pray believing.

Tomorrow is Palm Sunday. I invite you to join me in being present for the events of that final week of Jesus' earthly life, seeing them
through the eyes of one who waits to be healed. Please bring with
you anything in your life that needs healing.

Loving Lord Jesus, we bring You our disabilities and our pain. Please
touch us with Your healing Presence.   —Marilyn Morgan Helleberg

23

SUN   **Palm Sunday**

And they that went before, and they that followed, cried, saying,
Hosanna; Blessed is he that cometh in the name of the Lord.
—Mark 11:9

On Palm Sunday, our church joins with the congregation down the
street, and we all process from their church to ours, following the
Cross, waving palm branches and singing, "Hosanna!" Then we
worship together. My back wouldn't let me be in the procession this
year, so I waited in a pew. In the silence, as I began to hear the first
faint cries of "Hosanna," I closed my eyes and imagined myself
right there in Jerusalem on the day of Jesus' triumphal entry into the
city.

Because it hurts to walk, I wait at the bottom of the hill trying to sort
out my thoughts. People have said this man can heal, and I want so much
to believe it, but unless I see it myself. . . . Besides, the crowd's so big, and
there are so many worse off than I, like that little girl over there, so pale
and limp in her mother's arms, and that paralytic man carried here by his
friends, and that young woman who can't stop crying. Even if this man
can heal, I doubt he'll notice me.

There's moaning among us as we watch the other people tearing palm
branches from nearby trees and throwing their cloaks onto the road. They
say this Jesus is to be the new king. I wonder if he'll be like Solomon or
another Caesar. I suppose he'll be dressed in purple robes and riding a fine
steed.

Wait! What's this? A plain-looking man wearing simple clothes, riding
on a donkey! And isn't that the tax collector and some ragged fishermen
walking beside him? Yet it must be the man called Jesus because they're
waving the palm branches now and shouting, "Hosanna!"

Oh, those eyes! They looked right into mine, as though he knew me, as
if there were something in those eyes especially for me. King or not, I want
to keep following this man.

As the crossbearer enters the church now, followed by the singing
choir and congregation, a silent shout of joy wells up in my heart. "I
have been touched by the eyes of the King! He knows me! Hosanna!"

I'm just a common person, Lord, unknown to any earthly king. But You
have shown me the first step toward healing: trusting that You know me,
and that You care.   —Marilyn Morgan Helleberg

24
MON   **Monday of Holy Week**

My house shall be called the house of prayer....

—Matthew 21:13

Brrring! I slam my hand down on the snooze button of my alarm clock. I'd planned to go to daily Communion during Holy Week, but I've had a fitful night of pain. It's just too hard to get up. In fact, *everything* seems too hard these days. I have deep fears that I won't survive surgery. I have so many new fears—fear of surgery, fear of death, fear of a crippled life, even fear of my own anger. Lying in bed now, wavering among my fears, I start to doze, and I imagine myself in the outer court of the temple in Jerusalem.

Suddenly, as I wait among the hurting, a wild scene bursts out around me. A fierce man with fiery eyes and a whip in his hand storms past, flinging tables here and there, pouring out coins, cracking his whip of cords near fleeing animals! Cowering vendors scramble after clattering coins rolling across the paving stones. Animals run squealing away! Who is this man with eyes like fire, the strength of a lion and the fearlessness of God, whose voice rings out across the court: "My Father's house shall be called a house of prayer!"

Oh, I can't believe it! It's that Jesus again . . . and he's heading toward us, this strange community of now-cringing sufferers! Suddenly, I'm weak with fear. Could this be the same man whose eyes looked into mine with such compassion only yesterday?

But now he has chased them all out—the animals and their peddlers— and the temple stands clear and silent. Yet I feel no reverence: fear still quivers in my heart.

Yes, I must cleanse this temple that I am. To make room for reverence, I need to drive out fear and the other negative emotions that have set up shop within.

Lord Jesus, lend me Your power to cleanse my inner temple, and Your courage to let go of fear, that my soul may truly be a house of prayer. Amen.

—Marilyn Morgan Helleberg

25
TUE   **Tuesday of Holy Week**

What sign showest thou unto us? . . .   —John 2:18

"Do something, Lord! Please!" Sitting in my blue prayer chair by the window, trying to find the least painful position, I cry out to God in anguish. "You said if I'd pray believing, my prayers would be answered. Yet I've prayed and prayed for healing, and it doesn't happen. Why, Lord? Why?" As I close my eyes and beg for some sign that my prayers are heard, I find myself once again at the Jerusalem temple.

Leaning against a white marble wall in the outer court of this magnificent building, begun forty years ago and not yet finished, I'm struck by the glint from the gold-plated walls inside, bright in the morning sun. Talking quietly with others among the sick, I can still feel some fear from yesterday. Yet I've come here again, just in case Jesus shows up and just in case he really can heal people.

Oh, I think that's him, just inside the temple door, talking to the scribes and priests. They're firing questions at him now. "By whose authority did you drive out the money changers?" "If a man dies and his wife remarries, whose wife will she be in heaven?" "Should a man pay tax to Caesar?"

Then someone asks, "What sign can you show us to prove you have the right to do these things?"

What sign indeed, *my heart echoes.* Show me!

"Destroy this temple," comes the answer, "and in three days I will raise it up."

What can he mean? Destroy our precious temple, forty years in the building and still not done! Who does he think he is, anyway? Master of both the temple and the law?

And yet—oh, there's something splendid and strong about him that moves me and draws me to him, as if he held the answer to all my questions and my pain. For today, that will have to be sign enough for me.

It's not the kind of sign I'd hoped for, but it is the sign He's given: Despite all my questions and my fears, this hurting body is a temple of His love, and today He gives me strength to bear whatever pain I must.

When I'm hurting, Lord, let me enter the temple of Your Presence, that my weakness may be swallowed up in Your strength!

—Marilyn Morgan Helleberg

26
WED   **Wednesday of Holy Week**

"She has done a beautiful thing to me."   —Mark 14:6 (RSV)

"Hi, Mom!" It's Karen's cheery voice on the phone. "We're bringing you lunch today, if you don't mind fast food." Over her protests, I insist on paying for the food. Her salary's rather small, and she's done so much for me since my injury—errands, grocery shopping, some household chores. . . . Not easy, with an eighteen-month-old baby! Besides, I find it so hard to let others serve me, even when I'm ailing.

When they arrive with the food, my granddaughter Saralisa's face beams as she hands me a pretty bouquet of pink carnations! I smile at my little sweetie but then turn quickly to Karen. "Oh, no, you *shouldn't* have!" Too late, I see, with a stab of regret. Little Saralisa's face has fallen. And though I try, I can't make it right.

Resting after lunch, I imagine myself outside an open window of a house in Bethany, my ego smarting because I had to lean on friends to make the trek.

A young woman carries an alabaster jar into the house and interrupts the meal by breaking her jar and pouring its contents over Jesus' head! That scent! Someone in our group says it's pure nard, as costly as a man's wages for a whole year! A few of Jesus' friends begin to grumble and one of them— some say his name is Judas—complains loudly, "Why wasn't that oint- ment sold and the money given to the poor?"

But now the woman sits at Jesus' feet, gazing up at him with the most incredible love in her eyes, the silent eloquence of her spontaneous act still gracing the air. And this man Jesus, so fierce with the money changers, so tough with the scribes and priests, quietly accepts her gift with love, *say- ing, "She has done a beautiful thing to me."*

How could I not have seen it before? Today, He has shown me that gratefully to accept what another offers is to give the greater gift.

Lord, when I'm tempted to say, "You shouldn't have!" let me remember to say instead, "You have done a beautiful thing for me."

—Marilyn Morgan Helleberg

27
<u>THU</u>   **Maundy Thursday**

Not as I will, but as thou wilt.   —Matthew 26:39

"I've decided to dismiss you, Marilyn," says my physical therapist. "I don't think anything short of surgery will do it." I feel as if the last door has slammed as I hobble out of his office choking back tears. Back home in my prayer chair, I pour out my anguish. "I don't want surgery, Lord! With my heart arrhythmia, I might not survive. Please take this away without it!" As if in answer, all the darkness within sweeps me into a vision of another dark night.

My friends have carried me here to the foot of the Mount of Olives. The stillness of Passover hangs heavy in the air as we wait concealed among the olive trees outside the place called Gethsemane. I've about given up on being healed by Jesus. Yet somehow, I simply want to be near him.

By the light of the Paschal moon, I see Jesus and three others move away from the rest. Then he leaves these three, too. He's all alone now. Oh, something's wrong! He stumbles and falls forward, leaning against a boulder and, with a cry of anguish, looks toward the silent heavens and begins a groaning agony of prayer. I wait, not knowing why.

Suddenly, I hear him cry aloud, "Abba, Father, all things are possible unto thee; take away this cup from me!" My heart pulses in my throat, echoing his prayer: "Yes, my God, take this cup of pain from me!" But now he adds another line. "Nevertheless, not as I will, but as thou wilt." Oh! I don't know whether or not I can truly pray that prayer. . . .

I'm jolted out of my thoughts by the sudden approach of a swarm of men with torches and swords. Jesus stands facing them as one among them approaches and kisses him. Now the others come forward to grab him. A scuffle breaks out between the newcomers and Jesus' companions, then suddenly subsides. They tie Jesus' hands like a thief and take him away. All of his friends are left behind.

My heart is still pounding as I return to my prayer chair. I'm finally ready to pray the rest of Jesus' prayer. "Father, not as I will, but as thou wilt." Suddenly, something inside of me shifts, and I know that my prayer has been answered. It's okay to have the surgery. I'll be all right.

Thank You, Lord, for the prayer that is all prayers in one. My heart now trusts enough to pray authentically, Thy will be done.
—Marilyn Morgan Helleberg

28
FRI   **Good Friday**

Father, into thy hands I commend my spirit. . . .   —Luke 23:46

Clock ticking. Time dwindling. Tomorrow is the day of my back surgery. I can't sleep, and there's a falling sensation in my chest. I feel like a child again, wanting my daddy, a doctor who was able to heal all my hurts. But my father is dead, and I barely know the surgeon who'll be cutting into my spine tomorrow. I feel so alone, so vulnerable, as I close my eyes and find myself on a hill outside Jerusalem, a hill called Golgotha.

It's a clear and windless noon, but dust stirred by the crowd sticks in my throat. The smell of sweat rises on waves of heat, as soldiers shout and shove their three prisoners to the top of the hill. Iron beats against iron now, as spikes are driven through the prisoners' hands. Then up! With a loud shout and a grunt, the soldiers hoist the crosses high, until they stand, three stark gashes, against the now darkening sky.

A woman near me starts to cry, and a silent scream rises in my heart. He's broken now, betrayed, scourged, crucified, this man they thought would be the new king, this man I'd hoped would heal me. I want to turn away, but I see a woman there—they say it's his mother—and she does not turn away. If she can bear it, surely I must, for I, too, have come to love this man of compassion and courage.

Time hangs heavy. He has spoken a few words I've not been able to hear. Now his arms tighten, his head strains upward, and he calls out with a loud voice, "My God, my God, why hast thou forsaken me?" Oh, yes, Jesus, I know! I know. I, too, have felt abandoned by my God.

The inching minutes crawl. Now his tongue flicks to wet his lips, he glances upward, and with a loud voice, cries, "Father, into thy hands I commend my spirit." His head drops forward, his body goes limp. He's dead now. Dead. And a part of me has died here, too.

My Jesus died with His Father's name on His lips. Can I do less than pray His final prayer on this night before my surgery?

Abba, Father, You are here. I entrust You with my spirit. Amen.
                                        —Marilyn Morgan Helleberg

29
SAT   **Holy Saturday**

Lord, I believe; help thou mine unbelief.   —Mark 9:24

It's been three weeks since my surgery, but the pain is still there—back, hip, leg, ankle, foot. I'm discouraged, tired of hurting, tired of trying to keep hope alive, tired of unanswered prayers. I'd been so sure, the night the decision came to me in prayer, that God wanted to heal me through surgery. Now doubt and despair stretch before me like a desert. I close my eyes and find myself sitting on a sand dune in a desolate land.

My friends have brought me here to the desert by the Dead Sea so I could be alone with my thoughts. He was my last answer, the man who died on the cross yesterday. Now I'm not sure he ever healed anyone. People imagine things. Yet I can't help thinking about those eyes that moved me so, less than a week ago. It meant something then.

And the power *he displayed the day he drove the animals and the money changers out of the temple. Why couldn't he use the same power to get off that horrible cross? Then the day he responded to questions from the priests, there seemed to be a new voice of wisdom in the land. Well, now I'd like to have some answers myself! And when that woman anointed him with the costly nard, he blessed her. Could Judas have been right? Should the money have been given to the poor instead?*

Thursday night, he prayed to have his cup of suffering removed. Instead, it got worse! And I can't close my eyes now, without seeing a cross stabbed upright in the earth and the slow drip, drip, drip of his blood on the ground.

Well, what am I supposed to think? I don't know. I just don't know. I only know that I have loved him.

How deeply I feel, tonight, the sorrow of those who loved Jesus and lost Him. But more than that, I feel their doubt, because it is also mine. My only prayer tonight must be:

Lord, I believe; help thou mine unbelief. Amen.

—Marilyn Morgan Helleberg

30

SUN   **Easter Sunday**

He is risen. . . .   —Mark 16:6

It's 4:45 A.M. when the phone rings. My daughter Karen is calling to remind me she's picking me up for the sunrise service, but I'm just not up to it today. "No, I'm sorry. You go ahead. Thanks anyway." Alone now in the dark, I close my eyes but can't get back to sleep, so one more time I imagine myself in Jerusalem, this time inside the house of the one in need of healing.

I wake in pain to another day, with no particular desire to greet the dawn. Soon there's a commotion outside. My neighbor knocks and then enters. "Have you heard? Mary Magdalene—you know, that woman friend of Jesus—well, she says she went to the place where they laid his body, and the tomb was empty! And she even said she saw an angel who told her Jesus was risen from the dead! Imagine! We're going to the tomb. Do you want us to take you there?"

Oh, how much I want to believe it! And I'd like to see for myself. But I just can't risk being let down again. "Thanks, but you go on ahead. I'll stay here."

Alone now, I waver between hope and despair. "Lord God of Israel, I ask You: Could it really be true that Jesus has come to life again? How can I possibly know whether or not it's true?" As I pray, the room begins to get lighter, and the growing brightness seems to be greater than just the sun rising. A whisper of a breeze rustles my hair and brushes my cheek. Where did it come from, with the shutters so tightly closed?

Suddenly, I find myself enfolded in a light brighter and more golden than the burnished temple roof gleaming in the morning sun. What's come over me? I can't be sure . . . but my back! The pain is less than it has been in months, and I think I stand a little straighter now. But it's more than that: the clear, unbounded joy of a love so new and real and all-forgiving, I know it must be heaven-sent. Could Jesus be here with me? I can't explain it. And yet I know it, heart and soul and spirit. He is risen! He is truly risen! Hallelujah!

I hurry now to call Karen. Though I've missed the sunrise service, perhaps she'll go with me to the ten o'clock. I want to celebrate! I'm going to be fine now. I *know* it, body, soul and spirit. Jesus Christ lives!

Hallelujah! Hallelujah! Hallelujah! Amen.

—Marilyn Morgan Helleberg

31
MON

So then faith cometh by hearing, and hearing by the word of God.   —Romans 10:17

I had been going to church for years and years, as long as I could re-member. I had memorized creeds until they were reflexes and stayed awake for countless sermons. I wanted something in return, some-thing to tell me my praying wasn't just talking to myself, something to show me God was there.

Every Sunday I'd show up for choir practice, each time a little more frustrated, until finally I was there only because I liked to sing and I was one of only two altos in the choir. Singing "God Is Like a Rock," I thought, *Well, they got that one right. A great big rock, just sitting there. Can't go over it. Can't get around it. Can't just stand here beating my head against it either.* I didn't know what I was supposed to believe anymore. I didn't even know where to start.

On Easter morning, I was preparing to sing a solo, "Morning Has Broken," but with my black mood it could have been the middle of the night. *C'mon, God. You're all-powerful. Why don't You just* do *something! This isn't fair.*

A loud cry of "Easter! Easter! Easter!" pulled me abruptly from my thoughts. Pastor Schumm's Easter cheer was famous in Laguna Beach, California. Every Easter Sunday the canyon rang with it, and it seemed to get louder every year. It was almost time for the creed; I was on after that.

The congregation began reciting the words I had repeated for so many years. I couldn't remember a single word beyond "I believe." I pretended to study my music, hoping that Erika, the organist, wouldn't notice that I wasn't joining in. But as I listened, my eyes widened and I began to smile.

I believe in God, the Father Almighty, maker of heaven and earth. . . .

An answer. It had been inside me the whole time, but concentrating on myself, straining to discern inner voices, I couldn't hear it. Now, in the voices of my family, my friends and my neighbors, I could recognize it as my own. A simple answer, but where I needed to start. . . .

Start! My song! I needed to start my song! My sheet music was in place when I began, but I didn't need any help remembering the words. Morning had broken.

Father, with all of my questions and all of my doubts, help me to remember that all things begin with You. Amen.   —Kjerstin Easton

Everyday Wonders

1 _____

2 _____

3 _____

4 _____

5 _____

6 _____

7 _____

8 _____

9 _____

10 _____

11 _____

12 _____

13 _____

14 _____

15 _____

16 _____

17 _____

18 _____

19 _____

20 _____

21 _____

22 _____

23 _____

24 _____

25 _____

26 _____

27 _____

28 _____

29 _____

30 _____

31 _____

O give thanks to the Lord of lords:
for his mercy endureth for ever.
To him who alone doeth great
wonders: for his mercy endureth
for ever. —PSALM 136:3–4

April

S	M	T	W	T	F	S
		1	2	3	4	5
6	7	8	9	10	11	12
13	14	15	16	17	18	19
20	21	22	23	24	25	26
27	28	29	30			

1

LOVE IS . . .

Love . . . is not proud.   —I Corinthians 13:4 (NIV)

Jack Hinckley was a proud man—with good reason. Hard-working, churchgoing, family-centered, Jack was a self-made businessman active in Christian service organizations. His wife Jo Ann was a devoted mother, their two older children top students, the youngest a quiet, gentle boy who loved music and animals. Then in 1981, when he was twenty-five, this youngest son, John, traveled with a gun to Washington, D.C., and shot President Reagan and three other men.

Two years later, I spent several weeks in the Hinckleys' home in Colorado, working on a book about the early signs of mental illness, which they'd so tragically failed to recognize in their son. One day the Hinckleys were respected citizens, the next reviled, traveling under assumed names to visit their son as he awaited trial.

"Denying my name—it was like denying everything I stood for," Jack told me. His own father had died when he was two. "When my mother remarried, I remained a Hinckley to honor my dad's name. Now here I was, hiding it."

"And yet," I pointed out, "you're not hiding now." Jack and Jo Ann were giving up their home and their business to devote their lives to addressing the public about the mental diseases that fill a third of our hospital beds.

The change occurred, Jack said, because of a letter from a stranger. "Your name is mud anyway," the man had written. "What have you got to lose by going to bat for the mentally ill?"

His name, the name he'd been so proud of, was mud. "And now at last," Jack said, "God can use me. Long ago I gave my life to Him. But He can't use us, I'm discovering, all shiny and strong. It's the muddy things, the broken things, that do His work in a broken world."

God of love, what pride of mine is standing in the way of the work You have for me today?   —Elizabeth Sherrill

Editor's Note: We'd love to know what discoveries you've made in your own life that show you the wonders of God's love. Take the time to review your monthly "Everyday Wonders" and write us about one or two of the things you've recorded there. Send your letter to *Daily Guideposts* Editor, Guideposts Books, 16 East 34th Street, New York, New York 10016.

2
WED   *I am not alone. . . .*   —John 16:32

In these pages several years ago (April 11, *Daily Guideposts,* 1994) I wrote about the advantages of eating alone. Among the many letters I received were some pointing out that I might pray for those of my fellow diners who looked as though they needed help. I couldn't have agreed more, and the suggestion started me on an ardent campaign.

I prayed for lone diners and for families, and most of all for an old couple who ate but never said a word during their meal. I had singled this couple out in the piece I wrote, saying that I wanted to tell them, "Look, you might just as well be eating alone like me. Stop wasting each other. Please!"

It happened that I saw them again one evening and they were the same: nontalkative, wasteful. "Oh, God," I prayed, "give me the power to change them."

Their supper over, they passed by me on their way out. Suddenly, the lady was back. "Cheer up," she said. "We've been praying for you."

My mouth flew open. The couple was gone before I could respond, but they had left their mark on me. No longer do I pray for the problems I think people have. Instead, I pray that God will provide for whatever needs they have.

And there's one thing more: I try to look more cheerful. After all, someone might be praying for me.

Eating alone, Father, is a misnomer; there is always You. —Van Varner

3
THU   *Be patient in tribulation, be constant in prayer.*
                                        —Romans 12:12 (RSV)

I was shopping with my son Ross, just five then, and didn't notice he'd stopped to look at an Easter display of bunnies and brightly colored eggs. I had walked only a couple of aisles away, but far enough for him to panic a little when he realized he'd temporarily lost me. He suddenly ran up to me with a frightened yet relieved expression. "Mommy, where'd you go? I got too far away from you, and I got scared."

We hugged, he smiled again, and all was well. But I remembered what he said a few days later, when I was particularly worried about my trouble-plagued pregnancy. I'd been constantly afraid for my baby as I went through various tests. And remembering Ross' words, I knew what was wrong. *God, when I get too far away from You, I get scared.*

So I began to pray constantly, often feeling enveloped in the warmth of God's love. Even when Maria was born five weeks early (under five pounds but beautiful and healthy), I wasn't afraid. And in the time since, prayer has continually kept away the nagging fears that are a natural part of raising children.

In prayer, I see myself like Ross that day in the store, running to my loving Parent, reassured by His nearness and knowing I have nothing to fear. It's a simple truth even a child knows. The times I'm least afraid are the times I am closest to the One Who loves me most.

Lord Jesus, You lived and died and rose again so that we might come nearer to You. Let me always be close to You, for Your love casts out all fear.

—Gina Bridgeman

4 *That we may . . . find grace to help in time of need.*
FRI   —Hebrews 4:16

I once asked Gertrude, an elderly, well-liked elementary-school teacher, what her secret of success as a teacher was.

"If I have a difficult student in my class, I don't try to force my help on him or her," she said. "Instead, I ask the student to help me."

She explained that the tasks may be simple, such as asking the child to help shelve supplies or redecorate the bulletin board. But she makes sure that the child realizes the need is real, and she uses the opportunity to get to know the child better.

"Trying to help can sometimes be threatening. But if you ask for help, people know that you need and trust them. Once trust is established, then that person is more likely to accept your help in turn."

I remembered Gertrude's words when a standoffish woman moved into our neighborhood shortly thereafter. Instead of rushing back and forth with multiple plates of brownies and my "welcome transmitter" set on overload, which had been my *modus operandi* in the past, I waited until a family gathering at our house one Sunday afternoon. I asked our new neighbor if she could do us a favor by coming over and snapping a family portrait for our scrapbook. She did come, it broke the ice, and we became friends. Later, when she needed help during an illness, she felt free to call on me.

Father, help me to help others, and to let others help me.

—Madge Harrah

5
SAT

Let the morning bring me word of your unfailing love, for I have put my trust in you.   —Psalm 143:8 (NIV)

I don't like to clean my house.

There, I've admitted one of my most embarrassing shortcomings. A friend once told me to express my gratitude to God for each item in my home as I dust or vacuum it. It helped a little but, frankly, the only thing that really spurs me on is if I know that company's coming.

One Saturday, our friends Bob and Sue were supposed to come over at four. That morning, at eight A.M., already frenzied, I elbowed my husband. "We have to clean!" I cried. "We have to clean!"

Startled, Paul gamely got up, and we listed everything we had to do. It was a long list. We raced around vacuuming, dusting, polishing. I mopped; Paul swept. I cleaned the tub; he did the refrigerator. I washed a few windows; he wiped down the blinds. Finally, after several hours of frantic work, I said, "It looks good—and just in time. They'll be here at four." Paul looked at me blankly. "Who's 'they'?"

I stared at him. "Why, Bob and Sue, of course."

"Oh, I completely forgot they were coming," he said. My jaw dropped to my chest. "Then why did you think I woke you at eight to clean?"

He shrugged. "I had no idea! I just assumed that you had gotten into some kind of a cleaning frenzy, and I thought, 'Let's take advantage of it while it lasts!' "

After our laughter died down and we both agreed the house looked great, I added something else to my list of things to be grateful for: a husband willing to go along with his wife's odd 'cleaning mood'— even if he doesn't understand it.

Dear Lord, even when I don't understand why You're asking, let me be ready to do Your will.   —Linda Neukrug

6
SUN

Consider the lilies of the field, how they grow; they toil not, neither do they spin.   —Matthew 6:28

It was early April. My wife Barbara and I were in Nacadoches, in beautiful east Texas, with Nancy, then our only child. The whole world seemed to be in bloom. The roadsides on the drive from Fort

Worth were covered with wildflowers, the azaleas in the yards showed full color, and along the edge of the wooded areas redbud and dogwoods were at their peak.

I hadn't noticed much of this because I was tired from a stressful week and was preoccupied with the responsibility of speaking in a rather large church. On Sunday morning, as the three of us walked the short distance from our hotel to the church, I had my mind more on not being late and on my sermon than on anything else.

Nancy was only four, and her short legs made it hard for her to keep up. Finally, I turned to tell her that she was going to make us late and saw that she was standing looking at a gorgeous dogwood tree whose limbs shaded the entire sidewalk. Her eyes seemed to be taking in each blossom. Before I could scold her for being so slow, she smiled and said, "Hi, tree," as though she were talking to an old friend. I was ashamed of myself. I had been in such a hurry to get to church that I had missed my Creator's sermon growing by the sidewalk.

A lot of years have passed since then, but I've remembered the lesson my daughter taught me. Just yesterday, I stood at the kitchen window and thanked a little chickadee on the feeder for the way it lifted my spirit as it swooped in for a seed, then sat on a limb of the holly tree and ate it. I've even learned to talk to flowers.

Lord, let me see Your beauty in the beautiful things You have made.
                                                        —Kenneth Chafin

7   *Two are better than one. . . . For if they fall, the one will*
MON   *lift up his fellow. . . .*   —Ecclesiastes 4:9–10

In my office at Guideposts, in the bottom right-hand desk drawer lies an unsecret stash of Oreos, Nutter Butters, raisin oatmeal cookies (for the more healthily inclined) and Mystic Mints. The inventory keeps changing. Sometimes the supply runs low, and you can only find a few Fig Newtons; at other times it's a horn of plenty, with Chips Ahoy, Nilla Wafers, gingersnaps and butter biscuits.

Our Guideposts Cookie Drawer had its origins several years back when Mary Ann bought a package of Pepperidge Farm cookies and after having a few at lunch, brought them to me for safekeeping. "Anyone can have some," she offered generously. "Just keep them out of my sight!" Then Edward added some, and Ellie brought a pack of her favorite brand, and I picked up something at the supermarket. Those who contributed took a few, and those who took came back with more, so that now whenever you want a cookie, you can go to the drawer.

It's a good system. We pool our resources. We share our bounty. And when you withdraw a few too many cookies from the drawer, there are good friends nearby who can listen to you discourse on your bad habits—maybe even help you change them.

Someone once told me that you can't be a Christian by yourself; you need other believers to share your joys, help you weather your sorrows and keep you on the right path. In an odd sort of way, that's the fellowship we have at the cookie drawer.

Thank You, Lord, for the friends who make me whole.   —Rick Hamlin

---

8
———
TUE

"He who is faithful in a very little is faithful also in much. . . ."   —Luke 16:10 (RSV)

"Everything is so lovely," I told my friend Darilee at the end of the tour of her new bed and breakfast. She and her sister had purchased a grand, century-old mansion, and now she had painstakingly restored it and turned it into a new enterprise.

"But, you know," said Darilee, as we descended the mahogany staircase, "it's really the details that make the difference." Darilee had decorated each of the bedrooms and baths with great attention to detail. The cozy pillow in the bathtub; the wallpaper border under the window; the cheerful fern above the back stairs; the perfumed soaps delicately wrapped in colorful tissue had together turned the magnificent mansion into a warm, welcoming refuge.

Walking down to the lake with Darilee later, I thought about what she'd said about details. I'd read somewhere that, at the end of their lives, people often look back and realize that it was the little things in their lives that were really important.

"Maybe I should take the kids to the park next Saturday. And surely I can find fifteen minutes every day to spend with You, Lord," I whispered into the breeze. Somehow, I knew, these "small things" needed to take center stage. Because it's all those little things that really make up the whole of my life.

Father, help me to recognize that I cannot be given the "big" things until I've been proven faithful in the "little" things.   —Robin White Goode

9   *"The more lowly your service to others, the greater you are.*
WED   *To be the greatest, be a servant. But those who think themselves great shall be disappointed and humbled; and those who humble themselves shall be exalted."*
                                        —Matthew 23:11–12 (TLB)

A few years ago, I attended a celebration of the 125th anniversary of the Milwaukee Archdiocesan newspaper *The Catholic Herald.* At the reception, feeling somewhat cocky because I was one of the paper's regular columnists, I introduced myself to a number of guests. Then, as I nibbled on a piece of cheesecake, I studied the mementos and photos chronicling the newspaper's history that lined the office walls.

A tall, good-looking gentleman on my left was also looking at the display. Thinking perhaps he was one the paper's staff and anxious to let him know that I was one of the columnists, I asked, "So what do you do here?"

He smiled and said with a twinkle, "I empty the wastebaskets."

When he turned to face me, I noticed his Roman collar. I laughed. "Oh, sure, Father, and I bet you do a great job. What do you really do?"

Just then an acquaintance on my right said, "Your Excellency, I'd like you to meet Patricia Lorenz. Pat, this is Bishop Sklba."

I felt the color drain from my face, then immediately a whole new blood supply rushed upward. I was sure my cheeks were flashing neon red. "Oh, Your Excellency, I'm, I'm—"

Bishop Sklba interrupted with a hearty laugh as he put his arm around me. "Pat, it's my pleasure to meet you. And you know what? I really do empty the wastebaskets!"

As the bishop moved on to meet other people, I was moved by his humility, by his humanness and, mostly, by his sense of humor.

I learned a good lesson that day. I learned not to take myself or my position so seriously, and that a sense of humor and the ability to laugh at oneself are the mark of a truly great person.

Today, Lord, help me to put others at ease by being humble and humorous.
                                        —Patricia Lorenz

10
THU
And be ye kind one to another, tenderhearted, forgiv-ing one another, even as God for Christ's sake hath for-given you.   —Ephesians 4:32

"I can't stand it any longer!" I heard myself say. "I've resented Bart for twenty-five years, and it's driving me nuts!"

"Why don't you forgive him?" my friend Sam said.

"Forgive him? Are you kidding? He did a terrible thing to me! I'm not going to let him off that easily!"

Sam laughed affectionately. "Let him off that easily?" he said. "Why, he's probably out playing golf and doesn't even know that you resent him. Listen, Keith, when you resent people, you let them live rent-free in your head. Forgiving him could free you from that resentment."

"I know," I said, "but I've tried, and I just can't. What do you do when you can't forgive someone?"

"I imagine there's a conveyer belt, right by my desk, going up to God," Sam said. "I take a resentment I can't get rid of and put it on the conveyer belt in an imaginary grocery sack, pull the handle to start the thing, and send the sack and the resentment up to God."

That's the silliest thing I ever heard, I thought. But when I got home, I decided to try it. I put the twenty-five-year-old resentment in an imaginary sack, pulled the handle of the imaginary conveyer belt and said, "Lord, I'd appreciate Your taking this."

About five minutes later, I heard an imaginary plop, and the sack was back. "See," I said over the phone to Sam a minute later, "I *knew* it wouldn't work!"

"Send it up again," he said calmly. "You've had that resentment for twenty-five years. You can't expect to get rid of it in one try."

So, although I felt like an idiot, I sent that resentment up to God every day for two weeks. Then one day I sent the sack up and, to my amazement, it never came back!

Thank You, God, for forgiving me and helping me to forgive.

—Keith Miller

11
FRI
Cast your cares on the Lord and he will sustain you. . . .
                                      —Psalm 55:22 (NIV)

Recently, I read that the basic credo of time management is simply this: Never handle a piece of paper more than once. The author insisted you can save hours by dealing with each paper the first time it comes into your hands. I looked at the piles of papers on my desk, many of which I'd shuffled through several times already. *Handle only once? How?*

The article continued: Put each piece of paper in a definite place. Either toss it in the wastebasket, file it, pass it on, post it, or put it in a "to do" tray—anything—but don't pile up the papers to handle again.

My piling habit is connected to another bothersome trait: I'm a worrier. Just as I shuffle papers back and forth, I keep passing around nagging concerns in my mind. *Did we choose the right school for our daughter Elizabeth? Is this mole normal? What if it's not?*

"Put each in a definite place." Sitting at my desk, I close my eyes and give God each worry. I've read about the value of writing down prayer requests and keeping track of answers, but I've never taken the time to do it. Now, it seems like a good way to stop my mental "worry piling." Inspired by my clear desk (yes, I got rid of those piles!), I take a notebook and list people and concerns. Writing down each care releases it from my mental pile and kindles my faith that in God's providence, it will be provided for.

Thank You, Lord, for helping me to clear out my "worry piles" and commit each care to You.   —Mary Brown

12
SAT   *This mortal must put on immortality.*
                                    —I Corinthians 15:53

Not long ago, one of our Virginia cousins came down to attend the funeral of a family member. It was not a sad occasion, because she had lived a good and happy life, and died full of faith and confidence.

On the way back from the cemetery, our cousin said reflectively, "I remember the first funeral I ever attended. I was four years old, or thereabouts. My mother was in the pew beside me, and I tugged at her sleeve apprehensively. 'Is Uncle Fred really in that big box?' I wanted to know. Mother gave me a reassuring smile and a true answer. 'What he used to wear is in that box,' she said serenely, leaving me for the time being with a comforting vision of Uncle Fred's shoes and shirts and sweaters being carried off to some unspecified destination, but not—great relief!—Uncle Fred himself."

"What he used to wear. . . ." A gentle reminder that sooner or later, for all of us, the time will come when our souls leave the familiar confines of our bodies and move on into eternity. When that hour does arrive, what we've been wearing won't seem very important. It's the immortal part that counts.

Father, help us to live so that when the time comes, You can welcome us home.   —Arthur Gordon

13

SUN   *Encourage one another daily. . . .*   —Hebrews 3:13 (NIV)

We were seated around tables in the church fellowship hall following a potluck supper. Adults of all ages were sprinkled throughout the room, and we were having a wonderful evening sharing stories and memories with one another.

I was the discussion leader and had posed the question, "What is one of the most meaningful gifts you have ever received?" In response, several people had spoken of birthday presents, anniversary gifts or a favorite Christmas surprise. Then quietly Joe Jack Pearce raised his hand and stood up to speak.

Joe Jack is eighty-four years old and is the International Racquetball Champion in the eighty to eighty-four-year-old bracket. Pausing to gather his thoughts, he said, "Several months ago I received a phone call. It was from some boys I coached on a high school basketball team in 1941. Now in their seventies, they were having a reunion. They called to tell me how much I had meant to them and that I had helped shape their lives."

Joe Jack paused. There were other things he wanted to say, but his voice choked up. Shaking his head, he mumbled, "That just might be the nicest gift I ever received."

The room grew quiet. We were all thinking of phone calls we needed to make, people we wanted to thank for their influence on us. I left that night determined to give the gift of gratitude to the many people who have loved me through the years.

Dear God, help me to share my thoughts of thanksgiving. Amen.
                                          —Scott Walker

14
MON
Most important of all, continue to show deep love for each other, for love makes up for many of your faults.
—I Peter 4:8 (TLB)

I had been a snapping turtle all weekend. A longtime friend had been consistently critical of me for several months. Each encounter with her was abrasive, so much so that my feelings were constantly hurt, and I had reached the point where I didn't care whether I ever saw her again.

My family gave me a wide berth. Frustrated after several attempts at trying to cheer me up, my husband John buried himself in the newspaper, and my daughter Katrelya decided it would be a good time for a long hike. I had the feeling that because of me, they couldn't wait for the weekend to be over. *So be it,* I thought. I didn't care.

Mid-morning on Monday, the doorbell rang. It was the florist with a huge arrangement of flowers. Daisies, snapdragons, larkspur, baby's breath and my favorite, tiger lilies. The gift card read, "Just because! I love you. John."

I sat in the kitchen and cried. "How could he?" I muttered through the sobs. "I don't deserve these."

Teary-eyed, I phoned his office and thanked him. He chuckled, "I just figured you needed some extra loving today!"

How grateful I was that John did not let his frustration with me get in the way of his love for me! He set me a good example that I was determined to follow.

I called my friend. "Let's have lunch. My treat!"

Over salad and coffee she confessed, "I know I've been irritable lately. Thanks for not giving up on me!"

By loving in unloving circumstances, we reflect the wondrous love of Jesus Who, whether we're in a state of grace or disgrace, never gives up on us and never stops loving us.

"Where there is love, Lord, let me put love so that love may be maintained. Where there is no love, Lord, let me put love so that love may be created" *(St. Augustine paraphrased).*   —Fay Angus

15
TUE
He who gives to the poor will lack nothing. . . .
—Proverbs 28:27 (NIV)

I was feeling poor.

My wife Julee and I were walking west on 29th Street through the

April twilight after meeting with our accountant. We owed taxes. We owed our dentist for procedures not covered by insurance. We owed Marty's vet for treatment of an infected paw. Our savings were dipping. For the third month in a row we wouldn't be able to pay the full balance on our credit cards. And now we owed our accountant for giving us all this sorry news. "Where does all the money go?" I lamented.

Just off of Fifth Avenue we passed by a bedraggled young woman holding out an empty, fast-food coffee cup with a penciled dollar sign, the equal symbol and the word *food* inscribed on it. Julee subtracted a wrinkled dollar bill from her jeans pocket and added it to the woman's cup. Shock prevented me from reacting for a few paces, then I exploded. "You know what she's going to spend it on!"

My wife shrugged. "Everyone has to eat. I like to think my dollar goes toward a meal."

I wasn't about to let her off the hook that easily. "Shouldn't we be worrying about our own money predicament?" I insisted. Then I got in a dig at the heart of Julee's habitual do-gooderism. "You're just doing it to make yourself feel better."

Julee stopped in her tracks. "Yeah," she agreed, "in a way I do. To be able to give something reminds me of how much I have, and that makes me feel blessed. So I guess I *am* making myself feel better."

I stood there on the dusky street wondering if I looked as stupid as I felt. I had let the scaly anxiety of our tax-time finances get the better of me, as I seemed to do every April. God would provide for us. He always does. Through Julee, He had even provided something in His own way for the young beggar.

I no longer felt so poor.

Lord, let me not forget that Your blessings are to be shared.
—Edward Grinnan

16
WED
Then our mouth was filled with laughter. . . .
—Psalm 126:2 (NAS)

Minnie, our cat, adores a soft, fluffy white blanket of ours. Anytime we bring it out, she eyes it from afar, then slowly makes her way to it, trying to appear casual. If no one scolds her, she's soon curled up on the blanket as though it were her very own. Minnie isn't the only one who enjoys that blanket; it's also a favorite of my mother's.

Today, it took Mother ever so long to inch her way with the walker from the car to her recliner in our living room. I'd taken her to the doctor and the trip had required great effort. Each step resulted in tremendous pain. She forced a determined smile onto her drawn face. I moved ahead of her, propping pillows on the comfortable chair and then laying out the white blanket.

When Minnie saw Mother coming, she deliberately beat her to the blanket in the chair. Mother's pain seemed to precede her and fill the entire room. It was intense and had wearied both of us. Suddenly, Mother spoke in a sharp, commanding voice that startled Minnie and me. "Is *that cat* on my blanket again?"

I laughed, softly at first. Then my snickering turned into rippling, uncontrollable hee-haws. I laughed hysterically until I hurt. Mother paused with her walker and, to my amazement, also began to laugh. Minnie watched, wide-eyed. Mother bent over the walker as laughter overtook her. We both laughed helplessly and loudly until we could hardly speak. Occasional bursts of laughter continued to escape from us, like an important P.S. on a letter.

Gradually, the laughter ceased. But it had done an extraordinary thing. I felt better. I enjoyed preparing supper. Mother and I both smiled more during the meal. Things didn't seem so difficult. Loading the dishwasher was almost fun.

Lord, send laughter to rescue me more often. Amen.

—Marion Bond West

WORDS OF WONDER

God moves in a mysterious way
His wonders to perform;
He plants his footsteps on the sea
And rides upon the storm.

Ye fearful saints, fresh courage take;
The clouds ye so much dread
Are big with mercy, and shall break
In blessings on your head.

—WILLIAM COWPER

17

THU *If I must boast, I will boast of the things that show my weakness.* —II Corinthians 11:30 (NIV)

Linda sat on my newly upholstered den sofa and haltingly told me that she had always felt secretly inferior to others. "Karen, you always seem to have it all together," she said.

I tried to tell Linda that we're all quite human, but the words didn't seem to be sinking in. Then I remembered something an artist friend named Charlene had done for me.

I had been a newcomer in town; everyone I met seemed to dress so stylishly, their homes were well decorated and always neat. I had felt awkward, believing that I'd never fit in. One day Charlene invited me over to her home. "Come upstairs," she said. "I have something to show you." I followed her up the stairs, expecting to be shown some work in progress. Instead, she ushered me into her bedroom and showed me her unmade bed. "This bed is what I wanted you to see. Now that you know I'm not perfect, we can be friends."

I turned toward Linda and said, "I want you to see something." I took her by the hand, led her down the hallway and opened the laundry room door. The usual pile of dirty clothes was on the floor. I opened the washer to show her the wet clothes that had been lying in it for at least a day. By the time I opened the cabinet under the sink and a jumble of toys and crumpled paper fell out, Linda was smiling.

Linda used to think I was perfect. Now she just calls me her friend.

Lord, You know I'm not perfect. Help me not to worry about others knowing it, too. —Karen Barber

18

FRI *One of them [sparrows] shall not fall on the ground without your Father. . . . Fear ye not therefore, ye are of more value than many sparrows.* —Matthew 10:29, 31

All night I'd been unable to sleep. I got out of bed at sunup and decided to go out to sweep the porch. Perhaps keeping busy would help quiet my anxious thoughts.

Huddled against a back corner of the porch I saw a little mourning dove, the kind that frequented our backyard feeder. Its stillness, half-closed eyes and hanging beak told me it was sick or hurt. I tried to slide a saucer of water toward it, but it fluttered, frightened, to the back of the porch.

I went into the house, but I couldn't forget the little bird. *Perhaps it's hungry,* I thought. So I went back outside and tried to put a few seeds from the feeder near it. It beat its wings and plopped off the porch.

After lunch, my husband Bob and I found it sitting in the middle of the road. A car was coming! I dashed out, waving my arms to stop the car while Bob scooped it up with a piece of cardboard. As it was being lifted, the bird fluttered into the nearest bush. Thankful that it was out of the road, I motioned the car to move on.

Later that afternoon, I slipped quietly out the front door. There, under the same bush, was the little bird, surrounded by three others of its kind. They murmured their soft little mourning sounds and, occasionally, one fluttered its wings, flew up slightly, then landed again.

They came to rescue it! I thought.

As I watched, fascinated, two of the birds flew above it, circled and rose to the sky. The one I'd found on my porch flapped its wings, fell to the ground, tried again and flew unsteadily after the first two. The remaining birds followed.

For the first time in days, I felt a sense of peace.

Surely, Father, Your love extends to everything You have made, including me.
                                                              —Drue Duke

19 *He was oppressed, and he was afflicted, yet opened not his*
SAT   *mouth. . . .*   —Isaiah 53:7

There's something I know about myself that I don't like.

I don't like to suffer in silence. When I'm hurting, I like others to come alongside me, put their arms around me, pray with me, maybe even bring over a few casseroles. This tendency can quickly turn into self-centered suffering, better known as self-pity.

I had an opportunity to be reminded of that truth last weekend. While out riding my bike on Saturday afternoon, I hit some slippery gravel and took a nasty, hard fall on my right shoulder. I ended up in the emergency room, badly shaken and in great pain. After a series of X-rays, I actually felt disappointed when the doctor diagnosed a mere sprain. He sent me home with only a couple of pain pills.

What? Only a sprain to show for all this pain? For just a day at least, I wanted crutches. I wanted a cast. I wanted an hour in the hospital in traction so my pastor would hear of my plight and come pray with me. I wanted some dramatic "badge" that would validate my pain, something that would show I'd had a bad fall. I was like a child who wants to wear a bright Band-Aid to cover a tiny boo-boo on her finger.

The diagnosis of a "mere sprain" meant I had to suffer in silence. Yet as my husband Lynn drove me home from the emergency room and helped me find a comfortable position on the couch, I had the distinct sense that I was facing exactly what God had in store for me through this experience. So I winced my way through the whole next week, sometimes sharing my plight, but often not. And by the end of the week, even though I didn't have any casseroles, I found the blessing of suffering in silence. It brings me closer to God.

Father, when I am hurting, help me to take my eyes off of myself and to focus on You.　　　　　　　　　　　　—Carol Kuykendall

20
SUN　　*"A farmer went out to sow his seed. . . . some fell along the path. . . . Some fell on rock. . . . Other seed fell among thorns. . . . Still other seed fell on good soil. . . ."*
　　　　　　　　　　　　—Luke 8:5–8 (NIV)

There are fascinating people whom I meet periodically, people whose lives are exemplified by their passion to serve Christ. The ministry I work with has such a special person. Her name is Carolyn, but I call her the "Tract Lady." She is married and has three wonderful children, and is a delightful, compassionate person.

Everywhere she goes, Carolyn has a handful of pamphlets declaring her love of Christ, which she passes out to people she meets. And when she runs out of tracts and can't afford to purchase additional ones, she asks the church, the ministry or individuals to help underwrite the cost of more. She has developed her own megaministry. "Every opportunity to share my faith is important," she says, "because somebody might read this tract and give their life to the Lord."

I've heard some people say, "It's embarrassing to be with her."

Would I be embarrassed? I ask myself. Maybe. But I pray I can rise above my embarrassment and meet the challenge that the Tract Lady presents: to find my own creative ways to declare my love for Christ. I may not be comfortable handing out booklets as she does, but I can pray for her. I can really listen to people who come to me for help. And every opportunity, however small, that comes to me to share my faith and speak of God's love, I will seize with great verve.

Lord, help me to find my own personal ministry for You.

—Dolphus Weary

21

MON

"Master, you delivered to me two talents. . . ."
—Matthew 25:22 (RSV)

The hospital room was quiet, except for the hiss of oxygen and the churning of the IV machine. The TV on the other side of the room was mercifully off. I sat in the orange vinyl chair and reached out to take my father-in-law's hand.

In the time that I'd known him, Dad always had gentle hands. Years of retirement had smoothed the calluses he'd earned from years as a farm boy, a construction worker, a small-appliance repairman. Today, his hands were different. Months of severe illness had left them emaciated; water retention had inflated them so that his fingers looked like strings of puffy little sausages.

I talked to Dad gently, telling him how much we loved him. I sang "The Old Rugged Cross" and "Amazing Grace." And then suddenly I began to cry in frustration. "I can't do anything, Lord! I love this man, and I can't help him. Everything I have to give isn't enough! I can't do anything for him except hold his hand."

In the midst of my tears, I began to think of Jesus' mother and the beloved disciple, who couldn't do anything but watch at the foot of the cross. "But," a voice in my head said, "they were there. Sometimes that's the hardest thing God asks of us—simply to be there."

Simply *being there* is no small task. That day I went from thinking about "being reduced to" holding Dad's hand to seeing that holding his hand was a great gift and privilege. I began to distinguish between wanting to feel useful and being useful in the way God asks.

Blessed Lord, help us to overcome our own definitions of what it means to help, and to be where You call us to be.   —Julia Attaway

22
TUE

*Why beholdest thou the mote that is in thy brother's eye,
but perceivest not the beam that is in thine own eye?*
—Luke 6:41

I was sitting with a group from church, complaining about the messiness of our local roads. "Paper wrappers, battered coffee cups and beer bottles seem to sprout overnight," I said. "Why can't people take care of their garbage? There's a bag of trash at the end of my street that's been there two weeks. It looks terrible. I wish the people who live there would pick it up."

I went home with murmurs of sympathy echoing in my ears. Each day as I took my walk along the road, I fretted and fumed over that debris. Then one evening, as I approached the offensive bag, I noticed a familiar piece of paper, and then an ice cream container (my favorite flavor) and a yogurt cup. *Oh, no,* I thought in growing embarrassment, *this is my garbage.*

The bag had probably fallen from the collection truck as it rounded the corner, and here it had stayed for weeks. *My* garbage littering the road! In a humbler frame of mind, I went home and got a fresh bag. I cleaned up the papers and empty containers, and I asked God to forgive my overbearing righteousness.

*Father, on this Earth Day, if I can only see the litter in other people's lives,
remind me to clean up my own.*   —Susan Schefflein

23
WED

*It is my prayer that your love may abound more and
more. . . .*   —Philippians 1:9 (RSV)

Recently, I learned of a beautiful practice called the "Loving-kindness Prayer." It's for increasing one's capacity for love. Here's how it goes:

Begin by thinking of two good things you've done in your life (however small), and give thanks to God for using you. Then pray for a dear friend or family member. Next, pray for someone you feel neutral toward. Finally, extend your prayer to someone you feel has harmed you in some way.

I still find that last one to be the hardest, but the most *exciting* part is what's happened as I've prayed for the "neutral person," a clerk in a store where I often shop. I had no positive or negative feelings toward her. She was just there. The first thing that happened was that I noticed her name tag, so I began praying for happiness, good health and spiritual growth for Linda before I entered the store, as I passed her in the aisles, or as she waited on me or checked me out.

As time has passed, I've noticed a special warmth growing in my heart toward Linda. I feel a bit of secret joy each time I enter the store, and her face now lights up as we greet each other in the aisles. Instead of the automatic, "Have a good day," and "Thanks! You, too," Linda and I now converse a bit at checkout time.

But most important, the warmth, like a subtle perfume, seems to go with me out of the store. I've noticed people smiling at me more, and I've started to pay attention to others I'd taken for granted before. That's okay. I think it's time for me to find a new neutral person, anyway. Linda has moved up to friend!

Today, Lord, I pray the loving-kindness prayer for _____.

(name)

—Marilyn Morgan Helleberg

24
THU *A fool thinks he needs no advice, but a wise man listens to others.* —Proverbs 12:15 (TLB)

Greeek, greeek. An irritating, infuriating squeak had emerged from under the engine of our car, and it was driving me nuts!

Greeek, greeek. For weeks I scoured the underside of the car in my spare time and soon the entire underbelly was soaking wet with silicone spray and white grease.

Greeek, greeek. The noise continued to mock me.

One day, I was working on the car in the driveway, and my wife Sharon was hanging out clothes beside me. "Hear that, hon?" I asked, rocking the car up and down, but the noise wouldn't sound for her. "Here, let me put the hood down and try harder." I lowered the hood and rocked the car furiously. *Greeek, greeek.* "There, hear that?"

"Maybe it's in the hood," she suggested, "since it doesn't do it when the hood is up."

I shook my head. "It's not coming from the hood, dear, it's coming from under the engine. See?" I rocked the car. *Greeek, greeek.*

But when she went indoors, I checked the hood, just to be sure. It was the hood! Somehow the squeak had a ventriloquistic effect that had deceived me. A dab of grease on the hood latch ended months of frustration.

Sharon was right even though she knows nothing about cars. My "expertise" blinded me to what was obvious to her. Perhaps it would be good for me to be more open to other "nonexperts" when I'm trying to solve problems. I have nothing to lose by doing so, and I might very well get a fresh perspective on my frustrations.

Teach me, Lord, to consider good ideas, no matter what their source.
—Daniel Schantz

25
FRI

Praise the Lord. . . . He satisfies my desires with good things, so that my youth is renewed like the eagle's.
—Psalm 103:2, 5 (NIV)

On April 25, at eleven-fifteen A.M., my fiftieth birthday, I brought in the mail and became a senior citizen. It said so right inside the official envelope cradling a letter of welcome and my own personalized senior citizen card. I felt as if I'd swallowed an ice cube. I looked from the mail to the mirror above the hall table. Yep, I looked old.

I flung the card aside. But the label stuck and grew throughout the day, till I was trapped in it. *Senior citizen . . . gray, grim, grouchy.* When my husband Whitney bounced in the door, holding a brightly wrapped present, I burst into tears. "What's with you?" he asked. Well, he got the whole earful, and he laughed.

Whipping out his wallet, Whitney produced *his* senior citizen card. "I got it four years ago, remember?"

I hadn't.

"Know why you forgot?"

"Why?" I sniffed.

"Because it wasn't a big deal. It's just crossing a time zone."

So we took our senior citizen cards and got a discount at a fine restaurant. And we had a toast to being seniors *together.*

Lord, help me to face each new day with a youthful spirit.
—Shari Smyth

26
SAT

And if one can overpower him who is alone, two can resist him. A cord of three strands is not quickly torn apart.
—Ecclesiastes 4:12 (NAS)

It was a beautiful summer morning, but a solemn and sad occasion. A good friend had died suddenly, and my wife Joy and I found ourselves standing on a grassy knoll as he was laid to rest in the presence of his family and many friends. As the service ended, we stood quietly in the breezy sunshine, each one lost in his or her own thoughts. Next to me were two men I'd known a long time who had flown in from other states. One turned to me and said, "You know, if I died tomorrow, I don't know if my wife could find six friends who know me well enough to be my pallbearers."

I thought about that remark for several days, knowing it was also true for me. Like many men, I was so busy in my own life that I hadn't taken the time to grow deep friendships since leaving college. It became a priority for me this year to try to reverse that trend.

First, I sought out occasions where several of my acquaintances would be together, and I began to look among them for potential friends. Then I arranged breakfast once a week to cultivate the individual relationships. And lastly, I started to make more time for my two old friends to make sure we didn't drift apart. Simple steps, but the results have already been rewarding—adding the lasting treasure of good friends to my life.

Lord, help me to be the kind of friend whose friendship lasts throughout the journey of life.   —Eric Fellman

27

SUN   *By love serve one another.*   —Galatians 5:13

My son-in-law Jan Bortner is the men's tennis coach at Penn State, and by my reckoning an exceptional teacher of the game. He was a top college player, is good at explaining proper technique and patient with learners of the sport. He has tried to get me interested in tennis and I've dabbled at it, but old golfers are tough to convert. I joke among friends that after watching me swing a racket, Jan gave me a tennis tip: Stick with golf.

There are some fundamentals parallel to both sports, I've found— get in position to hit the ball, get prepared to hit it and follow through—and they have something in common with Christian discipleship. To serve Christ and others more effectively I need to practice the same procedures I do in golf.

1. *Get in position.* I can't do God's bidding holed up at home

watching TV or reading; I need to put myself on the firing line where need exists.

2. *Get prepared.* There is a Christian training ground for service, and it begins with Bible study and prayer. Unless I draw upon God's Word and listen for His marching orders, I won't be ready when opportunities come.

3. *Follow through.* The road to hell is paved with good intentions, someone said, and I need to do better following through on my commitments.

That, and keeping my head down when trying to hit a golf ball.

> *Coach me Lord, on the road of Christlike serving,*
> *Stopping for the wounded, instead of swerving.*
>
> —Fred Bauer

28
MON   *Use hospitality one to another. . . .*   —I Peter 4:9

A small oil painting, *Rainy Monday* by B. Lansing, hangs on our bedroom wall. Several years ago, my husband David bought the painting for me at a summer arts and crafts show in Cave Springs, Georgia.

Sheets of rain fall across the dark sky in *Rainy Monday.* Over to the right, smoke pushes out of the chimney of a little raw-board house on a hill. Light pours from the windows and makes golden puddles on the ground. More times than I can count, I have imagined myself making my way through the rain toward that little house. I reach the porch and the door flies open. I step into the light and find an open fire crackling in the fireplace. The rain pounds like rivets on the tin roof, but I am safe and dry.

Some would find my painting bleak, but it represents something very special to me. In a world that's often cold and sometimes downright cruel, I have the power to create little heavens of light right here: a student's favorite pot roast waiting as she returns home from college; the smell of lemon and cloves greeting an elderly neighbor invited for tea; cinnamon toast, warm for my spouse's arrival home from work; an extra place at supper for a widower from church.

Father, let my home overflow with the light of welcome each time You send a friend or stranger to my door.   —Pam Kidd

29

TUE *I thank my God . . . for your fellowship. . . .*
                                            —Philippians 1:3, 5

I was called to the home of a church member who wanted to donate items to our church fair. Having recently retired, I had time to volunteer and collect these things. Over coffee Mary said, "I'm eighty-five, and I'm legally blind. All my friends are gone, or they are in nursing homes. I'm totally dependent upon old-age services, and I don't like it. What do I have to offer?"

I had been asking myself that very same question and told her so. "I've been reluctant to call or visit friends. I feel like I am impinging on their time. I have all the time in the world, but they are still working or have other things to do. So most of the time I neglect them."

Then Mary said something about handling friends that opened my eyes. "Put all your feelers out," she told me, "and move slowly. You'll make mistakes, but it is better to make mistakes than to be neglectful."

What was it that Mary said about having nothing to offer? Her wisdom and friendship were gifts for my retirement hours. I left her home knowing that I had received a precious guide from a lonely lady who had felt she had nothing more to give.

Giving Lord, You speak to us through others. Thank You for helping a friend share her love and her wisdom.   —Oscar Greene

30

WED *Take therefore no thought for the morrow: for the morrow shall take thought for the things of itself. . . .*
                                            —Matthew 6:34

"You've got mail," the deep, synthetic voice says from the depths of my computer when I switch it on. A few clicks on little pictures and there are my daughter Charlotte's words, written late last night while struggling with a college paper.

Even in the closest knit families, you can't call your mother at one o'clock in the morning to complain of fatigue, to say college is just too hard, that holding down a job and studying gives you no time to have any fun, that your boyfriend is dropping out of school. But you can get it off your chest by sending electronic mail any time of day or night.

E-mail may be a standard feature of the modern office, with memos and spreadsheets flying coast to coast and computer to computer, but I haven't yet gotten used to the wonder of being able to share a thought, a poem, a prayer via cyberspace with a daughter whose life is rolling along hundreds of miles away.

How to respond? The screen looks so empty. No one trains mothers to be Ann Landers. "So glad to hear from you"? That sounds as if I'm pleased she has problems. "Wish I could help"? That's just admitting I'm useless. "I'll pray for you"? Is that comfort to a lonely and tired college student? I start to feel as if *I'm* the one who needs help!

Then, I think of it. Something to help both of us, perhaps. "Take therefore no thought for the morrow: for the morrow shall take thought for the things of itself." So I write that I love her and add these words from Matthew that say so much better than I can, "Don't worry. You are being taken care of."

And press another button: "Send."

Help us, Lord, to use all of Your gifts to stay close to each other.
                                                    —Brigitte Weeks

Editor's Note: Guideposts is now on-line! If you have a computer and a modem, you can visit Guideposts on the World Wide Web at http://www.guideposts.org. You'll be able to sample *Daily Guideposts* and our magazines, send prayer requests to our Prayer Fellowship, and write directly to our editors by e-mail.

Everyday Wonders

1 _____

2 _____

3 _____

4 _____

5 _____

6 _____

7 _____

8 _____

9 _____

10 _____

11 _____

12 _____

13 _____

14 _____

15 _____

16 _____

17 _____

18 _____

19 _____

20 _____

21 _____

22 _____

23 _____

24 _____

25 _____

26 _____

27 _____

28 _____

29 _____

30 _____

Many, O Lord my God, are thy
wonderful works which thou
hast done. . . . —PSALM 40:5

May

S	M	T	W	T	F	S
				1	2	3
4	5	6	7	8	9	10
11	12	13	14	15	16	17
18	19	20	21	22	23	24
25	26	27	28	29	30	31

1

THU

Devote yourselves to prayer, being watchful and thankful.
　　　　　　　　　　　　　　　　　—Colossians 4:2 (NIV)

Prayer has always been a central part of my life. Norman and I cultivated prayer as a regular part of everyday life, as regular as eating or even breathing. One habit of ours that surprised many people was keeping a prayer schedule. Whenever one of our children had an exam at school, or a job interview or a serious medical appointment, we would put it on our appointment calendar and stop wherever we were to pray for the situation.

Recently, I attended a meeting in which several leaders of an international religious organization were discussing their many difficulties. The list of problems was a long one. As each problem came up, a method of handling it was discussed and decided upon. Finally, one problem arose for which a solution could not be found. "Oh, well," said the chairman, "we'll just have to pray about that one."

I was struck by the fact that they were considering prayer only as a last resort. No prayer had gone into this problem and none was scheduled until the situation was hopeless. A phrase came to me: "Prayer should be our first resource, not our last resort." I spoke up in the meeting and asked that we spend more time in prayer for all our needs, not just the impossible ones.

Lord, on this National Day of Prayer, help me to make the habit of prayer a normal part of everyday living.　　　　　—Ruth Stafford Peale

2

FRI　**LOVE IS . . .**

Love is kind. . . .　　　　　　　　　　—I Corinthians 13:4 (NIV)

It was an invitation to fault-finding: a mother-in-law with an advanced degree in child-development and years at a children's clinic; a daughter-in-law who'd never so much as seen a jar of baby food. I was almost unbelievably innocent of household skills, let alone the care of a baby.

Before the birth of our first child, I enrolled in a course for new mothers, but even among fellow beginners I was sadly ignorant. The other women had questions about diaper pails and diaper services, while I wished the instructor would simply hold up a diaper so I could see what one looked like.

And it was to this woefully unprepared young woman that Mother Sherrill's first grandchild was born. She would look down at little John Scott in his bassinet ("What's a bassinet?" I'd asked in class), noting, I was sure, half a dozen things amiss. Too many blankets? Gown on backward? Underpad bunched up? And Mother Sherrill would say, "How comfortable he looks!"

Bathing, diet, feeding schedule, in every aspect of my mothering she found something to like, something to praise. Each time she left our little apartment I'd feel sure her tongue must hurt from biting it. Certainly, I wasn't doing things as she would have.

But each time she left I'd feel, too, that I was a bit more skilled, a bit more competent than I'd imagined. Not corrected by her expertise, however excellent, but growing into motherhood in the kindly sunshine of her approval.

God of love, You are gentle to our faults. Help me remember that what others need most from me is not my know-how but my caring.

—Elizabeth Sherrill

3
SAT

Then I realized that it is good and proper for a man to eat and drink, and to find satisfaction in his toilsome labor under the sun. . . . —Ecclesiastes 5:18 (NIV)

Today is Eppa Rixey's birthday.

Now, I know you're asking, "Just who is Eppa Rixey?"

He was a baseball pitcher. For twenty-one years, he toiled in Philadelphia and Cincinnati, pitching nearly 4,500 innings. In 1922, he won twenty-five games, the best in the National League. Of course, in 1917, he *lost* twenty-one games, the worst record in the league. All in all, Eppa Rixey won 266 games, which is mighty respectable. Then again, he lost 251 games. Only four pitchers have ever lost more games than Eppa Rixey.

And here's the kicker: Eppa Rixey is in the Hall of Fame, right between Sam Rice and Phil Rizzuto.

Now that you know who he is, you may be asking, "How did Eppa Rixey get into the Hall of Fame?"

Well, why not? I say, good for Eppa Rixey! Maybe his only claim to fame is that he played so long. That's no mean feat. Win or lose, on good days and bad, Eppa Rixey went out and pitched his innings. He didn't strike out that many, but he didn't walk that many, either. He was just another working guy from Culpeper, Virginia, trying to make a living at something he loved.

Now, he's mostly forgotten. And that's too bad, because we should honor people like Eppa Rixey. Today, May 3, should be a national holiday for all those working folks who shoulder their adequate talent and make a living. It's not a celebration of the mediocre (mediocre pitchers don't play for twenty-one years), but of those who do a fine, if unremarkable, job. We have statues and buildings and entire streets named after some really average presidents. Why not a day for the rest of us, whose only amazing feat is that we have survived?

Happy Eppa Rixey Day! Celebrate by doing nothing more extraordinary than being yourself. Now *that* is extraordinary.

Lord, help me to see the extraordinary achievements of everyday life.
—Mark Collins

4

SUN

"*Give, and it will be given to you. . . .*"
—Luke 6:38 (NIV)

Until my second son turned five, I'd been a lifelong hoarder. Then my husband Gordon suggested a little spring cleaning. "Don't you think it's time to pass along the baby things?"

I shook my head slowly. "How can we possibly give away the baby things if there's a chance we might need them again?"

Gordon stopped working on me, but God didn't. A financially strapped seminary student's wife had had a baby boy, and our baby clothes were perfect for him. I went into the attic and pulled out the box and gave myself a little pep talk: "If I ever need any of these again, God will provide." Then I bravely gave the box away. Next went the crib, the high chair, the blankets, the maternity clothes, everything.

Four years later, I was pregnant with our third child and completely without any baby supplies. *Well,* I thought, *I guess God will provide now.* He did. One by one, items started appearing. A friend passed along her entire maternity wardrobe; everything was a perfect fit. Another friend had a crib to lend me. Another neighbor was moving and gave us her baby swing, stroller, infant seat and slide.

One day, as I was taking a used terry cloth baby sleeper that some-one had passed along to me out of the dryer, I noticed some writing on it, stitched just across the breast in pink. I finally made out the words: *I'm heaven sent.* Of course, the words were supposed to mean that the baby inside the sleeper was sent from heaven, but I received them as a merry wink from God to me, a reformed hoarder.

God, help me to rely on Your provision, not my own.   —Karen Barber

5
MON *He calms the storm and stills the waves. What a blessing is that stillness, as he brings them safely into harbor!*
—Psalm 107:29–30 (TLB)

The Monday before my son Michael's wedding, the reminder board in my front hall listed seventeen things that needed to be done that day to prepare for the rehearsal dinner for thirty at my house the fol-lowing Friday and for the sixteen houseguests who would begin to arrive in three days. All I could do was shudder and ask God to send me a guardian angel to help me get everything done.

That morning, Wally and Shirley Winston pulled up in their RV. They were here to attend the wedding and spend a week in Wisconsin visiting old friends.

Shirley immediately saw the list on the board. "Well, let's get to work," she said. Wally gathered up brooms, the hose and my fifteen-year-old Andrew, and headed for the backyard patio to get it ready for the rehearsal dinner. Shirley and I headed for the grocery store. Then we started cooking. She not only thought up fabulous enter-tainment and food ideas, she also organized and set out everything while I was at the wedding rehearsal. She and Wally even stayed up late cleaning after the dinner party.

The dinner and the whole wedding week were a great success, but I could never have pulled it off alone. Through Shirley, Wally and my reminder board, God showed me how important it is to make our needs known to others—and that guardian angels don't always have wings.

Lord, give me courage to admit that I can't do it all alone. Help me to swal-low my pride and allow others to help me when I'm feeling stressed.
—Patricia Lorenz

6   *A merry heart doeth good like a medicine. . . .*

TUE   —Proverbs 17:22

I tend to take myself far too seriously, overanalyzing, pushing myself too hard, feeling guilty if I'm not accomplishing something worthwhile all the time. So recently, my daughter Karen gave me a writing tablet with hilarious baby pictures on each page. Here were kids with expressions that looked like little old men or women, tough executives, primping prima donnas, pity-me Pattys, you name it. Each had a caption under it, spoken as though by an adult.

The one that really cracked me up was a kid with tight lips and intense, I'll-do-it-if-it-kills-me eyes. The caption: "Stress got me where I am today. WHERE AM I?" I laughed till my stomach hurt! Then I pinned the little guy on the cork board over my desk. Whenever I find myself getting uptight, I just glance up at my little buddy and break into laughter.

Just in case you're one of those do-it-if-it-kills-me types, you might want to look for a cartoon that really cracks you up and pin it where you'll see it often. A merry heart might be just the medicine you need! Take it from one who knows, it'll do your heart good!

Lord Jesus, grant me the grace of a holy sense of humor. I'll begin by learning to laugh at myself.   —Marilyn Morgan Helleberg

7   *Praise the Lord, O heavens! Praise him from the skies! . . .*

WED   *Praise him, vapors high above the clouds. . . . And praise him down here on earth. . . .*   —Psalm 148:1, 4, 7 (TLB)

The rain awakened me in the early morning hours. It was fierce, thundering on the roof with such intensity that I wondered if we would spring a leak. "That's all we need!" I muttered as I snuggled deeper into the bedclothes. Earthquake. Fire. And now the possibility of flood. I was filled with foreboding and fear. Mother Nature was playing havoc with California, and I was not sure I had the stamina to ride out another disaster.

Within the hour, my husband John was out in the deluge clearing gutters and getting a siphon into the swimming pool so that it would not overflow and erode the hillside upon which our home is perched.

Watching him move the siphon hoses around I was suddenly struck by an unusual phenomenon. Although our pool is plastered white and the water in it is colorless, like the ocean it reflects the blue of the sky. That day, in spite of the overhang of black clouds and the sheets of gray torrential rain, our pool still reflected a brilliant azure blue!

"Thank You, Lord," I whispered. "No dark clouds can keep the promise of Your presence from shining through the heavens!" My foreboding suddenly lifted; my fear was gone.

Lord, when anxiety and fear bring a stormy season to my heart, help me to remember the brilliant azure blue of heaven piercing through the clouds.
—Fay Angus

8
THU
He was lifted up, and a cloud took him out of their sight.
—Acts 1:9 (RSV)

Yesterday, I flew from Atlanta to Dallas. Cruising at thirty-five thousand feet, I looked to see the highest clouds stretched majestically beneath me. Anticipating Ascension Day, I pondered some logical questions: *What does it mean when the Scriptures say that Jesus was taken up in a cloud? Where did the cloud go? Is heaven above the clouds? And what is heaven like?*

In a modern world of airplanes and space exploration, questions such as these assail every person who has the courage to think. And answers to such questions cannot always be found upon this earth. But questions aside, what I do know is that the followers of Jesus were visibly convinced that Jesus had returned to be with the One Whom He called "Father."

Soaring quietly above the clouds, I reflected that the ascension of Jesus is a glimmer of hope, a window of insight into eternal truth. It is God's promise that I, too, will be reunited with my Father when death has conquered my physical body. And though I do not understand it all, I remember the words of Isaiah 55:9: "For as the heavens are higher than the earth, so are my ways higher than your ways, and my thoughts than your thoughts." I embrace the mystery with faith.

Dear Father, give me the courage to realize that much truth is beyond my understanding. Amen.
—Scott Walker

9
FRI

And now, in my old age, don't set me aside. Don't forsake me now when my strength is failing.

—Psalm 71:9 (TLB)

"Oh, Dad, not again!" I said. For the third time in a week, he had spilled his orange juice all over the breakfast table. He had been reading the newspaper and turned a page, knocking the glass over. Startled, he looked up. Then he tried to use his napkin to wipe up the juice, which was rapidly heading for the edges of the table.

"That'll never do it!" I snapped, reaching for the roll of paper towels. While I blotted and washed and dried the table, he sat in his chair with his head bowed. I knew he felt embarrassed, but I was trying to keep my anger in check, so I said nothing. I needed time to think.

My stepfather is almost eighty-six, and it's still hard for me to accept that our roles are reversed. He used to be my support system. I can't count the hours he spent reading to me when I was a little girl, patiently explaining words I didn't understand. He taught me to drive when I thought I'd never get the hang of it. He encouraged me to reach for goals that seemed beyond me. He helped me to make peace with myself when I didn't reach them, and then to try again.

Now he looks to me to make his decisions—to tell him when to get a haircut, to remind him to shave, to keep track of his medications and to find his eyeglasses whenever he misplaces them. Most important, he relies on me to help him maintain his dignity. And I certainly wasn't doing that when I scolded him for spilling his juice. He depends on me, but he's not a child.

I apologized for snapping at Dad, and I also thought about a way I might help him. When Dad reads his newspaper, it's hard for him to concentrate on anything else, so ever since then I've been saying, "Dad, here's your juice," as I put down the glass. There haven't been any more spills. It's a small victory, perhaps, but to me it is a step toward becoming the support system for my dad that he always was for me.

Dear Lord, help us to be there for our parents in their time of need. Amen.
                                                    —Phyllis Hobe

10   *To all perfection I see a limit. . . .*

SAT   —Psalm 119:96 (NIV)

It sounds silly, I know, but for years, whenever I saw a clown making balloon animals, I was jealous. I wanted to dazzle children with
my skill at twisting balloons into bears, ducks and rabbits. Then one
day, a clown, noticing my curiosity, silently handed me a pamphlet
on making balloon animals. Armed with the pamphlet, I volunteered
for the next ASPCA benefit, to be held two months later. But after
hours of practice, I could only make one animal—a dog.

On the day of the benefit, I cringed as I handed the first eager child
a dog. And then I handed out another dog. And then yet another dog.
To add insult to injury, some of the dogs had no necks, some had
long necks and some had tails as long as their bodies. And I popped
more balloons than I inflated. Toward midday, I was just blowing up
balloons and handing them out without even bothering to twist them
into shapes. Kids, nudged by their parents, politely said thank you,
but I felt like a failure. *Please, God, let this time go quickly,* I prayed.

At the end of the day I was glumly packing up my few supplies—
the balloons, the hand pump—when I heard "Miss! Miss Clown!"
Three boys were yanking their little brother toward me. "Will you
make our brother a giraffe, too?" asked one of the boys. I stared at
the dog I'd given them. *I suppose, with its misshapen neck, it does look
like a giraffe.* Another boy ran over. "Look!" he said with a wide grin.
"She made *me* a horse!" *Hmmm . . . I can see the resemblance. But what
about that child over there? I gave him a plain long balloon.* As if on cue,
he shouted happily, "And she gave me a snake!"

Happily, I unpacked my things. "One more *snake* coming right
up!" I said.

*God, when something doesn't go perfectly today, let me take whatever I can
from it—let me see the snake in the plain old balloon.*

—Linda Neukrug

11   *Her children arise and call her blessed. . . .*

SUN   —Proverbs 31:28 (NIV)

Mother raised four of us children, and I've never doubted for a moment the godly influence she continues to have on each of our lives.
But at a community gathering a few years back, I learned all sorts of
interesting tidbits about her.

"Your mother is the 'Mother Teresa of Madison Avenue,' " a lady announced, referring to the street where my parents still live. Oh, I knew she went grocery shopping for shut-ins, but I never realized that by clipping coupons and careful shopping, she stretched the fixed incomes of those seniors to include ground beef and fresh fruit.

"I knew a different side of your mother," another woman recalled. "When she was a single teacher straight out of college, they assigned her to a country school so far up the 'holler' they had to pipe in sunshine. There wasn't much entertainment for those kids, and one December she stayed up the whole night with the family of one of her pupils to watch their Christmas cactus bloom. They talked about that for years."

"I'll never forget the time her brother was in the Army during World War II," the first lady said. "Not many of us women drove back then, but that didn't stop your mother. She hopped right in her car and drove those back roads clear from West Virginia to Texas to see him. When I asked her if she was afraid, she said she borrowed a fellow's tweed cap so she'd look like a man behind the steering wheel."

My practical, cautious, serious mother—the one who wouldn't let us go off to school until we'd had our morning dose of oatmeal—had done all that?

On this day set aside to honor mothers, why not take a moment to celebrate the many roles your own mother has played? Like a fine diamond, she's a woman of many sparkling facets, "blessed" in ways you may never have imagined. And all this time, we thought she was just "Mom"!

Lord, what a priceless, enduring treasure my mother is. Thank You.
—Roberta Messner

12
MON

Cast your bread upon the waters: for thou shalt find it after many days.   —Ecclesiastes 11:1

Someone once ventured that no kindness—no matter how small— goes unnoticed by heaven, and I'd like to think God smiles when He sees us helping each other. Amazing, isn't it, how one little caring gesture can halo a day. A short note from a friend today had such an effect on me, and I wanted to pass on the feeling.

When a neighbor commented on the beauty of our Virginia blue-bells, I offered to share some. It seemed the neighborly thing to do considering my crop came from Agnes Braden who used to live just north of us, down a stony path through the woods. Agnes is gone now, but her flowers remind my wife Shirley and me of her friendship.

For several years, we didn't have much commerce with the Bradens, René and Agnes. They were retired and seemed to stay pretty much to themselves. Oh, we'd wave and chat when we passed by on walks, but I didn't know much about them until their health started to fail. Then, because their children lived far away, we and other neighbors began looking in on them. One of Agnes' joys, I learned, was her flowers—especially wildflowers.

One spring day, when I was admiring a spectacular stand of trumpet-shaped blooms in her woods, she answered, "Oh, yes, Virginia bluebells are lovely this time of year." Then she invited me to "take some for your place," and so I transplanted a few stalks.

That was several years ago. Today, Agnes' gift has multiplied several times over, and clusters of these blue beauties can be seen everywhere I look. That's the way it is with thoughtful acts and deeds. They have a way of spreading all over the place.

> *Impress upon us, God, that . . .*
> *What we sow, we reap*
> *What we give away, we keep.*

—Fred Bauer

13
TUE *For we do not have a high priest who cannot sympathize with our weaknesses, but one who has been tempted in all things as we are, yet without sin.* —Hebrews 4:15 (NAS)

"This is just a simple little quiz," I mutter to myself. I have to pass a short written exam in order to get my chauffeur's rating, so I can continue to drive the outreach teams for Central Christian College where I teach.

For someone taking a "simple little quiz," I am awfully nervous! I studied the guidebook fifty times, underlining important parts. I drilled myself with flash cards. I spent most of last night rehearsing the answers instead of sleeping.

My hand shakes as I receive the test from the officer. She looks at me in an all-business way, and I wonder if I look as coldly at my students.

Twenty minutes and ten fingernails later I am finished. My face is burning, and I'm breathing like a runner. I lay the test in front of the officer. She grades it swiftly.

"You passed," she says matter-of-factly, then she smiles. "Barely."

I feel as if I just escaped the jaws of death and humiliation. Thank God I don't have to do that every day.

The experience set me to thinking about my work. As a teacher, I'm used to being the examiner; I'd forgotten what it feels like to take a test. But now I can see things from my students' point of view. Next time I give my students a "simple little quiz," I'll be more sympathetic and understanding.

Thank You, Father, for giving us a High Priest Who knows what it's like to be tested.
                                                              —Daniel Schantz

---

WORDS OF WONDER

In wonder-working things, or some bush aflame,
Men look for God and fancy him concealed;
But in earth's common things he stands revealed,
While grass and flowers and stars spell out his
    name.

—MINOT J. SAVAGE

14
WED

Blessed are they that mourn: for they shall be comforted.
                                                              —Matthew 5:4

One day, a couple of years ago, I stopped off at my bank to use the ATM. As I entered the alcove, the man ahead of me turned and said, "I'll be done in a minute." I smiled and nodded.

When he had finished and I was stepping up to the machine, he spoke again. "Are you from West Medford?" (Most of the African-American families in our area live in West Medford.) Again I nodded. "Do you know Whitfield Jeffers?" I said yes, so he introduced himself. "My name is Ralph Penta. Jeff and I worked together in the fire department for ten years."

Ralph and Jeff had both worked for Robby, another friend of mine and a retired fire lieutenant who had recently lost his wife of sixty-three years. I asked Ralph if he knew about Robby's loss.

"Yes, I know Robby, and I knew his wife. My own wife died in 1989. After all this time, it's still hard to talk about it. While she was alive I took so much for granted because she was always there. Now I miss her every day." Then, changing the subject, he asked, "How is Jeff?"

I swallowed hard and said, "He lost his wife, too. A few years ago, she was crossing the street between two cars. One backed up and hit her. Her death was devastating for Jeff and for our whole community."

Ralph's words and Jeff's loss reminded me again of how precious my fifty-three years with Ruby have been. We shook hands and Ralph said, "I'm going to call Jeff and Robby tonight."

In that tiny alcove, something beautiful happened. A chance encounter would reunite three lonely widowers, and Ralph's words opened my eyes and increased my gratitude for what I have been given.

Use our moments to bring us closer, Father. Like Your love for us, they are precious.   —Oscar Greene

15
THU *Even there your hand will guide me, your right hand will hold me fast.*   —Psalm 139:10 (NIV)

After we learned about the reoccurrence of her cancer, my mother said matter-of-factly that she didn't want to go through the kinds of treatments the doctors usually prescribed. But she did agree to have an MRI.

While the test itself wasn't painful, lying on the hard table was terribly uncomfortable for Mother's spine. I asked the technicians to allow me to remain with her, and to my surprise they agreed. I was instructed to sit on a stool by Mother's feet. I could even hold them if I liked. We were left alone in a very small, very cold treatment room. As Mother disappeared into the shiny machine, her feet were the only parts of her that I could see or touch. I held on to them gratefully.

Numbers flashed on the huge machine showing the length of each test and how much time remained. We couldn't talk because of the thunderous noise it made. Mother had been instructed to lie perfectly still. Periodically, I squeezed her feet.

Two technicians peered in at us through a window in the wall of the tiny, cold room; I felt as though we were in a scene from *Star Trek*. After a long time, one of the technicians came in and pulled Mother out of the machine as if she were removing a cake from the oven. Mother smiled gratefully, thinking it was over, but the technician pushed her back in. It was only half over. Again I grabbed hold of Mother's feet.

The entire procedure took almost two hours. When it was finally over, the technician gently helped Mother off the table and into a wheelchair. Mother said softly, "Thank you, dear. You did a fine job." Then she reached for the young woman's hand—and kissed it. The startled technician bent over and gave Mother a good, long hug.

There's nothing quite like a human touch, is there, Lord? Is that why You became one of us? Amen.   —Marion Bond West

16

FRI   *Ask, and it shall be given. . . .*   —Luke 11:9

For some time, my husband David and I had been talking to God about our concerns for our daughter Keri.

"Father," we would pray, "Keri wants to go to medical school. We want to guide her in the right direction and help her understand what she can accomplish. Can You help us?"

God answered with a flourish.

"Keri, would you be interested in working in my office this summer?" Dr. Lois Wagstrom casually asked one Sunday after church.

Within weeks, Keri was home from her freshman year at Birmingham Southern and working eight-hour days in Dr. Wagstrom's plastic surgery practice. And Dr. Wagstrom, we were discovering, was fast becoming a lot more than an answered prayer.

"I love to watch Dr. Wagstrom perform surgery," Keri remarked one night. "I don't think I would be as happy in any other branch of medicine."

On another evening, she said, "You know, Dad, for the first time in my life, I actually want to learn biology and chemistry. After talking to Dr. Wagstrom, I can see why it's important."

Tales of Dr. Wagstrom's generosity, her kindness, her impressive Christian ways came often into our conversations. Keri's job was not only providing her with motivation; she had found just the kind of hero I hoped God might send, a doctor whose primary reason for being was to help others.

Of course, none of this ensures that Keri will stick to her goal, excel in college, make it to medical school and become a surgeon. But that's not what we prayed for. We asked God that she might see what she could be. He sent a beautiful, in-the-flesh role model to show her the way.

Father, You put good people around us to show us how good we can hope to be. Thank You for using them to answer our prayers. —Pam Kidd

17
SAT
He brought you water out of hard rock. He gave you manna to eat in the desert. . . . —Deuteronomy 8:15–16 (NIV)

Elizabeth's sleepy little head nuzzled into my chest as she nursed her way back to sleep. *How amazing,* I thought, *I'm feeding her from my own body.* It was probably one of the most complicated things I'd ever done in my life, and yet I couldn't even feel my body making milk. God took care of it, as long as I drank enough fluids and got enough rest. I hardly had to think about it at all.

I touched the down on Elizabeth's scalp, marveling at the incredible gift of her life. Whatever I might be called upon to sacrifice, I was eager to sacrifice for her sake. I would gladly give her my own self, if need be.

Then I thought again about the milk, and it occurred to me that I *was* giving her myself. When we truly give ourselves, we're only giving others what God has given us. When we truly give, we hardly have to think about it at all.

Blessed Lord, help me to give to others, as You have given to me.
—Julia Attaway

18
SUN
And there were dwelling at Jerusalem Jews, devout men, out of every nation under heaven. . . . every man heard them speak in his own language. —Acts 2:5–6

A weekend meeting I attended in New York adjourned unexpectedly on Saturday night. My friend Marion and I, both from rural areas, weren't able to catch earlier flights, so we decided to attend church together the next day.

I called several churches to inquire about service times, but I got no information until I reached the message machine at Community United Methodist Church in Jackson Heights. "Please worship with us," a friendly voice invited. "The Chinese service is at nine, English at ten, Spanish at eleven-thirty and Korean at one."

We went at ten, and what a surprise! The congregation was a veritable United Nations! The organist was Hispanic, the lector Greek, and the altar flowers had been given by a Chinese family. People wore suits and dresses and gracefully flowing saris, embroidered shirts and kimonos. When we sang the lovely hymn "Lord, You Have Come to the Lakeshore," voices were raised in Spanish as well as English.

During fellowship time, a Korean worshiper greeted me. "I'm surprised to see so many nationalities," I commented, "since you offer worship in four languages."

"Oh, some people go to *all* the services!" he said. "It's wonderful to spend the whole day praising the Lord with different people in different ways!"

I left for the airport and the long trip home with a song of praise— a Spanish one—in my heart.

Thank You, Jesus, that we can praise You in different places, languages and ways.   —Penney Schwab

---

19
MON

Be glad and rejoice. Surely the Lord has done great things.
                                                    —Joel 2:21 (NIV)

The mailman had left five or six large boxes stacked up inside the front porch. *It's here,* I thought as I raced down the driveway. A couple of weeks before, I had received a most unexpected phone call from the head of a big crafts company in Arkansas. She had been reading *Daily Guideposts, 1996,* and had come across the devotional I had written for March 25 about a knitting project for Oxfam, the international relief agency. I have been involved in knitting sweaters for displaced children, mostly in Africa, for some years and had written of the rich rewards the work had brought me.

Yarn is costly, and my small sweaters have been knitted from the most inexpensive materials I could find on sale racks or begged from friends. That was about to change. "We have quite a lot of discontinued yarn in our stockroom," the lilting Southern voice on the phone told me. "And I was reading about the sweaters you make. It's all real wool, and I was wondering if you could make use of it?"

I was speechless. It was too good to be true. Now I wouldn't have to scrounge around for yarn and use up little pieces that sometimes didn't quite go together. And she was offering me pure woolen yarn—a joy to knit with and hold in one's hand and, of course, extra warm and comfortable for the wearer.

How did that story, that thoughtful reader and that surplus yarn all come together? A small miracle, maybe, but to me an especially moving one. I thanked her breathlessly and gave her my address. And now here it was, just as she had promised. The boxes beckoned me to pull out the yarn and imagine transforming it in its many glowing colors into knitted messages of support and hope.

Lord, remind me that the unexpected is always a part of Your plan.
—Brigitte Weeks

20
TUE

This is the covenant that I will make . . . saith the Lord; I will put my laws into their mind, and write them in their hearts: and I will be to them a God, and they shall be to me a people.   —Hebrews 8:10

Mid-afternoon is the most important part of the day at our house. That's when the postal truck arrives to drop off our mail. I quickly shuffle through magazines, papers, ads and circulars and look for personal letters from family and friends.

The kettle has been kept on low rumble until the mail arrives. Treasured letters deserve to be savored and served with a cup of tea, a cookie, a footstool and an easy chair. After all, what I'm holding is an author's original, limited edition, signed and dated, too, written just for me.

As I read, I visualize the writer: a grandson's struggle manipulating an unruly pencil (and its eraser) as he begins, "Dear Grandma, How are you? I am fine." Then he tells of his delight in having driven in the winning run in Little League. I share a granddaughter's excitement about her engagement, how wonderful Keith is, what her ring is like, the wedding date. When one friend writes, she tucks in helpful hints before sealing the envelope. Another sends news of my former neighborhood plus items about her family.

But these aren't the only letters that interest me. I also read some written long ago by men named Paul, John, Peter, James and Jude. "Epistles," the Scriptures call them.

These beloved correspondents tell of their activities, just as my friends do. They, too, include practical advice on making my life more abundant. And they bring news of home, where Jesus is waiting to welcome me and all who love Him.

Yes, letters from family and friends are treasured. But so are those from Jesus' apostles. So much so, in fact, that as I read my tea often cools and my cookie is forgotten.

Thank You, Lord, for all the letters in Your Word. It seems each one is written just for me.
                                                          —Isabel Wolseley

21
WED

The Spirit itself maketh intercession for us with groanings which cannot be uttered.   —Romans 8:26

Enter your login name, my computer says, the green letters glaring at me from the black screen. I type in, *Fhaml,* my name as far as the computer is concerned. Then it says, *Enter your password,* a more exciting prospect, making me feel as though I am a spy entering a secret command center. I type in the secret word we've shared for a month. *Password invalid,* I'm told. *You have five grace login(s) to change your password.*

"Drat!" I say to myself, searching my mind for new passwords. I've used up the names of immediate family members and pets and distant relatives. What other names can I remember? Suddenly, I have an idea: *I'll pick someone from my prayer list.*

Would you like to change your password? (Y/N). I type "Y" for yes. There's a friend I've been meaning to pray for all week, **Scott.** The code is entered and repeated. **Scott.** I close my eyes and pray. Good, I'm logged on.

A month passes, and my password is remembered every day. By month's end, when that formerly dreaded message, *Password invalid,* comes up, I think of someone else I need to remember regularly. Thus, over the months, I've prayed for a friend in financial trouble and a heart attack patient and my son Willy's school chum who is caught in an ugly custody battle. I close my eyes while the computer issues its mysterious grinding, as mysterious to me as the workings of intercessory prayer. However it works, I know, when I open my eyes, that spiritually at least I've logged on.

Dear Lord, today I pray for ————————.
                          (login name)

—Rick Hamlin

22

THU   *Pride only breeds quarrels. . . .*   —Proverbs 13:10 (NIV)

When my son Jonathan was seventeen, he went to the hospital for minor surgery on his shoulder. As he lay in his hospital bed, waiting for the operation, I tried not to look at the grungy, beat-up baseball cap he was wearing. Everywhere he went he wore that hat, while I flushed with embarrassment. Our arguments over it grew increasingly fierce.

Even when they wheeled him down the hall for surgery, he kept the hat on. *Why, Jon?* I kept thinking. Ahead loomed the double doors of the operating room, which was as far as I was allowed to go. *Be with him, Lord,* I silently prayed.

Suddenly, I felt something in my hands. "Will you keep this for me, please, Mom?" Jon's eyes were pleading as he pushed his beloved cap toward me. The nurse covered his black hair with a surgical cap and the doors swallowed him. I carried the hated baseball cap past tempting trash cans to an empty waiting room, laying it on the seat next to me. The hat and I waited. And waited. Two hours, then three. Too long.

"Dear God," I prayed, tears falling, "please don't let anything go wrong. I thank You for Jon . . . for his kindness and loyalty, for how hard he's worked to overcome learning disabilities."

I looked over at the filthy cap: so small on the seat, so big to me. Suddenly, it wasn't the cap I was seeing, but the grungy dirt of pride that had made an issue of it, that said, *What will people think of me if I let him wear this thing?*

Just then, the surgeon burst into the room, still in scrubs. He was smiling. "Jon's fine, Mrs. Smyth. It just took a little longer than we expected. You may go to the recovery room to be with him." Carefully, gratefully, I carried the cap down the hall, not caring who saw it. For whatever reason, it was important to Jon. And that was more important than my pride.

Lord, clothe me in humility so that I remember that what's in the heart is most important to You.   —Shari Smyth

23
FRI   *The Lord your God ... loveth the stranger. ... Love ye therefore the stranger. ...*   —Deuteronomy 10:17, 18, 19

When I was ten years old, I became a Girl Scout. I had been a Brownie, had "flown up" and gotten a new, green uniform. I had even named one of the small groups—the Road Runners. I was also the only "colored" girl in the troop. I don't remember the other girls being unfriendly, and I wasn't unfriendly to them. But there was a definite aloneness that I felt. I longed for someone who looked like me to join.

Now that I'm older, I know that skin color is only a small part of who a person is. I remember when I wanted to know my colleague Laura better. With a simple statement—"We should do lunch sometime"—and her eager nod of assent, we opened the door to friendship. Over lunch, we talked about our husbands, our desire for more education and our ongoing struggle to put God first in a world that demands so much from us.

It didn't matter that Laura and I were of different races. By the time we finished lunch, we could see we were alike in so many other, important ways.

I'm glad I responded to the warm feelings I had for Laura. Being friendly—creating space for friendship to grow—is the way to go for me. I keep finding friends who "look like me" after all.

Jesus, help me to take down the superficial barriers that separate me from others.   —Robin White Goode

24
SAT   *All the days ordained for me were written in your book before one of them came to be.*   —Psalm 139:16 (NIV)

Our daughter Amy Jo married her high school sweetheart last year, in a flurry of white lace and endless lists. It was a hectic and exciting time, but as the day of the ceremony drew near, I began to wonder just what "giving away" your only daughter meant.

What would it be like, knowing that this would not be her *real* home anymore? Would she be happy? She and Randy were different in many ways. And how would he fit into the family? Exactly what kind of mother-in-law would I be? Would I gain a son or lose a daughter? And what about my husband Gary and me? How would our relationship change?

When the big day came, I was careful to tuck a lace hanky into my beaded purse, just in case the tears began. The string quartet played the wedding march as Gary walked a beautiful Amy Jo down the aisle. He looked handsome in his tux. After he had placed Amy Jo's hand in Randy's, he sat down beside me. I glanced at Gary; his eyes were brimming with tears. A handkerchief . . . did he have one? Just then, Gary reached into the inner pocket of his tux and pulled out a neatly folded wad of toilet tissue—one he had no doubt tucked in at the last minute.

I linked my arm in his and smiled. Amy Jo and Randy would be just fine. Because different can be good. And love can be lasting. I tapped the toe of my sequined shoe against Gary's cowboy boot, knowing that the best things between us would always be the same.

O Father, You are the Constant in all the changes of our lives. Help me to celebrate that!   —Mary Lou Carney

25
SUN *Every man shall give as he is able, according to the blessing of the Lord. . . .*   —Deuteronomy 16:17

It was stewardship season, but I wasn't squirming. In fact, I was quite comfortable. "Hey, Keri," I whispered to my little sister, "you're tithing this summer, aren't you?" I smiled righteously at her as I dropped my check into the plate. I'd been out of college for a year, and I took pride in tithing my ten percent.

Out of the corner of my eye, I noticed Jerry Adams, a member of our church who has cerebral palsy. He seemed to be fumbling for something. His effort seemed painful. I thought about getting up to help him, but then I remembered his determination to be independent. "Jerry works very hard at a sheltered workshop," Michael Stevens, a man who sometimes assists Jerry, had told me several weeks before. "He's proud that he's able to make a few dollars of his own each month, in spite of his disability."

After the service was over, I made my way out to the fellowship hall to visit with friends. Later, I walked through the sanctuary on my way out. There, in the same spot, sat Jerry in his wheelchair. He was still so focused on whatever it was that he was trying to remove from his pocket that he didn't notice me standing near him. I watched for several minutes until he finally got his hand in his pocket and pulled out a crumpled dollar bill. He slowly rolled his chair up to the altar and dropped the dollar into the offering plate.

As Jerry left the sanctuary, I walked up to the altar and looked into the plate. The check that I had been bragging to Keri about seemed so little compared to Jerry's wadded-up dollar bill. And I prayed that one day I would be able to give as much to God as I had seen Jerry give.

Lord, my gifts to You are tiny compared to Your blessings. Help me to give from my heart.   —Brock Kidd

26
MON
I know, O Lord, that a man's life is not his own; it is not for man to direct his steps.   —Jeremiah 10:23 (NIV)

As a young man living in a small town with very few opportunities, I struggled with the problem of poverty. I dreamed of escape, of a better life somewhere else. So I made a promise to leave Mississippi and never return. But God brought me back to minister to the community I had once wanted to abandon.

Now that our daughter Danita is in medical school, people are asking me if she will return to Mendenhall and work in our health center. Curious about what her response would be, I asked Danita myself. She said, "I'm trusting God to guide me, and if He guides me back to Mendenhall, I'll come back gladly. If He leads me to another community where there is a Christian health center serving the poor, I'll be content to serve there, too. Wherever He leads me, as long as I can be a witness for Him, I'll be happy."

My heart was overjoyed after listening to Danita's response. I trusted God to direct my steps over thirty years ago, and I'm glad that Danita is allowing Him to direct hers.

Lord, help me to know Your plan for me, and then order my steps to go where You would have me go.

—Dolphus Weary

27
TUE
"Nevertheless not my will, but thine, be done."
—Luke 22:42 (RSV)

Until my friend Sarah called I thought I was having a bad day. The things I wanted to happen at my office weren't happening—at least not the way *I* wanted them to—and all morning I had been shooting God what could only be called metaphysical dirty looks. Then the phone on my desk burbled.

Had Sarah not identified herself, I never would have recognized her voice. She was crying. "I just needed to call someone," she said.

"Bad day?" I asked.

"Bad life," she retorted. I knew through our mutual good friends that Sarah's mother was gravely ill, and that her job had changed, and that she and her fiancé had recently postponed their wedding. My own problems began to shrivel.

"What happens," she wanted to know, "if the things you hope for most in your life, the things you've dreamed about since you were little, are not part of God's plan for you?"

It was not a question I was prepared for in the middle of a busy workday, and I groped for something reassuring to tell Sarah. But while I was fumbling with a well-meant platitude, she interrupted me and answered her own question. "I guess the thing I have to pray for is to accept God's will for me."

I knew Sarah well enough to know that she really didn't believe that she was having a bad life, and that when she hung up the phone she would do exactly what she said: Say a prayer of acceptance rather than a prayer of demand. What she probably didn't know was that because of her call I would be praying the same prayer.

God, You made me flexible so that I can bend. I must remember: Thy will, not mine.   —Edward Grinnan

28
WED
They are those who, hearing the word, hold it fast in an honest and good heart. . . .   —Luke 8:15 (RSV)

Our daughter Tamara phoned her dad one evening to relay the news that she'd been involved in a minor automobile accident while riding with her college roommate. A teenager had run a red light and rammed their car, pushing them up onto the sidewalk. Tamara had bruised her knee on the dash, and her friend Katherine ended up in a neck brace for a few days.

About a week later, an insurance adjuster for the other driver showed up. He offered a substantial amount for Katherine's totaled car and assured them their medical bills would be taken care of. After speaking with Katherine about other compensation, he turned to Tamara and declared, "We're prepared to offer you five hundred dollars for pain and suffering." She certainly could have used it; in another few weeks she was leaving for Israel on a study tour with a group from her school.

Tamara looked him in the eye and answered, "I can't take your money. I didn't have any pain and suffering. All I got out of the deal was a bruised knee and a good story." The adjuster was taken aback. People usually don't refuse financial settlements unless they intend to sue. I was startled, too. I thought about how hard it would have been for me to turn down that "free money." Tamara, however, knew it was not right to claim it.

I know one thing without a doubt. That insurance representative will not forget my daughter. And the next time I'm tempted to "take all I can get," neither will I.

Lord, an honest heart is pure gold all by itself. Teach me just how valuable it is to You.
                                                              —Carol Knapp

29
THU

Carry each other's burdens, and in this way you will fulfill the law of Christ.   —Galatians 6:2 (NIV)

Monday night last week, our twenty-two-year old son Pete called from the Air Force base where he was stationed. "It really looks as if I'll have a crack at F-15 pilot training! Five slots are going to open up, and the officers say I have a good chance of getting one!"

Then came his call on Tuesday morning. "Mom, the doctor says the tests they ran when I was so sick last month show that I have a very rare virus in my system. It's contagious and has no known cure."

Within hours, my husband Bill and I had alerted every friend we could think of. Over the next two days, we could feel their prayers around us as an overwhelming peace. Despite our anxiety, we were able to sleep normally, knowing that others were carrying our burden.

On Thursday, the new test results came in. "You can breathe, Mom!" We could feel Pete's grin over the phone. Yes, he had the virus in his body—it was a blessing it hadn't killed him when he was so very sick the month before—but now his body was healing itself. And the initial read of the lung X-rays showed no damage. What he was suffering from this time was a cold.

Relieved and happy, we called and wrote to thank the friends all over the world who had prayed for us. And as we shared our joy in Pete's good news, we passed on the prayer needs others had given us along the way. Bill and I had become part of a vital organism, the body of Christ, interceding with the Father for our brothers and sisters.

Lord, thank You for intercession and intercessors.   —Roberta Rogers

30
FRI
Greater love hath no man than this, that a man lay down his life for his friends.   —John 15:13

I remember Uncle Mack as a quiet man. Aunt Frieda, his wife, could talk for half an hour without stopping for breath, but Mack rarely said anything. He would sit in an easy chair on the edge of our family gatherings, taking in the sometimes raucous debating of the adults and the occasional squabbling of the children with tired, heavy-lidded eyes. When he did talk, there was an edge of impatience in his soft voice, as if the effort to speak was costly.

Mack seemed to live inside a great fatigue. In part, this was the result of the heart disease that would eventually take him. But there was a deeper tiredness, a sadness that predated the disease and perhaps even helped produce it. When I was old enough to put the question into words, I asked my father what was wrong with Uncle Mack.

"We were both in the Italian campaign in World War Two," Dad said. "I was in an antiaircraft battery in the Anzio landings and the battles that followed, and they were pretty rough, but your Uncle Mack had it worse. His unit was part of the advance across the Rapido River.

"The river was only about fifty feet wide at the widest, but the Germans had removed all the cover and diverted water from upstream to create a marsh. Their side of the river was heavily fortified. The attack began at night, in a fog. It lasted for two days. When the battle was over, every GI who had made it across the river had been killed, wounded or captured.

"Mack's never been able to get over that battle, to get over the sight of his buddies dying around him. He's always tired because he has trouble sleeping at night—he's afraid to dream."

Lord, when I'm tempted to think of Memorial Day as just the beginning of summer, don't let me forget how much my freedom cost.

—Andrew Attaway

31
SAT *I am the root and the offspring of David, and the bright and morning star.* —Revelation 22:16

It had been months since my mother's death, and I still couldn't seem to pull out of my grief. In spite of feeling bleak, I attended a friend's retirement party. My friend sensed what I was going through and took me out to the deck to look up at the star-filled sky.

"When sailors are lost," he told me, "the first thing they do is look for the North Star. It comes out first, and it's bright. You can't miss it. You can fix all the other stars by its location and find your way. There it is, right up there." He pointed toward it.

"I think you need a North Star in your life now. You need to focus yourself on Jesus. Just get Him in your sights, and you can't be lost."

My friend was right. He knew that I needed to focus on something outside myself, on a power greater than my own. He said a prayer for me right there, his soft words echoing out among the pine trees. "Dear Lord, Susan is depressed. Help her to find Your star. Lift her spirit and help her trust in You and follow You. We know You will bring her from darkness into light."

My depression didn't clear that minute, but I felt a glimmer of hope that my situation would get better. It did. Now, every time it grows dark, I look for the North Star, and I think of my friend's words.

Thank You, Father, for Jesus Your Son, Who lights my way along the darkest paths.

—Susan Schefflein

Everyday Wonders

1 _____

2 _____

3 _____

4 _____

5 _____

6 _____

7 _____

8 _____

9 _____

10 _____

11 _____

12 _____

13 _____

14 _____

15 _____

16 _____

17 _____

18 _____

19 _____

20 _____

21 _____

22 _____

23 _____

24 _____

25 _____

26 _____

27 _____

28 _____

29 _____

30 _____

31 _____

Beloved, let us love one another:
for love is of God; and every one
that loveth is born of God, and
knoweth God.   *—I JOHN 4:7*

June

S	M	T	W	T	F	S
1	2	3	4	5	6	7
8	9	10	11	12	13	14
15	16	17	18	19	20	21
22	23	24	25	26	27	28
29	30					

1

LOVE IS . . .

Love does not rejoice in unrighteousness, but rejoices with the truth.   —I Corinthians 13:6 (NAS)

Roy Baliles was a fifteen-year-old Georgia farm boy when he was stopped one night on a dark road by two men with drawn guns—no uniforms, no badges. Terrified, Roy drew his own gun and shot one of them dead. The men, it turned out, were police, and Roy was sentenced to life imprisonment. Ankles shackled so he could barely shuffle, Roy swung a sixteen-pound sledgehammer on a chain gang from dawn to dark.

After four years of good behavior, the shackles had come off. And when Roy learned one day that his mother was ill, he simply went home. He was sure the police would come for him right away. When they did not, the nineteen-year-old began to run—from job to job and from state to state.

He was working as Roy Standley at a cotton mill in Gastonia, North Carolina, when he met Ellie. They married, bought the little brown-shingled house where I was sitting with them now, had two children. Townspeople knew Roy as a loving father, a caring neighbor. Only Ellie knew of the sleepless nights, the never-ending fear.

Roy was thirty-six when a passerby from Georgia recognized him and reported him to police. This time he didn't run. "By then I knew the Lord. I knew He wouldn't let us go on forever, living a lie." Roy was returned to Georgia to resume serving his life sentence.

Then something amazing happened. A Gastonia newspaper carried the story of the fifteen-year-old who'd never had a lawyer. Neighbors circulated a petition. Ten thousand people signed it, including the mayor and the chief of police. Ellie took the petition to the Georgia Prison Board, and Roy was granted parole. "The warden told me, 'You're a free man.'"

"The words were truer than the warden knew," Roy told me. "Free from prison, yes. But so much better than that—free to have the terrible thing I'd done out in the open. Free to tell the truth and be loved in spite of the worst I'd done."

God of love, You promise that the truth will make us free. Help me to bring the dark places of my life into the sunlight of that promise.

—Elizabeth Sherrill

2 *The Lord is good, a strong hold in the day of trouble; and*
MON *he knoweth them that trust in him.*   —Nahum 1:17

Today, I put my thirteen-year-old son Drew on a bus bound for New York City. He wasn't traveling alone. Forty classmates and four adult chaperons went with him. But New York City is a long way from our small Texas town. A world away. And all of the big city dangers suddenly rushed through my mind. It was hard to say good-bye.

Driving home, I felt anxious and uneasy. My mind flashed back twenty-eight years to a scene in the Atlanta airport. I was seventeen years old and departing to spend a summer in Honduras helping to set up medical clinics. I was excited about this grand adventure and embarrassed when my mother hugged me, shedding a few quiet tears. Now I know how she felt. It is tough to let go of your children.

At the deepest level, life is a matter of trust. Each day I have to decide whether life is good or bad; whether God is caring or distant; whether humanity is sane or depraved; whether life is fleeting or eternal. And I must choose whether to trust that God loves my children more than I do, regardless of what life brings their way.

I put Drew on a bus today because I had no other choice. The time had come. He must begin to learn how to make his way in the world. And I must trust that the God Who has sustained me will sustain him as well.

Dear God, I trust to Your eternal care those whom I love. Amen.
—Scott Walker

3 *If we hope for what we do not see, we wait for it with*
TUES *patience.*   —Romans 8:25 (RSV)

One of the things I've always tried to impress on my children is that every living thing has a reason for being. There is an economy in nature; God didn't put anything on earth without a purpose. A story that came my way the other day seems to bear out these truths.

A building contractor in the Northeast constructed some condos on old farmland along the seashore just outside of a metropolitan area. The houses were quickly purchased, mostly by city folks who moved in and found the dwellings to be perfect in every way save one. There were snakes in the fields nearby—big, ominous-looking corn snakes.

"Get rid of them," the fearful newcomers implored. The builder said he could eradicate the harmless reptiles, but there was a downside. One of the benefits of corn snakes is that they feed on rodents, keeping rat and mouse populations under control. His warning, however, fell on deaf ears, and the residents insisted the snakes be eliminated. Result? The condos soon had a rodent problem.

Though I don't like to admit it, I often react like the snake fearers when a problem comes my way. I don't try hard enough to understand it or probe deeply enough to see if there may be some hidden benefit in my discomfort. I simply want God to eliminate those thorns and cockleburs from my space—the sooner the better! My greatest need at such times is patience . . . and that may even include putting up with a few corn snakes.

> *Give me wisdom, God, that trusts You night and day,*
> *Faith to admit both fears and doubts—and still obey.*
> —Fred Bauer

4
WED   *Behold, we put bits in the horses' mouths, that they may obey us; and we turn about their whole body. . . . Even so the tongue is a little member, and boasteth great things. . . .*
—James 3:3, 5

Laurie clenched the saddle horn with her small fists, her eyes brimming with angry tears. She was a beginning rider, and we had been practicing at a low trot in the arena. The mistakes common in younger riders—pulling in on the reins, grasping the saddle horn, kicking the horse in the kidneys—had all surfaced during Laurie's lesson. In her fright and frustration, she began yelling at Bugsy, her experienced bay, blaming him for going too fast. When he pranced a little, none too happy at being yelled at, Laurie shrieked.

I told her to dismount and untied Bugsy's lead rope, disappointment in my pupil showing in my jerky movements. I loosened the cinch and watched as Laurie removed the horse's bridle. When I saw how she carelessly tugged the leather strap over Bugsy's ear, my anger bubbled to the surface.

"When are you going to learn to have some consideration for your animal, Laurie? If you want the horse to do something for you, you have to ask him nicely. Communicate clearly with him, the way you learned. If he's doing well, tell him so. Let him know you appreciate him. If he misbehaves, correct the problem and move on. You can't expect him to be perfect."

Laurie sniffed and mumbled something into the tack she was carrying.

"I'm sorry, I couldn't hear you. What did you say?"

The little rider sighed and said, "That goes for people, too."

She was right: I had been guilty of the very things I had warned her against. Softly, I apologized. It took another couple of lessons before Laurie trotted well, but she got there. And in the meantime, Bugsy and Laurie were both a lot happier with each other and with their teacher, who learned that there was a lot more to teaching a skill than just knowing how to do it.

Father, when I try to teach others, teach me that love comes before knowledge.   —Kjerstin Easton

5
THU
Train up a child in the way he should go: and when he is old, he will not depart from it.   —Proverbs 22:6

This year I bought a hat. Given that few people wear hats these days, unless you count the backward baseball caps firmly glued to the heads of most males under twenty, this was not a routine purchase. I'd never done such a thing before in my life.

The hat is made of straw. On the brim is a collection of silk flowers, giving the overall effect of an upside-down bouquet perched on the top of my head. I've only worn it once: to my eldest son Hilary's graduation from college.

It was hot that summer day in Montreal. Photos were taken, speeches delivered, parents introduced, and then the day was over.

For me, holding my head and my hat high, it was intensely special. Hilary had made his father and me proud in the knowledge that we had fulfilled at least the first part of our contract as parents. We had delivered to the world a son, by no means perfect but at least equipped with a college degree and affectionate family, baptized, confirmed and with the basic training to become a useful, Christian adult.

Now that, I felt, deserved a hat.

May our children grow and prosper, Lord, under Your guidance and protection.   —Brigitte Weeks

6
FRI

"For if you love those who love you, what reward have you? Do not even the tax collectors do the same?"
—Matthew 5:46 (RSV)

"The problem with you, Julia," my boss began, "is that you think your opinion means something." To keep my jaw from dropping— or snapping—I bit my tongue. My boss treated me like a disposable diaper. It was maddening, and her often erratic demands were making me feel increasingly insecure.

Fortunately, one of the blessings of working in a large city like New York is that churches leave their doors open for people to stop in and pray. Each day at noon, I fled from my office to the quiet of an old church around the corner. There I'd stumble into a pew, throw myself on my knees and pour out my troubles to God.

Boy, did I pray! *Blessed are those who know their need of God. . . .* I was sure I was going to have a nervous breakdown if God didn't help me. I prayed for patience and humility. I prayed for wisdom and fortitude. I prayed for guidance with my career.

After several months, I was no longer seeking sanctuary in the old church; I was simply looking forward to my time with God. With a sense of wonder, I gave thanks for this transformation. "So why not pray for the person who made it possible?" asked a voice in my head. I was aghast. In months of praying, I'd never once prayed for my boss.

Many years have passed, and my former boss is still in my prayers. Whenever my prayer life feels dry, I start by praying for her. Then I go down the list of everyone else I don't particularly like. Suddenly, God and I have a lot to talk about.

Blessed Jesus, help me to remember that You died on the Cross for other people besides me.   —Julia Attaway

7
SAT

He that giveth, let him do it with simplicity. . . .
—Romans 12:8

One of the few recipients of my untithed largess is a beggar who works the corner across the street from Macy's. He sits on a plastic milk crate at the subway exit, where I pass him on my way to work. An empty paper coffee cup in his hand, he gives me a boisterous "Hey, man!" and I drop in a few coins (all except quarters, which I save for parking meters and the Laundromat).

We talk about the church shelter where he sleeps and the soup kitchen where he eats and the clothes he picks up from rummage sales. Sometimes he disappears for a couple days, and when I wonder where he's gone, he reappears and tells me about the hotel room he found or the friend who took him in for a few nights. Usually, his eyes are clear, but sometimes they're clouded by alcohol, and then I can guess what a losing battle he fights.

One warm June day as I was taking the subway to Yankee Stadium with my two boys, I heard some rowdy shouting on the train. I gritted my teeth, wondering what urban misfits my children were being exposed to, when one of the loud fellows walked past us and stopped. "Hey, man!" He looked me in the eye with a more-or-less lucid gaze. My beggar friend! We slapped low and high fives. "Who's this?" he asked, pointing to tow-headed Timothy leaning from a straphanger's pole like a rider on a carousel.

"That's my son," I said.

Then he bent down to Timo and exclaimed, "Your daddy's a good man!"

So why do I give to beggars? Well, you never know how your gifts will come back to you.

Lord, let me never miss an opportunity to give.   —Rick Hamlin

---

8   *As every man hath received the gift, even so minister the*
SUN   *same one to another, as good stewards of the manifold*
grace of God.   —I Peter 4:10

"Every desire of the human mind is a prayer uttered to God and registered in heaven." I first read these words of Ralph Waldo Emerson many years ago, but it's only recently that I've really come to understand them—through a boy named Andrew.

Andrew is an acolyte at our church. He was salutatorian of his high school class. He holds the school math team's all-time scoring record. He was on the science team, and he was the winner of the school's Grand Science Award. He was a member of the National Honor Society. He served on the editorial board of the school newspaper. He also found time to play the violin in the Greater Boston Youth Symphony and to be a member of the school tennis team.

"I wanted to be a good student," Andrew said. "I saw the names of the past winners on the Grand Science Award, and I wanted my name there, too. It took sacrifices. I studied on weekends, I missed television shows, I couldn't spend much time with my friends. But even that wasn't enough. I had to believe I could be a success."

But there's more to Andrew than the drive to succeed. On the Sunday after graduation, Andrew came to church with his mother. When he was called up to receive the parish scholarship, Andrew and his mother were nowhere to be seen. I was concerned about them. After the service, we went into the parish hall for coffee. There in the kitchen were Andrew and his mother. I asked Andrew where he had been during the service.

"When we got to church, we opened the bulletin and saw that we were down for providing coffee. So we hurried to the store for doughnuts and cookies, and then rushed back to church to make the coffee and set the tables."

It didn't matter to Andrew that he was going to be recognized for his academic and social merits. There was a greater need to be served . . . his fellow congregants.

Father, help us to strive prayerfully for excellence, not for applause, but to serve others better.   —Oscar Greene

---

9
MON
For we are his workmanship, created in Christ Jesus unto good works, which God hath before ordained that we should walk in them.   —Ephesians 2:10

"Don't throw that away. Put it in the rag bag. You never know when it might come in handy."

I heard those words often during my growing-up years, and as I look back on those days, I'm amazed at how often something useful was pulled from that old rag bag. Once it was a few pieces of a worn-out shirt and a red bandanna that Dad knotted into a tail for my kite. Another time it was a stained tea towel I tied to the end of a stick to carry my lunch hobo-style during a hike. Strips from threadbare sheets became bandages to wind cut thumbs or fingers into miniature mummies. Even unwearable overalls escaped oblivion. They were torn into inch-wide lengths, rolled into balls, and eventually braided into rugs.

Now, whenever I find myself feeling worn and a bit threadbare, I remember how helpful our old rag bag really was. It gives me confidence that God will find ways in which I, too, can still come in handy.

I can't thank You enough, Lord, that—no matter what—I will never become useless to You!
                                                    —Isabel Wolseley

10
TUE   *He maketh me to lie down in green pastures. . . .*
                                                    —Psalm 23:2

A friend of ours vacationing in the mountains of North Carolina offered one day to help his wife, who had a bad cold, by taking the family laundry down to the village.

"But you've never set foot in a Laundromat," Martha objected between sniffles.

"Oh, there must be directions on the machines," said Robert. "You just take it easy. I'll be right back."

But soon he ran into trouble. He had brought no soap. Thinking that management provided it, he helped himself to a large cupful from a box standing on a shelf.

"Young man," said a gimlet-eyed old mountain lady, "that's my soap, not yours. What's more, you've taken far too much. If you put that in your machine, we'll have suds up to the ceiling!"

"Oh," said Robert, abashed, "I didn't know. This is the first time I've ever been to a Laundromat. I'm sorry to be so green."

The shadow of a twinkle came into the old lady's eyes. "Well," she said, "if you're green, you're growing. Here, give me that cup of soap. Now, which is your machine?"

Robert says the encounter taught him that little mistakes caused by inexperience aren't to be regretted. They're something to learn from. They're a sign of life.

If they're green, they're growing. The good Lord made plants like that. He made human beings like that, too.

Comforting thought, isn't it?

Lord, help us not to be discouraged by little failures when they come our way.
                                                    —Arthur Gordon

11

WED

Jesus . . . said . . . "I have come as light into the world. . . ."
                                        —John 12:44, 46 (RSV)

One evening recently, while I was taking care of my little granddaughter, Saralisa discovered a most spectacular toy: Grandma's
flashlight! She found out that just by pushing a lever she could cause
light to shine! Of course, we turned off all the lights and played with
our new toy, flashing it all over the room, across the ceiling, into
Grandma's mouth, into her own eyes, shining it through our fingers
to turn them red, giggling and squealing with delight through it all.
Next she shined it on my old dog Oscar, and then, one by one, on
the photographs of family members that hang in my family room,
naming each one.

Later, after my little one was asleep, I sat there quietly thanking
God for the shining wonder I'd seen in Saralisa's eyes and for the joy
it gave me to be "in on" her marvelous discovery. Then it occurred
to me that prayer is like that light beam. Even in the darkest passages
of life, we can shine the light of Christ on those we love, and upon
ourselves as well.

I'm going to make this a part of my evening prayer time, and it will
be a good way to teach Saralisa how to pray for others, too.

*Loving Christ, Light of the world, may my prayers tonight beam Your love
into the lives of* _____, _____, _____. . . .

                        (write in names)
                                        —Marilyn Morgan Helleberg

12

THU

I have a message from God unto thee. . . .
                                        —Judges 3:20

Just a few minutes from downtown Nashville, the Radnor Lake Natural Area is an unspoiled forest encircling an eighty-acre lake. As the
sunlight filters through the trees and falls on the trail, God seems a
little nearer and sometimes a little easier to hear.

It is a Thursday in mid-June. My daughter Keri, home from college after her freshman year, is working long hours at her summer
job. After work, we often meet at Radnor for an evening walk. Today,
I'm early. Tense and edgy, I'm perched on a split-rail fence in the
parking lot, watching for Keri's old car to turn the corner.

I feel awful because earlier in the day I lost my temper and said something hateful to a colleague who was critiquing my work. Then, at lunch, my husband David asked me to make a phone call for him and, irritated, I almost bit his head off saying no.

Keri swings in, and we're off. The trail is cool. We walk along not saying much, until Keri asks, "Momma, did you notice that sign?"

"No, I didn't even see a sign," I reply, still edgy.

"Back there, where the trail forks, there's a sign that says, 'Fragile forest. Stay on path,' " my daughter answers.

"Uh-huh," I say.

"Momma, pay attention. That's an awesome thing to think about. You know, life is fragile and that's why it's important to stay on the right path. Isn't that what you're always telling me about prayer? Keep talking to God, tell Him how you want to be, be honest with Him when you mess up. If you're careful to stay on the path, you won't hurt other people and you'll be happier."

Of course, I tell myself, *I'm off the path! I overslept this morning and missed my prayer time. Without prayer, I lost peace. Without peace, I had no patience. No wonder I'm such a grouch!*

"You're right, Keri, it's a great sign."

Father, today I thank You for the messages You sometimes send me in unexpected and wondrous ways.   —Pam Kidd

13
FRI

Remember his marvelous works that he hath done, his wonders. . . .   —I Chronicles 16:12

Recently, my friend Lurlene and I ended a shopping spree in downtown Chicago by having dinner and a late-evening stroll down Michigan Avenue. Big-wheeled carriages and plumed horses lined the curb. Couples in evening clothes hurried toward the theater. In front of a large department store, a mime-magician performed. He swished colored scarves from his sleeve, made balls disappear from under cups and produced streams of coins from behind his ear, between his fingers—even out of his nose!

This latter trick particularly delighted a young boy standing near me. Then he noticed the black top hat the magician had placed on a nearby stand. "What's that for?" he asked me.

"Money," I replied as patrons tossed coins and bills into the black hat.

The boy's eyes widened. "But what does he need with our money? Anytime he wants, he can pull a coin from thin air!"

I thought about that small boy the next day as I began my devotions. God *has* everything, *is* everything, *can do* everything. And yet He wants something from me—expects something from me. My devotion. Gratitude. Praise. Obedience. And in return, I get, well . . . *everything!* What could be more wonderful and magical than that?

O Creator and Sustainer, I praise and submit to You. Work Your wonders in my life!
                                                    —Mary Lou Carney

14
SAT

This is my commandment, That ye love one another, as I have loved you.   —John 15:12

My daughter Wendy and I took a trip to Grenoble, France, to visit with friends she'd made on a previous school-sponsored trip. During dinner at the home of one of the families, the father, a slight man in his fifties with dark, pensive eyes, shared the only English he knew. It was the song "Happy Birthday to You." He sang the whole thing in an emotional, off-key tenor, while the rest of the family smiled and nodded. "Where did you learn it?" I asked through Wendy, who spoke French.

During World War II, he said, he was having a fifth-birthday celebration when the air raid siren sounded. Somehow he got separated from his family and found himself running, alone and crying, down the street. An American soldier intercepted him and took him to a safe place. The soldier spoke only a little French. But he managed to learn that it was Pierre's birthday. While the planes droned and the bombs fell, the soldier balanced the boy on his knee and taught him the song. Pierre forgot his fears. After the raid, the soldier returned the boy to his home. Pierre never saw the soldier again.

"But I sing the song often, and I remember here," Pierre said, pointing to his heart. An anonymous soldier had pulled a terrified little boy to safety and, while the noise of death rained down, found a way to lock out fear. No medals for this . . . except the memory in Pierre's heart. A half century later, it's still polished bright.

Lord, as I observe Flag Day, help me to remember the good things done by those who have carried our colors.   —Shari Smyth

15
SUN

Listen, my sons, to a father's instruction; pay attention and gain understanding. —Proverbs 4:1 (NIV)

I don't know what kind of wedding-day advice most fathers give to their sons, but this is what my father told me. "Always keep oil in the engine. You can run out of gas, you can run out of water, but you can't run out of oil."

I laughed, as he knew I would. Cars had always formed a bond between my father and me, a bond made particularly strong when we restored a '74 VW Beetle together. Everything that could have gone wrong did. Nothing matched—the different-colored fenders and ill-fitting bumpers were cannibalized from other Beetles. And the engine, despite claims to the contrary, went back a lot further than 1974. What we spent in time and money on that car is incalculable, but what it cost us physically is something else again.

Early in our restoration, I was eager to show off to my not-yet-wife, so my father and I decided to impress her by starting the engine. She was more impressed by the ambulance that showed up to take my father to the hospital—he had pinched off the top of his finger in the VW's v-belt. And the first thing he said in the emergency room was, "Did you hear it click? It almost started. Did you hear it?"

Yes, Dad, I heard it. And I heard your advice at Calvary Church. And I think of how much you've taught me, not only about the satisfaction of getting an old car through yet another state inspection, but about pride and accomplishment in little victories. I learned the importance of working on the things I value; I learned the prudence of proper maintenance. I've learned—slowly and incompletely—to take care of the things I love, and I don't mean just cars.

Happy Father's Day, Dad!

God, our Father, You are the pattern of all earthly fatherhood. Thank You for my father, and help me to know You better through knowing him.
—Mark Collins

16
MON

A true friend is always loyal, and a brother is born to help in time of need. —Proverbs 17:17 (TLB)

Right after fifteen-year-old Andrew talked me into practically shaving his head at the beginning of the summer, he talked two of his friends into doing the same thing. Safety in numbers, I presumed.

"Please, Mom, Brian and Paul really want you to cut their hair like mine. School's out. It'll be cool!"

I looked at the boys, each sporting sun-streaked, four-inch-long haircuts. "It's okay, Mrs. L. Shave it off!"

I insisted they call their parents for permission, and then for the next hour I ran my electric clippers over each head until just an eighth of an inch of fuzz remained. During each haircut, I got to know my son's friends much better. I became very well acquainted with Paul's two stubborn cowlicks, and as we talked about school and his part-time job, I gained a new respect for his hard work at the tree nursery. When I nicked Brian's ear, I made noises over him like a mother hen, then heard about his plans for the future and about his family. His gentleness and quiet sense of humor impressed me.

That night after the boys left, Andrew asked, "Mom, do you like my friends?"

I'd never told my son what I thought about any of his friends; not Paul, Brian, Nick, Dave, Bert, Tracey, Heather, Tiffany or Cheryl. I sat down with Andrew and went down the list, pointing out what I thought were the best qualities of each: Bert's friendliness; Tracey's bubbling personality; Heather's openness, etc.

Throughout that school year, Andrew's friends filled our home with their infectious laughter, constant chatter and empty stomachs, and by its end, they had become my friends, too.

Lord, help me to be a friend to my children's friends and to welcome them into my home and heart.   —Patricia Lorenz

---

WORDS OF WONDER

Life has loveliness to sell,
    All beautiful and splendid things,
Blue waves whitened on a cliff,
    Soaring fire that sways and sings,
And children's faces looking up
Holding wonder like a cup.
                                    —SARA TEASDALE

17
TUE   *Yet now there is hope. . . .*   —Ezra 10:2 (NAS)

I dreaded taking my mother to the oncologist. They often had the bedside manner of robots. Mother's own physician had asked her just to talk to this doctor. She had agreed.

We didn't even make small talk waiting in the examining room. Then he entered the room: tall; wearing a sharp suit—no white jacket; enormous smile; direct eye contact; good, casual body language, like an athlete. He was obviously comfortable with us and liked his work. He began asking Mother medical questions. She ignored the questions and said, "I'm an old woman. Eighty-six last week. I've had a good, full life. . . . I'm not afraid of —"

"Mrs. Grogan"—the doctor spoke gently, enthusiastically, leaning slightly closer to her face, looking directly into her eyes—"you look fifteen years younger than your age. You and your daughter behave much more like sisters than mother and daughter. I want to talk to you about *life.* You have a lot of living to do! What's more, I want you to take the radiation treatments. They won't cause side effects. We're going to get rid of this wheelchair." His joy seemed to fill the small room.

My mouth fell open. Mother smiled a slow, skeptical smile that soon grew to be genuine. The doctor touched her shoulder and was gone. We left the examining room and started down the hall. If I hadn't been pushing Mother in the chair, I probably would have skipped to the car, like Dorothy going down the Yellow Brick Road.

On our way out, we stopped at the nurse's desk to set up Mother's next appointment. I couldn't help sharing my joy. "What a marvelous doctor!" I told the nurse. "He's given us such hope."

"Yes, he's very special," she replied. "He's a cancer survivor himself."

Father, help me to be a messenger of hope. Amen.

                                —Marion Bond West

18
WED   *My sheep hear my voice. . . .*   —John 10:27

"If I'm supposed to do God's will," I asked my friend Paul, "how am I supposed to find exactly what His will for me is?"

"Besides reading the Bible," Paul said, "I listen for ten minutes every day with a spiral notebook and write down everything that comes to me. At first, all I wrote down were all kinds of seemingly unspiritual things. I was tempted to give up, but I remembered that Jesus is interested in every part of our lives. Besides, it takes time to learn to hear God's voice in all the thoughts that go through our heads."

Although I was skeptical, I tried listening for ten minutes a day. The first thing that came to me was, "Wash your car."

After several weeks had passed, I realized that in the first five minutes I was getting a complete list of everything I needed to do that day. But I also began to hear things like, "Write songs," "Write a novel," "Spend more time with your kids and grandkids." So during the past few years, I have written the lyrics to a musical play and a novel, and each year, Andrea and I have started taking the children and grandchildren on a "Granny and Granddaddy summer camp" trip.

I don't know if all these things are from God, but listening for Him like this has made me feel much closer to Him and has given me a quiet sense of doing His will.

Thank You, Lord, for sending a Counselor to make You and Your ways known to me.   —Keith Miller

19
THU
"The gardener. . . . cuts off every branch in me that bears no fruit. . . ."   —John 15:1–2 (NIV)

The half-mile narrow trail around Lake George in the high Sierra to our favorite fishing hole is beautiful but treacherous. Laden down with fishing gear and haversacks, my husband and I walked carefully beside flaming red fireweed and gold California poppies, digging our heels into the crumbly shale to keep from sliding down the steep bank.

"Hold on to a branch to steady yourself as you come down!" John called up as he waited for me at the water's edge. Stepping down from a large rock, I grabbed for a branch and was gingerly groping for a foothold when I slipped. Suddenly, I was falling, and with an ominous snap the branch I was holding on to broke. I skidded down the rocky bank and would have plummeted into the lake had John not been there to catch me.

"Are you hurt, honey?"

Yes, I was hurt.

I limped painfully back to our van for the bumpy ride to the local hospital. X-rays showed that I had cracked my tailbone, not seriously, but enough to cause discomfort for several weeks.

"For heaven's sake, lovey," John said, "you should have known better than to hold on to deadwood."

Unable to fish with John for the remainder of our vacation, I had lots of time to think about what he had said. I discovered that I had held on to deadwood not only by the lake, but in the rest of my life, too. The "if only I had" of regrets and guilt. Resentments. A grudge held on to for years and years. "Lord," I prayed, "help me to let go of the deadwood in my heart."

Now I've learned to reach for living branches that will not let me down. On the lakeside trail, they're branches growing green. In my heart, they're faith and forgiveness.

Dear Lord, help me to prune the deadwood from my life.   —Fay Angus

20
FRI

Blessed are his children after him.

—Proverbs 20:7 (NIV)

When Norman and I approached our twenty-fifth wedding anniversary, we held a family discussion to decide how our anniversary would be celebrated. We decided that we would have a reception at Marble Collegiate Church on Fifth Avenue in New York City, where Norman had been pastor for twenty-three years. Invitations would go to personal friends, and we would announce to our congregation that all were welcome. Twelve hundred people came! Our children, Margaret, twenty-two, John, nineteen, and Elizabeth, thirteen, were all in the receiving line.

We celebrated our thirty-fifth anniversary in the same way. But as we approached our fiftieth, the children descended upon us and said that they had had it: No more huge receptions! Norman and I respected their plea. The whole family went to Switzerland and celebrated our anniversary in Interlaken.

Our son John reserved a private dining room, ordered the dinner and was emcee for the evening. He called on each one around the table to describe the family incident that meant the most to him or her. It was wonderful! I will never forget listening that night as our children and grandchildren shared their favorite memories. Our grandson Andrew, then eight, came last. Taking a deep breath, he said, "My happiest moment is . . . right now!"

That fiftieth-anniversary celebration was our most memorable because of the love we were able to share as a family. America needs a rebirth of families, and the key to that rebirth is love. Today, make time to write, telephone, pray for and send loving thoughts to everyone in your family.

Dear Lord, today help me to renew the bonds of love that hold my family together.   —Ruth Stafford Peale

21

SAT

And he that sat upon the throne said, Behold, I make all things new. . . .   —Revelation 21:5

My wife Sharon looked at her heirloom wristwatch lovingly. "I just hate to part with this." She hugged it tightly. "It was my high school valedictory award, and they don't make watches like this anymore." She held it up to my face. "See, it's white gold, and look at all the detail!" She sighed. "But it's a windup model, and it's worn out."

"Why don't you see if the jewelry store has a quartz watch that looks like it," I suggested—sensibly, I thought. She looked at me as if I had suggested plastic surgery on her nose.

But she went to the jeweler's and came home singing. "Tamara, the clerk, said I could keep this watch and simply have Mr. Sterrett install a new quartz movement in it for about a hundred dollars!"

I was happy for her, and I thought the clerk's idea was a first-rate approach to change in this mind-spinning world of insecurity: Keep the best of the old, and add the best of the new. Don't discard something of real worth just to be up to date.

It was an approach I could apply to my taste in music, for example. I much prefer the old church hymns to most contemporary Christian music. I know the words to most of the old hymns, and there are powerful feelings and rich memories attached to them. And yet I also like the sounds of modern instruments. So, I shop for tapes of old hymns done in new arrangements by modern groups. Some of them have actually enhanced my appreciation of the old tunes and given new meaning to the old lyrics.

Whenever I'm threatened by something new, I pause and ask myself, *How can I incorporate this into my old ways?* Sometimes the answer is "I can't." But often enough the answer is "very easily" when I really look for it.

Lord, in the midst of changes let me be open to Your renewing Spirit while holding fast to Your unchanging truth.   —Daniel Schantz

22
SUN
As many as I love, I rebuke and chasten. . . .
                                              —Revelation 3:19

The invitation was from Jenny. As I stood at the mailbox, looking at the elegant ivory envelope, my thoughts went back a few years to when I was her Sunday school teacher.

While her parents thought she was safe in class, Jenny had found many opportunities to slip away from Sunday school to visit with her friends. I prayed to find some way to persuade her to stay. Then I remembered Miss Nabors.

Miss Nabors taught me English at a time when I was giddily excited at being part of a group of smart-aleck girls who I thought were wonderful. One day she told me, "You've done good work in my class until recently. Now I find it completely unsatisfactory. Drue, please take a closer look at your new companions. Do they really represent what you want to be?"

Her words made me think more clearly about my friends and my own goals in life. I buckled down, studying to improve my grades and my teacher's opinion of me.

The next Sunday morning, I stood in the doorway of the classroom to prevent Jenny's leaving. "Are you going out again today?" I asked quietly.

"Someone's waiting for me."

"Someone's waiting for you here, too," I told her. "Jesus is waiting. I believe He's disappointed that you never stay to meet Him."

She looked at me quizzically, then frowned slightly.

"Won't you please stay today?"

The transformation in Jenny was not immediate. But she began to stay in the classroom and started taking part in the lessons. Soon Dan, a fine young member of our church, began escorting her to the morning services.

I opened the envelope and prayed a silent thanksgiving. Then I walked back into the house and sat down at my desk to accept the invitation to Jenny and Dan's wedding.

Heavenly Father, give me the wisdom to help the wayward to walk in Your ways.   —Drue Duke

---

23
MON
Speaking to yourselves in psalms and hymns and spiritual songs, singing and making melody in your heart to the Lord.   —Ephesians 5:19

At first, it was funny. Whenever I wasn't concentrating on anything, I was mentally singing either a TV commercial or the theme song from a TV program. I had been sick at home for almost three weeks. After sleeping most of the time for the first week, I had started to watch afternoon reruns and some evening programs. The commercials had a dreadful sameness to them, and by the third week the jingles in my head became annoying.

Going back to work helped some. Then, at the end of my first week back, I joined the small choir at church, which sang gospel and Scripture songs to taped accompaniment. The song we practiced was new to me, so we went over it several times on Saturday and before church on Sunday. The result was that all Sunday afternoon and into Monday morning I was no longer singing commercials, but uplifting words of Scripture that praised the Lord.

Now I understood why Paul told the Philippians to fill their minds with "whatever things are true . . . lovely . . . if there be any praise, think on these things" (Philippians 4:8).

Lord, help me to fill my mind and heart with words and songs of praise.
                                                  —Mary Ruth Howes

---

24
TUE
The righteous care about justice for the poor, but the wicked have no such concern.   —Proverbs 29:7 (NIV)

A few years ago, I was walking on the beach in Southern California with some friends, when suddenly a Jaguar passed us. "What a beautiful car!" I said. "They cost a fortune. I guess anyone who can afford a car like that must have it made."

"I know the owner," one of my friends said. "Would you like to meet him?"

"Of course," I answered quickly. Perhaps I could interest the man in supporting our ministry work.

The next day, we went to visit the Jaguar owner at his house. After we had talked for a while, he asked me what I did. I told him about what our ministry was doing for the poor in Mendenhall, Mississippi.

He looked at me and said, "Dolphus, I thought that you were an intelligent young man, but now I see that you're crazy, wasting your time trying to help poor people. They don't deserve your or anybody else's help."

I wasn't prepared for his response; he didn't speak with anger or bitterness in his voice, but with an unemotional contempt for the poor. I didn't argue with him, I just concluded the conversation as quickly and politely as I could and left the house.

After I left, I thought about what he had said. For a brief moment, my mind was full of questions: *Is what I'm doing the right thing? Can I see concrete results from our work? Should I continue working with the poor?*

But then I remembered the words of Psalm 113:7–8 (NIV): "He raises the poor from the dust and lifts the needy from the ash heap; he seats them with princes, with the princes of their people."

Immediately, my moment of despair lifted. If God's response to this world's castaways is to raise them up, then I should continue to make it mine as well.

Lord, help me to remember that we were all poor before You redeemed us.
                                        —Dolphus Weary

25
WED

A man's pride shall bring him low: but honor shall uphold the humble in spirit.   —Proverbs 29:23

"Hey, Darrell, what's the record for passing the exam?" I asked my boss.

"I don't know, Brock, seven or eight weeks."

I smiled. "I'll take it in five."

It was my third day as a sales assistant in the investment division of a Nashville bank, and in an attempt to set myself apart, I had committed myself to a practically impossible feat: pass the Series Seven licensing exam for investment brokers in five weeks. The test is six hours long and contains five hundred questions.

I studied like a madman: during my lunch hour; staying late at the office; even through weekends. "Hey, Brock, how's the studying coming?" my boss would ask.

"No problem," I would answer. "I think I'm ready for the Seven right now!"

The bank enrolled me in a weeklong crash course in Atlanta, and there I finally realized I was in trouble. On the last day of the course, we had a practice exam. I failed miserably. By then, the test was ten days away, and I knew I probably wasn't going to make it.

Three days before the test, I was so terrified of failing that I couldn't concentrate. I abandoned my studies for a walk with my father. "Brock," he said, "it's time to stop trusting yourself and start trusting God."

I went to my room and prayed: "Lord, I've really messed up. Whatever happens, use it to bring me closer to You."

On the day of the exam, I felt strangely calm. The test was given on a computer, and after I answered the last question, I paused. Pass or fail, I knew everything would be okay. Then I hit the enter key. It took the computer about a minute and a half to figure out my score— the longest minute and a half of my life. Finally, it displayed the result: PASS.

Believe me, there wasn't anything cocky about the words of thanks I was whispering to God.

Lord, help me to remember that pride will always get me in trouble—even if You sometimes break my fall.
                                                    —Brock Kidd

26

THU

Crave pure spiritual milk, so that by it you may grow. . . .
                                                    —I Peter 2:2 (NIV)

When my husband and I were on our honeymoon fifteen years ago, we ran into a young couple we thought we'd like to spend some time with. Unfortunately, they shot down every suggestion we made. Did they want to see a movie? "Greg and I are not the kind of people who enjoy going to movies. We like plays." Swimming? "Frances and I are not the kind of people who like to swim." Well, then how about a late breakfast? "Greg and I go to church in the morning and then have lunch—we are not the kind of people who eat a late breakfast."

We chuckled over how set in their ways they appeared to be. But I stopped chuckling when I heard myself turn down a burrito because "I've never had one and wouldn't know whether to eat it with a fork or fingers." And when I said no to a motorboat ride, stating firmly, "Every time I've gone on a ferry I've felt a little queasy. It'll probably be worse on a motorboat."

At that, my English-born husband laughingly reminded me of a popular advertisement I'd seen in his native land. It was a man explaining his views on a product: "I've never tried it because I don't like it."

Thinking it over, I decided that I wasn't quite done exploring the kind of person I am—and I hope I won't be done exploring until God decides to call me home. "I'll try a chicken burrito," I announced, "but not until after our motorboat ride."

Let me grow by trying something new today, God—a new food, a new friendship, a new prayer. And may I never discover the "kind of person" I am once and for all!
—Linda Neukrug

27
FRI

Walk about Zion, and go round about her: tell the towers thereof. . . . that ye may tell it to the generation following.
—Psalm 48:12–13

Over the years, it's been a great sadness to me that I have not been blessed with children. Although I've taken great pleasure in the children of my friends and family, I've always had a sense of something missing: a link connecting me to the future.

This summer, as I traveled homeward to Ohio for our first Manchester family reunion, I thought again of the joys I had missed. Greeting the family, meeting children who looked just like their parents did the last time I saw them, I was touched by the way a whole new generation of children listened to our stories, receiving our memories.

My nephew's little boy Nicholas shyly put his hand in mine. "Would you like to see the view?" I asked, pointing toward the cupola at the top of my grandparents' house.

"Oh, I'd like that," he answered. "How far can you see from that funny room?"

"You can see all the way to forever," I said, and we traveled together up the winding stairs through the attic to the highest point of the old house. How I had loved this place when I was small!

Nicholas and I looked out at the fields stretching away into the distance, the wheat ripening as it had for the past hundred forty years under our family's tilling. Nicholas smiled at me and cried, "Look, Aunt Susan, we can see a million miles from up here!"

I smiled, too. Maybe this was why my great-great-grandfather had built this little windowed box at the top of the house, so that each new crop of children could see the land with a fresh vision. A new generation had come, and a part of me would go on into the future. I suddenly felt very certain of that and squeezed Nicholas' hand.

Lord, thank You for renewing our spirits in the wondering eyes of children.
—Susan Schefflein

28

SAT   *The Lord's voice crieth unto the city....*   —Micah 6:9

I'm a little tired today. Last night I had one of my bouts of insomnia, worrying about a million things and nothing at all. Every stray sound became torture, and—as anyone who's ever been to New York can attest—this is not a quiet city.

I turned on my air conditioner to muffle the noise outside. Desperate, I dug out some earplugs. No relief. *How will I function at work tomorrow? Lord, I need my rest!*

Suddenly, I found myself flashing back to the first time I ever spent the night in New York, years ago at a friend's apartment high above Park Avenue. I lay awake listening to the sounds of the streets drifting up. It was exciting, this concord of taxi horns, rushing subways, howling sirens, the general *swoosh* of traffic and the mingling of a thousand conversations. "It sounds just like the movies," I scrawled on a postcard home the next day, tired but feeling proud that I, a Midwestern exurbanite, had been baptized into the urban lullaby of New York.

The memory prompted me. I pulled out my earplugs, shut off the air conditioner and cracked the window. Then I lay back, listening, remembering, surrendering.

Yes, I'm tired today. Maybe I'll close my door this afternoon and steal a catnap at my desk, twenty-one floors above New York. Then again, maybe I'll just crack my office window and listen to God's tumultuous world in action and His voice in the din reminding me that life—even its noise—is a gift.

I must always try, Lord, to listen for You everywhere.
—Edward Grinnan

29
SUN

Inasmuch as ye have done it unto one of the least of these my brethren, ye have done it unto me. —Matthew 25:40

My friend Kenneth Lawrence knew exactly what he would do when he retired from the railroad. He and his wife had bought a lot overlooking the fairway of a golf course in the beautiful Texas hill country. He planned to build a house, move from Houston and play golf every day. His golfing buddies who were years from retirement envied him.

He had one small problem. At the time he retired, his wife Nelda, who was a professor at the University of Houston, had two more years to teach. Kenneth had good health, lots of energy, time on his hands and a pickup truck. Our church was helping relocate families from Vietnam and Cambodia, and someone enlisted Kenneth to collect furniture that church members had donated for the apartments. He soon discovered that the refugees had a host of other needs, and he found delight in helping them learn how to live in their new country.

When Nelda retired, they built their new home and moved to Kerrville, to what many thought was an ideal retirement. One Sunday, after they had been gone two years, I saw them in church and figured that they were just visiting. When I asked Kenneth, "How's the golf game?" he told me that they had put the new house up for sale and were moving back to Houston.

"I discovered that playing golf with my friends every day wasn't as much fun as I had anticipated. And I realized that helping those Asian families start over was the most fulfilling experience of my life."

Dear God, help me to look beyond fun to find fulfillment.

—Kenneth Chafin

30
MON

My voice shalt thou hear in the morning, O Lord; in the morning will I direct my prayer unto thee, and will look up. —Psalm 5:3

One day while my husband Larry and I waited together in a doctor's office, I read him some excerpts from a magazine article about how to build a better relationship with your companion. One of the suggestions was to try for at least four minutes of meaningful conversation a day, minutes where you focus your full attention upon the other person, listen to what is being said, and respond in a caring and appropriate way.

The next morning at breakfast, after Larry and I had exchanged mundane comments about the weather, he asked, "Does this count as a meaningful conversation?"

"Sure," I said.

"*Whew*, that's a relief," he replied. "Only three minutes to go."

We both laughed, but later I got to thinking, *Just how meaningful are my conversations with God, Who should be my most important companion of all? Do I pray every day? When I do pray, do I really listen, really contribute, or have my prayers become mechanical over the years, no more spontaneous than chats about the weather?*

That article was right: It is important to nurture a relationship—with a spouse, a friend and, most of all, with God.

Four minutes of meaningful conversation. Four minutes of attentive prayer. I can do that, even on the busiest day. Starting today.

Father, my attention is focused on You. Let's talk.   —Madge Harrah

Everyday Wonders

1 _____

2 _____

3 _____

4 _____

5 _____

6 _____

7 _____

8 _____

9 _____

10 _____

11 _____

12 _____

13 _____

14 _____

15 _____

16 _____

17 _____

18 _____

19 _____

20 _____

21 _____

22 _____

23 _____

24 _____

25 _____

26 _____

27 _____

28 _____

29 _____

30 _____

He delivereth and rescueth, and he worketh signs and wonders in heaven and in earth. . . .

—DANIEL 6:27

July

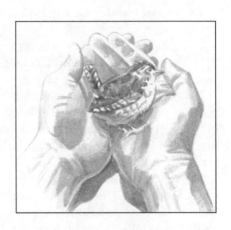

S	M	T	W	T	F	S
		1	2	3	4	5
6	7	8	9	10	11	12
13	14	15	16	17	18	19
20	21	22	23	24	25	26
27	28	29	30	31		

1

LOVE IS . . .

Love . . . is not irritable or resentful.

—I Corinthians 13:5 (RSV)

When I arrived at Dick Riley's home in Springfield, Pennsylvania, he was propped up in the mechanized bed where he'd lived ever since he fell from a ladder seventeen years earlier. He'd been only twenty then, working as a housepainter to support his wife and the baby that was on the way.

Paralyzed from the neck down, he could have turned bitter and self-pitying, taking his resentment out on those around him. "I did react that way at first," he told me. "My tongue was about the only thing I could move, and I turned it on anyone who stepped into that hospital room."

One day, a nurse was struggling to change the sheet beneath him and Dick was carping as usual, calling her "slow" and "clumsy," when he heard something that checked the flow of fault-finding. The nurse was crying. Dick couldn't turn to look at her, but he found himself wondering suddenly what other troubles she had—besides one very disagreeable patient.

Lying as she'd turned him, facing the wall, he told her he was sorry. "For the first time since the accident I realized there was something I could do for someone else."

He asked the nurse about her family, her work, her dreams. . . . It was the moment—and it was only a moment, then—when Dick took his eyes off his own misfortune. Such moments came more and more often, first with other patients in the hospital, then in the rehab center where he regained partial use of one arm, today in the accounting service he runs from his bed.

"Whatever our limitations, everyone on earth—my wife, our son Dicky, me—has something to give." For him, he said, the gift might be a smile, a prayer, a sympathetic ear, a bit of bookkeeping. "You can't hold on to resentment while you're opening your hands to give.

"Don't forget," he reminded me as I stood up to go. "Call me for help when it's tax time."

God of love, what have You given me that I, in turn, can give away today?

—Elizabeth Sherrill

2
WED

We took sweet counsel together, and walked unto the house of God in company.   —Psalm 55:14

On the subway one morning, groggy-eyed and running late as usual, I took out a worn green pocket edition of the *New Testament* and *Psalms.* Around me others shook open their tabloids with headlines that screamed of unspeakable tragedies. The doors slammed closed, and I found myself distracted by the percussive effect of the Walkman music blaring in one youth's ears. Feeling rather alone, I turned to my book and read through three psalms.

Just as I was preparing to close my eyes, the woman sitting next to me asked, "May I borrow that?"

"This?" I asked, holding up the tattered volume.

"Yes," she said. "I left mine at home."

"Of course," I said.

When I closed my eyes, I could hear her turn the soft pages, and the noise blended in with the train rolling over the tracks, sounding as holy as a hymn sung in a country church. Even here, on a rush-hour subway, in the middle of a crowded city. Even here, where I had somehow forgotten there were other travelers looking for the Lord.

"God bless you," she said, handing me back the book when we came to her stop.

"You, too," I said, ready to face the day.

Help me remember, Lord, I am always part of a church without walls.
                                                      —Rick Hamlin

3
THU

"So if the Son sets you free, you will be free indeed."
                                              —John 8:36 (NIV)

As I drove to work one June day, I noticed a scraggly mutt dodging coal trucks and scrounging for food along the busy highway. He was there again when I drove home. I began to see him regularly as I traveled to and from work; he seemed to grow thinner with each passing day. I asked around and learned that his name was Spanky and that his owners had moved away, abandoning him to the sporadic care of strangers.

For a week, my husband Mark and I tossed a scared Spanky peanut butter sandwiches from our car window. I longed to take him home and care for him. "That Spanky's a wild thing," a man told me one day. "Why, he'd never go home with you folks."

But on Independence Day weekend, I lured Spanky—his fur matted with fleas, filth and cow manure, and his eyes circled with fat ticks—into my car with a Moon Pie. Once we got home, he wolfed down two cans of tuna and licked my hand when I assured him we had an appointment with a top-notch groomer and veterinarian.

I left Spanky in the backyard with all the comforts of home and went out to run an errand. But when I returned, the yard was empty. He'd jumped the tall white picket fence and run away. An exhausting search proved futile. Then, at ten that night, we found Spanky thumping his tail on the front porch. Spanky was home!

I suppose one reason I feel such a kinship with Spanky is that he reminds me a little of myself. How many times have I, too, in the name of freedom, developed a wandering eye? But these days, I'm trying to trust the Lord's provisions for my needs even when they don't exactly match my wants. And like Spanky, I'm learning that loving boundaries aren't nearly as confining as I once thought.

For straying dogs and Christians, there's no place like home.

Dear Lord, I guess I look pretty scraggly when I go my own way. Help me to see that my true freedom lies in You.   —Roberta Messner

4

FRI

Thou hast been honorable, and I have loved thee. . . .
—Isaiah 43:4

Whenever the Fourth of July comes around, I remember a talk I once heard. It was given by Gen. Mark Clark, and the subject he chose was honor. Honor, the general said, is the ability to put morality ahead of expediency, duty ahead of self-indulgence, and to do this instinctively and every time. But, he added, this shining quality does not occur spontaneously in people. It has to be learned. Parents have to teach it. Schools have to teach it. Churches have to teach it. Unless they do, our society will begin to crumble.

The sense of honor that our ancestors knew, the general said, has become weakened and diminished in our own times. The reason may be that we no longer understand how important honor is in the conduct of our daily lives. The men who signed the Declaration of Independence did understand. In the last line of that document, so dangerous to the signers, all of them pledged to one another "our lives, our fortunes, and our sacred honor." To them, honor was not just some casual concept. It was *sacred*.

That was how those brave men understood the meaning of the word in their day. Somehow, we must recapture it for ours.

Father, help us to make honor the bedrock of our lives.—Arthur Gordon

5
SAT

First of all, then, I urge that supplications, prayers, intercessions, and thanksgivings be made for all men.
—I Timothy 2:1 (RSV)

"Lord, please help us get back in touch with our son."

That had been my daily prayer for at least six months.

Although Eric and his family lived only forty miles away and we did see them at occasional family gatherings on Sunday afternoons, Eric had become a stranger. Morose, silent, he would slump into a chair and stare into space, ignoring the family chatter. Larry and I knew he worked hard six days a week and was exhausted on Sundays, but the silence seemed to go beyond fatigue. If we could just talk to him alone. But it never seemed to work out.

Then came the time for the annual Fourth of July family get-together at our cabin in the Colorado mountains, one of my favorite family events of the year. I bought food and began cooking. But one by one, I got phone calls from eleven different family members explaining why they couldn't come: unexpected work deadlines; other commitments; car trouble; summer school. Disappointment filled my chest with an ache akin to flu. "Why, God?" I asked.

I found out why when only one guest showed up at our reunion: Eric. For three days, Larry, Eric and I worked, played and talked together in the serenity of the high country. Eric shared concerns about his job, his finances, his children. By the end of the visit, Larry and I both felt closer to our son than we had felt in years.

A prayer. God's answer, far exceeding anything I had dreamed of.

Father, as I pray today, I place my trust in Your greater vision.
—Madge Harrah

6
SUN

Consider it all joy, my brethren, when you encounter various trials.   —James 1:2 (NAS)

Last summer, I was under intense pressure due to a reorganization at work. Nearly every job assignment was scrambled and resorted.

Many of the changes made my colleagues and me feel pulled in several directions at once—and none of those directions appeared to be forward!

Around the Fourth of July, my youngest nephew John came out from Minnesota for a visit. One evening I was in my usual spot, hovering over the barbecue grill trying not to burn dinner, watching John play catch with my oldest son Jason. Jason was throwing the ball everywhere except right at John and then laughing as John jumped up, dove down, lunged left and right. Finally, I had enough and called out, "Hey, Jason, quit teasing John and make some good throws!"

Immediately, John replied, "It's okay, Uncle Eric. Jason is just helping me make some great catches."

His reply started me thinking in a whole new way about work. Monday morning I began telling my colleagues that all the changes gave us an opportunity to show our skills in new areas. Slowly, our attitudes changed and several great "catches" produced some great results.

So when life throws you a curve, practice making great catches.

Lord, help me to see my problems today as opportunities to let my faith and abilities stretch and grow.   —Eric Fellman

---

7   *Hear counsel, and receive instruction, that thou mayest*
MON *be wise in thy latter end.*   —Proverbs 19:20

During the 1930s, our fifteen-room home in Williamstown, Massachusetts, was an inn and a haven for African-Americans seeking summer vacations. One of our first guests was Mr. Scott, who spent the summer of 1935 at our house.

I liked Mr. Scott. Short, pleasant and talkative, he was always neatly dressed in a suit, tie and white shirt. He worked as a chauffeur for a wealthy widow, and also owned a little restaurant in White Plains, New York. In my eyes, Mr. Scott was a success. His diamond-studded ring was all the proof I needed. But best of all, he didn't have to go to school. He was free!

One day, Mr. Scott asked, "How's school, Oscar?"

"I don't like it," I answered. "I'll be glad to get out and go to work like you!"

Mr. Scott's smile vanished. "You'd better like school," he scolded. "It's the only time in this life you'll receive something you need that's free. Growing up brings responsibilities. Go to school, and you won't have to be at someone's beck and call like me."

The passion with which Mr. Scott spoke startled me, but I heeded his words. Although opportunities for blacks were few in 1935, I began to work and to study. I discovered Booker T. Washington and George Washington Carver. I went to college, and when I graduated in 1941, the economy was recovering and I got a job in Illinois.

Mr. Scott's challenge still rings in my ears, as inspiring now as it was sixty-two years ago.

Thank You, Lord, for the gift of wisdom in the words of those around us.
—Oscar Greene

8
TUE   *They understood not . . . and were afraid. . . .*
—Mark 9:32

Our dog Bandit doesn't bark often, so when he does, we listen. You can understand then why we were perplexed the day he fell into a fit of hysterical barking. "What in the world is wrong, Bandit?" my daughter Keri asked as she tried to console our eleven-year-old pet. My husband David and I scoured the yard for some ominous stranger when we heard the noise up in the sky.

Overhead was a lovely, rainbow-colored hot-air balloon. It was so close we could actually see the faces of the passengers and hear the *whooshing* sounds as the gas filled the balloon. In the following months, hot-air ballooning became increasingly common in our area and Bandit's uncontrollable outbursts continued. *Why did the balloons elicit such a response from an otherwise calm, collected dog?* we wondered.

Then, one night, an awful nightmare woke me into imagining a snowballing succession of unmentionably terrible things that could happen to my family. After a few minutes of sheer terror, I knew that I had lost my hold on reality. I slipped out of bed, went to the living room and pulled out our big family Bible. In the Psalms, I found solace. Verse after verse assured me that the worst imaginable tragedy— even death—was only temporary. We are all in God's good hands.

Around noon the next day, Bandit's barking started again. I went out in the yard to comfort him, and in that moment, I understood his turmoil. To me the beautiful red and yellow balloon represented an incredible adventure, an untamed freedom; to Bandit it had become a living, breathing monster. He didn't understand what it really was, so the balloon frightened him . . . just as death had fright-

ened me before I stepped back and saw what it really was; a journey
to God.

*Father, Your love surrounds us; there's no need to fear. Help us hold on to
that truth.*   —Pam Kidd

9
WED *Blessed are those who hear the joyful blast of the trum-
pet, for they shall walk in the light of your presence.*
                                              —Psalm 89:15 (TLB)

After our long, gray, cold winters, summertime in Wisconsin is welcomed like a long-lost friend. Fresh breezes from Lake Michigan, just
a mile from my house, temper the sunny eighty-degree days, creating perfect weather.

One glorious July day I sat on my deck just soaking in the sounds
of summer. First I heard the roar of a jumbo jet that had just taken
off from Milwaukee's Mitchell Field two miles north of my house.
Then the birds. Melodic blue jays, twittering finches, cawing crows,
all scarfing up vittles from my four bird feeders. Next I heard the man
down the hill making sad, guttural, unintelligible sounds caused by
the debilitating stroke he'd suffered the year before. Finally, the magnificent electronic carillon of the church down the block. Twice a day,
at one and six P.M., four or five pieces—hymns, gospel songs, clas-
sical and seasonal music—carry with the wind across the fields and
road to lift our spirits.

As I listened carefully to those four sounds, it seemed that the voice
of God was giving me some powerful advice:

*Stop complaining about airplane noise. It doesn't upset you when you're
in a plane going to visit a loved one. Be patient now, and let these passengers enjoy their travel.*

*My birds are chirping happily because you feed them. Don't neglect them
in the winter when the deck is covered with snow.*

*The man down the hill needs your patience and your help. A kind word
to his wife and an offer to mow their yard would be a good idea.*

*Just because you're not a member of the church with the magnificent
bells doesn't mean you shouldn't be neighborly. It's time you let them
know how much you enjoy the music.*

*Lord, today and every day, open my ears so I can really hear the sounds of
Your world, listen for Your voice and act on Your goodness.*

                                              —Patricia Lorenz

10
THU

Lips that speak knowledge are a rare jewel.
                                —Proverbs 20:15 (NIV)

I spend a great deal of my time on the road. Being away from my family so much is a real sacrifice, and at times I've questioned the value of all my traveling and speaking. But a few years ago, when I spoke to a mission group in Florida, that all changed.

I spoke to them about reaching out to people across the barriers of race, nationality, economic status and disability. After the meeting, several people stayed to ask me questions, but I didn't sense any enthusiasm for my message. Tired and discouraged, I returned to Mississippi.

A few weeks later, I received a phone call from Gaile, a member of the Florida group. "Dolphus," she said, "you might not remember me, but what you said about reaching out to people who are different has changed my life. I work in a camp ministry that has worked only with upper-middle-class kids, and I'm revamping our entire program so that it's more sensitive to people who are different. Would you consider coming to speak at our camp?"

A year later, when I returned to Florida to address the mission group, I added a visit to the camp to my schedule. Gaile beamed with joy as she greeted me. I met her father, who was the founder of the camp. He was overjoyed by the remarkable changes he had seen in the camp—scholarships for the poor, racial integration of both staff and campers—and in his daughter's life.

I had no idea that what I had said a year before would produce such abundant fruits. And now, whenever I'm tired out with traveling and those doubts return, that experience reminds me that I can make a difference.

Lord, use me to speak Your Word to others and help me leave the results to You.   —Dolphus Weary

11
FRI

Cast all your anxieties on him, for he cares about you.
                                —I Peter 5:7 (RSV)

I walked into our apartment and found my wife Julee sitting cross-legged on the couch, riveted to the TV. She was watching a rerun of a show on which she had appeared under crisis circumstances three years before.

"Not so nerve-wracking this time around, is it?" I joked.

"Are you kidding? Feel my palms." Her hands were clammy and trembling.

I will never forget the original broadcast. Before a live national audience, Julee was singing material she had never performed live before, with a band she had never worked with and as a last-minute substitute for an artist who had withdrawn from the show under great public controversy. Edgy record-company executives and hysterical agents fueled the crisis atmosphere backstage. At the center of the maelstrom, utterly confident and serene as airtime neared, was Julee. *Why, watching a harmless rerun, was she a nervous wreck now?*

We talked about it during the commercial break. "Remember what a mess I was after dress rehearsal?" Julee recalled. "I went to my dressing room, threw everyone out, sat in the dark and begged God to take over. Until the time I went on, I sat there telling God I couldn't do it without Him. When they announced my name, I wasn't the slightest bit nervous."

Most of us don't get the opportunity to watch reruns of our great crises in life. Three years later Julee was having a delayed reaction to the anxiety that almost destroyed her performance that Saturday night before she entrusted herself completely to God. I couldn't help wondering what a rerun of one of my own crises might look like, and if I would be able to see myself reaching out for God and receiving His help.

Suddenly, Julee's voice filled the living room, as pretty and as flawless as ever. She relaxed. "Now I remember what to do," she said. So did I.

With each new problem I face, Lord, the first step is to remember how You never fail me when I ask for Your ever-present help.

—Edward Grinnan

12

SAT   *Be not afraid, only believe.*   —Mark 5:36

I spent last summer visiting my Aunt Judy in North Carolina. One evening my stomach began to hurt, and over the next couple of hours, the pain seemed to get worse and worse. Finally, Aunt Judy, a nurse, said that we needed to go to the hospital. After I had waited an hour or so in the emergency room, the doctors told me that I had appendicitis and that I needed surgery immediately.

I was more than five hundred miles from home, away from my father and my grandparents, and to make matters worse, I'd never been hospitalized before. I was afraid. While I waited in a dark room by myself for the results of the X-rays, I asked God to protect me and to be with me through the operation. While I was praying, the image of my mother, who died when I was in the eighth grade, came into my mind. I remembered how she had held my hand and prayed for me when I was sick, and how her prayers and her presence had assured me that I would be all right. And then my fear left me and I felt a great peace.

After being prepared for surgery, I was put on a gurney in my hospital gown and little blue cap. Aunt Judy walked beside me as I was wheeled to surgery. As she was leaving me at the entrance to the operating room, she looked at me intently and said, "Honey, for all these years you've looked exactly like your father. But just now, I think you look just like your mother."

Lord, thank You for those who have been my examples of prayer.
—Hollie Davis

13

SUN

Let us offer the sacrifice of praise to God continually. . . .
—Hebrews 13:15

My husband Lynn and I went off to the mountains for an overnight last weekend. We had looked forward to this mini-getaway for weeks, but things seemed to go wrong right from the start. It rained; I scratched my eye with my contact lens; we lost our checkbook.

On Sunday morning, we decided to go to a small local church because we heard they had a good pastor, a *Don* somebody. But I was feeling a little grumbly as we walked across the parking lot in a drizzly rain and entered the church, just as the praise music started.

Soon a young man stepped up to the pulpit. I assumed he was the popular pastor.

"I'm sure you're wondering where Don is this morning," he began. "Well, he's in the hospital. While playing softball with the church team on Friday afternoon, he slid into home plate and broke his ankle. It required an operation, so I'm your pinch hitter in the pulpit." He grinned. I didn't. In fact, I rolled my eyes at Lynn and chalked up one more disappointment.

But the pinch-hitter preacher got right into his sermon, talking about slaves and masters and employer-employee relationships. The topic seemed a long way from my needs at that moment, and my thoughts started wandering away . . . until I heard a question.

"Do you sometimes wonder what God's will is for you?" he asked. "It is clearly stated in the Bible: *'Rejoice always, pray constantly, give thanks in all circumstances; for this is the will of God in Christ Jesus for you'* (I Thessalonians 5:16–18, RSV).

"Now you'll notice God is not telling us to be thankful *for* all circumstances, but *in* all circumstances. Even in the midst of difficult or unpleasant circumstances, we can rejoice and pray and always find something for which to thank God."

I sank down in the pew, because I knew he was talking directly to me. For the rest of the service, I thought about all the things I'd forgotten to thank God for, like the time with Lynn, and miracles like contact lenses, and for a pinch-hitter preacher who said exactly what I needed to hear.

Father, forgive me for being grumbly in the midst of plenty of reasons to be thankful.
                                                            —Carol Kuykendall

14
MON

When we cry, "Abba, Father!" it is the Spirit himself bearing witness with our spirit that we are children of God.
—Romans 8:15–16 (RSV)

Standing by our mountain bikes on the outskirts of Waco, Texas, I noticed that my ten-year-old son Luke needed to tighten the straps on his helmet. With a few adjustments, the straps fit snugly under his chin and we were ready to ride on a ten-mile trail.

Thirty minutes later, we were poised on the top of a narrow ridge staring down a nearly vertical path leading to the Brazos River Valley below. "We've got to be real careful," I cautioned Luke. "This is a dangerous path. Follow me, and take your time."

I made it to the bottom safely, but Luke didn't. I looked up to see him careening down the slope. His front wheel hit a tree root, and he was flung into the air. He hit the ground hard, and his head flew back and smacked against a rock.

Dashing up the hill, all that I could hear was an awful silence. There was no cry of pain or fear. Just silence. Reaching his side, I could tell that Luke was stunned but not unconscious. He was confused, beginning to stir, the breath knocked out of his lungs. Suddenly, I heard a little incoherent voice whisper, "Daddy, I need you to hug me. Hug me."

The good news is that Luke was not seriously injured. He suffered some scrapes and bruises and owes his life to a cracked helmet. But I will never forget his words, "Daddy, I need you to hug me."

For all of us, life sometimes grows out of control. We get banged up and injured. Words don't make sense. Sometimes the most honest prayer we can say is, "Father, I need you to hug me. Just hug me."

Dear God, thank You for being a shepherd Who holds me in Your arms. Amen.   —Scott Walker

---

WORDS OF WONDER

And to my listening ears,
All nature sings, and round me rings
The music of the spheres.

This is my Father's world;
I rest me in the thought
Of rocks and trees, of skies and seas,
His hand the wonders wrought.
                    —MALTBIE D. BABCOCK

15
TUE

I will now turn aside, and see this great sight. . . .
                                              —Exodus 3:3

Our trip had been wonderful. My husband Don and I rode a narrow-gauge train from Durango to Silverton in Colorado, floated down the river near Lake Powell in Arizona, and hiked to Emerald Springs in Utah's Zion National Park. We planned to visit the North Rim of the Grand Canyon, but by Thursday afternoon, I was ready to go home.

"I've got tons of work to do before I go to the office Monday," I told Don, "and it will take hours just to wash our vacation clothes. How 'grand' can a canyon be, anyway?"

"Grand enough that I've looked forward to seeing it for years," Don said firmly. "Your work—and wash—can wait."

So, after a day of hiking and mule-riding, we stood together holding hands as the setting sun slowly bathed the awesome canyon in glorious shades of gold, pink, purple and, finally, the gray shadows of night. *We almost missed this,* I thought as we returned to our car in darkness, *because I was thinking about laundry.*

Back home in Kansas, evidence of God's creative power still surrounds me. Bold flashes of jagged lightning, fields of sunflowers with upturned faces, even swirling brown "dirt devils"—all invite me to "turn aside" from work and routine and be renewed by my Creator.

Lord, thank You for the great and small marvels of nature that turn my heart toward You.   —Penney Schwab

16
WED
Thy faithfulness endures to all generations. . . .
—Psalm 119:90 (RSV)

Last July, I helped host a reunion of my mother's family, the Bantas. Though Mother died in 1976, three of her brothers and sisters were there, as well as four later generations. My grandparents have a total of seventy-six descendants at this time. I couldn't help marveling at the fact that all of these people existed because of two people who fell in love and married ninety-nine years ago.

As my cousins and I talked, we discovered that we'd raised our families based on similar values (for example, going to Sunday school and church was not negotiable), and some of the same faults (our sense of reserve caused a cut-off of hugs and kisses at adolescence), and that these patterns had repeated through the generations.

Recently, as I was baby-sitting my granddaughter Saralisa (a typical, try-my-wings two-year-old), she started pulling books out of my bookcases onto the floor. I jumped up, about to scold her, when I remembered my grandparents' home library. So I sat down on the floor with her, told her how special books are, showed her each one, let her hold them and encouraged her to help me put them back. The last one to go back was my grandmother's family Bible. I held it close to my heart, and then let Saralisa hug it before we placed it back on the shelf.

Saralisa now has her own little space on the bottom shelf, with a few of her books, including a children's Bible story book. And she leaves my books alone. Thanks, Grandmother Banta!

Help me always to remember, Lord, to interact with those I love as if the future depended on it. Because, of course, it does.
—Marilyn Morgan Helleberg

17
THU

O Lord, you have examined my heart and know everything
about me. . . . you know my every thought.
                                        —Psalm 139:1–2 (TLB)

The phone was shrill, a sudden interruption to the quiet cool of twilight and the steady rhythm of the sprinklers wetting down the sun-parched earth. It had been a scorching California day with temperatures topping one hundred degrees.

"I need to walk." My friend's voice quivered, and I could sense the hurt. "Just walk. Not talk."

"Meet you on the boulevard," I responded. I raced down the hill, and we met at our favorite corner, near a bush of night-blooming jasmine heavy with scent.

It was a silent walk, broken only by the birds chirruping as they bedded down for the night and the staccato beat of my short steps as they tried to match the stride of my long-legged friend. As we started off, her head was held high, her chin jutted defiantly out. Then, suddenly, she drooped. She bent her head down and bit her lips as tears welled up in her eyes. I was consumed with questions, but I remembered her emphatic, "Just walk. Not talk!"

"Help her, Lord," was all I could pray.

We walked for nearly two hours, pausing now and then on the sidewalk, with not a word exchanged. Tramping back through the darkness, we reached her kitchen door. Abruptly, she turned, and we put our arms around each other. "Thanks for not asking," she said with a small smile, "I'm okay now." And with that she went in.

I will never know what was bothering my friend that night, but I don't need to know. Simply being there was enough.

When pain is too deep for speech, Lord, help me to listen to the silence of
the heart.   —Fay Angus

18
FRI

Behold, the kingdom of God is within you.
                                        —Luke 17:21

In Trento, Italy, on a steamy July morning, I took the children into the city to buy groceries and post letters. The congested city throbbed with traffic and noise—backfiring motorcycles, blaring horns, construction work.

At the bakery, the grocery and the drugstore, we loaded Mark's stroller. But the post office! It wasn't where the map showed it. Or I'd misread the map. We turned and headed in the opposite direction.

The sun beat down. The exhaust of the buses closed in on us. I pushed through the crowds, wilting in the heat. Mark fussed. My head throbbed like that drilling jackhammer we were passing. Turning a corner, I spotted the open door of a church. We stepped inside and found quiet coolness.

With the street noise muffled and the flickering candles and Cross of Christ before us, peace engulfed me. Elizabeth and I lighted candles, knelt and asked God to help us find the post office. Longing to stay in the quiet peace of the church, I looked up at the Cross. *My peace I give you.* Refreshed, I stepped back into the heat. As we walked along the smelly, noisy streets, God's peace prevailed in my heart. And, yes, we found the post office.

Back home in our suburban Michigan house, it's Trento again, crowded and noisy, jammed with tasks, telephone ringing, children whining, frustrations blaring. But on the refrigerator hangs a picture postcard of a little Italian church to remind me: Take the first open door in the day—even if only for a few moments—pause, close your eyes, and sink into that quiet place in your heart where His Presence can renew you.

Oh, Lord, in the busyness of each day, You hold open a welcoming door. Help me go inside, find Your quiet Presence, and carry Your peace into the din of daily life.   —Mary Brown

19
SAT

"But when you pray, go away by yourself, all alone. . . ."
—Matthew 6:6 (TLB)

Mother rarely complained, even though she was still confined to her wheelchair. The only thing that seemed to bother her was that she couldn't do anything for others.

As a pastor's wife, I'm responsible for putting together the weekly bulletins for our Sunday service. One Saturday night, when Mother saw me getting ready to fold the bulletins, she exclaimed, "Oh, let me do that!" I told her the job would only take me five minutes, but she was adamant.

Mother took the bulletins and had me wheel her into the kitchen and over to the table. After awhile, I passed and saw her still methodically folding the bulletins. "I can't believe you haven't finished," I said. "Why is it taking you so long?"

"Is there a time limit?" Mother answered, smiling.

"No, but how can it take you so long?"

"I'm fine, doing it my way," she said, creasing one bulletin at a time ever so slowly and deliberately.

"Is this hard for you?"

She sighed and stopped for a moment. "No, it's not hard at all. I like doing it. If you must know, I'm praying for each person who will open a bulletin tomorrow. Everyone who comes to church will have been prayed for. I thought I could do it secretly here in the kitchen."

I slipped quietly out of the kitchen and left Mother to her prayers.

Father, help me to take all of this day's tasks and turn them into prayers.
—Marion Bond West

20
SUN

"When you pray, go into your room and shut the door and pray to your Father who is in secret. . . ."
—Matthew 6:6 (RSV)

I was almost five years old. The room was dark. My mother was sitting at the side of my bed, her hand touching my head on the pillow. She was saying a prayer.

I had always loved those quiet moments. All day long I had to act tough and strong so that my dad and my older brother wouldn't think I was a sissy. But during those few minutes alone with Mother each night, I could relax and be what I was—a tired little boy.

Just as she was about to leave, Mother looked at me thoughtfully and sat back down. "Johnny," she said, "it's time you began praying. God is listening for you to talk to Him, just as I do."

"You mean God's actually listening for *me* to say something?"

She nodded her head.

I squeaked a loud whisper, "You mean He's right here in this room?"

She said, smiling, "Yes, and He's forgiven you for all your sins and loves you very much." She leaned down, kissed me on the forehead and left, closing the door.

I peered into the blackness; I was really frightened. I thought of all the things I had said and thought and done in that room alone with the door closed—things I wouldn't want God to know about. Then, just as I thought I was going to have to call out in fear, I remembered what Mother had said: "God has *forgiven you* for all your sins—and He *loves you* very much."

I quickly whispered my first prayer: "Thank You, God." And my spiritual journey had begun.

Lord, keep me always thankful for Your gifts—and especially the gift of mercy.   —Keith Miller

21
MON

Cast all your anxiety on him because he cares for you.
                                    —I Peter 5:7 (NIV)

On a cool summer evening, I walked alone up a rutted dirt road, pocked with holes, stones and branches. It led along a forsaken place, edged with woods and fields and curtained by dusk. I'd fled to this place to escape the strain of my husband's business problems. They seemed to be running away with us both.

Over the crest of the hill appeared a tall, strapping man and a little girl, about four, walking an enormous German shepherd. The dog pulled on the leash, while the man held him back. The man's long legs, next to the child's small steps, seemed barely to move.

"Hello," I said as I neared them.

The little girl looked up at me with a dimpled smile as she held onto the leash. "This is my dog, Bear. I'm walking him."

"I see," I said, my eyes moving from the man's strong hold on the leash to the child's hand behind his. The man smiled knowingly at me. I smiled back, sharing the secret that he bore the brunt, allowing only as much tug as the child could grasp.

As I made the needle-sharp turn into the dark, wooded descent to my house, I held in my mind the picture of the man shielding the child from more than she could handle. In the rustle of pines, I heard my Father's voice, "Would I do any less for you?" Those gentle words put my husband's "run-away" business problems into place . . . leashed to the hand of a loving God Who allows just enough tugs to mature our faith.

Father, help me to see that the tensions of life reach me through Your loving hand.   —Shari Smyth

22
TUE

His thunder announces the coming storm; even the cattle make known its approach.   —Job 36:33 (NIV)

I dearly love storms, but I admit they can be dangerous, so I'm grateful for the way God always warns us of the imminent tempests: thunder for our ears; dark clouds to catch our eyes; wind to slap our faces. Time to take cover!

Long before the days of satellite weather forecasts, our forefathers recognized many signs of an approaching storm: birds flying close to the ground; cattle lying down; leaves showing their backsides; smoke descending instead of rising; insects becoming aggressive; ditches smelling bad; sounds traveling farther. They were even attuned to bodily changes, such as aching teeth or a melancholy mood.

> Hark how the chairs and tables crack!
> Old Betty's joints are on the rack.
> Her corns with shooting pains torment her . . .
> Twill surely rain.

What is true of storms is also true of relationships. There are almost always warnings of trouble brewing between me and my students, my wife, or my boss: the cloudy countenance; unexpected thunder-anger; verbal wind or just that certain coolness in the air. If I ignore these warnings, I may be setting myself up for a full-blown storm that may permanently damage the relationship.

So I'm trying to develop more sensitivity to these warning signs. This afternoon, I plan to visit with one of my students who has been cool to me for a week. It's probably nothing to worry about—she's likely got relationship problems or financial troubles. But it can't hurt to spend a few minutes chatting, and it might head off a serious problem.

Lord, make me sensitive to brewing storms.   —Daniel Schantz

23
WED   *We count them happy which endure. . . .*   —James 5:11

"Look, I really don't have time for this. Don't bother calling again!" *Click.*

You would think averaging a hundred of these "cold calls" each day I'd be used to having people hang up on me. A couple of months before, when I was promoted to my present position of institutional broker, my boss Darrell had said, "It's a great opportunity for you, Brock, but it's not going to be easy." He was right. Building a clientele from scratch is definitely not easy.

My day begins when I arrive at the office at seven A.M., where I look through *The Wall Street Journal*. At seven-fifteen, we have a brief meeting to discuss the bond market and the particular bonds that will give our customers better yields. My problem is that I need customers to sell those bonds to! After the meeting, I hit the phone. My territories are Ohio and Kansas.

Today, after several hang-ups, feelings of rejection began to make me doubt my abilities. Desperately, I decided to pray: "God, I sure could use some encouragement right about now." Suddenly, I remembered some advice I had received last Sunday from George Allen, a friend from my church and a very prominent Nashville businessman.

"Brock, I've been hearing good things about you," George had said. He encouraged me and told me that he believed in me. "Just keep sawing that wood, Brock. Just keep sawing wood."

"Thanks, God," I said, feeling amazed that He had answered my prayer so quickly. Back to "sawing wood," I smiled as I picked up the phone and dialed the number of a bank in Kansas. Already, I knew that if this one hung up, I would be one call closer to a customer who needed exactly what I had to offer.

God, help me to endure the rough spots of my job. Let hope click in every number I dial.   —Brock Kidd

24
THU

Look carefully then how you walk, not as unwise men but as wise, making the most of the time. . . .
—Ephesians 5:15–16 (RSV)

One of my favorite childhood memories is of the Pacific National Exhibition, held each year in Vancouver, British Columbia, Canada. The thrill of any fair is hard to beat: cotton candy; jugglers throwing knives; circus elephants. But for me, the highlight was going to see the roller coaster!

Each summer, I stood at the foot of the high wooden trestle and yearned to hop aboard. I never did, though. I was just too scared. I'd content myself with another go-round on the Ferris wheel and tell myself there was always next year.

The years passed, and I started taking my children to the PNE. Each in turn conquered the roller coaster, teasing me to join them. Each year I answered, "Maybe next year."

But this year I didn't have that option, for this was the PNE's last year at the old Exhibition Grounds. My fifteen-year-old son took me over to the roller coaster to gaze up at the trestles. Nothing had changed in nearly forty years. I still yearned to go; I was still too scared. I don't know that I ever did agree; Blake just took me over and pushed me through the line.

Wow! We rattled down that seventy-three-foot drop at more than a hundred miles per hour. I thought I was going to fly out of my seat! I loved it!

We went a second time, and while hurtling through the air, I thought of all the fun I'd missed in life because I have a bad habit of living as if I always have "next year" to do the hard things.

But coming home from the PNE I realized that time does run out. We can't keep saying "next year." So I made a new resolve—to seize each opportunity that presents itself. Now, not next year!

Father, help me to live more wisely, making the most of my time instead of squandering passing days on misplaced fear.   —Brenda Wilbee

25

FRI

Forgetting what is behind and straining toward what is ahead.   —Philippians 3:13 (NIV)

"Bobbi, I hate to bother you, but something has happened. Could you come up for a few minutes this evening?"

My neighbor Roye Caldwell so seldom asked for help that I knew it must be serious. It was. I had just settled into her armchair when she said quietly, "I'm going blind."

Roye and I had gotten to know each other when she lost her husband Walt less than a year before. A few months later, the supervisory nursing position she had held for more than twenty years had been eliminated, leaving her without work at fifty-eight. Now, diabetic retinopathy had suddenly taken most of her sight.

Because Roye is fiercely independent, I knew what it cost her over the next months to call me to drive her places and to be her "eyes" as we went in and out of stores and doctors' offices. She refused to hold my arm when we went out—she didn't want to look like a blind person. Walking just behind me, she made her way across parking lots and up stairs without looking down at all. She looked straight ahead, watching what she could see of me and obeying my quiet suggestions and warnings. She was trusting her steps to the one she had chosen to guide her.

Right now, it's hard to understand all the things the Lord is doing in my life. I can "see" a little, but what I don't understand is scary, hidden. But I remember Roye watching the shadowy outline of my back, listening for my "Step up" and "We turn here," and doggedly obeying. Then I listen for a quiet voice and move ahead in faith, knowing we will arrive safely.

Lord, help me to hold fast to You and to move forward a step at a time.
—Roberta Rogers

26
SAT
Wash me, and I shall be whiter than snow.
—Psalm 51:7

I'm sure I'm not the only one it happens to. I put on a suit fresh from the cleaners: That's the day someone removes the "Fresh Paint" sign. I wear a tie for the first time: spaghetti sauce. It happened again to a pair of chinos, not expensive, but brand-new.

That Saturday morning I felt crisp and clean as I came down to breakfast with my friends, the Hambletons, who had invited me for the weekend. Breakfast over, my hostess gave me a metal pail and directed me to a blackberry patch where I had offered to pick enough for that evening's cobbler.

"Oh, my," Merrill exclaimed when I reappeared a full pail later. My pants were a sight. She rushed me to the basement where she got to work with some stain removers and a whirl in the washing machine. The purple stains were no longer vibrant, but they were there.

And that was that so far as the chinos went. I couldn't wear them and something told me that I couldn't abandon them, so they hung in my closet, unworn. Until the day that I determined to organize my wardrobe. I picked up the trousers, fully intending to put them among the discards, when, suddenly, I stopped. Looking at the faded stains, I thought of all the errors I'd made in life, some of which I'd never admitted to anyone. Not only did I keep the chinos, but as a reminder of my past mistakes, I put them on and wore them in public.

That was a long time ago. I still have those pants, but it would take an eagle eye to see the stains. Repeated washings have done the trick. But I know. And I am humble.

Father, I know You have forgiven, but I need to remember that You need to.
—Van Varner

27
SUN

Yea, though I walk through the valley of the shadow of death, I will fear no evil: for thou art with me. . . .
—Psalm 23:4

"I'm going through a Slough of Despond," a friend reported tongue-in-cheek one day. After being "downsized" from her previous job, she was having trouble finding a new one.

"But you will reach Celestial City," I prophesied. We both chuckled at the references to John Bunyan's famous book *The Pilgrim's Progress.* This seventeenth-century classic relates the trials Christian, Bunyan's protagonist, had after he left the City of Destruction on his way to heaven. There was the Hill of Difficulty; the Valley of the Shadow; the Valley of Humiliation; Doubting Castle, where he was held in prison by Giant Despair; and Vanity Fair, where Christian's friend Faithful was martyred.

Few books have had the staying power of Bunyan's allegory, which underscores the fact that no one's life is trouble-free. No follower of Christ knew that better than Bunyan himself. In 1660, at the age of thirty-two, this itinerant tinker-turned-minister was imprisoned for preaching without a license. He spent most of the next twelve years in jail, but there was one redeeming thing about it: He used his confinement to write *The Pilgrim's Progress,* which at one time was, next to the Bible, the world's most widely read book.

"All things work together for good to them that love God, to them who are the called according to his purpose," I can imagine Bunyan quoting Romans 8:28. I know of no verse more fortifying for the forlorn.

If you are wading through some Slough of Despond today, climbing some Hill of Difficulty or facing some Valley of Humiliation, take heart. Like John Bunyan's hero Christian, you, too, will find the Celestial City.

> *When my progress is thwarted, Lord,*
> *Arm me with Your Spirit's sword.* —Fred Bauer

28
MON

For all the law is fulfilled in one word, even in this; Thou shalt love thy neighbor as thyself. But if ye bite and devour one another, take heed that ye be not consumed one of another.
—Galatians 5:14–15

When my wife Barbara and I lived in Houston, I served on several committees in the Fort Worth-Dallas area, so I became a regular on commuter flights. One evening as I was standing in line at the airport ticket counter, I noticed a very interesting thing about the ticket agent: He got the customers' names, took their credit cards, wrote their tickets and pointed them to their gates without ever looking at them. I decided to see if I could get him to look at me.

As the man in front of me left for his gate, the agent said, "Name?" I didn't respond. Then, still without looking up, he ran his hand around on the counter, hoping to find my credit card.

Finally, I said, "Would you mind looking at me?" He seemed startled, but he looked up. I asked him if he realized that he had ticketed the six people in front of me without ever looking at any of them.

"You want to know why I do that?" he asked. "As far as the people in this line are concerned, I might as well be a machine. If they could punch the information in on my nose, then twist my ear and have the ticket come out my mouth, it would be fine with them."

I stood there for a moment, speechless and sad. People so often live up—or down—to the expectations we have of them. When we treat them like machines, they start acting that way. Jesus challenges me to treat everyone I meet with love. It isn't easy, but as I walked toward my gate, ticket in hand, I decided to work on it, one person at a time.

Lord, help me to value the person in everyone I meet.

—Kenneth Chafin

29
TUE *The Lord . . . remains faithful forever.*
—Psalm 146:6 (NIV)

Several years ago, two old friends paid me a two-week visit with their five-year-old son Stephen. One day in the house, Stephen asked me to kiss his finger, saying matter-of-factly that he'd gotten a booboo and it wasn't bad enough to run upstairs to get a Band-Aid. I said spontaneously, "Stephen, I like you!" He looked up at me briefly, smiled and went back to his red blocks. I didn't even know if he'd heard or understood what I'd said.

Two days later, Stephen's mother said, "The funniest thing happened today. Stephen and I were outside your house, and your neighbor asked if we were having a good time and how long we were going to stay. Stephen piped up, 'We were supposed to stay two weeks, but we might stay a lot longer—a year or more.' I was shocked. I said,

'Stephen, this is Paul and Linda's house. We can't stay longer unless it is all right with them.' And he said, 'Oh, I know it will be all right with Linda. She likes me. She told me she did.' "

Stephen had faith that my liking for him would not change. And despite my insecurities and fears, I'm trying to live with a faith like his in God and in the people He's put into my life.

Help me trust, today, God, that my friends will always be there for me. And that You will always be there for me, too.   —Linda Neukrug

30 *"His father saw him and was filled with compassion for*
WED   *him; he ran to his son, threw his arms around him and*
kissed him."   —Luke 15:20 (NIV)

In 1906, Jason Manchester, my great-grandfather, built a round barn on our family farm in Auglaize County, Ohio. It was quite a phenomenon, and visitors came from many miles away to see it. As a child, I enjoyed playing there. We would run around and around the circular oak floors until we were dizzy.

Although there are no longer animals to eat hay from the circular troughs, my cousin Tim continues to use the barn every day for drying and storing grain. I'm sure my great-grandfather would be proud to see how the barn has remained useful throughout the century. It's become a symbol of stability in a world of change.

I've read that the Shakers originated the round barn design to convey their spirituality and love of God. They believed it captured a bit of heaven. As I walked round and round the barn on a recent family visit and marveled at its shape, I felt that the Shakers were right: The circle expresses a sense of completion, the wonderful perfection of God's creation.

I remember asking, when I was little, how God could be everywhere. Our minister, a gentle person who understood my puzzlement, said, "Think of the way your dad picks you up and holds you when you're afraid. That's what God does with everyone everywhere. He holds the whole world in His arms." The round barn speaks to me of the special way we are connected to each other through God's love. We are all being held in the circle of His arms.

Lord, when it seems that I'm just going around in circles, help me to stop and feel Your arms around me.   —Susan Schefflein

31

I know that there is nothing better for them than to be happy and enjoy themselves. . . .

—Ecclesiastes 3:12 (RSV)

I should have known it wasn't going to be the usual sedate stroll around the fairways when we had to search high and low for the rickety little signs leading to Sleepy Hollow Golf Course. When we pulled up, it looked exactly like what it was: an old homestead disguised as a golf course.

"Where's the clubhouse?" my mother asked.

I pointed to a small utility building and said, "I think that's it." A note on the door informed us that the owner was off mowing the driving range. I could see him jauntily shifting gears on his full-sized tractor. I hiked out to tell him we needed to rent clubs.

How our laughter rang out that bright summer day, soaring over the course as free as the pair of eagles high overhead. One thing was for certain: None of us were going to see any eagles in our golf games! Instead, we watched my son slice his yellow ball into the biggest dandelion patch I've ever seen. Minutes later my mother and I, in a feeble attempt at self-preservation, crouched behind a burly cottonwood as this same son took a mighty swing and, sure enough, nailed that very tree. The ball (an orange one this time) rebounded into the cold creek, where his sister went wading after it.

Maybe Sleepy Hollow has changed since I was last there, but I hope not. It's nice to play a course that has personality. It helped us shed our seriousness. We actually began to anticipate the next misadventure, instead of concentrating on perfecting our swings. It was the most fun I've ever had in a golf game.

Lord, it's amazing how enjoyment crops up when we quit dictating how things ought to be. P.S. Exactly where did that yellow golf ball land?

—Carol Knapp

Everyday Wonders

1 _____

2 _____

3 _____

4 _____

5 _____

6 _____

7 _____

8 _____

9 _____

10 _____

11 _____

12 _____

13 _____

14 _____

15 _____

16 _____

17 _____

18 _____

19 _____

20 _____

21 _____

22 _____

23 _____

24 _____

25 _____

26 _____

27 _____

28 _____

29 _____

30 _____

31 _____

I have loved you, O my people,
with an everlasting love; with
lovingkindness I have drawn you
to me. —JEREMIAH 31:3 (TLB)

August

S	M	T	W	T	F	S
					1	2
3	4	5	6	7	8	9
10	11	12	13	14	15	16
17	18	19	20	21	22	23
24	25	26	27	28	29	30
31						

1

LOVE IS . . .

[Love] always trusts. . . .   —I Corinthians 13:7 (NIV)

DoraMae was one of my little shadows. Every counselor had them, in this Catskill Mountain camp run by the YWCA for inner-city kids—the little girls who tagged after you everywhere.

The camp ran on a shoestring; as swimming counselor, I'd fashioned "achievement badges" from safety pins and colored foil. Blue, I decided, for treading water, green for floating, gold for a dog paddle.

Alas, for even these modest goals! Buses from New York City discharged the campers, a new group every two weeks, tear-streaked and terrified. These children were frightened of cows, of the night-drone of cicadas, and above all, of the wide flat expanse of the lake—the biggest open space most of them had ever seen. By the end of the first two weeks, I was awarding blue badges to those who waded in up to their knees, green for waist deep, gold to anyone who would bend down and put her whole face in the water.

"Look!" I'd say, floating on my back. "The water is supporting me! Water will hold you up." No one dared to try.

DoraMae arrived with the fourth group, a love-hungry child who could not get enough of holding my hand. She got her blue badge at the end of her first week, green and gold ones the second.

"DoraMae," I said as she waded in nearly up to her chest on her last day at camp, "if I hold my hands beneath you, will you lie back in the water?" Without a word, solemn brown eyes on mine, she leaned against my hands. Slowly, I lowered her until the water was bearing most of her small weight. Her eyes never left mine as the lake lapped about her shoulders, her ears. . . .

"If I take away my hands," I told her, "the water will hold you up." Her eyes grew wider still. "I won't let you go under! My hands will be just underneath. Do you want to float, DoraMae, just for a minute?" Not a sound came from her, just a look in those dark eyes that I've held in my heart ever since. A look of absolute, unquestioning trust.

And for a minute . . . two minutes . . . three . . . a small girl floated in a brand-new element while the mountains cheered.

God of love, give me the courage to face the unfamiliar, rejoicing that Your arms are underneath.   —Elizabeth Sherrill

2
SAT

And from his fulness have we all received, grace upon grace.   —John 1:16 (RSV)

Our church lies only a block from our walk-up apartment in Brooklyn. While my father-in-law lived with us, it seemed a mile away. Dad's brain injury had left him with a shuffling walk and a form of dementia similar to Alzheimer's. The logistics of getting him dressed, fed, slowly guided down two flights of stairs and up the street to church each Sunday morning were a nightmare.

One Saturday, after a particularly bad Dad week, my husband Andrew stayed home while I went off to "church sit" so that the building would be open so passersby could stop in. I was feeling a little sorry for myself that day, and I welcomed the chance to spend two hours—preferably alone!—in the church. The building was quiet, and I was weary. I became distracted from my prayers, mulling over the diminished quality of Dad's life and the effect it was having on Andrew and me.

Soon a middle-aged man I recognized as a new parishioner came in. I didn't expect him to know me, but he stopped to talk. "I've wanted to meet you," he said. "You see, one of the first people I noticed when I visited this church was your father-in-law. I saw how people showered him with affection and love, even though he was feeble and confused. And I thought, 'This is the kind of place I want to be.'"

So Dad was the reason he decided to come back to church! My frustrations melted in the face of this sudden view of God's grace at work. In spite of—and maybe even because of—Dad's infirmities, God was working through him to beckon others to a life of faith.

Lord, help me to remember that each day in each person's life is a sacred gift from You, designed with exquisite purpose and filled with riches that are not always ours to see.   —Julia Attaway

3
SUN

Him that overcometh will I make a pillar in the temple of my God. . . .   —Revelation 3:12

My daughter Rebecca's speech is peppered with malaprops. "I bought one of those A-*frame* dresses today," she announced one evening. Another time she said, "I saved a magazine article for you, Mom. It's about the earth's rotation on its *axle.*"

A few months ago, she was in tears when she called. "Vic died this morning," she said, "and I don't know what our church will do without him. He sang in the choir and was always helping people. He was an absolute *statue!*"

"The right word is *pillar,*" I told her smugly. "A statue is something that just stands there."

Later, though, I looked up both words in the dictionary. *Statue* was defined as "a three-dimensional representation of a person, produced by sculpting, molding or casting." And *pillar* had several meanings: a "firm, upright support" was one of them, but so was "an ornamental statue."

As a Christian, I ought to be both a statue and a pillar, I thought. *I can't provide firm, upright support for other people unless I allow Christ to mold me into His image.* And maybe the first step in that molding is admitting I'm not the family's sole authority on words . . . or compassion.

"Honey," I told my daughter, "I'm so sorry about Vic. I know you'll all miss him. And by the way, you were right. He was a statue!"

Heavenly Father, thank You for using my child to teach me more about You.
—Penney Schwab

4
MON

Blessed are all they that put their trust in him.
—Psalm 2:12

It was past bedtime, and a sultry summer storm thundered in the distance. "I'm scared," my son Timo said to me after I tucked him in and listened to his prayers. I understood. When I was five years old, thunder and lightning scared me, too.

"I'll stay right here until it's gone," I said to him in the dark, lying down on the rug next to his bed.

The ceiling fan spun overhead, and outside the trees shivered in the wind. A flash of lightning illuminated the room and silently I counted to myself, "one thousand one, one thousand two, one thousand three," clocking to see how many miles away it was. *Crack,* came the thunder. Not a very close one. More rumbling followed, like pins falling in a distant bowling game. Then came the rain, spattering in hard drops on the warm sidewalk, spitting on the leaves, finally spilling from the eaves in a torrent. Timo was already asleep, but there I lay listening to the sounds.

How comforting the storm was, cooling the air from the summer heat, relieving the atmosphere from the pressure that had been building all day. Closing my eyes, I felt the tensions of the workday wash away. And like Timo trusting that I would be beside him as long as the storm persisted, I knew God was there.

"What took you so long?" my wife Carol asked when I finally returned to the living room.

"I said my own bedtime prayers."

In You, Lord, I put my trust.   —Rick Hamlin

5   *I meditate on all that thou hast done. . . . I stretch out my*
TUE   *hands to thee. . . .*   —Psalm 143:5–6 (RSV)

Every morning my wonderful dogs help remind me of a lesson in prayer I recently learned.

More or less at the crack of dawn, I crawl out of bed to leash up Sally, my peppy cocker spaniel, and Marty, my big yellow Lab, for their walk. But first they indulge in a morning ritual: stretching. Marty starts by doing his forelegs, then stretching out his hips and back legs, taking his time, carefully preparing his body for the rigors of his walk. While I get on my coat, Sally likes to jump up and use me to stretch against. After their walk, I rush over to the gym for a quick, heart-pounding workout. On the way I squeeze in some prayer.

This all came to an irritating halt recently when I sustained a painful case of tendonitis in my lower right leg. "You've got to do your stretching," the trainer admonished me. I hate to stretch. It might be fine for dogs, but I am impatient with it. "Stretching before you work out prepares the muscles. It opens them up so they can grow," he explained.

For the next week I stopped at the gym only to soak my leg in the whirlpool. I was chagrined to find myself still squeezing in my morning prayer, rushing through it like just another chore to cross off. A friend to whom I mentioned this situation remarked, "Isn't meditation before prayer a little like stretching before exercise? You need to put yourself in God's presence before you can talk to Him." My friend—and the trainer—were onto something. *Stretching helps open up your muscles so they can grow.*

That is why, when I watch Marty and Sally stretch out now before their morning walk, I remind myself: *Take your time. Stretch your mind and soul for God before you pray. Open up and prepare to grow!*

God, work with me to stretch my prayer muscles. —Edward Grinnan

6

WED

"Well done, good and faithful servant. . . ."
—Matthew 25:21 (RSV)

My longtime friend and prayer partner Carolmae Petersen has just been told she has two months to live. I am still reeling from the shock of it. Carolmae has never been a complainer. Though she'd been having stomachaches for a while, she brushed that aside and continued to live her full, very active life, which has always been centered in service to God and other people.

When she first learned she had cancer (less than two weeks ago), I prayed with her, and as always, her wonderful faith glowed in the dark. Her only tears that day were for her husband and grown children. On Sunday and again on Tuesday, Carolmae was at the church taking care of her altar guild duties. I imagine she'll continue to do that as long as she can.

And I'll continue to pray for God's will in her life, for relief from pain, and for peace of mind for my dear friend and her family. But I have no great anxiety about Carolmae's future. She has lived a life of faith, with great integrity, a life knit together by her love for Jesus, deep prayer and service to others.

Carolmae once gave me a lovely painting of the transfigured Christ, which now adorns my home. I know that when her earthly life is finished, she will be met by a gentle Being with soulful eyes and the radiance of love shining all about Him. And when He says, "Well done, good and faithful servant," she, too, will be transfigured.

My Lord and my God, may I be inspired to live the rest of my life as though I had two months to live, two months in which to express my love for Your Son. Amen. —Marilyn Morgan Helleberg

7

THU

Share with God's people who are in need. . . .
—Romans 12:13 (NIV)

When my husband Bob's job began to involve traveling around the state, he realized that unexpected problems—car trouble, overnight trips, bad weather—might require ready cash. To be prepared, he tucked some money into a separate compartment of his wallet as a "just-in-case reserve." For several months, the money stayed put.

Then one day Bob was eating lunch at a fast-food restaurant in Birmingham, Alabama, when a young man came in and asked to see the manager.

"Do you have any work I could do in exchange for a few sandwiches?" he asked.

"We have no jobs open," the manager snapped.

"Please," he implored, "not for myself. For my wife and children."

"Like I said, no jobs!"

"The car has enough gas to get us to my wife's family tonight. But the kids are hungry and . . ." His voice trailed off as the manager walked away. For a moment, the man sat dejected, then left the restaurant.

Bob overtook him near the car where his wife and two crying children waited.

"I overheard," Bob told him. He pressed the just-in-case money into the stranger's hand. "I want you to take this and find a restaurant where you can all have something to eat."

"We aren't beggars," the man said, clutching the money. "My company phased out my job, and now I'm looking for work. Please give me your name and address and I'll mail this back to you as soon as I can."

"Don't return it to me," Bob said as he shook the man's hand. "When you get back on your feet, find someone else who needs help and pass the money along."

Later, Bob and I prayed for the jobless man and his family and for others like them. We decided to increase our emergency fund, and we asked God to provide opportunities for each of us to be "just-in-case representatives" for Him.

Keep us thankful for Your good gifts, Lord, and help us to pass them along.
—Drue Duke

8
_____
FRI

O Lord our God, the majesty and glory of your name fills all the earth and overflows the heavens.
—Psalm 8:1 (TLB)

"Mom, you're supposed to do 'Hawaii Five-Oh' when you turn fifty. It's a tradition. I'll pay your airfare," my oldest daughter Jeanne said.

And so we went, Jeanne, her boyfriend Canyon, my youngest son Andrew and me, on a dream vacation to Hawaii for fifteen glorious days. On the morning of day twelve we rented ocean kayaks, the only way to get to the most spectacular snorkeling spot on the Big Island. We kayaked a half-mile across the bay and spent the day smiling at a *gazillion* Technicolor fish underwater.

Around four P.M., we climbed into our kayaks for the return trip, the only living souls in that part of the Pacific Ocean. Exhausted, we lollygagged across the calm, crystal clear water.

Suddenly, huge fish were popping out of the water just ahead of us. Dolphins! Dozens of them! We paddled like crazy to get closer, then sat silently when we reached the spot where they were playing.

I looked at Jeanne and Canyon in their kayak. They were speechless. As we sat motionless in that great ocean, the dolphins jumped out of the water, spun in the air and dove back in headfirst. They seemed as happy to see us as we were to see them, and for thirty minutes or so, we four were spellbound.

Finally, Canyon whispered, "This is unbelievable. It's definitely a 'God moment.' "

I nodded as six sleek dolphins, in perfect synchronization, glided within feet of the kayak Andrew and I were in, waggled their fins almost in a wave, then headed out to sea.

Lord, thank You for the "God moments" here on earth that are a preview of what eternity with You in heaven is all about.   —Patricia Lorenz

9

SAT

Let not your heart be troubled: ye believe in God, believe also in me.   —John 14:1

For years I observed the actions of others without acting or speaking. I withheld information, ideas and decisions, fearing they would cause disagreement. I wanted to be liked, and I wanted to avoid unpleasantness.

Then a dear friend said, "When are you going to get off that fence? When are you going to be yourself? When are you going to reach out and take a stand?"

Her words jolted and puzzled me, until I happened to read *My Larger Education* by Booker T. Washington, written in 1911. Washington suggested that the best means of destroying race prejudice was by being useful to others; any man or woman with something to offer would be accepted. And in order to be useful, it was necessary to be open and truthful.

Slowly, I gained the courage to make my thoughts known. I spoke out about what I thought our church needed during our seventeen-month search for a new pastor. When I felt weighed down by the burdens I was carrying, I was able to say no to additional responsibilities. When I heard people speaking emotionally and irresponsibly, I was able to challenge them.

My friends noted the change; they admitted that they had had to find out what I was thinking by reading my eyes, my facial expressions and my tone of voice. They had sensed the conflict between my words and my heart.

I felt better after climbing down from the fence. The tottering wasn't easy. Now I'm free to be true to others and to myself.

Father, may the words of my mouth truly express the feelings in my heart.
                                                            —Oscar Greene

10
SUN   *In whose hand is the soul of every living thing, and the breath of all mankind.*   —Job 12:10

"My prayer life is not working well," I told my friend Sam.

"Why?" he asked.

"Well, I pray for all kinds of things to happen, and most of them don't."

"What kinds of things?"

"Like telling God to stop a friend from marrying a woman he was dating. She obviously wasn't right for him." I laughed. "I guess I thought God needed that last bit of information to do His work properly."

Sam, who is very honest, said, "Sounds to me like you're trying to get God to be your errand boy—to do *your* will. Sort of backward, isn't it? I thought the whole idea of prayer was to learn *His* will."

"Oh, that hurts!" I said. But I knew he was right. I was playing God under the guise of prayer. "But," I went on, "if telling God what I want Him to do about peoples' lives isn't the way to pray, how should I pray about them?"

Sam shrugged. "Well, here's an example. When I pray for my kids, in my imagination, I put one of them at a time in my cupped hands. Then I imagine Jesus in the room, and I take each child and lay him or her quietly in His cupped hands—and I don't say anything. I don't even know God's best for *me,* much less for other people. So I figure the best thing I can do for people I love is to put them in God's hands every day."

Now, that's the way I pray, too.

Lord, let me trust in Your will for those I love—and for me.

—Keith Miller

11

Lift up your eyes on high and see: who created these? . . .
—Isaiah 40:26 (RSV)

For three nights in a row we gather on a quilt in the cool backyard grass, craning our necks to scan the sky for shooting stars, participants in the annual summer light show known as the Perseid meteor shower. It's been a tradition since my husband Paul and I watched the August skies together on our first date. Now the four of us—Paul, Ross, Maria and I—lie on our backs waiting and watching, wondering who will be first to glimpse a shooting star.

"I see one over there! Ooh, look, another one," Ross jabbers. "Wow, that's so cool!" he says, in his precocious, six-year-old way.

"They are amazing," I say, as one just slips into view. We all quietly marvel at God's great wonders.

Just then Maria laughs, her bubbly, giggly, baby laugh. Our dog Cookie is licking her toes, and she is delighted. We all laugh, too, at such a sweet blessed sound.

"God sure loaded Maria up with happies tonight," Ross says, and Paul and I exchange a smile at such innocent wisdom, as we marvel at God's smallest wonders.

I look around me and realize I don't have to search the skies for the wonders of God's love. They lie right beside me, in the cool grass of my own backyard, on a hot summer night.

Loving Creator, thank You for Your wonders, great and small, that touch my life and bring great joy.   —Gina Bridgeman

12

Every good and perfect gift is from above. . . .
—James 1:17 (NIV)

I was in graduate school and short on money back in 1986, and I really couldn't afford flowers for Ginny, a fellow nurse in her early thirties who was in the final stage of cancer. Then I spotted a coupon in the local newspaper offering a dozen long-stemmed roses for only five dollars in celebration of the fortieth anniversary of Spurlock's Flowers.

By the time I got to Spurlock's, the long line of customers snaked halfway around the block. "Wait till my girlfriend sees these," said a delighted young man in the line. "I never had enough money before." "Mine are for my Aunt Nan," announced a pigtailed girl in braces, clutching her ragged coupon and a pink vinyl purse. It took me nearly an hour to reach the head of the line.

When I delivered my breathtaking red roses to the cancer unit at St. Mary's Hospital, I passed several smiling faces also bearing the coveted long, slender boxes. Quietly, I handed the roses to Ginny's weary mother, who arranged them in a plastic water pitcher. Standing at the edge of the doorway, I heard a faint, groggy moan from the once delicate body of my friend, now swollen and jaundiced from cancer. "Who loved me enough to bring me roses?"

I've often wondered just how many others felt like royalty that day. What I do know is that I wouldn't have been able to give Ginny that one last gift had it not been for Mr. Spurlock's generosity.

Since then, I've looked for ways to help others to be givers. At my summer yard sale, for instance, a little girl asked me the price of a gold-framed picture of a mother reading to her children snuggled on her lap. Spotting the quarter in her hand, I answered, "How about twenty-five cents?"

"My mama's birthday is today," she said with a grin as we completed the transaction. My spirits soared, and I breathed this prayer as the two of them headed home hand in hand:

Dear Lord, You are the Source of all gifts. Thank You for those who help us to be givers.   —Roberta Messner

13

WED *Water will gush forth in the wilderness and streams in the desert.*   —Isaiah 35:6 (NIV)

As our boys have grown older, I've moved from fishing trips to college search trips. Last summer, Nathan's desire to visit the large universities in Arizona came at a time when a lack of devotional reading and personal prayer had left me feeling particularly spiritually dry. During our tour of the University of Arizona in Tucson, I learned a lesson about dealing with dryness.

The student guide warned us that the temperature was 112 degrees so we needed to drink a lot of water during our walk around the immense campus. "You may not feel that you need a drink," he said, "but believe me, you do. The desert air draws the water out of you, and you don't know it because the dry heat keeps you from sweating."

Just an hour later, one young girl who had not paid attention to his warning fainted right in the middle of his description of the Student Health Center. With a little shade and some cool bottled water, she was fine in just a few minutes. The guide didn't need to repeat his warning again; every drinking fountain along the way was well visited.

I was struck by the parallel between what I was feeling spiritually and the effect of the desert. I was feeling faint, not realizing that life's pressures had drawn the vitality right out of me, and I hadn't known the remedy was simply to take more frequent sips of the cool, Living Water.

Lord, thanks for providing streams of living water able to refresh me in any desert.   —Eric Fellman

14
THU

In everything commending ourselves as servants of God, in much endurance, in afflictions, in hardship, in distresses. . . .   —II Corinthians 6:4 (NAS)

It was early evening. My husband Gene had gone to a meeting, so Mother and I were at home alone. I went to Mother's room to check on her. "Mother?"

"Here," she answered from the bathroom.

She was on the floor, half sitting up. I asked a stupid question: "What happened?"

"I've fallen and I can't get up," she replied in the voice of the woman in the TV commercial.

I sat down on the floor beside her, remembering the times my first husband Jerry had fallen when his brain tumor had made walking suddenly impossible. We had spent a lot of time on the floor.

"How long have you been here?"

"Maybe twenty minutes."

"If you can lie down on that towel, I think I can pull you into your bedroom." She held on with all her might, and I pulled with all of mine. She wanted to get out of her clothes and into a gown. We huffed and puffed and managed that, but she was still on the floor.

"Do you think you're hurt?"

"No, I believe I'm better. I think the fall helped something in my back." Then she added, "I'm not senile, am I?"

"No, you definitely aren't."

"But I'm not much better after radiation. What are you going to do with me?" A suggestion of fear appeared around her eyes.

"I'm going to put you in the attic!"

Relief and the hint of a smile quickly replaced the fear. We made five attempts to get her up. I wondered why I felt so calm; maybe it was because she seemed so calm.

"You always did fall well, Mother."

"Thank you." She shot me a smile.

On the sixth try, she made it up onto a chair, and then she stood in her walker.

"Don't you want to go to bed?"

"No, I want to sit in the living room. It's such a pretty room."

So she sat in the living room. I covered her with her favorite white blanket, and she was soon asleep.

Lord, when I reach the limits of my strength, help me rest uncomplainingly in Your peace. —Marion Bond West

15
FRI

But other [seed] fell into good ground, and brought forth fruit, some a hundredfold, some sixtyfold, some thirtyfold. —Matthew 13:8

When my wife Rosie and I returned to Mendenhall in 1971, we worked in the youth ministry. Many of the young people we worked with became frequent guests at our house. When they went off to college, we would visit them regularly, and Rosie would often bake cookies for them so that they could get a taste of home at their far-away schools.

I received a phone call one day not long ago from one of those young people, Derek Perkins, inviting me to speak at a national Christian youth conference in Pasadena, California. I really wanted to attend the conference. But when I looked at my schedule, I realized that the conference date was close to our twenty-fifth wedding anniversary. I talked to Rosie about it, and we agreed that we should go. We had planned to take a trip to Mexico to celebrate our anniversary, and it wasn't difficult to adjust our airline reservations to fit in the trip to California.

Derek introduced me when I spoke at the conference. Because his own father, John Perkins, the founder of our ministry, had to travel so much, Derek said, I had become a second father and big brother to him. "After my mother and father, Dolphus Weary is the man most responsible for my being who I am today," Derek told the young people. "I hope I can have the same kind of influence on some of you."

I was astonished. I had no idea of the influence our relationship had had on Derek. And I was reminded that working with young people is one of the most important things I can do, because it helps to make the world's future. It may have results that I can only come to know years later, if at all. It's up to me to plant the seeds; God will give the increase.

God, today, help me to plant seeds of faith and hope in the lives of the young.
—Dolphus Weary

16
SAT

For all have sinned and fall short of the glory of God. . . .
—Romans 3:23 (NIV)

When I was staying in North Carolina this past summer, several of the young people I made friends with were surfers. After a good deal of coaxing, they succeeded in persuading me to try surfing myself. I paddled out on the board, and after several attempts and a lot of coaching, I managed actually to catch a wave and ride it for what my friends say was at most a second.

Being up on the wave was a thrill, but what really amazed me about the experience was the fall. Suddenly, I was under the water, falling off the eight-foot wave. The water bubbled and churned around me, rolling me along at its will, until I was vaguely aware that the surface was somewhere to my right. In the midst of that fall, when I felt most helpless, I became aware of the power of God.

How many times have I "fallen" because I haven't depended on God? How many plans have I made, how many projects have I tried to organize that have fallen apart because I wanted to do them on my own? Sometimes those falls were just embarrassing; sometimes they were deeply humiliating. But I needed each and every one to bring me back to God, to show me that I must rely on Him. I'm learning to appreciate stumbling.

Lord, thank You for using our mistakes to draw us closer to You.
—Hollie Davis

WORDS OF WONDER

I Will Not Hurry

I will not hurry through this day!
Lord, I will listen by the way,
To humming bees and singing birds,
To speaking trees and friendly words;
And for the moments in between
Seek glimpses of Thy great Unseen.

I will not hurry through this day;
I will take time to think and pray;
I will look up into the sky,
Where fleecy clouds and swallows fly;
And somewhere in the day, maybe
I will catch whispers, Lord, from Thee!

RALPH SPAULDING CUSHMAN

17
SUN
Lord, now lettest thou thy servant depart in peace, according to thy word.   —Luke 2:29

"Andrew, the nursing home called. Your dad is back in the emergency room."

I set the telephone down and shook my head to clear away the cobwebs, although it was eleven A.M. Then I put the phone back to my ear.

"He's got some kind of internal bleeding, and the nursing home sent him back to the hospital. I'm going over there to see him." The hospital our priest was talking about was miles away, across the river in Brooklyn. I had called him from a booth outside a hospital in Manhattan, where my wife Julia had been in labor for five hours.

Dad was suffering from a battery of complaints: a broken hip; cancer; kidney failure; a deepening mental confusion and disorientation. Julia and I had been praying that he would live to see the baby, his first grandchild, but now that seemed impossible.

"Father," I asked, "please tell him the baby's on its way, and that I love him and I wish I could be with him."

Elizabeth Rose was born at four the next morning, pink and beautiful as the sunrise. I called Father Cullen to give him the good news and find out how Dad was doing.

"It was amazing," he said. "For just a moment, his confusion lifted. When I told him about the baby, he understood me. And he said, 'Tell them I bless the baby.' "

> *Just as I am, without one plea*
> *But that Thy blood was shed for me.*
> *And that Thou bidd'st me come to Thee.*
> *O Lamb of God, I come, I come.*

Every night, when I get sixteen-month-old Elizabeth ready for bed, I sing her that old Gospel song. She heard it for the first time when she was a week old, at her grandfather's funeral. He never got to see her or hold her, but he knew she was coming, and he left her the only gift he could give her—his love.

Father, thank You for the love that knits the generations together, here and in eternity.   —Andrew Attaway

18

MON   *The Lord is my shepherd; I shall not want.* —Psalm 23:1

This year, to mark two significant milestones in our lives, my husband Lynn and I planned a major celebration. Our milestones: turning fifty and entering the season of the "empty nest." The major celebration: a two-week trip to England with our good friends Wayne and Joyce, who were celebrating the same milestones. We'd never been there before. In fact, we'd never been away from home for two whole weeks.

We spent the first week in London, scurrying through museums and historical buildings. The second week we were in the Cotswolds, where we wandered for hours on friendly footpaths that crisscross the gentle rolling hills and lush green pastures, bordered by stone fences and dotted with grazing sheep.

On our first morning out, we stopped in a wooded area and each found a walking stick—ordinary branches, gnarly, sturdy and just the right length for each of us. Through the week, those walking sticks became our companions, going everywhere with us. We bonded to those sticks, and as we neared the end of our week, we talked of taking them back to Colorado.

On our last afternoon, we set out with our sticks for our final walk through the countryside and lingered to watch the sun set over the rim of a distant hill. In the waning light, we reluctantly retraced our steps through the pasture, paused to take one last look at the grazing sheep and then crossed over the last stone fence. On a whim, we decided to leave our four sticks there, leaning up against the fence, like an offering to the next travelers.

Now that we're back home in Colorado, I cherish the memory of leaving those sticks as a reminder of how God would have me face the passing seasons of my life: relishing each segment, celebrating the milestones of change and leaving behind what's been outgrown. That allows me to enter a new chapter with an open hand, ready to receive whatever God has in store for me.

Jesus, You are my shepherd, and as I enter a new season, I know that I shall not want.   —Carol Kuykendall

19

TUE   *For he is like a refiner's fire. . . .*   —Malachi 3:2

My husband George loved to build fires. Especially at our summer home on Lake Erie, where we had seven acres right by the water, and were given special permission to burn our trash.

One morning I noticed there were rainbows in the fire. Spurts of purple, green and vivid rose sprouted like flowers among the tongues of orange and gold. "What in the world are you burning?" I asked him.

"Oh, just some junk I found in the garage," he told me. "Trash, pure trash. All of it very dirty and useless."

He poked the fire and was rewarded by a fountain of leaping colors. "Mostly some old plastic containers of hair dye, cosmetics, dried up tubes of oil paint."

"No wonder!" I exclaimed. "They were intended to make somebody or something beautiful. And now just look! They're succeeding!"

Like *us*, we suddenly agreed. Like people, created in such innocence and beauty, so often getting lost, life-smeared, discouraged, forgotten . . . yet with God's beauty still somewhere within us, waiting to be salvaged, to burst into flame and flower again.

For the fire of God's love does not destroy, it purifies and cleanses. Like silver and gold, melted and molded by fire, we can be rebuilt to rise up stronger, finer, shining; no longer worthless, but precious, ready once again to contribute to the beauty of the world.

Dear Lord, let me recognize the value in every seeming throwaway. Let me see the beauty within, and stretch out my hand to help You light Your restoring fires.
                                                          —Marjorie Holmes

20
WED
God has given each of you some special abilities; be sure to use them to help each other. . . . —I Peter 4:10 (TLB)

One of the great highlights of our summer is when friends invite us to a concert under the stars at the famous Hollywood Bowl. They provide the box seats, and we bring the picnic dinner. It's an enchanted evening of friendship, food and glorious music.

One of my favorite concerts featured the extraordinary music of LeRoy Anderson. Two white-gloved, tuxedo-clad gentlemen came to center stage as featured artists. One stood at an elegant Grecian column on top of which was his small instrument; the other sat at a linen-covered bench, facing his. The conductor raised his baton and launched into the hilarious Anderson Concerto for Typewriter and Ding Bell. "Click, click, click, click," then "zing!" as the manual typewriter carriage was returned. "Click, click, click, click, zing!" The violins' strings sang, the brass was spectacular, but on cue the entire orchestra deferred to the one white-gloved finger that rang "ding" on the small, hotel-desk ding bell. The audience thundered their applause.

I was ecstatic! I, the musically nontalented, had found instruments I could play. Why, with a bit of practice, it is possible that one of my dreams could come true. I could play in a symphony orchestra. Thank heavens I haven't thrown out the old typewriter. And somewhere around the house, I know we have a ding bell!

Thank You, Lord, that however small or seemingly insignificant our gifts, You can weave them into Your glorious symphony.   —Fay Angus

21
THU   *The joy of the Lord is your strength.*   —Nehemiah 8:10

My Great Aunt Ella lived on a dairy farm in the rolling hills of Lancaster County, Pennsylvania. One day, when I was eight, I went to visit. Her faded brown eyes were clouded with the "blues" she got now and again. She stood at the old-fashioned wooden sink, her work-worn arms resting on the rim, a heavy sadness stooping her thick shoulders. I followed her gaze through the dark kitchen window to the sun-splashed field where Guernsey cows grazed, their eyes pools of contentment. Aunt Ella's lips were moving, as if in prayer.

Feeling helpless, I left her and went outside to the field, tramping through the fragrant tangle of grass and weeds, an ocean of sky overhead. *What could help Aunt Ella?* My eyes landed on a jeweled butterfly resting on a milkweed, as fragile and breathtaking as a touch of joy. *That's what she needs,* I thought. But when I reached for the butterfly, it flew away.

Disappointed, I returned to the kitchen. Aunt Ella was rolling pie dough, the sharp contours of her face softened, a tiny sparkle back in her eye. She smiled at me, patting a stool beside her. I climbed onto it, relieved that she'd found a glimmer of joy.

I remember that day vividly; its lesson is lodged in the shadowy part of me that sometimes gets depressed. If, like Aunt Ella, I look outward, away from the darkness in me, to God, I'll find a touch of joy, which is all I need to jump-start my soul. Whether it comes on the wings of a butterfly, the words of a prayer, or watching a child at play, it's there, in the pockets and folds of each day, fragile and strong.

Lord, teach me that joy is as close to me as You are.   —Shari Smyth

22
FRI
"I will turn their mourning into gladness; I will give them comfort and joy instead of sorrow."

—Jeremiah 31:13 (NIV)

Today is Ralph and Kristi's fifth anniversary. The week before their wedding, my wife and I had been having a fight about some old hurt that hadn't fully healed. We stood on opposite ends of our mutual wound, angry, stubborn and ready for trench warfare.

Then something happened. The day before the wedding, Kristi was rushed to the hospital. She had Guillain-Barré syndrome, a virus slowly paralyzing her from head to toe. She had awakened to find that her legs didn't work; her arms had gone numb by noon. If they couldn't stop the disease, she'd need a respirator soon.

The next day we filed into the chapel. Instead of a flower arrangement, the altar was decorated with a large-screen TV. Ralph and Kristi had wed earlier in her hospital room, and we were gathered here for the video replay. We watched as the bridesmaid read Kristi's vows for her, and Ralph, a man not known for tears, choked through his part, stopping twice to weep. Then the screen went blank. Stunned, we all retreated to the reception hall.

And then, odd as it sounds, we partied. We danced. Ralph's mom sang "Sunrise, Sunset." We danced some more. The best man ruined his rented tux with champagne and sweat. And somewhere in there, my wife and I laid down our weapons. No more pained looks or steely attitude. We danced the slow dances. The wound closed. It was as if we knew the stakes: Cherish each other this moment, because next week. . . .

Kristi recovered. The only lasting effect of the disease is a dizzy feeling when she plays too hard with her kids. Her oldest girl likes to play dress-up. When my wife and I bring our kids over to play, Kristi's daughter Molly disappears into her room and emerges in a wedding dress. And I see that wedding again, the one without the bride, when we finally understood how precious it all is.

Happy anniversary, guys. *L'chaim*—to life.

Lord, thank You for the gifts of love, unique and irreplaceable, which You have given me.   —Mark Collins

23
SAT

*Whatever you do, work at it with all your heart, as work-
ing for the Lord....*   —Colossians 3:23 (NIV)

I'd always wanted to learn how to swim, but just when I'd learned
the basics in a required swimming class in high school, I had a frightening setback. At the beach one day, two boys—strangers to me—
came rushing up, scooped me up by my arms and legs, and threw
me in the ocean. Even though I wasn't harmed, I became terrified
of the water.

For years after that, I wanted to swim, but I knew that it would
take more than practice to get me over my fears. So I prayed to have
my fear released, and even hunted down a swimming teacher who
had a strong faith. When I called to arrange a private lesson, I felt
relieved when she said, "I always pray with my students—it allevi-
ates fear." I suppose I pictured the two of us praying for the first hour.
But when I met her, things were different.

"Hi!" Patty said, smiling and taking my hand. "Where's your
swimsuit? And your bathing cap?"

"My—" I stumbled over my words. "I didn't think I needed to
bring them. I thought we were going to pray!"

Patty laughed. "Linda, we *are*—but we're also going to swim!" She
gave me some instructions (and I'll admit they didn't sound very
"spiritual" to me!): "Go out and buy a bathing cap. Go out and buy
a swimsuit. Put on your bathing cap and swimsuit and get into the
pool every opportunity you get. And practice what I teach you every
single day. *Then* pray!"

After weeks of prayer and practice, I finally, fearlessly, swam across
the pool!

*Lord, when I need Your help with some task today, let me pray to You—
and then get to work.*   —Linda Neukrug

24
SUN

*Be careful for nothing, but in everything ... let your re-
quests be made known unto God.*   —Philippians 4:6

"I'm worried," I told my friend Virginia. "Our old car is about to take
its last gasp, but with all our other bills, we can't afford a replacement. Or anything else, for that matter. How will we ever manage?
We need a new roof, too. If God really is preparing a place for His
followers, we could use one right down here!"

"Tell the Lord," Virginia answered. "He can be trusted to take care of all your needs."

I wasn't convinced, so I tactfully changed the subject to the neighborhood party we'd both attended the night before. That summer evening, one of our next-door neighbors had invited everyone on the block to a potluck at their place. We adults had sat and chatted while our kids raced around and played noisy games.

It was not until Virginia and I finished our visit that I suddenly recalled something that had happened at the close of the previous evening's get-together. As darkness came the children's commotion diminished and, one by one, they tired. Our three-year-old John crawled into his father's lap. He quickly fell asleep, as did several others his age, so the party soon ended.

Instead of waking John, my husband carried the sleeping boy to our house. While we were readying him for bed, he drowsily came to, looked around and then asked, "How did I get here?"

"Daddy carried you home," my husband answered.

Why should I ever worry, Lord, when I have such a caring heavenly Father.
—Isabel Wolseley

25
MON

Train up a child in the way he should go: and when he is old, he will not depart from it. —Proverbs 22:6

Rummaging through the remnants of an estate sale, I came across a box of letters grown yellow with age. One letter was written in 1910 by a twelve-year-old boy about his father. As I read the letter, I resolved that this young boy's thoughts would not be destroyed by time.

My father has influenced me most. He has a good disposition and is very mild. He is firm and means what he says, is just and honest.

I have many reasons for liking him. He is kind to me and only harsh when I deserve it. He never whips me, but talks to me, which does me more good than a whipping. He gives me money to spend and takes me places with him, which I enjoy very much. I am sure nobody could be any kinder to me than he is.

If it is to be that I shall live to be a man of twenty-one, I hope I shall have all the traits of my father.

This boy grew up to become a prominent judge and community leader. His aspirations to be like his father made him a great man.

I purchased the letter for a dollar and framed it. It reminds me that the most important thing that I can give to my children is my example.

Dear Father, keep before me this day Your example as revealed through Your Son Jesus Christ. Amen. —Scott Walker

26
TUE   *He that doeth good is of God. . . .*   —III John 11

Since we began taking walks every summer morning at 5:30, my daughter Keri and I have made a discovery. A sort of subculture comes to life on the streets of our neighborhood at that early hour.

Rounding the first corner, we expect to meet Stick Man. We call him that because he always carries a big hiking stick to ward off the more ambitious dogs. Next we see Manners Man. "Good morning, ladies," he always says with a courtly nod. Then there are the Talking Ladies. They walk fast, talking to each other, and never seem to notice us. Bicycle Man is also a regular. But our favorite early-morning character is an affable man whom we've come to call Christian. We call him that because he often wears shirts with religious logos on them.

Christian has a unique habit that Keri and I have come to admire. Some of the walkers and runners carry weights. One man, Coffee Man—well, you can guess what he carries! But Christian always has a large bag in tow. We have seen him stop to pick up everything from a tiny nail to a six-pack of empty beer bottles.

The more sensible people who sleep late drive off to work or take later walks along clean, unlittered streets. None of them knows that Christian has been there before them, quietly making the neighborhood better without any fanfare or thought of recognition.

Father, I am a Christian by name; let me also be a Christian by habit.
—Pam Kidd

27
WED   *A time to laugh. . . .*   —Ecclesiastes 3:4

Yesterday, my fifteen-year-old and I were shopping for school clothes. I was tired and grumpy, and I had a sore foot. As I hobbled out of Ross's Dress For Less, Blake asked, "Want a piggyback ride?"

My first inclination was to decline. But then I thought, *why not?*

He squatted low just as I used to do for him. I lunged up onto his back just the way he used to lunge up on mine. Then he hefted me high with a bounce and jogged on down the parking lot, with me squealing and uncertain and hanging on for dear life. Suddenly, he started to whirl in circles. I found myself spinning around and around, screaming my head off with exhilaration!

Blake, surprised at my delight and laughing at my foolish fears of being dropped, carted me all the way to the car and very gently set me down. "Mum, you're so silly."

He was secretly pleased, of course, that he'd jarred me out of my doldrums. I was, too. Because while driving to the next store, looking for those elusive jeans he wanted, I realized that the task no longer seemed so exasperating. And my sore foot didn't hurt as much either—at least, it didn't bother me as much. I had forgotten the energy of play and the bond forged by shared laughter!

Thank You, God, for the gift of laughter. Help me to remember to sprinkle in playtime while doing my chores.   —Brenda Wilbee

28
THU *The wolf and the lamb will feed together, and the lion will eat straw like the ox. . . .*
—Isaiah 60:25 (NIV)

My friend Bernice was distraught over her impending divorce. "There are times when I don't feel very lovable," she confided. "The thing is, sometimes I don't act very lovable."

I had no reply. Many times I, too, have needed to be loved, yet I've acted in ways that deserved just the opposite.

That afternoon, browsing in a local store, I saw a pair of white ceramic salt and pepper shakers shaped like kneeling angels holding lambs. I thought a gift might cheer Bernice up, so I hastily bought a pair without opening the box or undoing the bubble wrap the shakers were packed in.

The next morning, when I started to wrap the gift, something told me to take the angels out of their box and look at them. The pepper shaker came out first, just as I'd remembered it from the display—a sweet, tranquil lamb gently cradled in an angel's arms.

Then out came the salt shaker. Something wasn't right about it:

There was a long, skinny tail hanging down over the angel's sleeve; the animal's face didn't look pointed enough and its ears were too upright and rounded. Then I looked at the animal's feet hanging over the angel's arm. They were definitely round-toed paws, not hooves! This angel was placidly and lovingly holding a lion cub.

I wrapped the gift and drove straight to Bernice's. When she opened the box, I said, "Look, Bernice. One of these angels is holding a lamb, the other is holding an unruly lion cub. Whether we're lions or lambs, the angels aren't afraid to hold us in their arms."

Thank You, Lord, for wrapping me in Your arms, even when I'm not very lovable.   —Karen Barber

29 *There is a right time for everything: A time to be born, a*
FRI *time to die. . . .*   —Ecclesiastes 3:1–2 (TLB)

We lived together for thirteen years, my dog Clay and I. He was four months old when he came to me, afraid to take a step on a New York sidewalk, ignorant about how to climb a staircase, but in no time he was running with me through Central Park. My little Honda became his kennel and his means of seeing the world; my apartment was our home, the foot of my bed his resting place, night or day.

The years went by. The time came when his arthritis prevented him from climbing onto our bed, and I would feel his cold nose summoning me to get up again to lift him. By then, well-intentioned friends were saying, "He's in pain." And I would look at him and see that he was not complaining—and I couldn't think the unthinkable.

Summer came, and a hot Sunday night in August. A sound wakened me. Clay was not at the foot of the bed. I went into the living room. He lay there panting in a circle of wetness expanding on the carpet. He raised his head and looked at me; a long, telling look.

I lifted him up and took him to the Honda, and we drove through the empty streets. At Sixty-fourth Street a hospital waited, and though it was two o'clock, a friendly woman was on duty. She led him away. I never saw him alive again.

I miss him to this day, and yet I cannot grieve, for in that look he gave me was the knowledge that his time had come. God gives His creatures a finite span of years. We're fortunate if we've used them well. And so I think of thirteen years in which I was given patience and loyalty that I didn't always deserve but accepted as willingly as Clay took to a Frisbee.

Thank You, Father, for the gift of dogs. Their stay with us is short, but their gifts remain our whole life long.   —Van Varner

30 *You have taken off your old self . . . and have put on the* **SAT** *new self, which is being renewed in knowledge in the image of its Creator.*   —Colossians 3:9–10 (NIV)

"The fall ham class starts next week . . ." My husband Bill let the sentence hang in the air.

For several years he had quietly been asking me to join him in his hobby of amateur radio. The whole idea seemed overwhelming to me: Bill understood things like picofarads and wavelengths; I did not. But this year the hole in our marriage loomed large. We were growing apart. Bill had his interests, I had mine. Maybe God was nudging me, sending me a message to take this first step.

Reluctantly, I signed up for the ten-week course. I understood a little, cried a lot, memorized the answers for the written test and passed the Morse code. When my novice license arrived, I was still wondering how I was going to use my new skills.

My first two months as a ham were uneventful. I couldn't work up the courage actually to talk to anyone. Then one day I found myself alone in our family room with our small, long-distance radio. Above the static, I heard someone calling "CQ! CQ!" over and over. I knew this meant that the caller was looking for someone—anyone—to talk to. Gingerly, I picked up the microphone and gave my call sign: "This is KA3VNK!"

From the moment that ham in Texas responded, I was hooked, and in the next two months, I talked to people in more than sixty countries. I still don't understand wavelengths and picofarads, but the communications skills I've gained have enriched my life in countless ways. And I'm communicating better with my husband, too. Joining Bill in something that means so much to him has brought a new sense of sharing into our marriage.

I'm glad that when God transmitted His message, I received His signal!

Thank You, Lord, for challenging me to grow and grow closer to those I love.   —Roberta Rogers

31 *For now we see through a glass, darkly. . . .*

—I Corinthians 13:12

"Has anyone seen my sunglasses?" I asked plaintively, going from room to room in the old Virginia house where we were spending Labor Day weekend. A chorus of "No" that sounded more like "Not again" came from various family members and guests. A beautiful day—and I needed those sunglasses badly.

"I'll go and get the paper," I volunteered, and I drove into the nearby town. Only the convenience store was open that Sunday morning. They had a big stack of papers and—relief—two pairs of sunglasses by the cash register. I took the smaller pair and cheerfully paid $4.50.

In the car I scratched off the price sticker and put them on. The world was suddenly transformed. I hadn't looked at them closely, but the mirrored glasses turned out to be tinted yellow and transformed everything around me into a world lit by surreal, glare-free sunlight.

Driving slowly back along the same country road, I marveled at how different everything looked. The trees seemed green and fresh, the red barn in need of paint looked picturesque instead of shabby. I decided that I liked this view much better than the somber, muted green landscape of my lost glasses. It sparkled with possibilities.

New sunglasses were such a small thing to make so large a change. But sometimes that is all it takes: Looking at life through fresh lenses can make all the difference.

Lord, may we continually see life afresh and wonder at its blessings.

                                                    —Brigitte Weeks

Everyday Wonders

1 _____

2 _____

3 _____

4 _____

5 _____

6 _____

7 _____

8 _____

9 _____

10 _____

11 _____

12 _____

13 _____

14 _____

15 _____

16 _____

17 _____

18 _____

19 _____

20 _____

21 _____

22 _____

23 _____

24 _____

25 _____

26 _____

27 _____

28 _____

29 _____

30 _____

31 _____

We love him, because he first loved us. —I JOHN 4:19

September

S	M	T	W	T	F	S
	1	2	3	4	5	6
7	8	9	10	11	12	13
14	15	16	17	18	19	20
21	22	23	24	25	26	27
28	29	30				

1
_{MON} **LOVE IS . . .**

Love is patient. . . . —I Corinthians 13:4 (NIV)

I thought of Len LeSourd, my boss for many years at *Guideposts* magazine, when I set out for a walk recently with my two-year-old grandson. *I* set out for a walk, that is. I was headed for the park down the street where there are ducks and a sandbox and a swing set.

But at the end of the driveway there was a white stone that Spencer had to sit on. A few feet away, a puddle to step in. A blue jay feather, a blown dandelion, the ring from a pop-top can . . . and we'd almost reached the driveway next door!

Patience is a gift of God to parents and grandparents, but the patience I found myself remembering was Len's. He had long since set out on the walk of faith, and how he must have wanted me to get on to the great things that lay ahead. Yet he never pressured me to move faster than I was ready to go.

When I came to the magazine in 1951, I was like Spencer, stuck at the start of the journey, tracing and retracing the same few steps, stopped by trifles, giving my attention to the details and not the goal.

"I don't have your kind of faith," I'd say, as I listed the stumbling blocks holding me back.

Len didn't argue, didn't knock down my objections. With the serenity of faith, he had a single reply. "I can wait, Tib. I can wait."

God of Love, on this Labor Day, I'm grateful for those in every workplace who, like Len, point the way to You. —Elizabeth Sherrill

2
_{TUE} *Whatever you task, work heartily, as serving the Lord. . . .* —Colossians 3:23 (RSV)

Judging by the number of people I know who have voluntarily made mid-life career changes, there must be a lot of unfulfilled folks in the workplace. So I am always eager to hear about workers who have found their true calling and are passionate about it.

Not long ago, on a trip to Africa, I met a man who seemed to be consummately happy with his occupation. I came upon him in Mombassa, Kenya, on the Indian Ocean, at a famous woodcarving center. Hundreds of carvers were gathered there, paring, sawing, filing,

and sanding blocks of mahogany and ebony into animated treasures—trumpeting elephants, stalking lions, charging rhinos. They
all seemed to be talented artisans, but one carver's enthusiasm made
him stand out. Sitting cross-legged on the ground beneath a canvas
fly to protect him from the hot sun, he was a sanding dervish. Saw-
dust wrapped him in a tawny cloud as he put the finishing touches
on a magnificently detailed bull elephant.

"That's a beautiful piece of work," I told him. Then, noticing
more unfinished elephantine-shaped blocks at his feet, I asked if he
carved any other animals.

"I only do elephants," he replied, smiling, "because elephants are
what I do best."

What a treasure to know one's calling and be satisfied in it! And
for those of us still searching, I know one thing for sure: We can serve
God by serving others wherever we are. He may have some other place
for you and me tomorrow—a larger role, a more important station, a
more exciting task—but today He asks us to be faithful where we are.

> *Through Your wisdom and Your grace,*
> *Show me, Lord, my serving place.*

—Fred Bauer

3
WED

*I will hope continually, and will yet praise thee more
and more.*   —Psalm 71:14

Today, John and I celebrate our fortieth wedding anniversary. That
means that for 14,600 mornings, give or take a few, I have sipped
my coffee out of a fine bone china cup decorated with pale lavender
prairie crocus, the official flower of the province of Manitoba,
Canada.

The cups were a wedding gift from John's Aunt Belle. "The crocus is the first flower that pushes up through the snow," John had
explained as I carefully lifted them out of their tissue-paper wrapping.
"It's a symbol of hope, that winter will soon be past and the new life
of spring is just around the corner."

"How beautiful." I traced my fingers over the delicate, etched
flowers. "Perfect for my morning coffee." And so began my marriage,
with a promise of hope put into each new day by Aunt Belle's crocus cups.

I had crocus cup in hand as dawn crept over our Sierra Madre hills and I nervously timed the contractions that were coming swift and fierce. I shook John awake. "This is it. The baby's coming." That afternoon, our first child, a daughter, was born! "Grow her gentle and strong, like the prairie flower," I prayed.

The day of the terrifying 6.9 earthquake, my hands were once again wrapped around the small lavender flowers of Aunt Belle's china cup. The chimney toppled, walls cracked, and a suffocating, blinding dust rose from the shaken earth. An icy fear froze my heart. I sent up a prayer like a small quivering shoot reaching desperately for the sun. Thank God, the family was okay.

Aunt Belle died four years ago. But now, sipping coffee from the last of her crocus cups (the others having long since broken), I still think of her daily. In good times and in bad, her prairie flowers have put praise and hope into each new day.

When fear and uncertainty ice over my heart, dear Lord, let me reach up to the sunshine of Your loving care.   —Fay Angus

4

THU   *They will still bear fruit in old age, they will stay fresh and green.*   —Psalm 92:14 (NIV)

When I was in the first grade, we lived in a rented house on a farm and I walked several miles to school. The house had neither running water nor electricity, and I do not remember there being books of any kind. My first writing was done with a pencil on paper from my much-prized Big Chief tablet, a Christmas gift that had cost a whole nickel.

Now I write on a computer and save my work on floppy disks. But it's not always easy. Every now and again, all sorts of things I didn't plan on appear on the screen and I can't figure out how to erase them. Sometimes the computer won't talk to the printer. And every so often, a few hours of hard work seem to disappear completely into outer cyberspace.

So what keeps me from unplugging everything and reverting to my Big Chief tablet? The thought of a friend's grandchildren writing their term papers on a computer; my engineer son Troy's excitement about getting me plugged into the information superhighway and his promise to help; the enthusiasm of a retired acquaintance who enrolled in a computer class at seventy.

It's a challenge to master the skills that will enable me to use my computer effectively. But if I want to keep going, I've got to keep growing. Maybe it's time for me to connect my fax and learn how to use the modem.

Father, help me to be constantly learning new things, which enrich the life You gave me.   —Kenneth Chafin

5
FRI
As we have therefore opportunity, let us do good unto all. . . .   —Galatians 6:10

I had just returned home from raking leaves and mowing lawns. I was bone weary, yet I smiled when Mother opened the kitchen door and the aroma of baked beans and corn bread rushed out to meet me. "A Miss Rosetta Davidson will be coming up from New York to spend two weeks with us in September," Mother said.

I frowned. Two young lady guests, schoolteachers from New York, had just left, and their visit had been tense. They seemed to be bored and disappointed. "This town is too quiet," one of them had said. "I'll be glad to get back to New York, where people are civilized," her companion replied.

I made up my mind that I'd be pleasant, but that I'd give Miss Davidson a wide berth. She arrived on a September afternoon that was chilly even for Williamstown. That evening we all sat in the kitchen and talked. Miss Davidson appeared to feel at home. She told us that she was a secretary and that she had heard about us from an engineer who had stayed at our home.

After Miss Davidson had been with us for a few days, Mother told me, "If you ask her to go to the movies with you, I think she'll say yes." I was eighteen and very shy. I trembled as I asked Miss Davidson to go with me, and I was overjoyed when she accepted. We went to see *Showboat*, and after the movie stopped to enjoy ice cream sodas. On the way home we talked, and I felt completely at ease. It was my first date with a young lady.

The next week was magical. On Sunday, Miss Davidson sat next to me at church, and when I returned to school, she helped me with my homework. By the time she returned to New York, I had grown very fond of her.

If I had avoided Miss Davidson because of the way two other New Yorkers had behaved, I'd have missed out on a lovely friendship, and on a memory as rich as the aroma of Mother's cooking.

Lord, thank You for teaching me to treat each person as precious and unique.   —Oscar Greene

6
SAT

Beloved, it is a loyal thing you do when you render any ser-vice to the brethren. . . .   —III John 5 (RSV)

When Baltimore Orioles shortstop Cal Ripken, Jr. broke Lou Gehrig's record for most consecutive games played (2,131), I read several articles about other great sports feats. But the one that stayed in my mind was about offbeat records, the ones that don't get world-wide publicity. Like the Englishman who ran nearly thirty miles in four hours and eighteen minutes—while balancing a fresh egg on a spoon. Or the man who holds the record for standing still, more than fifteen hours. How about 177,000 consecutive pogo-stick jumps? Or the woman who walked seventy miles balancing a milk bottle on her head?

It all makes me think about the "record holders" I know who also don't get the recognition they deserve. Like my friend Joann, who by calling and saying, "Can I have the kids this afternoon?" has come to my rescue more times than anyone. Or Grandma Hazel, who's cooked more meals and baked more cookies for lonely church new-comers than the record keepers could count. Or a man I know who surely caused a record number of smiles and giggles when he sent a box of toys and clothes to a family who had recently lost everything in a fire.

The feats of these people may not make any record books, but if statistics were kept for the works our Lord most values, like love, gen-erosity and compassion, they, and others like them—surely some you know—would go down in history.

Dear God, continue to bless and strengthen the record holders in our daily lives, and gently remind us to thank them for their selfless achievements.
                                                        —Gina Bridgeman

7
SUN

"Rise in the presence of the aged, show respect for the el-derly and revere your God. . . ."   —Leviticus 19:32 (NIV)

I could feel my grip tightening around the steering wheel. I was in Ohio on business, and that day I had driven more than three hun-dred miles, meeting with different prospects in banks along the way. I just wanted to go back to my hotel room and crash. But that wasn't possible. Knowing that I was going to be in Cincinnati that night, I had arranged to take my grandmother out to dinner. Now I wished that I hadn't.

Because she lived in Ohio and we lived in Tennessee, Dad, Mom, Keri and I only saw her once or twice a year. It was always great to be with her, but I had never spent time alone with her. To be honest, I felt too tired to go through the courtesies that are necessary when you're around someone you don't see often.

I located the retirement complex where my grandmother lives, and the look on her face as the door swung open made me glad that I had come. After "Mam-ma" asked about my day and pulled some worries from me, I felt my anxiety beginning to dissolve. She was interested in me. Really interested. Without the slightest effort, she was the one exercising courtesies, and I felt much better. We talked about everything from investing, to politics, to faith. Soon the two of us were joking about the weekly get-togethers she enjoys with her friends, cards flying, laughter floating, rotating from one person's apartment to the next.

As we went out for dinner arm in arm, I discovered that a really wonderful person had been at the edge of my life for twenty-three years. If I have my way in years ahead, Mam-ma will move closer to the center.

Lord, on this Grandparents Day, knit together the hearts of grandchildren and grandparents. —Brock Kidd

JEHOVAH JIREH: GOD WILL PROVIDE

Last year, when her seventeen-year-old daughter Kendall faced an unusual health problem, Carol Kuykendall faced the challenge of trying to help her through it. The experience seemed filled with painful contradictions: yearning to take charge and change the circumstances, yet recognizing her helplessness; wanting to model strong faith, while sometimes questioning her own trust in God; sympathizing with Kendall's pain, while enduring the pain of watching her suffer. Yet as Carol looks back on their daily struggles through that dark experience, she sees how God provided for them each step along the way . . . and she is touched by the wonders of His love. Je-

hovah Jireh—*those are the words that Abraham spoke on the top of Mount Moriah when he realized how powerfully God meets us in our struggles and provides for our needs when we surrender to Him.*   —The Editors

8

God Provides . . . Knowns in the Unknown

"For I am going to do something in your days that you would not believe, even if you were told."   —Habakkuk 1:5 (NIV)

I walked by the patio door on the Saturday of Labor Day weekend and saw my seventeen-year-old daughter Kendall sitting in the sun, reading a history book and running her fingers through her long blonde hair. "Mom, my hair is falling out," she called to me, and sure enough, as I got close, I could see several strands hanging limply from her fingers.

"Oh, don't worry," I assured her nonchalantly. "We all shed some hair at the end of the summer."

Kendall had just started her senior year of high school. She's our youngest, the last one living at home, and she looked forward to this busy year, with all the privileges and traditions of being a senior. She was a co-captain of her varsity basketball team, in several choirs at school and church, and involved in many other activities. She planned to study lots over this long weekend because she wanted to do well in some tough classes. Yet all weekend, as she sat reading or talking on the telephone, I saw her running her fingers through her hair.

Then on Monday evening, as we drove home from a Labor Day picnic with friends, I saw a large bald spot on the side of her head.

"What's the matter?" she demanded as she noticed my reaction. And then she looked in the car mirror and burst into tears.

We all knew something was terribly wrong, but since it was about ten P.M. when we got home, we decided to wait until morning to call a doctor.

"It will be all right," I tried to assure Kendall, but she dragged out our old cot and sleeping bag, as she used to when she was a little girl and felt sick or frightened and wanted to sleep in our room. She set it up next to our bed and pulled the sleeping bag up around her like a cocoon. Her dad and I said a prayer with her and then turned out the light. She reached for my hand in the dark and soon fell asleep.

But I did not. All I could think of were my fears of the unknown, which started to grow huge in the darkness.

After what seemed like hours, I sensed a simple command: *When faced with what you don't know, cling to what you do know.* So I began to recall, one by one, the knowns in the midst of all the unknowns, and finally fell asleep with these thoughts in my mind:

Father, I don't know what tomorrow will bring, but this is what I do know: that You love us. You will never leave us. You have gone before us. You are sufficient to meet our needs. —Carol Kuykendall

9
TUE   **God Provides . . . A Mountaintop Promise**

"Come to me, all you who are weary and burdened, and I will give you rest."   —Matthew 11:28 (NIV)

The doctor peered intently at Kendall's scalp with a magnifying glass, asked a few questions, then stepped back and used some words we'd never heard before.

"It's an autoimmune disease called *alopecia areata,*" he said. "For some unknown reason, Kendall's immune system has started attacking her hair follicles. At best, she'll get only patchy bald spots. At worst, it could mean total loss of body hair. Sometimes the hair grows back. Sometimes it does not. Sometimes it starts all over again, even if it grows back. It's a baffling condition. Though it is not life-threatening, it is life-altering. There is no known cause and no cure and no way to predict what course it will take in Kendall's case. We'll merely have to wait and see."

Later, walking back across the parking lot, Kendall's eyes filled with the tears she'd held back in the doctor's office. "I'm scared, Mom. What if I lose all my hair?"

"You won't, but we'll pray and we'll manage, Kendall," I said as I hugged her, feeling the tension of balancing possibilities with faith and encouragement. We'd brought two cars since she had come from school and I had come from work, so we climbed into our separate vehicles. As I drove ahead of her, I could see her in my rearview mirror, looking at herself in her mirror, lifting and touching her hair. She looked so sad, but I couldn't reach her to comfort her. I felt totally helpless.

As a mother, I'd been in this place before—up against circumstances I couldn't control or change—and I knew what I had to do. I had to surrender this child and the outcome of this problem to God, just as Abraham surrendered his son Isaac to God on the top of Mount Moriah. Abraham was called by God to surrender his child as a sacrifice. To prove that he trusted God, he trudged up the mountain with his son. Just as the boy was about to die, God provided a substitute sacrifice, a ram caught in the bushes nearby. Abraham called that mountain *Jehovah Jireh,* "God will provide," a powerful promise to parents like me.

Just before I turned the corner into our driveway, I prayed:

Father, I surrender my child to You. The outcome of this problem is uncertain, but I trust You, and know that even if we face our worst fears, You will provide. Please help me to keep my eyes wide open for those provisions along the way.   —Carol Kuykendall

10
WED   **God Provides . . . Tools Along the Way**

"But take this staff in your hand so you can perform miraculous signs with it."   —Exodus 4:17 (NIV)

Over the next few days, Kendall continued to lose her hair, and we began to deal with the reality of living with this strange disease. The mornings seemed the worst: waking her up when sleep protected her from remembering; encouraging her to get ready for school when she begged to stay home; trying to assure her that she looked nice as she walked out of the door, wearing an old baseball cap pulled down to her ears. As we began this journey, I felt confused about my role. *What am I supposed to surrender, Lord? What am I supposed to do?*

I shared my question with a co-worker one morning when she asked about Kendall.

"I think God expects us to pick out the parts of a prayer that we can control and surrender what we can't control to Him," she said. "And He certainly expects us to use the tools He places in our paths along the way."

I thought of her words all afternoon. Abraham surrendered his child to God, but he took charge of some of the circumstances, which made the journey easier. He took along his donkey and a couple of servants and an ax to chop the wood. Undoubtedly, he chose the best route up the mountain, and decided how long to travel each day.

I, too, could take charge of some things to make our journey more comfortable. I could take Kendall to buy some more hats this afternoon, and even start finding out about wigs. I could gather information from other people who have lived with this disease. I could contact her teachers and school counselor to keep them informed. And I could keep my own calendar of obligations to a minimum so that I could be more available to her. I couldn't control the outcome; I had to surrender that to God. But I could pick out some parts that I could control, and use the tools He provided to make the journey easier for Kendall.

Father, grant me the wisdom to see Your provision of tools along this path.
—Carol Kuykendall

11
THU   **God Provides . . . Through His Promises**

He will not let your foot slip. . . .   —Psalm 121:3 (NIV)

"Does God even care?" Kendall asked when I found her sitting alone on the floor of the family room on a Saturday night. She'd stayed home from the high school football game because she didn't feel like going anywhere. "Is He mad at me because I'm not learning something that He's trying to teach me? Is that why this keeps getting worse?"

I sat down beside her, and we both leaned back against the couch while I tried to convince her that God loved her. But I could tell that I wasn't getting through.

"I just don't think God cares," she said as she got up and went into her bedroom and closed the door. Her faith seemed to be dwindling because she didn't believe God loved her anymore. It was not my words she needed, but His.

So I got up early the next morning and searched the Bible for just one comforting reminder of His love that I could give her for the day.

"When you pass through the waters, I will be with you. . . . When you walk through the fire, you will not be burned," I found in Isaiah 43:2 (NIV). I wrote it on a yellow "stickee" and posted it on her bathroom mirror.

The morning after that, I did the same thing. "After you have suffered a little while, [the God of all grace] will himself restore you" (I Peter 5:10, NIV). This yellow stickee went on her backpack.

The next day, I found "For I know the plans I have for you . . . plans to give you hope and a future" (Jeremiah 29:11, NIV).

As I posted these yellow stickees on her calendar or history book or the bagel in her lunch bag, I prayed they would remind her that God cared for her. I couldn't tell right away if they were making a difference, but sometimes I found them gathered together in a pile by her bed.

I discovered something else, too. The process was making a difference for me! As I looked for reminders of God's love in the Bible each morning and wrote them down for Kendall, they became provisions for me, too, like toeholds of stability on the side of a slippery mountain as I walked alongside her.

Father, Your promises of love are powerful and nurturing provisions. Thank You.   —Carol Kuykendall

12
FRI   **God Provides . . . Safe Places of Comfort**

A voice was heard in Rameh . . . Rachel weeping for her children. . . .   —Jeremiah 31:15

I stood at the counter of a small photography studio one clear autumn afternoon. "I've come to pick up Kendall Kuykendall's senior pictures," I told the lady.

"Sit down," she said warmly, with a gesture toward a round table. "My husband usually takes care of this, so it might take me a minute to find your order." She disappeared into the back while I seated myself in the empty room.

"What a blessing you had her pictures taken before all this happened," many friends had told me. I agreed. But this still seemed a bittersweet task. Kendall had asked me to pick up the pictures because she could not bear walking into this place where she had come only a month earlier, when life had been so different.

The lady reappeared with a large envelope. "Here we are, I think," she said as she sat down beside me and spread the pictures across the table. "Is this your daughter?" she asked. I looked into about thirty radiant faces of Kendall, with sparkling eyes and a joyful smile I hadn't seen for weeks. The reality of the difference shocked me. And so did my response. I cried.

The lady looked surprised, but she reached for my hand as my tears came flowing out. And this kind stranger just let me cry. Finally, I regained my composure and told her about Kendall.

"I'm glad you could cry," she said with a gentle smile as she gathered the pictures back into the envelope and handed it to me. I wrote out the check, thanked her and left.

It all happened so quickly, but I carried the memory of God's provision of comfort with me for days; a total stranger, who wasn't even supposed to be there, who gave me a safe place to cry.

Father, You know when and where we need safe havens to cry. Thank You.
                                                        —Carol Kuykendall

13
_{SAT}   **God Provides . . . Answers to Prayers**

My peace I give unto you. . . .   —John 14:27

Early one morning, I walked through a park in our neighborhood. Dry yellow leaves floated down from the trees, and I felt an edge of nippiness in the air. Usually, I love autumn, but this year everything looked parched and lifeless to me.

I'd started off on this walk with some tough questions for God. Friends all over the country were praying for Kendall, but still her condition progressed unmercifully. She had dropped out of most of her activities at school, and in spite of some counseling, she'd grown frighteningly quiet. It seemed like our family was trying to navigate in the middle of a raging storm, and God's silence felt like total abandonment.

When the raging storm battered the boat on the Sea of Galilee and the disciples were frightened, Jesus calmed the storm and changed the circumstances. Why won't You calm our storm of difficulties? Why won't You answer our prayer for peace? I asked God as I walked. Again, I sensed no answer. So when I got home, I opened my Bible in search of the description of Jesus and the storm, and I made a surprising discovery. There are two descriptions of storms on the Sea of Galilee with the disciples. In the first, Jesus calms the storm. In the second, Jesus stands on the shore and watches the disciples suffer. Finally, He walks out across the water to them, but He doesn't immediately calm the waters. He calms the disciples instead.

Suddenly, the truth hit me. Sometimes Jesus brings peace by changing the circumstances, by calming the storm. Other times He allows the storm to rage and changes His children by giving them strength in the midst of the circumstances. Over the next few days, as I began to apply that truth to our storm of difficulties, I started seeing some subtle answers to prayers. The sound of Kendall's laughter while talking on the phone one day. Her answer to a cousin's question of "How are you?"

"My situation hasn't changed much," she said, "but I think I'm getting better about accepting it."

Thank You, Jesus, for eyes to see Your provision of answered prayers, even when they are not what I expect.   —Carol Kuykendall

14
SUN   **God Provides . . . Hope**

I have put my hope in your word.   —Psalm 119:114 (NIV)

September, one year later: I'm sitting in a circle of women, mostly strangers, at a meeting. The leader suggests that as a means of introducing ourselves, we provide a word-picture that identifies where we are in life. My turn comes.

"I'm a child running through a park on a beautiful autumn day. I sit down cross-legged in a pile of crunchy leaves and gleefully toss them above my head, reveling in autumn as the leaves float down around me."

This is a picture far different from the one I lived in a year ago. Today, I can look back and see a whole year full of God's provisions during a difficult time.

At this moment, Kendall is away at a Christian college, something that seemed impossible a year ago when she sometimes felt too self-conscious to leave the house. Today, she has hair on her head, a tangible display of God's goodness, and though we don't know what the future holds, we know where we are today, and relishing that is enough. I'm thankful, and filled with God's provision of hope.

Hope is believing what Abraham must have known as he trudged up the side of Mount Moriah: that when a parent faces his worst fears, God will provide. That's a promise . . . and hope is believing God's promises.

Today, I feel like a little girl again, delighting in the joy of autumn. Winter might be just around the corner, but springtime will always follow.

Lord, You will provide—today and always.   —Carol Kuykendall

WORDS OF WONDER

Song of the Creatures

Most high, almighty, good Lord,
    to You belongs praise, glory, honor, all
        blessings—
    to You alone, most high, belongs all
        reverence.
No man can fully speak of all Your
        wonders. . . .
                    —ST. FRANCIS OF ASSISI

15
MON

Behold a ladder set up on the earth, and the top of it reached to heaven. . . .   —Genesis 28:12

The morning is absolutely stunning as I walk along. Several days of late-summer rain have left the sky a clean blue and the grass and trees as green as spring. The honking of a small flock of geese traveling overhead is the only indication that this is mid-September and fall is near.

Today, a portion of my prayer time has been spent thanking God for our mended roof, and as I approach our driveway, I see my husband David up there, checking out the repairs. When we bought the house, the flat roof looked pretty, with its sloping eaves of cedar shakes. The leaks were minimal at first, but they worsened with the years. One summer night, so much rainwater poured in through our bedroom closet that we had to catch it in our big picnic cooler. The estimate to fix the roof was a whopping seven thousand dollars. With our daughter Keri in college, coming up with that much cash seemed impossible.

Then our son Brock, with much prayer, made a shrewd investment with a bit of our retirement savings and netted just about enough to cover the repairs. And here's David, on this beautiful day, standing up on the new roof. "How's the view up there?" I ask.

"Better than you can imagine," he answers, smiling. "Come on up and see for yourself."

I make my way up the ladder, shaky at first, but David's there, offering a hand. And finally, I'm standing two stories high, with my feet planted firmly on an answered prayer. The view is very good.

Father, so often I fail to trust in You. When my troubles shake the ladder, keep me climbing to Your Presence.   —Pam Kidd

16 *Set a guard over my mouth, O Lord, keep watch over the*
TUE *door of my lips!*   —Psalm 141:3 (RSV)

When my son Michael and his bride Amy returned from their honeymoon, they stayed at our house before moving to the town where Michael would be working as the director of a high school band.

One night, Amy, who'd been giving Michael haircuts all through college, said, "Don't you need a haircut, honey?"

Michael, who was getting ready for two weeks of active duty with the Wisconsin National Guard, said, "I think I'll get a haircut at the barber tomorrow."

Trying to be the frugal wife, Amy said, "Michael, that's ten dollars! I'll do it."

We all went out onto the patio. Amy started clipping; Michael started grumbling; I was watching.

Michael began. "Put that other attachment on the clippers! You're going to make it too short."

"No, I'm not. This is the attachment I always use."

"No, it isn't. You're not going to get it right."

Oh, no, I thought, *their first marital fight.*

"You wouldn't talk to the barber like that. Why can't you be nice and just tell me how you want it?"

"I'd be happy to tell the barber what I want, but you won't let me go."

At first, I wanted to side with Michael. *Maybe he should have gone to the barber. She's obviously not cutting it the way he likes.* Then I was on Amy's side. *She's trying so hard and she's doing a great job. Why can't he just appreciate her efforts?* But something, a guardian angel on my shoulder, perhaps, kept me from speaking any of those thoughts. Instead, I changed the subject to break the tension and before long, all three of us were chatting like old friends.

Before supper that night, Michael scooped his wife into his arms, apologized profusely and told her it was one of the best haircuts he'd ever had. He promised never to complain again when she got the clippers.

Lord, when those around me bicker and I'm tempted to add fuel to the fire, help me to be a healer instead.   —Patricia Lorenz

17
WED
Bless the Lord, O my soul, and forget not all his benefits.
—Psalm 103:2

I seem to be at a crossroads in my life, and for some time I've been praying for direction. "How can I best serve in my remaining years, God?" Surely, our Lord has some great and far-reaching plan for me!

But a surprising change of focus came to me this afternoon, as I sat at the dining table with my friend Mona. She'd brought peonies and lemon pie, and we shared tea and soulful conversation. How I relished the sweet tanginess of the pie, the lovely scent of the rose-pink peonies and the quiet soul-sharing of the afternoon!

This evening, as I sit in the soft darkness with only a candle glowing, I know that this day has been graced with holy moments. And it occurs to me that my reason for living need not be some monumental purpose. Perhaps those holy moments, when the ordinary connects the soul with God, are reason enough for living.

In his book *The Grateful Heart,* David Steindl-Rast writes that "to give thanks is to bless, and we are called to be blessers." *Yes!*

O Great Creator, help me to look for You in the ordinary, that I may be a blesser! Lord, bless this house, my family, the apple tree outside my window, the jogger running by. . . .   —Marilyn Morgan Helleberg

18
THU

"I will give him a white stone, with a new name written on the stone which no one knows except him who receives it."   —Revelation 2:17 (RSV)

Names are funny things. My nieces Clare, twelve, and Rachel, nine, were born in Korea and adopted from an orphanage while they were infants by my brother and his wife. I'm proud of the girls—they are happy, talented, well-adjusted. They are true survivors, rescued by love.

Clare can sometimes be difficult, though. She's the artistic one, sensitive and a bit temperamental. When she is in one of her moods, she has been known to sequester herself in her room, pull down the little sign on the door that says "Clare" and replace it with a placard bearing her Korean name. Until the tempest has passed, she will respond only to her Korean name and no other. She is very stubborn about this.

At first, Clare's behavior alarmed everyone. *Was she unhappy with her Americanization? Didn't she like her family?* We have learned to go along with her, though, and eventually the Korean sign comes down, "Clare" goes back up, and all is well. Clare, I think, just wants us to see her for who she is.

I've come to agree with her. I doubt that God only calls us by the names we call one another. He knows us as His unique, singular creations. And when I think about the people I love most in my life, I don't necessarily think of them as names. I think of them as the people behind the names, the essence.

My niece Kim Yu Sun taught me that.

God, guide me to see the people in my life just as You created them.
                                                    —Edward Grinnan

19
FRI

"You will seek me and find me; when you seek me with all your heart, I will be found by you, says the Lord. . . ."
                                    —Jeremiah 29:13–14 (RSV)

There's something to be said about making affirmations and thinking positively.

It was midnight, and I was on foot in a part of Manhattan I didn't know. I'd been enjoying the San Gennaro Festival in Little Italy with friends. We'd been pushed by the crowds through the narrow streets

filled with vendors' carts, had eaten a magnificent Italian meal and
had started for our respective homes along with throngs of other festival goers. I got on the subway to get to the World Trade Center
where I'd catch a PATH train to Jersey City. But the subway came
to a complete halt—a power failure. Everyone managed to get out,
and then I walked for blocks, my feet killing me in my dressy shoes.
And I was still a mile or two from the World Trade Center and my
train home. Fear rose in me. *I'm not going to get home.*

Then, in my desperation, I changed my tune. *You work for Guideposts and Norman Vincent Peale,* I told myself. *Now is the time to practice the power of positive thinking.*

I straightened my shoulders, walked determinedly forward, saying—and praying—with every ounce of energy I had, "I *will* get home
all right. I *will* find a taxi. There *will be* a taxi. Thank You, Lord."

And there was—at the next intersection. "Could you drive me to
the World Trade Center?" I asked.

"No," said the driver. "I'm a New Jersey cab—just brought a fare
over. I can't work in New York."

"That's wonderful!" I exclaimed. "I want to go to New Jersey.
Could you take me back?"

We made a deal, and within minutes I was home.

I'd faced my fear head on and put my whole heart into believing
that God would provide for me—and He did.

*Lord, as I face the future, I affirm with all my heart that You have every-
thing I need.*
                                                    —Mary Ruth Howes

20 *Thou dost show me the path of life; in thy presence there*
SAT *is fulness of joy. . . .*   —Psalm 16:11 (RSV)

Living in Missouri farm country, I have developed a deep reverence
for the men and women who cultivate the earth. Even with modern
equipment, farming is still backbreaking work, and all the members
of the family have to help. Yet they seem to do it with pleasure, and
I admire the clever ways they coax fun out of sweat.

Take haying, for example. Most farmers have gone to large, 1,500-
pound bales that they leave in the fields all year round. Often they
arrange them artistically, and in the winter the fields look like they're
full of giant frosted-wheat biscuits.

Troy Easley, one of my students, described the fun he has with haying. "When it's time to feed the cows, the challenge is to drop a bale downhill, so that it unrolls like a carpet. Sometimes a bale will roll into a pond, where it floats and makes a wonderful raft for swimmers." He tells how his farmer friends will line up bales so that they look like an enormous caterpillar or like a train. "They even decorate the bales with plywood cutouts, making them look like people or animals or their favorite basketball players."

If farmers can find laughter in hard labor, I ought to be able to find the fun that's hidden in my job. This fall, I plan to spend a little more time joking around with my students. I might even put some cartoons on my exams. I need to be a little less serious. In the long run, I think I'll be a better teacher.

Lord, no matter how hard the job, let me work with a ready will and a light heart.   —Daniel Schantz

21
SUN   *Everyone should be quick to listen, slow to speak. . . .*
                                              —James 1:19 (NIV)

When we lived in Tübingen, Germany, kind Frau Faessler, wife of my husband's professor-host, invited me to a tea for faculty spouses. Fearful that my German was inadequate, I wanted to decline her invitation, but she reassured me. "Oh, don't worry, my dear. Most of the ladies speak English. But if you want to improve your German, keep the conversation in German as much as possible. Even if you can't speak much, as you listen you will learn."

Following her advice, I gave brief responses in my primitive German, then asked questions to keep my companions talking. As I strained to understand their answers, I found Frau Faessler was right—I learned many new words that afternoon.

A few weeks after that faculty tea, we returned home to Michigan. The next Sunday I asked my ten-year-old Sunday school students to tell me about their summer vacations. The kids began speaking a "strange language," difficult for me to understand. They talked about hanging out at the mall, and several had started "going out" with boyfriends or girlfriends. I was about to exclaim in consternation, "But you're too young to date!" when Frau Faessler's words came to mind: "As you listen, you will learn."

I began to ask questions. I abandoned my usual talking-teaching role and listened. Soon the conversation drifted to their fears about growing up and their questions about God. I gave brief answers and asked more questions to help clarify their thoughts. I spoke as little as possible, yet we had one of our best "talks" ever!

Father, in every conversation help me to be a responsive listener, an eager learner.   —Mary Brown

22
MON

We don't even know what we should pray for . . . but the Holy Spirit prays for us. . . .   —Romans 8:26 (TLB)

At long last, I was ready to run. For years, I'd toyed with the idea of running as a good way to get some exercise, but now I'd actually gone out and bought a spiffy running outfit. I'd even asked my husband Gene to help me pick out proper running shoes. Hoping that I looked the part, I stepped outside and smelled the morning air.

To my surprise, I saw other people—neighbors of ours and even strangers—running the route I intended to take. Now I faced a dilemma: *How do I greet a fellow runner? Is there some kind of special runner's language I need to learn?* I decided that a simple "Hi" would do.

Before long, somewhat short of breath, I called out my first cheerful "Hi" to two women I knew slightly. "Morning!" they both sang out in perfect unison. The next person I passed spoke to me first. "Morning," he said. Sure now that "Morning" was the appropriate greeting for runners, I shouted it to the next one I met. "Hi!" she called back, smiling. Undaunted, I tried again, this time with a man and his golden retriever. "Morning," I said, hopefully but a bit less enthusiastically. "Gonna be a hot one today," he announced like the local TV weatherman.

It took me awhile, but I finally discovered there's no rhyme or reason to what runners say to each other. Now I just say whatever I feel like saying or simply smile or wave. The words aren't important; it's the act of communicating that counts.

That bit of information has carried over into my prayer life. Sometimes I become self-conscious about what I'm saying to God. Then I remember my morning run and leave the words to Him.

I'm not certain exactly how to pray today, Father, and I'm going to trust You to help me. Amen.   —Marion Bond West

23
TUE

Let us lay aside every weight, and the sin which doth so easily beset us. . . .   —Hebrews 12:1

"Here, Mom, check this out." Brett handed me his new dirt bike. It was amazingly light. "Only weighs twenty-two and a half pounds!" he said with pride.

All summer Brett had worked on that bike, adding special shocks, titanium nuts, a stronger stem. And always he was careful of weight. By the end of the summer, I realized why. On Labor Day weekend, Brett loaded his bike onto the back of his pickup truck and took off for Colorado. His goal was to ride across the Rocky Mountains.

"I can do it," he said as he hugged me before leaving. "I'm in great shape—and there's not an extra ounce on this bike!"

It was true. That bike was featherweight because Brett had been careful of everything he'd added. No unnecessary fluff. No flashy adornments. No extra baggage.

Am I traveling as lightly? I thought in those following weeks as I waited for a Colorado postcard. *Am I keeping things as lean as I should? Is Christian simplicity just a concept I applaud but don't practice?*

By the time that postcard did arrive, I'd made a few adjustments of my own. I'd stopped reading every sale brochure. I'd decided not to carry all my charge cards with me. I'd even cleaned off a few shelves and given away some lovely things.

With God's help, I'll learn to practice daily simplicity—and become a lean, *clean* traveling machine!

Dear God, remind me that I am a sojourner here on earth. Let me pack light and walk right as I travel toward my heavenly home with You.
                                        —Mary Lou Carney

24
WED

I have showed you kindness, that ye will also show kindness. . . .   —Joshua 2:12

Late at night, I pulled off the interstate highway to refuel my car at a convenience store. Summer was merging into fall and a crisp chill was in the air. When I entered the store to pay for the gas, I saw a small kitten huddled by the door, meowing and hungry. *Somebody dumped her,* I thought. *It'll be a tough winter for the little thing.*

Standing in line at the cash register, I looked at the back of the old man in front of me, one of America's homeless. His flannel shirt was tattered and filthy. Long, stringy hair hung down to his shoulders. He was stooped and bent.

As he picked up a package of cupcakes, I thought, *I bet this fellow hardly has a dollar to his name, and he's buying junk food. Seems like he'd make better use of his money.*

The cashier broke in, "Can I help you, sir?"

The man placed his purchases on the counter and asked, "Is that cat yours?"

"No, he's a stray. Been here a couple of nights too long."

"Well then, sir," the old man replied, "I want to get these here cupcakes and this cat food. I believe me and the cat are both hungry. You got a can opener?"

I was stunned and humbled by this poor man's love. His actions spoke louder than twenty sermons.

Dear Lord, soften my heart and help me to love as You love. Amen.

—Scott Walker

25

THU   *"And be at ease. . . ."*   —Proverbs 1:33 (NIV)

Today, reading is my most treasured form of relaxation. But it hasn't always been.

A few years ago, I was holding down two part-time jobs, and the pace had me feeling frazzled. Over coffee one afternoon, I told my troubles to a co-worker. "If you want to relax," she said, "read the *Thrush Green* novels. They're written by a woman named Dora Saint—she uses Miss Read as a pen name. You'll be transported to a slower, more relaxed time and place. There are about thirty of them, all set in an imaginary English village as seen through the eyes of the village schoolteacher."

Between jobs, I went to the library and took out a copy of *Gossip* from *Thrush Green*. That evening, I brewed a pot of spiced tea, sat down with the book and began reading. I loved it! The next day there was more tea and another volume. I read another. And yet another. I started hounding my librarian for more books, asking her to phone me as soon as anyone returned one. "I've read seven so far!" I boasted to my friend. "Now, if I can read one a week, I'll be done with the whole series in just—"

My friend started laughing. "Linda, listen to yourself. You're beginning to treat your hobby the same way that you treat work. Why not treat it as you do that cup of spiced tea you're drinking? Slow down—sip, don't gulp."

I laughed at myself, but I took her words seriously. I'm proud to say that several years later I *still* have not read my way through that series of wonderful books.

Today, Lord, may I sip, not gulp, and slowly savor those activities that give me pleasure.			—Linda Neukrug

26
FRI

"For my power is made perfect in weakness."
			—II Corinthians 12:9 (RSV)

"Oh, God, how am I going to do this?" I plead. "I don't want him to have to know." I am waiting at two A.M. for my husband Terry to pull in the drive after his long workday. His best friend of twenty years has died suddenly, at age forty-six, and it's left to me to tell him. My whole body trembles as I hear his step on the stairs. "God, give me the strength," I beg. "He and Gary were so close."

When the words come, they have the gentleness of Christ, and finally, after hours of numbed disbelief, I am able to stroke my husband's bowed head and cry. In the morning he dials Gary's wife, and now the sobs that he's held back shake him. I hear him say, "It's so hard; I loved him, too."

Five days go by. Gary's memorial service is in Washington state, and Terry is doing one last thing for his friend. He's giving the eulogy. Back home in Alaska, I pray, "Lord, he can't do this without You. You know he's not good in front of large groups, and this is Gary he's saying good-bye to. Empower him, Jesus."

In the early evening, the phone rings. My mother is on the line saying, "The church was packed, and Terry did such a wonderful job. He said some really good things—things that helped everybody. I was glad I was there." We finish our conversation and I sit, still clutching the phone, feeling incredibly proud of my husband. He's just done what seemed impossible for him, and he's done it with strength.

I think about all that God has done for us—taking what was weak and hurting in Terry and me and touching it with His power, making us able to stand when we were bowed down. In times of trouble, God has shown us that He is truly a Friend beyond all measure.

Jesus, when we are bowed down inside and think that we cannot possibly stand, come to us with power and strength and show us that we can.
			—Carol Knapp

27
SAT

Now we see but a poor reflection; then we shall see face to face. Now I know in part; then I shall know fully. . . .
—I Corinthians 13:12 (NIV)

After our second child was born, my wife insisted that we needed a new kitchen. So we refinanced our house and put the extra cash into renovation. To save money, I suggested that we reuse the old lumber in the new kitchen. The contractor agreed—as long as I removed the nails and stained the wood myself.

My initial nail-removing technique was awkward: yanking and yelling. Every nail fought extradition. And it's twice as difficult when an infant insists that you stop every few minutes to rewind Big Bird's jack-in-the-box. Finally, I developed a rhythm: hammer the point of the nail, turn the beam over, pull the head up, then pry the nail out. Hammer, turn, pull, pry. It became a little song: *Bang! Zip! Squeak! Ping!* as I flung the bent nail into an empty infant formula can.

The worst part of the staining was the fumes, which cause both headaches and hives. And my kids didn't help; they insisted that I jump in the leaves *right now.* (When a two-year-old pulls on your pinkie, it's useless to argue.) But with the can of stain resealed, my head began to clear, and I could see the progress. While I was busy pulling nails and staining, a new kitchen had arisen. Unable to lift my eyes from my own work, I didn't see how far we had come, only what I had yet to do.

And in those intervening months, other things had happened. My youngest daughter had begun to walk; my oldest daughter had learned to count to twenty. Intent on my renovation work and the immediate "Daddy tasks," I hadn't seen how far they'd come, how fast they'd grown.

Lord, when I grow too absorbed in the details of my journey, help me to lift up my eyes to see where I've been and where I'm going. —Mark Collins

28
SUN

Now there are diversities of gifts, but the same Spirit.
—I Corinthians 12:4

We have a friend who asks us to Sunday midday dinner now and then, and she always stimulates us with a provocative question or two. The other day she said, "You know how we Americans love to designate special days to commemorate certain ideas or events—Memorial Day, Thanksgiving Day, Flag Day and so on. Well, if you could decree a national holiday, what sort of day would it be?"

We all offered ideas, but the one I liked best came from a guest who said that he would decree a national Diversity Day. "Most of the time," he said, "we take diversity for granted. I think we should set aside a day to ponder it and be grateful for it. Consider this land of ours. We're all Americans, we all watch the same TV programs and elect one president. But think of the wonderful differences that remain. Different climates, accents, foods, architecture. Different manners, values, life-styles. It's out of these splendid differences that the color and character of this marvelous country really emerge.

"And that's just one example," he added. "Think of the infinite inventiveness of the Creator of all things. No two individuals alike. No two snowflakes alike. No two sets of fingerprints. No two days alike, not even two hours. How extraordinary this is! We should set aside a day to be thankful for it."

Diversity Day. I think the gentleman has a point.

Lord, grant us the wisdom to be constantly amazed and delighted and enchanted by the diversity You have placed all around us.

—Arthur Gordon

29
MON   *Every one helps his neighbor, and says to his brother, "Take courage!"*   —Isaiah 41:6 (RSV)

For much of my life I was a city person. I lived in big apartment houses and never got to know my neighbors. A lot of city people are like that. We aren't unfriendly. We just try to guard our privacy because, living so close together, we have very little of it.

During the early years of our marriage, my husband and I lived on New York's East Side. Apartments were hard to come by in those days, and tenants seldom moved out. So when the apartment above us was vacated and a new tenant moved in, we noticed. The newcomer was a young woman who lived alone. My husband and I used to see her on the elevator and sometimes at the bus stop. From our respective apartments, we could hear each other's footsteps, sneezes and laughter, yet we never said hello or even nodded at each other.

One evening after work, I rode in the elevator with my upstairs neighbor, without saying a word, and got off at my floor. I was in my apartment for only a few minutes when I heard her door close, and then something fall. I thought I heard a moan, but I wasn't sure. I waited, listening, but heard nothing else. *Oh, well,* I thought, *she probably dropped something.* At that moment my husband came home, and when I mentioned my concern to him, he thought we ought to investigate.

Feeling like busybodies, we went upstairs and knocked on the young woman's door. It swung open, and we saw our neighbor lying on the floor unconscious. When I rushed to her side, my husband used her telephone to call the police. They arrived just ahead of an ambulance. It turned out that the young woman was in a diabetic coma. "She might have died if you hadn't found her right away," the paramedic told us.

Our young neighbor recovered, and when she came home we learned her name. It was Doris. We also learned that she had no friends or family in the city. Putting our privacy aside, we sort of adopted her into our family. We have remained friends with Doris to this day, even though we now live many miles apart.

Privacy is still important to me, but not as important as being a good neighbor.

Lord Jesus, teach us to look after each other just as You look after us. Amen.
—Phyllis Hobe

30
TUE

For I know that through your prayers and the help given by the Spirit of Jesus Christ, what has happened to me will turn out for my deliverance.   —Philippians 1:19 (NIV)

Before electronic mail came into vogue, my husband Mark was communicating with people all over the country by e-mail. "It's quick and to the point," he explained, "and you don't have to hunt down an envelope and stamp, or go to the post office to mail it."

"Give me a handwritten note any old day," I countered. "I don't ever intend to talk to people on a computer. How impersonal!"

Then at the hospital where we both work, an e-mail group was established for sharing inspirational thoughts and special prayer requests. I began logging on at the start of my workday, and while I never initiated a message, I found myself caring and praying for people I'd never even met. Coming to work itself had a new joy.

When I developed new health problems, I desperately needed prayer myself. Yet I was so terrified that I couldn't talk about it. One day, I dashed off a quick plea for prayer on e-mail. "I'm battling pain and discouragement," I confessed to the computer. "Please, please pray for me."

I've never seen an answer to prayer arrive so fast. Within minutes, co-workers began stopping me in the hall, offering everything from assistance with projects to home-cooked meals to little gifts on my desk.

These days, I still prefer the charm of a handwritten note, but I'll never forget the words of encouragement that appeared on that "impersonal" computer screen from my new prayer partners.

Lord, we thank You for new developments in technology. We dedicate them to be used in ever-new ways for Your glory. Amen. —Roberta Messner

Everyday Wonders

1 _____

2 _____

3 _____

4 _____

5 _____

6 _____

7 _____

8 _____

9 _____

10 _____

11 _____

12 _____

13 _____

14 _____

15 _____

16 _____

17 _____

18 _____

19 _____

20 _____

21 _____

22 _____

23 _____

24 _____

25 _____

26 _____

27 _____

28 _____

29 _____

30 _____

Thou art the God that doest
wonders. . . . —PSALM 77:14

October

S	M	T	W	T	F	S
			1	2	3	4
5	6	7	8	9	10	11
12	13	14	15	16	17	18
19	20	21	22	23	24	25
26	27	28	29	30	31	

1

LOVE IS . . .

[Love] always perseveres.   —I Corinthians 13:7 (NIV)

Loretta Bolger was baffled by the report from her son's preschool: "Benjamin doesn't recognize letters." At four, of course, many children don't. But this was a "lab school," Michigan State University's program for gifted youngsters. Ben, Loretta knew, had an unusually high IQ. That's why, in 1979, she'd taken an apartment near MSU in East Lansing, even though as a single parent this meant traveling back and forth to Grand Haven where the tree farm she ran was located. "But I felt a child as bright as Ben needed the stimulation."

Tests revealed "severe dyslexia," a disability that in its milder forms affects the reading skills of nearly one person in five. There followed frustrating years of seeking a school attuned to the problem. "The kids would call me Dumbo," Ben said, recalling those days. Teachers would keep him in at recess, writing a single word hundreds of times.

At last Loretta, who had a degree in education, began teaching him at home. Science, history, literature; year after year she read aloud to him six hours a day. At thirteen, with no formal schooling since the fourth grade, Ben presented himself at the University of Michigan in Ann Arbor. They tested him—someone read him the entrance exam—and admitted him. Now his mother read eight, nine, ten hours a day, working their way through the college texts.

When he graduated, first in his class, Benjamin had a new goal: law. The youngest student ever accepted at Yale Law School, he and his mother today struggle with thousand-page legal tomes. "Doesn't your voice ever give out?" I asked Loretta. "How do you keep it up day after day?"

Loretta thought a moment. "Trees don't give up," she replied. "Through storm, drought, blight, they stand their ground. Trees don't quit, and I guess mothers don't, either."

God of love, give me the faith that doesn't quit when the road is long.
                                   —Elizabeth Sherrill

2

For I have given you an example, that ye should do as I have done to you.   —John 13:15

Last fall, I spent the night with my oldest son Patrick and his family. At supper, four-year-old Ryan asked, "Grandma, aren't you going to eat any green beans? David and I are supposed to eat two bites of everything." I hastily put a big spoonful on my plate and choked them down, just as I'd done when Ryan's dad was four.

I had to leave at five-thirty the next morning for a speaking engagement, so when my travel alarm went off I dressed quietly and slipped out the door, hoping I wouldn't wake anyone. When I walked to my car, however, the silence was shattered by frantic barking from all three dogs. That evening I called Patrick to apologize. "I was awake anyway, Mom," he assured me. "I knew you were tired, so I set my alarm in case you didn't hear yours. Just as you used to do for me."

Just as you used to do for me. Last week, my son Michael spent an hour helping eight-year-old Melissa select the perfect pig for her 4-H project. Was it because his father had showed the same patience with him when he was eight? Did my sister Amanda's practice of sending cards and cheery notes inspire our daughter Rebecca to show the same thoughtfulness? And if I remember right, the "two bites" rule originated with my dad.

"Many good works have I showed you from my Father," Jesus says (John 10:32). The power of example is a theme repeated over and over in the Bible. I think it's to remind me that it's never too late to pass on a family model of kindness and care.

Lord, help me to be a good example . . . even if it means eating green beans.
—Penney Schwab

3

FRI   *Perfect love casteth out fear. . . .*   —I John 4:18

Our bedroom door slammed open, and the overhead light glared on.

"Can't a guy even get breakfast around this place?" demanded my father-in-law. "In the army, at least you got three square meals a day!"

It was two A.M. Andrew and I groaned. How were we going to get him back to bed? It wasn't the first time Dad had gotten confused about time, but it was certainly one of the more inconvenient. Groggy with sleep, we took the wrong approach. "It isn't time for breakfast, Dad. It's dark outside, see? Look, we're all in our pajamas! The clock says it's two, so it's not time to get up yet, okay?"

It didn't work. Dad heard all our arguments as what they were—arguments. The more logic we used, the angrier and more combat-

ive he became. As things escalated, we realized the need to take another tack. Instinctively, I made my voice gentler. Andrew got up and
placed a hand on Dad's shoulder. Quietly, calmly, we shifted to
soothing Dad instead of trying to convince him it was the middle of
the night. Eventually, he shuffled back to his room, where I tucked
him in with a hug and a kiss.

Perhaps if we had been less exhausted, one of us might have recognized that Dad had woken up confused and disoriented, and therefore afraid. Then perhaps we would have responded to his needs instead of reacting to his words.

*Jesus, the antidote to fear is love, not logic. Help me to speak simply with
the voice of Your heart.*   —Julia Attaway

4
SAT   *"In all things I have shown you that by so toiling one must
help the weak, remembering the word of the Lord Jesus,
how he said, 'It is more blessed to give than to receive.' "*
—Acts 20:35 (RSV)

Stirling, Scotland, is a medieval city. The roads either "round-about"
onto completely different routes, or they dead-end altogether. After
an hour of being honked at and getting totally lost, I pulled over to
calm my nerves. I was at my wit's end and near tears. To my surprise, a couple approached my car. "You look lost," said the man.
"Can we help?"

I handed him my map. "Can you tell me how to get to the train
station?"

"Well, it's about three blocks away, if you're walking. But if you're
driving . . ." He laughed.

His wife peered through the open window. "Would you mind if
we got in and showed you? Otherwise," she said, "I'm afraid we'll
set you on a goose chase."

"Oh, do you mind?" I exclaimed in relief.

Mr. and Mrs. Shaw not only got me to the station, they paid the
necessary parking fee! As I waved good-bye to these good folk, I
thanked God for people like the Shaws who were willing to help a
stranger.

Three days later, flying out of London, I noticed a young mother
with a baby. *Good luck*, I thought, remembering my baby-flying days.

Eight hours later, I saw her again, in Minneapolis. She looked tired and bewildered. The baby and all her luggage were clearly too heavy for her to manage. I had my own bags and was feeling stressed. But then I remembered Mr. and Mrs. Shaw.

I wiggled through the crowd. "Can I help you with something?"

"Oh, do you mind?" she exclaimed in relief. "Here, if you could just take the baby a minute." We had a perfectly delightful time—two women, a baby and our mountain of luggage—as we awkwardly, but with much laughter, maneuvered through customs.

"Thank you!" the young mother declared when we were at last ready to go our separate ways. "I'll never forget the fun we've had!"

I won't either.

Dear Lord, if someone needs help today, let me be the one.
—Brenda Wilbee

5
SUN

Incline your ear, and come unto me: hear, and your soul shall live. . . . —Isaiah 55:3

When I was still a newlywed, I met with a spiritual adviser, and one of the things he told me gave me pause: "You need to spend time with the Lord to be able to know Him—just as you need to spend time with your wife."

With those words burning in my ears, I returned home that night, and as Carol and I ate our macaroni-and-cheese dinner and talked about our respective days, I wondered, *How well do I know my wife?* We had managed to sort out who would write what thank-you notes for our wedding presents, and we'd figured out what to call our in-laws and where to put our joint checking account, but how well did I know Carol day-to-day?

Just then she got up to answer the phone. "Uh-huh, uh-huh," she said.

It's her mother, I thought. I could tell from her tone of voice, just as I could tell by her wary "Hello" if she had a salesman on the line. If she had laughed and exclaimed "I can't believe it!" I would have known it was her best friend. If she had expressed a delighted "Oh, hi!" I would have been certain it was my parents on the line. That's what came of spending time together every day.

"Uh-huh, uh-huh," she continued before hanging up without any formal good-bye—another hallmark of her chats with her mother, as though they were in one lifelong conversation, which, in effect, they were.

"It was your mother," I said.

"How did you know?"

"When you spend time with someone, you just can tell."

Lord, on this World Communion Sunday, help me to know You so I can recognize Your voice whenever I hear it in this world.   —Rick Hamlin

6

MON

Create in me a clean heart, O God; and renew a right spirit within me.   —Psalm 51:10

I entered college in the fall of 1937. I had received a scholarship and would be working to pay my expenses, but I still worried about money. And I was troubled by the voices I had left behind. Father had said, "We can't afford to send you to school. Remember, it's you who wanted to go. You're on your own." Shame swept over me; I felt selfish. I worried that because of me there might be less food on the family table.

There were other voices, too. Some whispered, "Why is he going to school? There's a depression on. There are no jobs." "Why is he going so far away? Why not go to school here at home?" Their questions troubled me. *Had I made the right decision?* I was filled with self-doubt.

College was all I hoped for, yet as a freshman I was doing poorly in my classes. Worry, shame and self-doubt sapped my energy and disrupted my thoughts. In desperation, I asked an upperclassman to tutor me. After a few sessions, he said, "You don't need help. You learn quickly, and you should be topping your class. What's bothering you?"

Reluctantly, I shared my troubled feelings. He listened and then said, "You've got to grow up. Stop thinking of defeat."

By listening to those disapproving voices, I had allowed the seeds of failure to take root in my mind. When I got back to my room, I wrote one sentence in my diary: "You must never think of defeat." Every day during my freshman and sophomore years, I read that sentence. It became a prayer. Gradually, its call to courage replaced the negative voices.

Understanding Father, open my ears to Your message of trust, confidence and perseverance.
                    —Oscar Greene

7
TUE
But as for me, my contentment is not in wealth but in see-ing you and knowing all is well between us. . . .
—Psalm 17:15 (TLB)

In 1995, I received a letter from the medical director of a Texas health center asking me to answer the question, "What is the key to contentment, fulfillment or happiness in life?" Seems he was preparing a book that would contain the answers to that question from "leaders and personalities all across our nation."

Well, I knew I wasn't a leader, so feeling rather perky that he'd proclaimed me, a mom from Oak Creek, Wisconsin, a "personality" in his form letter, I set out to answer the doctor's great questions.

First, I pontificated about how one of the main purposes of education should be to help us discover the unique talent God has given each of us. I continued, "Next, we need to find a career that utilizes our particular talent. When we work at something we're naturally good at, contentment, fulfillment and happiness automatically follow. For me, chocolate chip cookies and naps work well also."

I'm not sure I captured exactly what the good doctor had in mind for his book, but the more I thought about it, the more I decided my last sentence was the most important.

Then I thought about lots of other "little" things that make me happy: the giant willow tree outside my office window; a good steaming cup of Irish Breakfast tea; snorkeling; the new bike path that starts a block from my house; my son Andrew's big hug every morning as he leaves for school. All these "little" things and hundreds like them make me contented, fulfilled and happy.

Lord, help me to start each day by listing a few of the wonderful "little" blessings You've provided that make me happy. —Patricia Lorenz

8
WED
Seek him that maketh the seven stars and Orion, and turneth the shadow of death into the morning. . . .
—Amos 5:8

I have my father's eyes. We are so uncannily similar that I see him looking at me, through the mirror, out of my own face. Teasing eyes, sometimes whimsical, so much like his that I want to cock an eyebrow at myself and laugh out loud.

I miss my father. I was eight years old when he left my mother, and there is still a little girl in me who has missed him all my life. World War II wrought a havoc of separation in both our lives. He, an officer with the Royal Navy, was imprisoned by the Japanese in Hong Kong. My mother and I were imprisoned in Yangchow, China.

From time to time, I curl up in a big brown chair that holds me snugly and fill the hollow in my heart with his letters. They are pitifully few, yellowed at the creases and torn from all my foldings and unfoldings through the years. Some were sent on Red Cross forms, from prison camp to prison camp.

> The stars will hold us together, Sweetness! No distance can ever separate us as long as there are moon and stars. Wherever you are, look up at the night sky and know I am looking at the very same stars, thinking of you and loving you.

All are signed, "Your stranger Daddy."

We survived the prison camps. My mother and I were repatriated to Canada. My father, ravaged by starvation, his tall frame whittled down to a mere ninety pounds, returned to Australia. I never saw him again.

But wherever I am, I can find my father in the night sky. He left me a legacy of stars! There, the arms of heaven spread out to encircle the earth. All I need to do is look up and remember: The same twinkling stars, the same bright moon, were shining on us then and are shining now around the world and out into eternity.

Thank You, Lord, for the benediction of stars that tuck me in at night with the sweet gift of love and remembrance.   —Fay Angus

9

THU

"By this kind of hard work we must help the weak. . . ."
—Acts 20:35 (NIV)

When a tornado blew through our town of Moberly, Missouri, on the Fourth of July, it came right down our street. My wife Sharon and I hid in the basement. In a few seconds it was all over, and we climbed out of the basement and looked around.

"Look at all the fallen trees!" I gasped. "And smashed cars! And there's someone's roof in our street!"

"Our neighbor's gazebo has vanished," Sharon noted, "but our house seems to be intact. Thank God for that."

We were overwhelmed by the power of the storm, but even more impressive was the powerful response of people to the emergency. Homeowners stepped outside, gave one "gee whiz" look around, then immediately began picking up trash and tree limbs. No one stood around moaning. There was no time for that because streets needed to be cleared and houses checked for injured people.

"Gimme a hand here!" a stranger called out to me, and I grabbed the other end of a tree and dragged it out of the road. In minutes, hundreds of men appeared in our neighborhood with chain saws and pickup trucks, and the area soon sounded like a bumblebee convention. Power and light crews worked all night using powerful lights; roofing crews joined together to cover holes in housetops with plastic and tar paper. Friends and relatives came from all over the state to help, and rescue organizations set up refreshment and first aid booths on the street.

It's October now, and every time I find a roofing nail in the driveway I remember the storm. But I also remember the glorious outpouring of human kindness.

When I see my neighbor's need, Lord, let me always pitch in and help.
—Daniel Schantz

10

FRI

Speak and act as those who are going to be judged by the law that gives freedom. . . . Mercy triumphs over judgment!
—James 2:12–13 (NIV)

Between 1935 and 1944, I served as president of the Women's Board of Domestic Missions of the Reformed Church in America. My duties included traveling around the country to speak at the annual women's meeting of each of the church's synods.

During the summer of 1941, Norman and I spent two months in Hollywood, where he was technical adviser for the movie *One Foot in Heaven* with Frederick March. The film was being made at the Warner Brothers studio, and our participation received considerable publicity.

Shortly after the film was completed, I started on my tour of the women's meetings. When I arrived in one town in Iowa, the president of the women's board informed me that I would not be allowed to speak at their meeting: I had been in Hollywood, and the women of their community disapproved of the motion picture business.

What was I to do? After careful consideration and much prayer, I went to see the women's board president. "I accept your decision," I told her. "But I must tell you that I am a member in good standing of the Reformed Church in America, and as such I am entitled to enter your church and attend this meeting."

I sat quietly in the back row of the church. Some of the women, seeing me there, came to sit with me. Through the kindness and courtesy of those Iowa women, God enabled me to be enthusiastic and happy in spite of rejection. I actually enjoyed the meeting very much.

Lord, when I experience injustice, let me witness against it with serenity, not with anger.   —Ruth Stafford Peale

11
SAT

"Bring the whole tithe into the storehouse. . . . and see if I will not throw open the floodgates of heaven and pour out so much blessing that you will not have room enough for it."
—Malachi 3:10 (NIV)

Saturday morning I sit at the kitchen table with my five-year-old daughter Elizabeth, a pile of dimes, her piggy bank (actually a wrinkled brown dog) and a box of church envelopes. We are disbursing her first allowance, a hefty one dollar!

"Why are you giving me ten dimes, Mom?"

"Well, this is how your grandpa did it with me."

I remember Saturday mornings years ago, another kitchen table, a pile of nickels, my own bank and a question: "But why do we put a nickel in the bank and give a nickel to church, Daddy?"

"Because we give God one-tenth of what we earn, and we save one-tenth." Then Dad stacked the coins to show how ten percent of fifty cents is a nickel.

The clink of a coin in the bank followed, then the solemn sealing of the church envelope and Dad's proclamation, "Now you have forty cents left to spend however you want!" Forty cents! An enormous sum in those days of penny candy and nickel soda pops. I'd pick up the nickels and dash off on my bike to the corner root beer stand.

As Elizabeth seals her church envelope, puts Wrinkles back on the shelf and runs to show Daddy her bulging coin purse, I smile and am encouraged. Alex and I are to tackle revising our budget this week. Our expenses are increasing, but our income is not. Still, I'm reminded of Dad's good math. God's timeless formula works in any age. If we give to God first, what is left will be enough.

Help me to give unselfishly to You, Lord, and to trust Your promise to provide.   —Mary Brown

12
SUN

He giveth snow like wool: he scattereth the hoarfrost like ashes.   —Psalm 147:16

The congregation had a good chuckle one Sunday in mid-October when our pastor asked how many were depressed by the season's early snowfall. Alex, our exchange student from Brazil, quipped, "Not *de*pressed—*im*pressed!"

His comment recalled the previous evening when the swirling flakes had contributed to the rescue of our dog. KC had been missing for hours. I assumed he was off romping in the woods with another dog or visiting a nearby house where he could usually persuade a couple of little boys to come out and play. A chow-golden retriever mix, he has an eager, trusting disposition.

About ten-thirty P.M., Alex and my daughter Brenda, inspired by the new-fallen snow, were taking a walk along the power-line trail when they were startled by a muffled yipping. They turned back, uncertain in the dark of what was down there. Then Brenda called, "Wait! What if it's KC?"

It sure enough was. Somehow he'd climbed into an abandoned pickup truck, poked his head through a small opening in the floor where the manual transmission had been removed and couldn't get it out. He'd yelped himself hoarse calling for someone to come rescue him. It wasn't easy, either. He was really stuck.

For Alex, the snow that evening had been a novelty. For KC, it became the catalyst for rescue. For me, it was evidence once again of God working in the unseen details of our lives, responding without our asking—creating solutions before we know we need them. It's a year-round message that I hope will forever *im*press me!

Praise You, Father, for Your watchful care over the seen and unseen in our lives.   —Carol Knapp

13   *Reproach hath broken my heart; and I am full of heavi-*
MON   *ness. . . .*   —Psalm 69:20

One morning, forty years ago, when I had just begun teaching, I was sitting in my office opening the mail. Among the normal business letters and the usual advertisements, I discovered an anonymous letter evaluating my teaching. It disturbed me that there was no signature. But what bothered me even more was being told that my teaching could stand some improvement.

I hadn't entertained the idea that I was perfect, but I wasn't eager to have someone point out my weaknesses. I loved teaching and was trying to bring a fresh approach to the classroom, and my inexperience had made me vulnerable to criticism.

The letter hurt enough that I took it home to my wife Barbara and asked her what she thought I ought to do about it. She read the letter carefully and handed it back to me with a question: "Did you skip the first paragraph?" As I carefully reread the letter, I realized that the student had begun it with, "I'm sure that you are aware of the many good points of your teaching," and had then listed several complimentary examples.

While I was absorbing the rest of the letter, Barbara added, "It seems to me that you allowed the one suggestion for improvement to completely outweigh all the good things the student said about you." She was right. I'd been so fixated on that one negative comment that I hadn't even seen the positive ones.

Lord, help me to keep everything in perspective—including myself.
                                                    —Kenneth Chafin

14   *I will be with thee . . . when thou walkest through the fire,*
TUE   *thou shalt not be burned. . . .*   —Isaiah 43:2

I wanted to take my grandchildren for a walk through the replica of a volcano in Albuquerque's Museum of Natural History.

Four-year-old Kristen sniffed the sulfurous fumes, listened to the roar that rolled through the volcano's low dark doorway and refused to go any farther. "There's a tiger in there!" she cried.

I tried to convince her otherwise, but without success. Finally, I took the other children through the volcano while Kristen stayed outside with a friend. When we exited, Kristen ran to us with tears streaking her face. "I thought the tiger had eaten you," she sobbed.

The other children clamored to go through the exhibit again, but Kristen once more stayed outside. When we came out that time, my friend reported that Kristen was missing. We hunted frantically among the surrounding displays. Then, to my astonishment, I saw Kristen emerge alone from the volcano, face pale, chin high. "Grandma, you were right," she said. "There is no tiger in the volcano."

Awed by her bravery, I asked, "How did you find the courage to go in there?"

"God held my hand," she replied.

Father, no matter what I have to face today, please help me remember that You are with me.   —Madge Harrah

---

WORDS OF WONDER

Wonder

Wonder is the attitude of admiration for life's
    beauty, perfection, and subtlety.
Wonder is the attitude of awe in the presence
    of life's vastness and power.
Wonder is the attitude of reverence for the
    infinite values and meanings of life, and of
    marveling over God's purpose and patience
    in it all.
Thus wonder leads to the birth of construc-
    tive imagination and vision, and soon issues
    in the more triumphant verbs I see and I
    believe.

—GEORGE WALTER FISKE

15
WED   *"A burnt offering to the Lord, a pleasing aroma, an offering made to the Lord by fire."*   —Exodus 29:18 (NIV)

I'm at a stage in my life where my body goes through changes without warning. I know this time will pass, but right now it seems endless. Sometimes the "changes" are so intense that they bring with them all kinds of fears and anxieties. Yesterday was one of those days, and by the time my husband Bill and I headed out to pick up my car at the repair shop, I was feeling overwhelmed by worries. While we were stopped by a light, I let out a deep sigh.

"What is it, honey?" Bill aksed.

"I feel so inundated with fears right now. I don't seem to have any control over what's going on in my body or my life, and it scares me."

"Tell me some of your worries," he asked gently, so I did. Instead of trying to talk me out of them, Bill was silent for a moment.

"I think maybe you ought to put them all in a basket and offer them up to God."

After we picked up my car, Bill went on to run some errands, and I drove home alone. I went into the dining room, sat down at the table and wrote every fear, silly or serious, on a slip of paper. Finally, I found a small bread basket in the kitchen and carried my pile of papers out to the backyard in it.

"Lord, as the Israelites gave things up to You by burning them, I'm giving You these fears to handle." I dumped the papers on the ground and set them on fire. As the tiny smoke trail went upward, peace settled on my soul.

Lord, thank You for the peace that comes when I surrender my worries to You.
                                                    —Roberta Rogers

16
THU *If we confess our sins, he [God] is faithful and just, and will forgive our sins and cleanse us from all unrighteousness.*
                                                    —I John 1:9 (RSV)

When I was little, my best friend was Mike Armstrong, the kid next door. One day after school, when we were playing a game, I got very upset with Mike for cheating. Alone in my room that night I wished the worst things on him. Terrible things.

I awoke the next morning paralyzed with guilt. I knew what I had wished for Mike was a sin, and I had to tell it to a priest in confession. So that afternoon I went into my parish church, St. Dennis, and found a confessional that was lighted up.

The problem was I wasn't really sure of the exact name of the sin I had committed. Mentally, I ran my thumb down the Ten Commandments. There was one I didn't quite understand. *That must be it!* I decided by process of elimination.

When the priest slid open the confessional window, I got right down to business: "Bless me, Father, for I have sinned. Since my last confession I have committed one adultery."

Shocked silence.

This must be a really bad sin, I thought.

"How old are you, my son?"

"Eight, Father."

A soft chuckle drifted through the hush. Now what had I done? I was ashamed; I'd messed up my confession.

"Tell me about this sin," the priest prompted. All the terrible details of the things I'd wished on Mike came spilling out. I was crying when I finished.

The priest told me that what I had done *was* a sin, but not the one I cited. "The important thing is you're sorry," he reminded me, "and you are willing to be forgiven." For my penance he told me to shake Mike's hand and apologize.

Good religion is also good advice. Today, when I am troubled by something I have said or done, even if I can't exactly put my finger on it, I remember that priest's words, and I tell God I am sorry.

Father, I am willing to be forgiven. Your perfect mercy is my saving grace.

—Edward Grinnan

17
FRI   *And everyone marveled.*   —Mark 5:20 (NAS)

Mother's wheelchair stood folded up in a corner of the garage. She still used her walker occasionally, but mostly she used a cane. Then a routine bone scan revealed that Mother's cancer was spreading. The pills she'd been taking were no longer working. Her doctor suggested chemotherapy—to begin that very day. Mother declined graciously, as though she were refusing a second helping of her favorite food.

We went for a second opinion to a cancer specialist we had been seeing in downtown Atlanta. "Yes," he told us, "the disease does seem to be progressing some. But I go by a patient's overall appearance more than by sophisticated tests. Mrs. Grogan, you look marvelous. You're something else! I don't recommend chemotherapy now."

The next day Mother and I celebrated by going shopping. She, my husband Gene and I had been invited to the wedding of a dear friend, and we wanted her to look her best. At the mall, we spotted a marvelous cranberry-colored silk outfit that looked made for Mother. "It needs a scarf for the neck," she insisted. I made a mad dash for the scarf department and saw it right away—the only one they had that looked like it matched. It was perfect.

At the wedding reception, we sat at a small table covered with a linen cloth and fresh fall flowers. I offered to get Mother a plate of food from the buffet. "Let me get it," she said excitedly. Leaving her cane at the table, she disappeared into the crowd. Suddenly, I saw her waving to us from over by the piano. The pianist seemed to be about Mother's age; she played music from the Roaring Twenties. Mother danced a few steps of the Charleston and waved to Gene and me from across the room.

Father, each day is a new marvel. Thank You! Amen.

—Marion Bond West

18

SAT

With the ancient is wisdom; and in the length of days understanding.   —Job 12:12

When I'm not on the road traveling, I usually go to the office on Saturday to catch up on work during the quiet of the morning. One Saturday morning not long ago, my work was interrupted by a phone call. "Reverend Weary," the man began, "I just called to tell you that I pray for the ministry every day. I think that you and Reverend Fletcher are doing a great work."

"Thank you, sir," I responded, "and thank you for praying."

"I am eighty-seven years old," he continued, "and I helped Reverend Perkins, the founder of your ministry, when he first got started in the sixties. Many people fought him when he started telling us to register to vote, but I knew that what he was doing was necessary, and I stood with him to help the community."

By the time our conversation had ended, I had an idea for a new outreach: a house especially designed for retired volunteers, people with unique skills and the wisdom of years who would love to help out in a ministry like ours if we had a place for them to come to. I had not only been blessed and encouraged by this eighty-seven-year-old prayer warrior; I had been challenged to grow.

Lord, help me to remember that, young and old, we all have a part to play in building Your kingdom.

—Dolphus Weary

19
SUN
He leadeth me beside the still waters. He restoreth my soul. . . .   —Psalm 23:2–3

It was the kind of Sunday lunch my mother cooked when I was a child—pot roast, potatoes, gravy, carrots, rolls and a pecan pie. Pushing back from the table, I basked in the warmth of a good meal shared with family and friends and felt the tug of a nap. But not, my wife informed me, before the dishes were washed.

Filling the sink with hot, soapy water, I held the first plate gently in my hands, rubbing its surface until a squeaky lustre shone through the suds. Outside the kitchen window, a rainbow of autumn-tinged oaks swayed and sprinkled their leaves on the ground. Sparrows were fluttering around a bird feeder three feet away, and I could see a sparkle in their small, black eyes. As I reached for another plate, the smell of soap and the warmth of water flowed over my spirit and I was bathed in happiness; a simple, pure happiness that comes when the elemental needs of life have been met.

In a busy, high-tech world, it's important for me not to become separated from the joys of the simple. Though we own a dishwasher, it's a pleasure now and then to place my hands in soapsuds and feel warm water relax my soul; later, to crawl under quilted covers and drift off to sleep. Money can't buy such peace and happiness. And I can't afford to lose it.

Dear God, slow me down. Help me to feel the sun upon my face. Amen.
—Scott Walker

20
MON
Who is wise? He will realize these things. Who is discerning? He will understand them.   —Hosea 14:9 (NIV)

My nephew Brandon is four years old and not yet out of the stage where the boxes are better than the presents. It doesn't seem to matter what he gets, as long as it comes in a box. An ordinary cardboard box can become a car, change into a boat, then become a plane and, finally, a house. For Brandon, the possibilities are limitless: Every box is an opportunity for imagination and exploration.

I sometimes wonder how many opportunities I miss in life. I meet people every day without ever discerning their potential. Like the quiet girl in my class who, if I give her the time and effort, might become a good friend. Or my friend with a great curiosity about God who might make a good Bible study partner. I'm going to spend today using a little imagination and looking for the possibilities in the people I meet.

Lord, help me to help others realize the possibilities their gifts offer.

—Hollie Davis

21
TUE

The eternal God is your dwelling place, and underneath are the everlasting arms. . . .

—Deuteronomy 33:27 (RSV)

I turn the key in the lock of my apartment and open the door. For a moment, I expect the rush of a dog, his tail in a frenzy of greeting, but it's only for a moment. He hasn't been here for years. Tricked again.

I put the day's mail down on the table and, opening the door of the Seth Thomas, wind it. If I don't do it now, I'll forget it. I have an electric digital in the bedroom, but I like the sound of the ticking of the old family antique in the living room.

I pick up the mail and look through it. Junk mail, nothing there. I take off my coat and hang it in the closet. Should I call a friend for a bit of dinner, a movie? No, I don't think so.

The chair seems to welcome me; it's held my form more than any other. I sit in it, and I think about the day and the passions that went into it. Suddenly, the Seth Thomas chimes the hour. It startles me for a moment. Then I settle back, I look up at the wall with its pictures of relatives and friends. It's not loneliness I feel now, for I am content. I am blessed.

Home.

Father, I am grateful for the things I have; never let me forget to appreciate them.   —Van Varner

22
WED

And he will be like a tree firmly planted by streams of water. Which yields its fruit in its season, And its leaf does not wither. . . .

—Psalm 1:3 (NAS)

Every fall, the solitary, ancient maple tree that stands in front of our house puts on a glorious, red and gold display. Turning into our driveway after a long drive home from Massachusetts this fall, the brilliance of the setting sun on that beautiful maple tree made me stop the car and get out to gaze at the colors. I was in a reflective mood; seems I get that way more and more now that I'm on the far side of forty. The meeting I had attended was on the theme of "Turning Success into Significance," and my thoughts were focused on the qualities I needed to change in order to make my life really significant.

As I stood there, God seemed to say, "You want to know something about significance? Think about *My* maple tree over there." So I did, and three things came to mind:

Consistency. Year in and year out, the tree produces beautiful colors.

Perseverance. The tree has been performing long before I was born, and it will continue to show its colors when I'm gone.

Excellence. In some years, the tree is more beautiful than in others, but it is always beautiful.

Not bad for standing in the driveway, huh? At least my wife Joy called me in for supper before I started talking to the tree.

Lord, let my life reflect Your wonderful qualities, portrayed in Your creation all around us.   —Eric Fellman

23

THU   *God setteth the solitary in families. . . .*   —Psalm 68:6

When our teenage son Chris was called to the vice principal's office for putting a bumper sticker on the hood of a teacher's car, I felt like trading him in for someone of a less troublesome age. The sticker shenanigan had been one of those ill-thought-out, impulsive acts that was made worse when Chris tried to pretend that he hadn't done it.

His father and I grounded Chris: no TV, no phone, no going out after school. I was thoroughly aggravated with him, not only because of his misbehavior, but because his punishment required me to be an unwilling jailer during his long period of restriction.

That evening Chris came to me with a piece of notebook paper. "I need help with this scout badge requirement," he said. "I'm supposed to come up with ten reasons why I'm important to our family. I could only come up with two."

"Well," I replied, in no mood to talk to him, "you baby-sit."

"I already have that."

I thought a moment and came up with more chores that he did. "Mom," he said, "can't you come up with other stuff? You know, things that are really important. Anybody can take out the trash."

After another moment's thought, I said, "You know, you've got a great sense of humor. You don't just baby-sit, you entertain. And every time we move to a new house, you're the one that always finds something you're really going to like. And when you wear those old plaid polyester bell-bottoms, you make me remember not to be afraid to express my individuality."

Finally, all ten lines were filled in, and I wasn't so angry with Chris anymore. Yes, we were having a difficult time—it's hard work plowing through awkward ages and stages together—but I knew we'd be able to get through this latest crisis, too, as a family.

Thank You, Lord, for the love that makes me "really important."
—Karen Barber

24
FRI

All the ends of the earth shall see the salvation of our God.
—Isaiah 52:10

My twenty-five-year-old daughter Wendy was home for the summer, on a break from missionary school. With her extensive travels and her zeal for missions, she brought a global perspective into our home-body lives. Sometimes it was unsettling.

One night Wendy and I were praying together about the stories that had been in the news that day, including the worsening situation in Cuba. "Lord," I prayed, "bless those who are suffering. Bring peace and freedom to that land."

Then Wendy began, "I pray for Fidel Castro, that You would have mercy on his soul. Bring him to know You." A bolt of anger surged through me. The very name of Castro is synonymous with dictatorship and cruelty!

"Why did you pray for that man?" I sputtered when we had finished.

"Because Jesus said we're to pray for our enemies, and Castro certainly qualifies," she said with a grin.

Wendy's simple obedience put me to shame. Not only did she routinely pray for people in other countries, whom I tended to forget most of the time, but she had room in her heart for everyone, for the tyrants as well as for their victims. Simply because Jesus commanded it. Reason enough; and who knows, perhaps such prayers take wing and knock at the most hardened heart.

Lord Jesus, on this United Nations Day, broaden my vision to include Your whole world, especially those who seem furthest from redemption.

—Shari Smyth

Editor's Note: A month from today, on November 24, we will hold our fourth annual Guideposts Family Day of Prayer. We invite you to join our prayer family by sending your prayer requests, along with a picture if you'd like, to Guideposts Prayer Fellowship, PO Box 8001, Pawling, NY 12564.

25
SAT

Then shall all the trees of the wood rejoice before the Lord: for he cometh; for he cometh to judge the earth. . . .
—Psalm 96:12–13

When the fall leaves were at their peak, I visited Bob and Betty, a retired couple who live next to Fahnestock State Park in New York. We strolled through the woods and admired the great variety of trees growing in abundance—sycamore, maple, oak.

Bob picked up two acorns and handed them to me. "Here," he said, "plant these at your place. They'll remind you of us."

I took the brown nuts, wrapped them in tissue and carefully placed them in my pocket. "Thank you," I said, "I love the majestic chestnut oaks. If these seeds become trees, I'll name them after you two, and I'll always have a part of you with me."

As we gathered bouquets of red and orange leaves, Betty spoke thoughtfully. "We once lived next door to a woman who told us how much she admired our shade trees. I said, 'Plant some for yourself.' But she didn't want to. She wasn't going to go to the expense of planting trees for the next residents."

"How long did they live there?" I asked.

"Thirty years," Betty replied. "And in all that time they never had a shade tree."

Lord, the future depends on what I do today. Help me to leave a legacy of love to those who come after me.   —Susan Schefflein

26
SUN

And God saw every thing that he had made, and, behold, it was very good. . . .   —Genesis 1:31

The story goes that Norman Rockwell, the much-loved illustrator, once was asked if he considered himself a realistic painter. "Of course I am," Rockwell replied. He thought a moment and then added, "But I paint reality the way I'd like it to be."

Rockwell lived in the same world we all inhabit, a world that sometimes seems all too full of pain and suffering and injustice and cruelty. But he chose deliberately to focus on the good side of life: the warmth, the caring, the compassion, the generosity, the humor of ordinary people living ordinary lives. Perhaps that's why his work has such enormous appeal.

When the Lord handed over the world to us, the Bible says that He looked at it and "Behold, it was very good." If it is less so now, it is because we have made it so. But what men and women tear down, they also can rebuild, if they have the vision to start seeing the world the way they'd like it to be.

Why don't we start that re-visioning in our own lives today?

Help us to see our world as You meant it to be, Lord. —Arthur Gordon

27
MON

"Do not be afraid; do not be discouraged."
                    —Deuteronomy 31:8 (NIV)

I sat alone at the kitchen counter early this morning with my Bible, a hot cup of coffee and a blank sheet of paper, trying to convince God that I couldn't possibly tackle the project before me.

I simply can't lead that workshop next weekend. I can't stand up in front of all those people. I can't even start an outline, I told God.

In case God didn't hear me, I wrote *I CAN'T!* in large letters across the top of my paper, and then put down my pen, as if I expected Him miraculously to rescue me from this task. Suddenly, I heard a great *whooshing* sound in our chimney and watched in amazement as a bird dropped down and flew through the family room, whamming into the picture window. With a frantic fluttering, it aimed for another window and whammed into that one.

I panicked. *Yikes! I'm alone in this house, and I can't handle a crazed bird! What will I do?*

Actually, I knew the answer. I had no choice. I had to deal with the bird, scared or not scared. So I marched down the hall, got a large towel and quietly tiptoed back toward the bird, now fluttering against a window sill. I stood poised for a moment and then tossed the towel over it. It froze. I froze. Then quickly I scooped it up in the towel, carried the bundle to the patio door, pushed it open and flung the towel outside. Immediately, the stunned bird flew away.

I did it! I thought, feeling surprised and relieved.

I threw the towel in the hamper, washed my hands and sat back down at the table where I saw the words *I CAN'T!* I smiled. God works in mysterious ways to show me that I can do what I fear the most—even if I have to do it scared.

Father, You know my fears. Please give me the courage to do what I fear I can't do, especially when I have to do it scared.   —Carol Kuykendall

28
TUE   *For thou didst form my inward parts, thou didst knit me together in my mother's womb. I praise thee. . . . Wonderful are thy works!*   —Psalm 139:13–14 (RSV)

"Oh, what are you making?" asked the cheerful middle-aged woman with whom I was sharing the dentist's waiting room.

As I looked up from my knitting, I was briefly tempted to answer, "I'm just knitting a prayer," but settled instead for a polite, "It's a baby blanket for a friend."

And that was true. The red lacy square in my lap was a gift for my friend Colleen, who was expecting her first child in a couple of months. But it was also something else, quite invisible to anyone but me. It was a prayer that all would go well with this pregnancy, so long awaited and preceded by a couple of miscarriages. Each stitch, linked and twisted into the next, represented an individual instant of prayer: that the blanket's owner would be born safely, would grow and flourish, and that he or she would have a happy and fulfilling life.

Some people use beads to count prayers; others write prayers out on tiny pieces of paper and burn them or consign them to the winds. Parts of my personal prayer journal are woolen and wearable: the lavender blanket for André and Jenny (their daughter Lucia must be almost two by now); the yellow jacket for Susan and Bruce (Madelaine is going on five, and I'd better start praying and knitting for her sibling or I'll be too late); and a whole outfit in bright red for Jill and Peter (their twin daughters awaited an energetic baby brother seven years their junior).

Maybe one day I'll be knitting prayers for my own grandchildren, and if that time comes, no pattern will be too intricate, no yarn too fine and no prayers more heartfelt.

Dear Lord, thank You for the special joy of babies and the chance for parents to grow in wisdom and love with their children.   —Brigitte Weeks

29
WED   *But a certain Samaritan, as he journeyed, came where he was: and when he saw him, he had compassion on him.*
                                                        —Luke 10:33

"Mmmm. Mmmm," fourteen-month-old Elizabeth grunted as she pounded her hand on the seat of the big blue living room chair. In her language, this meant, "Daddy, sit down and read to me!"

"Can you say 'please,' Elizabeth?" I asked.

"Peess," she answered.

"Okay, honey," I said, and I sat down in the chair, prepared for a long haul. My daughter loves being read to.

Elizabeth went over to the row of books beside the chair and chose one of the Bible story books her grandmother had given her. She handed me the book, lifted her arms to be picked up and then settled down on my lap.

Her favorite story is "The Man Who Helped," a retelling of the parable of the Good Samaritan. The "Hurt Man," his wounds marked by cross-hatching in the picture, was lying in the road. With a "step, step, step," the first traveler approached him.

"Did he stop to help?" I read. Elizabeth nodded her head yes.

"No, he didn't stop. He kept going." Elizabeth gave a little cry of dismay.

A second traveler rode by. "Did he stop to help?" I read. Again, Elizabeth vigorously nodded yes.

"No, he didn't stop either." Again she protested. Then she bent down over the book and, cooing softly, patted the hurt man's wounds.

No matter how many times we read the story—and she sometimes asks for it twenty times a day—Elizabeth has the same reaction. She refuses to believe that anyone would pass the Hurt Man by. In her world, the merciful aren't the exceptions, they're the rule.

Lord, open my eyes to see the need around me and then give me a merciful heart.
                                                        —Andrew Attaway

30

THU

I pray also that the eyes of your heart may be enlightened in order that you may know the hope to which he has called you. . . . —Ephesians 1:18 (NIV)

The grimy, gray stone walls of the eight-hundred-year-old church sagged wearily, supported by construction platforms abandoned in the lunch-hour sun. In the cemetery, the weathered stones tilted among patches of dying grass and thriving weeds. Someone had spray-painted two of the headstones blue.

Inside stood ranks of pews, some shrouded in linen, others only in dust and cracked varnish. My footsteps echoed through the empty sanctuary as I made my way down the center aisle. The altar was an imposing wooden structure with faded, blue-clad figures trailed by sprays of wheat and grapes covered in flaking gold.

I turned to leave, depressed by the state of this rotting relic. The shadow of the crucifix hanging between the altar and the pews fell over me. Startled, I looked up. The choir-loft lights were on, and a woman sat at the old organ. She played a few scales and then began a piece by Bach. I took a seat in the front pew and looked up at the figure on the Cross. The carving of Christ was in disrepair like everything else, but His gaze looked lovingly at me.

In the better light, I could see that the altar was in the process of being restored. A half-opened carton off to one side revealed new hymnals. The organ fell silent, and I could hear the shouts of the returning construction workers outside. I stood and made my way toward the exit. Curious, I peeked under one of the linen shrouds—a recently refinished pew appeared. I stepped out, blinking in the sunlight. In the cemetery, an old man crouched in the path, carefully uprooting the trespassing weeds.

My sadness was gone, replaced by admiration for the love and labor being expended to restore and heal a beloved church. And I knew that what seemed to be signs of decline and decay were actually the heralds of resurrection.

Lord, when first glances tempt me to despair, keep my eyes alive to the signs of hope. —Kjerstin Easton

31

FRI   ***What man is he that will begin? . . .***   —Judges 10:18

I sat beside my husband Gary's hospital bed, watching the eerie glow of the heart monitor. What began as a nagging heaviness in his chest

OCTOBER 1997

had escalated into a trip to the Mayo Clinic for two operations to help unblock his arteries. Last night he'd suffered a mild heart attack.

I looked down at the large book lying in my lap. It was filled with diagrams and explanations, lists of medical terms and pharmaceutical side effects, and things we would need to know about subjects like occupational therapy and exercise. That morning I'd attended a class on diet and nutrition. Yesterday I'd joined a group for a lecture on "living with heart disease."

It was all so new, so overwhelming. Gary and I had been married for more than twenty-five years. He'd always been strong, active, the one I depended on. What would the future be? How could I even begin to make all the necessary adjustments and changes?

I wandered down the hall, where our son Brett was waiting for his turn to see his dad. Inside the waiting room I saw Brett sitting at a table, bent over a jigsaw puzzle. He had dumped the box, and the pieces lay scattered across the table. I stood in the doorway and watched as he worked, sorting and fitting the edges.

In a few hours, Brett would leave for the long drive back to college. But I knew that after he had gone, others would work on that puzzle. It would be days, perhaps even weeks, before it was done, before all the pieces fit snugly and the picture was complete. But that was okay. Sometimes beginnings are enough.

Father, You are the Source of all courage and comfort. When I am confronted with a frightening new challenge, help me to begin.
—Mary Lou Carney

Everyday Wonders

1 _____

2 _____

3 _____

4 _____

5 _____

6 _____

7 _____

8 _____

9 _____

10 _____

11 _____

12 _____

13 _____

14 _____

15 _____

16 _____

17 _____

18 _____

19 _____

20 _____

21 _____

22 _____

23 _____

24 _____

25 _____

26 _____

27 _____

28 _____

29 _____

30 _____

31 _____

For I am persuaded, that neither death, nor life, nor angels, nor principalities, nor powers, nor things present, nor things to come, Nor height, nor depth, nor any other creature, shall be able to separate us from the love of God, which is in Christ Jesus our Lord. —ROMANS 8:38–39

November

S	M	T	W	T	F	S
						1
2	3	4	5	6	7	8
9	10	11	12	13	14	15
16	17	18	19	20	21	22
23	24	25	26	27	28	29
30						

1

SAT **LOVE IS ...**

[Love] always hopes. . . .   —I Corinthians 13:7 (NIV)

Over the baby's screams, I could barely catch the words of the white-haired woman in the rocking chair. At eighty, Clara Hale was saying, there were days when she never left this third-floor bedroom that she shared with as many as four newborns at a time.

The screams continued. "It's the pain," Mrs. Hale explained, rocking the pink-blanketed bundle in her arms. "She's crying out for the heroin she got in the womb."

It would be weeks before the crisis of withdrawals passed. During this whole period, until each new arrival was four months old, the infants shared Clara Hale's bedroom. "Old folks don't need a lot of sleep."

Downstairs, in a sunny playroom, the scene was very different. Watched over by Hale House staff, three toddlers pushed toy cars around a rug, while an older child painted an airplane in a green sky. Healthy, lively, loved, the children remained at Hale House in Harlem, New York, as long as it took for their mothers to complete a drug recovery program. Nearly six hundred drug-addicted babies, at the time of my visit, had been loved into health by Mother Hale and her helpers.

"How can you be sure the mothers won't go back on drugs?" I asked. Crack cocaine was peddled on that very street. The world the children were returning to was dangerous, violent.

"Sure?" Clara Hale echoed. "I can't be sure. I can hope." She gestured at a shelf crowded with school photos: bright-eyed, eager kids— "her" kids. When the night of rocking is long, "I look at those pictures. Hope is the gift God sends into the world with every child."

God of love, on this All Saints' Day, let me light my small candle of hope in the great fire of this faith.   —Elizabeth Sherrill

2

SUN *Then He showed me the river of the water of life, bright as crystal, flowing from the throne of God and of the*
Lamb.   —Revelation 22:1 (RSV)

Just over a week ago, I was called to the home of my dear friend and prayer partner Carolmae, who has been dying of cancer. The family felt the end was quite near. Standing around her bed with them and a few close friends, we said some special prayers for her, and then Carolmae, with almost no voice or breath left, began to hum an old hymn, "Shall We Gather at the River." Two of us remembered a bit of the hymn, but we're both frogs! Nevertheless, we began to sing what we could remember of it. Then Carolmae asked for other hymns, and we two frogs continued to sing until our friend drifted peacefully off to sleep.

Carolmae lived eight more days. I sat up with her on the night before she died, so that her exhausted family could get a bit of sleep. She was awake most of the night, though unable to speak, so I just sat there, giving her sips of water, holding her frail hand, saying Psalms and praying for her, sometimes silently, sometimes aloud. Near dawn, she used our joined hands to pull me closer. As I leaned over her, Carolmae said, in the tiniest wisp of a voice, "I'll meet you at the River, Marilyn."

I'll treasure that memory—and trust that hope—for the rest of my life.

If you've lost a loved one or have a friend who is terminally ill, you might want to look up some of those wonderful old hymns and sing them. It'll make your heart radiant—even if you're a frog!

> Yes, we'll gather at the river
> The beautiful, the beautiful river,
> Gather with the saints at the river
> That flows by the throne of God.

Amen. Oh, yes! Amen!   —Marilyn Morgan Helleberg

3
MON   *"Lord, teach us to pray. . . ."*   —Luke 11:1 (RSV)

The baby was crying again. I tumbled out of bed, trying not to glance at the clock. The weight of my eyelids told me it couldn't be more than two hours since the last time I'd been up. But the hardest thing about feeding Elizabeth was that it took so long to burp her. Sometimes it was more than an hour before the air came up—and if it didn't, she would scream with stomach pain.

Pat, pat, pat. Rub, rub, rub. As I burped her, I remembered an article I'd read in a newsletter long before Elizabeth was born. It was written by the young mother of a colicky baby. "Whenever I have to walk the baby at night," she wrote, "I use that time to pray for all the mothers who don't have the patience to cope with a difficult infant."

The idea had appealed to me, and now, I thought, it was time to put it into action. But I quickly discovered that sleep deprivation wasn't conducive to heavy-duty prayer. I was simply too tired to have anything to say. So I decided to start small, with something familiar. I named someone on my prayer list. "Our Father, Who art in heaven. . . ." *Pat, pat, pat. Rub, rub, rub.* "Amen." I named another person. "Our Father. . . ." By the time Elizabeth burped, I'd prayed the Lord's Prayer on behalf of nearly two dozen people. She was sleeping peacefully, and soon, so was I.

Elizabeth is more than a year old now, so she wakes up less often and never needs to be burped. I occasionally find myself staring at the ceiling in the middle of the night anyway. I don't mind being awake. In fact, I sort of look forward to it. Those quiet times have become precious to me because of the simple prayers they help me offer.

Lord Jesus, You taught us to pray. Help us recognize how much of each day we can fill with prayer.   —Julia Attaway

4
TUE

Let each of you look not only to his own interests, but also to the interests of others.   —Philippians 2:4 (RSV)

My first thoughts were about newspaper and television coverage. A friend, Ron Turner, was running for Nashville's Metro Council. He had chosen me to be the sign chairman of his campaign. I felt that fame was imminent. And the publicity would help me with my new job at the bank.

I launched a fevered effort to recruit volunteers to cover the Thirty-third District with campaign signs. The first Saturday, while thirty people gathered in a scorching-hot parking lot to get their assignments, I was still at Ron's standing in front of the garage where the signs were stored. Ron was out of town, and he had left me with a faulty garage door opener. An hour and a half later, the sweaty volunteers set out, irritably clutching stacks of signs. My career as a political mover and shaker was launched.

Requests for signs were constant, but by now, my sign staff had dwindled to my sister Keri and a friend or two. Sometimes, when I was really desperate, I dispatched Mom and Dad on missions to unfamiliar streets where they hammered signs in the dark. All of my spare time was spent searching for out-of-the-way addresses where I could put signs.

At last, Election Day! We gathered to wait for the final tally and—Ron Turner was our new councilman! But where were the TV cameras, the reporters with microphones? At least my family and friends were here to listen to Ron's victory speech: "And now, most of all, I want to thank—where's the kid?" His eyes searched the room. I was ready to raise my arms in triumph to meet the applause. "My campaign chairman." Ron looked past me to the young man who had run his campaign.

That was it. I'd joined Ron's campaign for personal glory, and here I was, an anonymous face lost in the celebrating crowd. I'd lost sight of the reason we have elections in the first place: to put good, honest people like Ron into important public offices.

Lord, when You give me a chance to serve, keep me from being self-serving.
—Brock Kidd

5
WED *Let us search and try our ways, and turn again to the Lord.* —Lamentations 3:40

I love reading bumper stickers. Some of them are funny, some are surprisingly wise. Each one makes me wonder about the owner of the car and what experience in life has prompted him or her to project that particular message to the world. I saw an extremely interesting sticker the other day:

If you find yourself going down the wrong path, God allows U-turns.

That one made me think about my own life and some of the wrong choices I've made along the way. Such as the time I wrote an angry letter to a neighbor who, I thought, had abused my trust in a business arrangement we had made together. It was a scathing, self-righteous letter filled with bitter accusations. I not only wrote it, I mailed it.

Wrong decision. Soon thereafter, I learned that I had completely misread the situation and my neighbor was innocent. After many prayers and a lot of anguish, I went to my neighbor, apologized and begged her forgiveness. She did forgive me, and we were able to mend the breach and proceed with our plans.

Thank God for U-turns.

Heavenly Father, please help me to see my errors. And give me the wisdom and courage to correct them. Amen.   —Madge Harrah

6
THU

To make ourselves a model for you to follow.
—II Thessalonians 3:9 (NIV)

I have never been crazy about spiders, even harmless ones. But one day I was substitute teaching, and at recess a five-year-old girl cried, "Teacher, there's a big spider near your foot!"

I froze. Everything in me wanted to scream, *"Eek!"* Fortunately, another substitute teacher sized up the situation, scooped up the spider in a paper cup and said, "Isn't this spider interesting? Let's look." The twenty students immediately crouched so that their faces were only inches away from it (while I bent down one millimeter!). And all of us watched in wonder as the spider crawled off to weave a web in the corner.

Later I whispered to the other teacher, "Lucky you're so brave. I hate those creatures. Can you imagine what would have happened if I'd screamed? Panic is contagious."

"Calm is contagious, too," she said, adding, "I'm terrified of spiders, too, but when I looked up and saw twenty pairs of eyes fixed on us, I could just imagine the hysteria erupting from the children had I given into my initial reaction and screamed!"

Calm is contagious. I mulled that over. Despite her fear, she had become a calm role model for the children. And for me.

Dear God, let me demonstrate calm, not panic, in the face of a possibly chaotic situation.   —Linda Neukrug

7
FRI

The inspiration of the Almighty giveth them understanding.
—Job 32:8

When I was a teenager, a friend of my dad's said to me, "Your father would drop everything to come to the aid of a friend." Maybe because I was in my teens and too busy finding faults in "the old man," I didn't believe him. And even as I grew older and gained a more rounded picture of my dad, I didn't put much credence in his friend's words.

Then a year ago, when I had just come home from the hospital after surgery and my wife Carol couldn't be there because she was staying at a different hospital with our younger son, who had a broken leg, Mom and Dad called from California to see how I was feeling. "Pretty rotten," I confessed.

"Could I come out and help?" Dad asked. He's in his seventies and has had his own medical troubles, so I wasn't sure he should, but I could hardly object. An hour later he called back. "I'm taking the red-eye tonight. I'll see you in the morning." And at six-thirty, after flying cross-country all night, he pulled up in a cab in front of our apartment building. He had dropped everything—meetings, business appointments, golf games, friends—to wash dishes, change sheets, do laundry, cook meals and take care of his ailing son.

"Dad," I said at the week's end when I was feeling much better and he was on his way back home, "I can't thank you enough." But what I was really grateful for was this chance to see him as his friend had seen him—devoted, supportive, ready to help at a moment's notice. I was finally grown up enough to recognize him for who he really is.

Help me, Lord, to see the members of my family as clearly as You see them.
                                                          —Rick Hamlin

8

SAT

Children are a gift from God; they are his reward.
                                      —Psalm 127:3 (TLB)

One Saturday night, when I was about seven years old, I'd gone to bed at my usual time, eight or eight-thirty. By nine-thirty, I was into a deep, sound sleep.

"Pat, wake up," Dad whispered as he shook my shoulder. "Are you awake? We want you to come out to the kitchen."

"Huh? Why, Daddy?"

"Your mom and I decided to have root beer floats, and we don't want you to miss out. Come on, honey. There's a big 'brown cow' out there for you."

I padded to the kitchen in my big, pink, fluffy slippers and plopped down next to Mom at the old wooden table. I watched Dad scoop the vanilla ice cream into the blue, brown and yellow mugs that had been in my mother's family when she was a girl. The foam from the root beer tickled my nose as I chatted with my folks about school and our family plans for the coming holiday season.

I never felt more loved than I did that night in the kitchen as I groggily slurped root beer and ice cream with my parents. Why? Because Mom and Dad wanted my company enough to wake me up so I could be there. That one simple act did more for my self-esteem than anything I can remember before or since.

Today, Lord, help me to think of a way to do something special for my child, grandchild or young neighbor. —Patricia Lorenz

9
SUN
We sat down and began to speak to the women who had gathered there. —Acts 16:13 (NIV)

After a few months as a novice radio amateur, I was no longer content to talk on just the long-distance bands allowed by my license. I wanted to be able to use the little hand-held radio called an "HT" (for Handy-Talky), so with much prayer I took and passed the next written exam. I was now a "Tech," a Technician Class ham, and soon I received a new call sign, N3IAR.

Soon, I began hearing new call signs used in daily transmissions between a husband and wife. She, NOLJZ, would call him, KB6IC, to see how his trip to work was going. They talked after the usual rush hour when the band was quiet and they wouldn't interfere with other conversations. From bits and pieces of their chats, I gathered that they were now living near our area of White Plains, Maryland, and that she was, like me, a stay-at-home mom.

Remembering how lonely it can be in a new place, I waited until the very end of their conversation one morning and then nervously called, "NOLJZ, this is N3IAR. My name is Bobbi. Do you copy?"

"Yes, N3IAR. This is NOLJZ. The name is Karen. Hi."

"Hi, Karen! I've heard you and your husband on the radio often lately. Are you new here?"

"Yes, we just moved from Omaha."

And so we talked for a while. Before signing off, I asked, "Why don't we meet at the mall for coffee soon?"

"Oh, that sounds great!" she responded.

We talked several more times that week. Within days we figured out how to recognize each other by sight rather than by voice and arranged to meet one morning after the kids were off to school. Before the coffee was finished, we both knew that we had found a friend for life.

Lord, thank You for new friends and the unique ways in which they come to us.   —Roberta Rogers

10
MON

Now you are the body of Christ, and each one of you is a part of it.   —I Corinthians 12:27 (NIV)

About twelve years ago, a small group of black people walked into an all-white Southern Baptist church near us in rural Mississippi and sat down to wait for the Sunday service. One of the deacons walked over to them and asked them to leave. Seven years later, that same church was asked to have a joint Easter service with a black church in the area. The young leaders of the congregation said yes, but some of the older people reminded them that blacks were forbidden to attend by the church's constitution. It took a year for that constitution to be amended, but at last a joint worship service took place.

Recently, the Southern Baptist Convention confessed that as a denomination its racial practices had been wrong, and it asked the black community for forgiveness. My immediate reaction was *It's about time!* But my second thought was *Praise God! Now the world has one less excuse not to follow our Lord. Let's move on.*

It's easy enough to focus on our divisions, but God challenges you and me to be bridge-builders. Although there are times I wish that things would change faster, someday the church will look and act like the body ordained by Christ and described by Paul in I Corinthians 12:27. And if you and I take the initiative to be reconcilers, we will have helped to make it so.

Lord, help me to reach out across every difference to my brothers and sisters in Christ.   —Dolphus Weary

11
TUE

Who shall separate us from the love of Christ? Shall trouble or hardship or persecution or famine or nakedness or danger or sword?   —Romans 8:35 (NIV)

Before I became a registered nurse, I thought war ended on the battlefield. But when, at the age of twenty-three, I began caring for veterans, I learned differently.

As I made my two A.M. rounds on my first night on duty, I found a patient leaning over his bedside table, his face buried in his hands. He'd been a prisoner of war during World War II. "I can't get back to sleep, nurse," he told me. His face was flooded with fear. "They've discovered that the cancer's moved to my liver. Would you read the Twenty-third Psalm to me?"

When I had finished reading, I continued down the hall. A veteran of the Korean War wheeled himself to the bathroom. He wore a navy blue baseball cap with the words *I Love America* emblazoned in red. In his lap was a patchwork quilt made by the hospital volunteers from woolen fabric scraps. It dangled down the side of his wheelchair where his left leg used to be.

At three-thirty A.M., I took a fresh cup of coffee to a frail, elderly lady sitting in a chair by the bed of her comatose husband, a veteran of World War I. She squeezed his limp hand and whispered "I love you" and talked to him about the morning glories spilling over their picket fence at home.

Just down the hall, a Vietnam veteran awakened from yet another nightmare. He'd fought on the front lines when he was only eighteen, and his best buddy had died in his arms. His faraway eyes told the story of a soldier with a slow, steady leak in his spirit. Still, he managed a smile and a "Thank you, nurse," when I hung a new bottle of IV fluid.

In just that one tour of duty, I'd cared for veterans of four different wars. These veterans, and all the others like them, wounded in body, mind, heart and spirit, became my teachers. Each time I pondered their sacrifices, I discovered something new about the price of freedom.

Lord, may all veterans and their families feel Your love in a special way this Veterans Day. Amen.   —Roberta Messner

12

WED   *Be transformed by the renewal of your mind. . . .*
                                        —Romans 12:2 (RSV)

My husband Terry and I once read the back page of a newspaper with ads from single men and women who were seeking to meet someone with similar interests. It was fun reciting the ads aloud, but when Terry suggested we compose our own, just between us, I felt awkward and ill at ease. Deep down I was afraid to know what we thought of ourselves. And even more terrifying, what if the people we were seeking weren't each other?

Over the next weeks I asked two friends to pray with me for the "renewal of mind" that Paul speaks of in Romans. I needed a fresh outlook so I could again appreciate my husband's qualities as those I would look for in a mate. Just as importantly, I concentrated on being the kind of wife I believed he would most hope to find.

God worked through the prayer partnership. Terry and I started liking each other again. We looked forward to being together. Our words and actions became affirming. Now, months later, we could write our married version of a "singles ad."

Mine read: "Young-at-heart wife with blue ribbons attitude. Needs self-sacrificing man who will make late-night emergency trips to store for chocolate. No mechanical aptitude—must be able to fix anything. Known to become lost in a book. Likes going to church. Interested in nature, fine arts, history, travel, most sports. Does housework only when necessary. Cooks great lasagna. Hates mustard."

Terry responded with: "Slightly worn husband, but with plenty of life left. Can repair everything but the crack of dawn and a broken heart. Needs regular maintenance—looking for partner who will take time for me. Reads Bible and other nonfiction. Cooks a mean breakfast. Not afraid to run a vacuum. Likes outdoor adventure, the Beatles, theater and symphony, a good laugh. Loves mustard."

Such has been the success of our campaign to renew our relationship that I can honestly say we plan on taking out lifetime subscriptions to each other.

Heavenly Father, earnest couple desiring to love You, and each other, seek new outlook through Your transforming grace.   —Carol Knapp

13

THU   *Then shall the righteous shine forth as the sun in the kingdom of their Father. . . .*   —Matthew 13:43

My friend Lynn was recently diagnosed with SAD, seasonal affective disorder. It seems her bouts with depression are directly related to the amount of sunshine she receives. Intrigued by this, I did some research on sunlight and was surprised at how necessary to us it is. In fact, in Ostrounoye—a village two hundred miles north of the

Arctic Circle that gets only minutes of sunlight on winter days—kindergarten students receive a daily dose of ultraviolet light to compensate for the lack of sun.

Lynn is undergoing treatment and doing better these days. But I've been wondering what I can do to help others who experience different kinds of darkness. My mother, whose days are filled with pain; my sister, who has known professional and financial problems this year; my friend, who is trapped in a difficult marriage. Can I be "sunshine" to them? A phone call, a card of encouragement, a pledge to pray for them each day. Maybe even an occasional plate of chocolate chip cookies and a few jokes!

Perhaps I can become a bearer of GLAD—news of God Loving And Delighting in His children. That's a truth that can brighten anyone's dark days—even mine!

Precious Jesus, You are brightness and goodness. Let me bask in Your glory and be a reflection of Your Sonlight. —Mary Lou Carney

14

FRI

Be ye doers of the word, and not hearers only. . . .
—James 1:22

I was sitting in a fast-food restaurant, bolting down a hamburger and preparing to lead a Bible study. Scribbling my thoughts on note cards, I glanced up when an unkempt young man plopped down at the next table. He fumbled in his soiled backpack for his coin purse and counted out the money for a meager supper. Destitute, he lived on the streets from day to day.

Unaware of my staring, he reached again into his backpack and pulled out a dog-eared Bible. He began to read, deliberately pointing to each word and slowly mouthing the syllables. My curiosity aroused, I stood up to leave and walked slowly behind him. He was reading from Psalm 16.

As I returned to my car, I hastily flipped to Psalm 16:1 and read, "Preserve me, O God: for in thee do I put my trust." The meaning of these words jumped off the page. This homeless man who had nothing trusted in God for everything.

Driving to the church, I also remembered the words of James 2:15–17 (NAS): "If a brother or sister is without clothing and in need of daily food, and one of you says to them, 'Go in peace, be warmed and be filled,' and yet you do not give them what is necessary for their body, what use is that? Even so faith, if it has no works, is dead, being by itself."

The same Bible that had comforted the afflicted now afflicted the comfortable. I knew God was talking to me.

Dear Father, may I not only study the Bible, may I live it, too. Amen.
—Scott Walker

15

SAT   *Fight the good fight of faith. . . .*   —I Timothy 6:12

Recently, my birthplace, Montpelier, Ohio, celebrated its 150th anniversary, and I returned for the festivities. It was a time for nostalgia for the four thousand townspeople who make up this community near the Indiana and Michigan borders, and it started me thinking about some of the people I knew there as a boy.

One of them was Babe Howald, the high school superintendent's wife. Memory whispers that her name was Thelma, but I never heard anyone use it. Every community, I suppose, has someone like Babe, an irrepressible, can-do person who, filled with civic duty, responds whenever a need arises. A large woman with a voice to match, she had been an outstanding athlete in the black-bloomer era of girls' basketball, and her love of sports never waned. She rooted hard for all the local teams, and even when victory seemed out of reach she never gave up. "You can do it!" was her trademark battle cry.

I'll never forget a high school football game we played against a much larger school on a distant field. It was a miserable, snowy November night, more suitable for skiing than for football. And we got clobbered. The score must have been 60–0. I know it was lopsided because I was playing! All either team wanted was to get out of the cold. By the fourth quarter, only a handful of shivering fans remained, one of whom was Babe. I didn't see her, but I heard her indomitable voice over the howling wind: "You can do it, boys!"

I'm uncertain if encouragers are born or made, but I believe God must have a special place reserved in heaven for all the Babe Howalds who lift our sights and urge us on.

> *Remind me, God, that . . .*
> *Encouraging words are a priceless gift*
> *To withered souls who need a lift.*

—Fred Bauer

Thanksgiving

Thank you for the tranquil night.
Thank you for the stars.
Thank you for the silence.

Thank you for the time you have given me.
Thank you for life.
Thank you for grace.

Thank you for being there, Lord.
Thank you for listening to me, for taking me
        seriously,
        for gathering my gifts in your hands to offer
        them to your Father.
Thank you, Lord.
Thank you.

—MICHEL QUOIST

16
SUN

"Make friends quickly with your opponent. . . ."
—Matthew 5:25 (NAS)

It was my first year of teaching literature at a small Midwestern school, which was in the process of changing from a Bible college to a liberal arts college. Many of the students were afraid of "secular" literature, even of the great masterpieces like Dante's *Inferno* or Plato's *Republic*. They not only resisted learning, but some of them were quite rude.

One Sunday afternoon, late in the first semester, Rachel Thompson, a fellow English teacher, invited a few of us from the college over to her house. To my dismay, one of the other guests was David, perhaps the most obstreperous and outspoken student in my literature class. My first thought was pretty much to ignore him, but he had with him an unusual hymnal. Every page in it was cut in two! The top halves contained tunes, and the bottom halves words, so any hymn could be sung to a variety of tunes.

Soon we were both at the piano, putting various tunes and words together, comparing notes as to our favorites, and talking about our past experiences. I found him a thoughtful young man, who had traveled thousands of miles from Ireland to attend an American Christian college. Before the evening was over, my animosity toward him had vanished.

On Monday in class, David raised his hand and asked to speak to the class. "I'm sorry," he said. "I want to ask Miss Howes' and your forgiveness for my past rudeness in this class. I've asked God to forgive me."

Because I had accepted him as a real person, not just as an unruly student, David had been able to see me as a real person rather than a hated teacher—and, in spite of my love for secular literature, as someone who loved God just as he did.

Lord, help me to remember that any "enemy" is really a potential friend.
—Mary Ruth Howes

17
MON

May the God of steadfastness and encouragement grant you to live in such harmony with one another. . . .
—Romans 15:5 (RSV)

How I longed for a call from my friend Katy. Each time I phoned her, it seemed that she had no time for me. Eventually, four months had gone by and we hadn't gotten together. I thought I had done something to displease her. And the awful thing was I couldn't talk to her about it.

I spoke with another friend about the situation. He looked at me quietly and said, "We can pray about it."

I was dumbfounded. I pray every day, but it hadn't occurred to me to pray about feeling rejected.

Later the next day, as I prepared to go home, the phone rang. It was Katy. "How are you?" she asked warmly. "I've missed you."

Suddenly, all the feelings I'd been holding in came pouring out. Katy was astonished. "Why didn't you tell me before?" she asked. "I'm not angry with you. Where did you ever get that idea?"

"I don't know," I replied, "but I'm awfully glad to find out it's not true."

When Katy and I had finished talking, I called my friend at his office to tell him what had happened. "Do you think it was the prayer that made her call?" I asked.

"I don't know," he replied. "But I do know one thing."

"What?" I asked.

"We're not supposed to give up. Not ever."

Father, how wonderfully You use my prayers to knit me to my friends. Help me to be steadfast in prayer and in friendship.   —Susan Schefflein

18

TUE   *For in the image of God made he man.*   —Genesis 9:6

As a writer, I try to avoid words of more than three syllables. Or even two. If you're reading, long words slow you down. If you're writing, they may sound pedantic. If you're speaking, they can make you seem pompous. And yet there's one word with six syllables that I have a lot of respect for: *verisimilitude*. It means having the appearance of truth.

The word is enormously important for a writer. If you're writing dialogue in a short story, the words must sound like words that were actually spoken, not just invented words originating in someone's imagination. They must have the ring of authenticity. They must seem true.

And what about people? Doesn't the word apply to them, too? If we're made in the image of God, as the Bible tells us, how close do we come to reflecting that perfect Being? How much verisimilitude do we have? Can we reach for more in our ongoing relationship with Him?

It's not an easy thing to achieve. But we have a lifetime in which to try.

Father, let the light we offer to the world be a faithful reflection of Your radiance.   —Arthur Gordon

19

WED   *And because ye are sons, God hath sent forth the Spirit of his Son into your hearts, crying, Abba, Father!*
      —Galatians 4:6

At age two and a half, my daughter Elizabeth was very attached to her daddy. When he had to be away at a weeklong conference, she happily waved good-bye at the airport Sunday night, not fully comprehending that Daddy wouldn't be home for a while.

The next morning, when she discovered that Alex was gone, she climbed up into his empty place on the bed, flung her head down on his pillow and sobbed. Nothing managed to cheer her up. She moped about listlessly; her usual singing and babbling vanished. Fortunately, Alex telephoned that afternoon. Elizabeth listened wide-eyed and afterward proudly proclaimed, "Daddy talked to me on the airplane!"

On Tuesday, she received a card in the mail from Alex and carried it around all day. When he called on Wednesday, she chattered exuberantly.

As Elizabeth cheered up, I began to flounder. Sorely missing Alex myself, weighed down with giving piano lessons and teaching special classes, the stress of single-parenting seemed too heavy for me. On Wednesday night, I clutched my Bible and moaned, "Lord, I dread the rest of this week."

Wait a minute, I told myself, *this is the first time all week I've opened my Bible or prayed*. During the next few days, I got up early to talk with *my* loving Father and found the strength I needed to face each day's demands.

Abba, Father, today and every day You come to me in Your Word.
					—Mary Brown

20
THU

"I give them eternal life, and they shall never perish, and no one shall snatch them out of my hand."
					—John 10:28 (RSV)

I lay in bed, the darkness swirling with fear over my nineteen-year-old daughter Sanna. Strong-willed and impulsive, she'd entered the party life and stopped going to church. I never knew what time she'd be home, or where she'd been. It was two A.M., and she was still out.

I crawled out of bed, pulled on a robe, padded downstairs to the living room and curled up on the sofa. The soft light of a half moon shone through the window on the empty corner where Sanna used to play with her dolls. One day, when she was three, she had sat in that corner, chattering sweetly to her dolls, while I sat at the sewing machine. Suddenly, I lifted my foot from the pedal and listened.

"Hi, Jesus," she was saying. "You've come to play dolls with me? Oh, goody!" Holding my breath, I watched as she stood and held out a little hand, her fingers curled as if clasping something tightly. "Come on, Jesus. I want You to have my best doll. She's upstairs." I heard Sanna disappear up the steps.

How safe I'd felt she was then. How scared I was for her now. A cold wind rattled the window. With a shiver, I looked beyond the glass into the darkness. In my mind's ear, I could still hear Sanna's little-girl voice welcoming Jesus. And I knew that since that day, when she took Jesus' hand, He had never let go. Wherever she was, He was, too. Because that's Who He is. I could rest in that. Sleep, even.

Lord, my security, for myself and my loved ones, is You.   —Shari Smyth

21
FRI
In all thy ways acknowledge him, and he shall direct thy paths.   —Proverbs 3:6

One evening, a few months ago, I was taking my dog for a late walk. Our route was along a quiet country road, with no houses on either side, only fields and woods. "Hurry up, Suzy!" I said whenever she stopped to sniff. It was getting dark, and I wanted to go to the library before it closed.

Finally, I decided we had gone far enough. "Let's go home," I said, turning around. But Suzy kept facing in the other direction. "Come!" I said, using a command that always gets results. Suzy didn't budge. She looked back at me, and even in the twilight I could see concern in her eyes.

From the fields around us, where the grass was waist high, I heard a high-pitched sound. I thought it might have been a bird, and when Suzy pulled in that direction, I went along with her. The grasses parted, and a tiny, black and white kitten stumbled toward us, crying pitifully. It was skinny and dirty, its face scratched by thorns. Suzy bent down to lick its head as if to reassure it. I picked up the kitten and carried it home, where it was only too happy to eat and fall asleep curled up next to Suzy. That scruffy kitten has now grown into a healthy, handsome cat named Dennis, who gives our family lots of joy.

On that first night I was disappointed because I was out so late that

I couldn't go to the library. But God had something more important He wanted me to do—and I've always been thankful that He helped me to stop and listen to His plan.

Lord, make me quick to change directions when I hear the sound of Your voice. Amen.   —Phyllis Hobe

22

SAT   *The Lord is good unto them that wait for him. . . .*
                                        —Lamentations 3:25

My friend Ronny has had a rich life, the fruit of her deep faith in prayer. During her seventy-six years, she has been a municipal worker, a church missionary, a director of Christian education and an interim pastor who brought healing to two churches.

I thought she had run out of surprises until she called with the news that she had opened the Lanier Mission House in Melrose, Massachusetts, in memory of her parents. "This has been my life's dream," she said. "I've prayed for this for more than forty years. I wanted to establish a haven for returning missionaries. A place that would welcome them, without cost, until they could get on their feet." And then she said, as she had so many times, "I believe in prayer. Isn't it wonderful?"

Ronny's words took me back to 1962, when I was working as an aircraft engine tester. I was working the night shift, the plant was noisy, and the work was grimy and greasy. During those hours I dreamed of being a technical writer. I took classes, studied hard and went on a lot of interviews. After each interview, I returned to the roaring engines, the oily parts and the night shift.

My wife Ruby sensed my disappointment and said, "Try not to worry. God may have a plan." So I worked and studied, and I prayed that God would help me handle my impatience. Finally, in June 1968, I was hired as a technical writer. After one week on the job, I knew why so much time had elapsed. I was writing about aircraft engines and without those six years in the plant, I wouldn't have known how to begin. Now I understood.

Yes, Ronny, prayer—and patience—make the difference.

All-knowing Father, teach us through prayer to trust Your master plan.
                                        —Oscar Greene

23
SUN

And all thy children shall be taught of the Lord; and great shall be the peace of thy children.   —Isaiah 54:13

The Sunday school class that my husband Bob and I attended had taken on the task of helping a low-income family. We soon realized that they needed spiritual as well as material assistance. The adults resisted, but they did give us permission to take the children to church. Pete, the little boy assigned to us, was a scrawny six-year-old with brown eyes in a solemn, seldom-smiling face.

One Sunday morning as the congregation gathered for the worship service, a woman sitting near us told a funny story involving her toddler. We adults enjoyed a good laugh, but Pete looked from one of us to another, bewildered. Cupping his hand in front of his face, he whispered, "Is it all right to laugh in church?"

I slipped my arm around his shoulders. "During the service, we sit quietly and listen," I explained gently. "But before the service starts, we talk together, and we often laugh because we're happy. Did you know that Christians are the happiest people in the world?"

His eyes were wide and piercing. "Why?" he asked.

"Because we know that God loves us. He sent His Son Jesus to prove it."

"How do you know that?"

"The Bible tells me," I said. "Do you have one?"

"No." he answered.

"If you like, I'll get you a Bible storybook that will help you learn about God and how good He is."

"I'd like that," he said.

The next morning, I went to the bookstore. As I thumbed through the colorful Bible storybooks, I wondered how many other children in our town had no books of their own.

Don't just wonder, my conscience challenged. *Find out!*

I left the store with six Bible storybooks in my hands, a firm resolve and a parting word to the bookseller: "Keep these on order. I'll be back for more."

Father, make us aware of the need for Your Word and give us the means to share it.   —Drue Duke

24
MON

My voice shalt thou hear in the morning, O Lord; in the morning will I direct my prayer unto thee, and will look up.
—Psalm 5:3

My mouth was a little dry and my voice a little shaky as I looked around at my colleagues and said, "I ask your prayers for my friend Frank—he's been out of work for almost two years now and is interviewing this week for a job." This was the first time I had made a prayer request at a meeting of the New York City Guideposts Prayer Fellowship.

Then I read from a couple of letters, one telling us of answered prayers and another beginning, "I read in the magazine where it said, 'May we pray for you?' " The mother of a drug-addicted son from a small town more than a thousand miles from the crowded streets of Manhattan went on to ask simply, "Please pray for us."

Prayer is very private and hard to describe in words. But picture this: The room is fairly large, the table oval; twelve or fifteen people are seated around it. I am there almost every week. I hate to miss it. Not so long ago, the idea of sitting down to pray with my colleagues once a week would have seemed like something out of science fiction. Already it seems a totally appropriate way to start the work week.

We meet on Monday morning at nine forty-five in the Guideposts New York City office and in our offices in Carmel and Pawling, New York. For an hour, we join through letters and prayers with the Guideposts family all over the United States and the world. (Letters have come recently from New Zealand, from South Africa and from Brazil.)

There's a special kind of spirit at work here each Monday morning, and those who have been touched by it know its strength and its comforting power. And if Guideposts is much more than just an efficient, well-run publishing company, it's because Prayer Fellowship is at the heart of who we are.

You have told us, Lord, that when two or three are gathered together in Your name, You will be in their midst. We thank You for Your presence with us and with all the members of our Guideposts family on this Family Day of Prayer.   —Brigitte Weeks

25
I have learned, in whatsoever state I am, therewith to be content. —Philippians 4:11

Soon after we were married, David and I moved to the mountains of eastern Kentucky to serve the poor. Very quickly, we learned that our concept of "poor" was a bit off-target. We came believing people were poor if they lacked material wealth. But God had a man named Taft Sargent waiting to teach us something different.

"Taft." Twenty-three years have passed, and the sound of his name still brings peace. He was a coal miner, hammered by black lung, dark mining tragedies, the death of a young son. Retired, he and his wife Beulah lived in a little house on a bit of land that clung to the side of a rocky hill. He had an old red truck, a huge garden, some chickens, a cow and a couple of pigs. That's about it for worldly possessions; yet, remembering Taft, I think "rich."

Taft had a "praying rock" up on the hill behind his house. Mornings, he went up there to talk things over with God. I imagine he spent a lot of time thanking Him for the fine turnips that were coming up in his garden or praising Him for a bumper crop of pumpkins—enough for all his neighbors. I don't imagine Taft ever actually asked for much. You could tell right away that he had all he needed and then some. Always, you left Taft and Beulah's with your arms full.

"Oh, you shouldn't give us all this," David and I would say, laden with jars of homemade jam, fresh churned butter, beans, corn and tomatoes.

"Why, we're just proud we have it to give," Taft would say.

To some, he was only a coal miner. To David and me, he was an extraordinary man of faith, deeply in love with being alive.

Father, help us to understand that if we're content with what You have given us, we can be instantly rich. —Pam Kidd

26
Never flag in zeal, be aglow with the Spirit. . . . —Romans 12:11 (RSV)

It was another hectic morning of another hectic day, and as the year drew to a close, I felt wrung out and uncertain about the future. Another birthday was about to happen and the holidays were around the corner, but I didn't feel much in the spirit of things. As I left my apartment for work, I saw my neighbor, a young man I'll call Charles, waiting in the hallway for the elevator.

Charles is dying of AIDS. He is literally skin and bones. He's in his early thirties but walks with a cane. His friends tell me that Charles' doctors want him in the hospital, but Charles postpones what he knows is inevitable. There is something gloriously tenacious and stubborn about Charles.

When the elevator came, I held the door open as Charles doddered in. We both studied a notice taped on the elevator wall: "Stunning Fire Island beach house for summer rent. Sign up now. Have something to look forward to and get you through the winter!" I glanced at Charles and felt uncomfortable. He would not be seeing another summer. But then I saw him brighten and tear off one of the phone numbers.

Outside, I helped Charles button up his overcoat and hailed him a cab. I opened the door as he eased himself in. I could tell he was in pain. But he managed a smile and a jaunty tip of his hat. "Thank you," he said.

Then he was off. And so was I, past the newsstand where people lined up for lottery tickets, past St. John's Hall where the homeless filed in for breakfast. I was feeling just a little bit like Charles. Stubborn and tenacious, and a bit more certain.

Make me see, Lord, how much You give me to look forward to, to help get me through the winters of my life.   —Edward Grinnan

27   *I can never stop thanking God for all the wonderful gifts*
THU   *he has given you. . . .*   —I Corinthians 1:4 (TLB)

It's good to feel grateful, but sometimes that's just not enough.

My father was a capable and dedicated minister, serving small-town churches throughout the Midwest. One church he served proved unrewarding. The members spoke up only to criticize, and he grew increasingly disenchanted with the work. Finally, he resigned and took another church not far away.

As soon as he had settled into the new parsonage, letters by the handful began to arrive from his former church.

"You were the best preacher we ever had. Why did you leave us?"

"We appreciated you more than you can know. You were a father to us."

I can still remember my father muttering to himself in a sad voice,

"If only those people had told me those things while I was there, I might never have left."

My father wasn't working for praise, but he was a human being, and few of us can do our best work without feeling that it's valued. That incident taught me early in life that it's not enough just to feel gratitude. There's a difference between "thanksfeeling" and "thanksgiving." Gratitude must be expressed if it's to have its best result.

If you're like me, you are probably grateful to many people, but you forget to tell them. This Thanksgiving I'm compiling a list of people to whom I'm going to send my thanks, beginning with:

My Father in heaven, from Whom I have received "every good and perfect gift," thank You.   —Daniel Schantz

28

FRI   *Be still, and know that I am God. . . .*   —Psalm 46:10

"Brock, you sure are quiet," my dad said. "Is something bothering you?"

It was the day after Thanksgiving, and my dad and I were headed to a camp in southern Alabama. The camp was owned by my uncle, and this was the second year in a row my dad and I were making the trip.

"I guess I'm stressed out about next week, Dad," I said, staring out the window. "It's gonna be pretty tough."

My dad nodded his head with understanding. The second business trip of my career was next week. It was a follow-up with the prospects I had met on my last trip, except this time I was to give each banker a presentation. My job was to tell them why they should do business with me.

The next day my dad and I were up early, before dawn. It was a cool morning, and there was frost covering the field. Thoughts of my trip came into my head. *How will I perform?* I knew the banks needed what I had to offer them, but would I be confident enough to do the job effectively? I became so worried that I began to pray. "Dear God, take away all of my worries and fears about next week."

The sun rose slowly, bringing the woods around me to life. Birds began singing; squirrels gathered nuts and playfully jumped from tree to tree. I saw a family of raccoons scurry toward the creek that winds through the forest. A glorious morning was beginning. The frost was melting, and I could feel all of my anxieties melting with it.

It was then, in that exquisite, singing stillness, that a verse I'd heard in church came to me: "Be still, and know that I am God."

Be still, Brock. Stop fretting and creating worries over the week ahead, God seemed to be saying in the morning's unfolding. *Be still, and know that I am God.* Such an obvious truth. Somehow, in the rushing and the chattering of telephones, the bleeping fax machines and stock prices, I had allowed this great truth of the ages to slip. Now, here in this quiet place, it had become clear again.

Lord, when I let the rush and push of my days get away, remind me of the medicine of stillness. Help me to be still and know that You are God.

—Brock Kidd

29

29
SAT

"Your people shall be my people. . . ."
—Ruth 1:16 (TLB)

For the first few years after we were married, Gene and I lived in Oklahoma, where his family lives. Although Gene's relatives always went out of their way to make me a part of the family, I often felt like an intruder. Sometimes I would step outside after dinner to give them a chance to reminisce alone.

One Thanksgiving, we were celebrating at Gene's daughter's home. After dinner, I took a slice of turkey and a cup of gravy outside to see if I could get Buck, the family dog, to eat. Poor Buck had developed a brain abscess after being kicked by a horse, and though the vet insisted that he not get dehydrated, Buck simply refused to drink or eat. Now he was lying beside the house, curled up in a tight ball. "Oh, Buck, please eat this, just a little," I said, but he would have none of it. I lingered with him, not even realizing that I was shivering from the cold.

Suddenly, I felt something warm around my shoulders. Above the strong wind, I heard Gene say, "Thank you. Thank you for trying." The heavy coat had been his first wife's, and it seemed to warm more than my body. A gentle, radiating warmth reached deep into my defeated spirit.

Pulling the coat tightly about me, I prayed, "Lord, please make Buck well for this family. Help him to drink." I dipped a finger into the gravy. Buck's tongue darted toward my hand. He licked the gravy off of my finger and then drank the entire bowl. Next, he consumed a pan of water, stood, shook off the blanket and ran to the creek for more. I jammed my cold, wet hands into the warm pockets of the purple coat and hurried inside to tell *our* family the good news.

You, Father, are the One Who truly makes us into families. Thank You for my family. Amen.   —Marion Bond West

THE CANDLES OF CHRISTMAS: HOPE, PEACE, JOY AND LOVE . . . AND CHRIST

One of the most beautiful customs of the Christmas season is the Advent wreath. Set in a circle of greens, four candles surround one central candle. On the four Sundays before Christmas, the candles in the circle are lit, first one, then two, then three and, finally, four. On Christmas Day, the center candle is lit to commemorate the coming of the Christ Child. Different Christian traditions give somewhat different interpretations to the four candles. During this Christmas season, Eric Fellman shares his tradition, which names them "Hope," "Peace," "Joy" and "Love."

—The Editors

30
SUN   **The Candle of Hope**

. . . Which is Christ in you, the hope of glory.
—Colossians 1:27

Today, we light the first candle on our Advent wreath, the candle of Hope. An old preacher I knew as a young man worked hard to give simple definitions to great words. His definition of *hope* was "acting on the expectation of success." For me, Joseph is the person in the Christmas story who best exemplifies hope. Against a background of scandal, difficult travel, danger and financial hardship, he kept moving his family forward. He listened to God's voice and, without anything but hope, set out for Bethlehem and then Egypt, before returning home to Nazareth. By doing so, he helped Mary to give birth to the infant Jesus in safety, delivered Him from the cruelty of King Herod, and raised Him in security and love.

As a father, I really relate to Joseph. Sometimes we fathers have to pack up and move with nothing but hope to sustain us. The day after Christmas 1984, I loaded our ten-year-old Plymouth with as much as it would carry and headed for New York and a new job. My wife Joy and the children were staying behind to sell our house, which was a nearly impossible task in Chicago in the winter. All we had was hope, and mine was pretty slim. All during the two-day drive through wind, rain and snow, I worried about the house. Like Joseph, I needed a word from God. It came through a pay phone at eleven P.M. and about eleven degrees.

Before even saying "Hello," Joy said, "Honey, I sold the house. You see, this young family came the day after Christmas, just the couple and their little baby. With all the cold weather, he wants a house right away. They don't quite have enough money to meet our price, but with the little baby and all, I thought we could come down some. Okay?"

A young couple with a new baby, the day after Christmas, with no place to stay? What do you suppose I said?

Dear Father, as I prepare for Christmas, renew my hope in the miracles You have planned for my life. —Eric Fellman

Everyday Wonders

1 _____

2 _____

3 _____

4 _____

5 _____

6 _____

7 _____

8 _____

9 _____

10 _____

11 _____

12 _____

13 _____

14 _____

15 _____

16 _____

17 _____

18 _____

19 _____

20 _____

21 _____

22 _____

23 _____

24 _____

25 _____

26 _____

27 _____

28 _____

29 _____

30 _____

The Lord thy God in the midst of
thee is mighty; he will save, he
will rejoice over thee with joy; he
will rest in his love, he will joy
over thee with singing.

—ZEPHANIAH 3:17

December

S	M	T	W	T	F	S
	1	2	3	4	5	6
7	8	9	10	11	12	13
14	15	16	17	18	19	20
21	22	23	24	25	26	27
28	29	30	31			

1

LOVE IS . . .

Love is . . . never selfish. . . .   —I Corinthians 13:4–5 (NEB)

We saw it as we drove south on Alabama Route 69, a glow in the December night. "What can it be?" I said to my husband—the map showed no town here.

Brighter and brighter it got as we drew close. Then, around a bend, there it was: a small frame house, a tumble-down barn, a hen-house, a fence, some trees—and each one outlined, festooned, glorious with Christmas lights. Thousands and thousands of colored bulbs transformed the night. We took our place at the end of a line of cars inching up the long dirt driveway, past the Nativity scene in the front yard, hearing the *ooh*s and *aah*s.

We stopped at the first motel we came to, and next day drove back to meet the creators of this splendor. Harold and Ruby Swindle answered our knock. Yes, they told us over mugs of coffee in the kitchen, the month-long display took money—new bulbs, the electric bill—and they didn't have much of that. Harold worked in a restaurant, Ruby in a cotton mill.

It took time, too: three months to put up the lights in the fall, all of January and February to take them down. "But Sis gets such joy out of it, we just can't stop." It was their daughter Sis, married now, who at age five, they told us, had insisted they hang Christmas lights on the porch "so people driving by can see them."

Each year they'd added a few more strings; each year as more people came to look, Sis's excitement grew. "Tell me how it looks, Mom!" she'd say. "Tell me about the children's faces!"

"Sis is blind, you see," her mother went on. "She's never seen a light. That's why she's so happy that others can."

God of Love, I want the joy You promised when You told us, "It is more blessed to give than to receive" (Acts 20:35).   —Elizabeth Sherrill

2

Be ready always to give an answer to every man that asketh you a reason of the hope that is in you. . . .

—I Peter 3:15

I recognized Irene's voice as soon as I picked up the phone. She sounded discouraged. "Papa is sick," she said. Her father, now in his eighties, had been admitted to the hospital.

"I'm so scared," she continued, beginning to cry. I could feel her grief, her fear. She was already missing him. Somehow, she knew: Her father would not make it.

I sat there, just listening. Irene had come to me for help, but all I could do was pray, and since Irene wasn't one of my Christian friends, I didn't feel comfortable praying with her. Perhaps she'd be embarrassed or offended.

But as I listened to her sobbing, I seemed to hear a deeper cry: *Pray for me! I called you because I knew you would pray.* Her need penetrated my foolish pride, and somehow I found myself praying aloud into the phone. Within minutes, she brightened.

"Thank you so much," she said. "I feel much better." And I did, too. Irene had taught me that offering others my help, in whatever way I can give it, is always better than withholding it.

Father, give me the courage to help others in any way I can.

—Robin White Goode

3
WED

And in every work that [Hezekiah] began . . . he did it with all his heart, and prospered.   —II Chronicles 31:21

Dad was the musical one in our family. As a young man, he had played the ukulele in a country string band, and at family gatherings he loved to sing in his pleasant tenor voice. Mother was another story. She had never learned to play an instrument or carry a tune.

One night, when I was about fourteen years old, Mom came back from a meeting of her women's club in a state of high excitement. The club was going to produce a fund-raising musical, and Mom would get a chance to sing in the chorus.

But as rehearsals began, her enthusiasm turned to anxiety. She was afraid she'd never be able to learn the music. Dad offered to coach her, but she was too ashamed of her singing to let him.

One night Mom asked me to show her how to use my tape recorder. I brought it out to the kitchen after supper and gave her a quick lesson. The light was still on in the kitchen when I went to bed that night. It was on every night for two weeks.

A few days before opening night, I wanted to use the recorder for a school assignment. When I rewound the tape and pressed the play button, I heard Mom's voice, more squeaking than singing:

Nine hundred and ninety-nine is our membership.
Nine hundred and ninety-nine just precise. . . .

Again and again, Mom sang that song, and by the end of the tape, although no one would have mistaken her for Ethel Merman, I could recognize the tune as "Seventy-Six Trombones."

On opening night, Mom took her place in the chorus. When the curtain went up, she seemed a little uncertain. But her voice, bolstered by all those nights of practice, gradually grew stronger, and by the show's end, her smile was brighter than the footlights.

Lord, when You call me to test my limits, give me a determined heart.

—Andrew Attaway

4

THU

Be content with such things as ye have. . . .

—Hebrews 13:5

Not long ago, my dad gave me *The Precious Present,* a wonderful book by best-selling author Spencer Johnson. It's the story of a man who spends his life seeking a treasure a wise old man has told him about, the Precious Present. "It is the best present a person can receive," the old man says, "because anyone who receives such a gift is happy forever."

So the man searches the world for this Precious Present until one day he discovers it is simply that: the Present. He finally understands what the old man meant when he told him, "When you have the Precious Present, you will be perfectly content to be where you are."

Lately, I can't get that story out of my head. As the mother of two young children, it seems my thoughts are always several steps ahead of the present. My daily calendar is often turned to tomorrow when today is not yet over. Working to be organized and efficient, I frequently find my mind wandering into the future. Listening to my son Ross read me a story at bedtime, I'm suddenly thinking about what's in my refrigerator to pack for his lunch tomorrow. As I'm rocking little Maria to sleep, my thoughts drift to the chores I can get done while she's sleeping. Instead of enjoying my son's excitement as he learns to read or the sweet, warm scent of my baby daughter, I'm already moving on to my next task.

God has given me so much to enjoy in my life, I don't want to miss any of it. So now when I'm snuggling my sleepy little girl and find myself thinking about that waiting load of wash, I say a little prayer:

"Thank You, Lord, for the Precious Present." And I have no doubt the future can wait.

Giver of all life, help me to remember the past and hope for the future, but to live now. —Gina Bridgeman

5
FRI

Jesus said unto him, If thou canst believe, all things are possible to him that believeth. And straightway the father of the child cried out, and said with tears, Lord, I believe; help thou mine unbelief. —Mark 9:23–24

Although thirty years have passed, I can still recall the anguish I felt when our son Kelly boarded the plane for Saigon. He was heading to a war on the other side of the globe. There would be no phone calls assuring us he was safe, no letters for weeks at a time. Never had I felt so helpless.

While Kelly still lived at home, I felt that his father and I were in charge. God had given us the responsibility of nurturing and protecting him. Now his life was completely in God's hands. I knew that the Lord's love and fatherly care would accompany Kelly across the Pacific, but it was hard to turn my son's life over to Him. Despite my faith and my determination to keep my gaze fixed on the Lord, I still worried about my son's safety.

Then a Scripture I'd memorized years before came to mind. It was the passage from Mark in which Jesus heals a possessed child. When Jesus asks the father of the boy if he believes, he confesses in anguish both his faith and his doubt. And in answer to that father's plea, Jesus heals his son.

That passage spoke to me now as it never had before. I didn't have to ratchet up my own faith and ignore my doubts and fears. My faith was in God's power, not mine; He would carry me through the dark days of waiting.

Kelly returned home safely from Vietnam, no longer an immature teenager but a confident young man. And when, mere months later, we anxiously waved good-bye as our older son John went off to war, we did so with renewed confidence that God would be with him— and with us.

Yes, Lord, as the Psalmist said so long ago, You are our refuge and strength.
—Isabel Wolseley

6
SAT

Surely you have granted him eternal blessings and made him glad with the joy of your presence.

—Psalm 21:6 (NIV)

Roscoe, my black Labrador retriever, came to me from Guiding Eyes for the Blind in Patterson, New York. He was eight weeks old, and I was raising him for them. When he was a year and a half, he would go back to Guiding Eyes to be trained to lead the blind.

As a future guide dog, Roscoe was a celebrity. He had his picture on the front page of our local paper, made appearances at schools and marched in a parade. He attended meetings, his health was closely monitored, and he had the best possible diet. When he was older, he wore a jacket announcing who he was, as I took him into supermarkets, restaurants and to church every week. People fawned over him.

Then came the day I returned him to Guiding Eyes for his training. I missed him dreadfully, but I was proud of what he was going to be. A week later, I received a call that Roscoe would be released from the program because he'd panicked at a gunshot.

My friends said it was a shame that Roscoe would never be a guide dog. "How sad," said the local newspaper reporter. "We were planning to do a spread on his graduation." Roscoe had no such sorrow. When I arrived at the Guiding Eyes office, he tore across the room, placed two big paws on my shoulders and showered me with kisses. He trotted to the car beside me, his whole body wiggling with happiness. He was with me; nothing else mattered.

Lord, help me to find my true joy in Your presence.   —Shari Smyth

7
SUN

THE CANDLES OF CHRISTMAS
The Candle of Peace

On earth peace, good will toward men.   —Luke 2:14

The second Sunday of Advent brings us to the candle of Peace, which my preacher friend defined as "a calming sense of Divine control." In the Christmas story, the word *peace* suggests Mary, the mother of Jesus. Repeatedly, in the face of humiliation and hardship, Mary takes unbelievable news with calm assurance, with which she "pondered all these things in her heart."

My paternal grandfather died when I was seven, but by then he had taught me to love fishing and passed on some of the best lessons that fishermen learn. One day I was sitting in a rowboat with him, our lines in the water, when the wind began to whip up waves on the lake. The boat began to rock, and I was frightened. But Grandfather stayed put, an anchor holding the boat in place and a lead weight holding his bait on the bottom. Finally, I blurted out, "Grandpa, shouldn't we go back? The fish can't bite in this bumpy water."

"Oh," Grandpa replied, "the waves don't bother the fish. Storms only affect the surface water. Down on the bottom, where the fish are, it is as calm as can be."

That's what Mary knew almost two thousand years before Grandpa taught me. Deep inside her, where she pondered the amazing things that were happening to her, her heart was at peace, and she could say to the angel, "Be it unto me according to thy word" (Luke 1:38).

Lord, let me feel Your presence deep within me this day and know the peace that dwells there.
                                                    —Eric Fellman

8
MON

The God of love and peace will be with you.
                              —II Corinthians 13:11 (RSV)

This year, instead of outlining my picture window with Christmas lights, I strung them across it, forming the word *LOVE*. If Jesus' message could be summed up in one word, it would be that one, and I liked knowing that my Christmas lights were passing on His love to neighbors and to all who drove by. But there was one problem. From the inside of the house, the letters were backward! And I wanted, most of all, for my family and friends to experience Christmas love *within* my home.

I thought of taking down the lights and going back to the old outlined window, but I was tired from a day of shopping and errand-running in Nebraska winter weather. I was also frustrated and upset with one of my sons, so I just gave up, turned off all but the backward LOVE lights, curled up in my recliner with Mother's afghan and listened to a tape of Christmas carols. When the music ended, I just sat in the silence, sensing Christ's presence, feeling thankful for this prayerful quiet time. And I noticed that, reflected on the glass door of my china hutch, were the lighted letters from my window turned around right!

How subtle is my God to remind me in this beautiful way that, when I bring my frustrations and upsets to Him in prayerful reflection, His love will turn them right again. Then a bonus! John walked in and said, "Hey, Mom! LOVE in the window—cool!"

"But it's *backward* from the inside."

"No it isn't!" John pointed to the mirror opposite the front entry, and there was LOVE again, turned around right. And, you know, I couldn't for the life of me remember why I'd been upset with my son.

Lord Christ, thank You for the transforming grace of quiet time with You, a grace that can soften my heart and right my distortions.

—Marilyn Morgan Helleberg

9

TUE

Be completely humble and gentle; be patient, bearing with one another in love.   —Ephesians 4:2 (NIV)

Almost all of the things which hang on the walls of my little office have happy associations; a watercolor of our barn at Windy Hill; an autographed picture that Billy Graham gave me years ago; a Ray Harm print of a raccoon watching a Carolina wren feeding; a picture that my dad liked.

But hanging above the sink is a framed postcard that recalls a painful experience. It was mailed to my office at the seminary by a man in a Midwestern state. At first, I thought it must have been a mistake, but the card had been handwritten and addressed to me. It explained how I could become a Christian.

That one postcard bothered me for days. Finally, I decided to write to my correspondent. I thanked him for his interest in my spiritual welfare and told him of my experience with Christ and my three decades as pastor and professor. Then, since we had never met, I asked him to tell me what made him decide that I wasn't a Christian.

Within a week his answer came, this time in a letter. He had read an article in which I had expressed my strong belief in the giftedness of women and had urged people not to discriminate on the basis of gender. "I didn't agree with you," he wrote. "So I figured you must not be a Christian." I saved his original postcard and eventually hung it where I would see it often.

Now, each time I step to the sink for a drink of water or to wash my hands, the postcard reminds me not to jump to conclusions about those with whom I disagree.

Dear God, help me to treat those who have different ideas as my brothers and sisters.   —Kenneth Chafin

10
There are different kinds of service, but the same Lord.
—I Corinthians 12:5 (NIV)

The wail of sirens and the sound of screaming pierced the cold morning air. The school bus lay on its side, filled with a tangled mass of bodies. Our own son David was in there. I stood helplessly on the sidewalk, but there was nothing I could do.

The sirens of fire and rescue units were real, but the accident in front of me was not. The bus was a hollow shell and the students were young volunteers smeared with stage-blood and sporting fake injuries. They were thoroughly enjoying the chance to scream without restraint.

My husband Bill, David and I were taking part in a local disaster drill, preparing for an event we hoped would never happen. During the two hours, each emergency-related service agency in the county would have a chance to play a part in the unfolding scenario. Our role as radio amateurs would be to provide communications between fire and hospital, Red Cross and sheriff, all those whose radio bands did not interface with one another's.

It was astonishing to see the speed and skill with which bodies were laid out, injuries tabulated (printed on cards worn by each "victim"), and triage begun. Bill played a distraught parent who was trying to get to his child and had to be restrained. David moaned and groaned on a blanket on the tarmac. I relayed information to another ham stationed at our local hospital and passed information on bed availability back to an emergency medical technician.

Over the next few years, Bill and I, and David when available, were able to take part in several of these staged events, helping with communications as needed. As we watched the emergency professionals respond, we grew to have a profound respect for their skill and their devotion. And we were thankful that these "disasters" were only simulations, but glad that God had given us gifts to use, if need be, in our neighbors' service.

Lord, help me to use the gifts You give me to serve You in serving my neighbors.   —Roberta Rogers

11
THU

"Look at the birds of the air: they neither sow nor reap nor gather into barns, and yet your heavenly Father feeds them. Are you not of more value than they?"

—Matthew 6:26 (RSV)

This has been a hard summer and fall. The lack of rain dried up my garden, except for a few very tall sunflowers. A venture that was supposed to help pay the mortgage has so far produced no income. My arthritis is acting up. An incipient ulcer keeps threatening my right eye! And before winter even officially gets here, we've had three snowstorms in as many weeks, with freezing weather keeping a foot of snow on everything.

In the midst of it all, I keep wondering what the future holds after I retire. There are times when I get very anxious. But when I look out into my little garden plot in the backyard, I am reassured by the presence of birds.

Even without water, my sunflower plants each developed suckers, and each sucker developed a flower. As they all turned to seed, the plethora of heads bent the plants over so that they stretched out along the top of the fence. The result: Even with all the snow, the birds have been having a feast in my yard. And I've been visited by cardinals and song sparrows, a rare occurrence. (I've kept the cats indoors as much as possible.)

If God can provide for the birds with such little help from you, I tell myself, *He will surely take care of you whatever the future holds.*

"Aren't you of more value than the birds?" Jesus asks me.

Yes, I am. And so I pray:

Lord, with Your help, I will trust Your goodness and Your loving provision for my needs.   —Mary Ruth Howes

12
FRI

He who sows sparingly will also reap sparingly, and he who sows bountifully will also reap bountifully.

—II Corinthians 9:6 (RSV)

A new secondhand furniture store had opened in our little town of Moberly, Missouri. We drove by to see it, but the windows were dark. "Must not be open yet," my wife Sharon observed with a shrug.

Several days later Sharon was walking by the store and noticed that it was still unlit, and yet a small open sign hung on the door. Curious, she stepped inside and browsed through the shadows. The storekeeper watched mysteriously from the darkened back room door.

"Do you have any lights around here?" Sharon finally dared to ask.

The manager flipped the switch. "I don't like to turn on the lights," he explained, "until I know someone is really interested. My light bill can run as high as one hundred fifty dollars a month."

Sharon and I got a good laugh out of the incident, but it made me pause and examine my own life for similar contradictions. How often do I try to flout the law of sowing and reaping, looking for a bargain or a shortcut? I have to remind myself that I can have the things I want, but only if I make an investment.

If I want more friends, I'll need to turn on the light of my smile.

If I want a better job, I'll need to invest in a more illuminating education.

And when I want to feel closer to God, I'll have to invest some time reading the Word of Light and talking to the Light of the World.

Father, sometimes I try to reap where I have not sown. Teach me to tap into Your riches by planting seeds of love and hard work.

—Daniel Schantz

13
SAT

Anxiety in a man's heart weighs him down. . . .
—Proverbs 12:25

Two years ago, I went to Washington, D.C., to visit a friend, and I left my two teenagers home alone. Phillip was sixteen, Blake fourteen. *Would they be all right? Would they get into an accident? What if something terrible happened at school? Would the house burn down? What if they trashed the house?*

I returned home eight days later at three in the morning. The boys had left on a lamp, there was a welcome-home note on the counter, the house was in perfect order. When I opened the door to my bedroom, I laughed out loud.

There was a man in my bed! A pair of blue jeans had been carefully laid out, with dirty socks for feet. A T-shirt made up the chest. Rolled-up posters worked for arms, mittens served as hands. The head was a Dave Barry book, propped against my pillow. A baseball cap topped everything off. And stacked on the T-shirt? A pile of presents.

Nothing untoward had happened. My boys had even missed me and gone out of their way to welcome me home.

Heavenly Father, help me to remember that anxiety is an unnecessary burden. —Brenda Wilbee

14
SUN

THE CANDLES OF CHRISTMAS
The Candle of Joy

I bring you good tidings of great joy, which shall be to all people.
—Luke 2:10

On this third Sunday of Advent, we light the candle of Joy for the first time. The old preacher defined *joy* as "a deep sense of well-being, not dependent on circumstances." I've always thought the shepherds were the most joyful participants in the first Christmas. They were almost outcasts, forced to live outside the city walls with their flocks, trying to keep warm under a rock outcropping on a cold winter night. Yet the angels came to them to announce the birth of Jesus.

In Pawling, New York, where we live, the winters vary between relatively mild and extremely challenging. Last winter was one of the latter. During a week in which more than three feet of snow fell and temperatures plunged to record lows, we were snowbound for two days, ordered by state authorities to stay off the roads. "Cabin fever" started to depress the family. One morning, we were gathered in the living room. Our middle son Nathan stood staring out the window at the blowing snow. Suddenly, he said, "You know, even though the snow is a pain in the neck right now, it's really beautiful."

He was right. We all gathered at the window to look out at the snow-capped evergreens and the graceful, sweeping ridges of snow (coming up over the top of the car!) that fell away to a smooth expanse across the yard and glittered in the brilliant sunshine. The sight of such beauty filled me with a joy that, though not as deep, was certainly a reflection of the joy those shepherds felt on that bitter winter night when they left the stable "glorifying and praising God for all the things that they had heard and seen" (Luke 2:20).

Lord, fill me this day with a joy that goes beyond my circumstances and looks ahead to the wonder of Jesus, Your gift to all humankind.

—Eric Fellman

15
MON

And suddenly there was with the angel a multitude of the heavenly host, praising God. . . .   —Luke 2:13

The longer I live in this motley metropolis of New York, the quirkier the trigger is that sets off the holiday spirit in me each year. When I first migrated here from the Midwest a decade ago, the obvious did it: Rockefeller Center's famous tree, the window displays at Lord and Taylor, the unerringly sharp Salvation Army band at the Plaza Hotel fountain, even the world's biggest menorah at 59th and Fifth.

I've become somewhat immune to these symbols, and in some years the spirit doesn't ambush me till the last minute. One frantic season it was my wife Julee's humming of "Silent Night," interrupted every time she licked a stamp for one of our Christmas cards. Another time it took a Santa playing drums in Herald Square with his crew of break-dancing elves. Last December, it was the sprig of holly hooked through the lapel of a policeman named Muldoon.

This year the powers that be canceled the traditional crèche and menorah displays at Grand Central Terminal, a nerve-center of our city. "What's next?" I asked a co-worker. "Arrests for whistling 'Joy to the World' in public?"

The next time I passed through Grand Central, I made it a point to stop and glare at the empty spot above the ticket windows where the "offending" displays had been. "Politics!" I muttered cynically. How had we sunk so low?

Suddenly, with the help of the terminal's cavernous acoustics, a small, impromptu choir of caroling schoolchildren swelled the air with "The First Noel." Nobody arrested them. Rushing people stopped to listen, strangers exchanged smiles. Even the newsstand man, a devout Muslim, hummed along. I'd been ambushed again. Christmas was here, and politics wasn't going to still it. It hadn't for two thousand years.

*Lord, Your birth reverberates through the centuries, its echo present in
every moment of our lives. Help me keep Your spirit alive inside me always.*
                                                        —Edward Grinnan

---

W O R D S   O F   W O N D E R

Before the paling of the stars,
Before the winter morn,
Before the earliest cockcrow,
Jesus Christ was born:
Born in a stable,
Cradled in a manger,
In the world his hands had made,
Born a stranger.
                            —CHRISTINA ROSSETTI

16
TUE   *When they saw the star, they rejoiced with exceeding great
joy.*   —Matthew 2:10

In December 1945, I was in El Paso, Texas, with Bob, my soldier-
husband, who was stationed at Biggs Field. The stores were decorated for Christmas. Everywhere, Yuletide music engulfed me,
conjuring up happy memories of family and friends gathered around
the big tree at my parents' home. I dreaded the bleak Christmas it
would be for us, alone in our little apartment.

One night Bob suggested that we go for a walk. I agreed; maybe
the crisp air would perk me up. As he swung open the apartment
house door, I saw something that made me stop to catch my breath.

Across North Piedras Street, against a background of dark trees
on Franklin Mountain, glowed a huge star of lights, the biggest star
I'd ever seen. "Merry Christmas, honey," Bob said softly.

I stood silently for what seemed like minutes before I could find
the right words. "Oh, Bob, thank you! Now I know how the Wise
Men must have felt when they saw the star on the first Christmas.
This star must be God's way of reminding me that Christmas, right
here, is His gift to us.

"I want Mrs. Blair on the third floor to see the star. She's been so lonely since her son went overseas. Let's ask her to walk with us."

"Of course," Bob said, as he put his arm around me.

I later learned that the "Star of Christmas," an annual gift to El Paso from the electric company, first shone in 1941. It is visible on land for fifty miles. I'll never forget the night I saw it from my front door and how it awakened my heart to the real meaning of Christmas.

Father, help me to remember that it's Christmas, no matter where I am, and accept my praise for the gift of Your Son.   —Drue Duke

17
WED   *They shall fly as the eagle. . . .*   —Habakkuk 1:8

The date was December 17, 1903. The place was Kitty Hawk, North Carolina. Orville and Wilbur Wright had just made history by keeping their flying invention in the air for a total of fifty-nine seconds. Elated, they rushed to the telegraph office and wired their sister in Dayton, Ohio.

"First sustained flight today for fifty-nine seconds," the message read. "Hope to be home by Christmas." Their sister was thrilled and hurried to the local newspaper with the great news and the telegram. And sure enough, the next day an article about the Wrights appeared in the paper. The headline, however, read: LOCAL BICYCLE MERCHANTS TO BE HOME FOR THE HOLIDAYS. The editor had missed the point—and one of the most important moments in aviation history!

Sometimes I'm like that nearsighted editor. My husband cooks a surprise breakfast—and I see the messy kitchen. My friend sends me a thank-you note, and I notice that it's late. I stew over the long distance bill for my son's calls home from college. So often I stop and ask myself: *What's the most important thing about this situation?* And it's hardly ever the details. More often it's the thoughtfulness behind the action or the generosity that prompted the gesture.

Focusing on the big picture opens up new attitudes for me, which can lead to positive changes in my relationships with family and friends, as well as with my heavenly Father. Who knows what could happen with that kind of thinking—you might say the sky's the limit!

O God, help me to filter out the unimportant, and teach me to see merit and mercy in everyday events.   —Mary Lou Carney

18
THU

I thank my God every time I remember you.
                                    —Philippians 1:3 (NIV)

Each year at Christmastime, a local theater hosts a "Festival of Trees" for the community to enjoy. Several years ago, a group of us nurses who work with veterans decided to decorate a tree in an effort to pay tribute to those who have experienced the pain of holiday separation because of military service.

"If you want to speak to people's hearts, remember, God is in the details," advised a veteran, herself a talented artist. And so we asked veterans and their families just what it was like to be apart at the season when all hearts turn homeward. Their responses sent us on a nostalgic hunt for furnishings and memorabilia of the World War II era.

We decorated a tree beside a cozy hearth with sparkling lights, patriotic sheet music and flags. A mother, lost in the memories of Christmases past, reminisced by the snow-curtained window displaying a "Son in Service" banner. She read a letter her son had written from a faraway battlefield, as the radio throbbed with Bing Crosby's "I'll Be Home for Christmas."

Folks of all ages lingered by our snug period room. But it was the details that joined their hearts in remembrance. "Look at those War Bonds, that old *Life* magazine, the 'V is for Victory' milk bottle," a lady remarked to a boy who checked out the old-time toys under the tree. "Why, that's just the way it was when your grandpa was in the South Pacific."

A man wiped his eyes with the back of his hand and gazed into the distance at some long-ago place and time. "My dad served in World War II, I was in Korea, and we lost our boy in Vietnam," he said. "This is for all of us. Thank you for not forgetting."

We ask Your blessings, dear Lord, on every home touched by the pain of separation this holiday season.   —Roberta Messner

19
FRI

Serve the Lord with gladness: come before his presence with singing.
                                    —Psalm 100:2

One Christmas, I got started on the idea of choosing a phrase from a Christmas song and adopting it as my theme for the season. The first year it was "And wonders of His love," a refrain from "Joy to the World." I focused on being in awe of the One Who began our world, coming into it and making Himself known. Then I looked specifically for the wonders of His love in my life. I saw acts of patience and kindness and forgiveness, and found myself wrapped in joy over the sheer fact of His love.

Another year I was struggling with things that were not right in my life, particularly certain attitudes. I heard "God Rest Ye Merry Gentlemen" and one line rang true for my situation: "To save us all from Satan's power, when we had gone astray." I felt that I had gone astray in a hidden part of myself. I needed the message of a Savior Who was able to battle for me and reconcile me to Himself. That Advent I dwelt on God's redeeming grace, opening secret sins to Him and asking for His salvation from them.

This year my Christmas song theme comes from "O Holy Night": "Till He appeared and the soul felt its worth." I would not have known my soul had worth, had Jesus not come to tell me so. I rejoice not only in what He means to me, but in what I mean to Him. I'm also trying to show others how valuable they are to me and how very valuable we all are in God's eyes.

Selecting a song theme for the Christmas season has focused my Advent meditation and enhanced my enjoyment of this "most wonderful time of the year." Why not try it? Perhaps the angels are trumpeting their own heavenly chorus for us—something like, "O come, all ye faithful."

"Son of God, love's pure light," shine on us in this sacred season.

—Carol Knapp

20
SAT   *Behold what manner of love the Father hath bestowed upon us. . . .*   —I John 3:1

The day I walked into that upscale Chattanooga, Tennessee, store, I was eighteen, fresh from my first semester in college and appropriately worldly. My father and I were there to choose a Christmas gift for my mother.

"Something in cashmere," I was saying to the saleslady as the door to the shop swung open and a waft of cold air introduced a ragged child.

Everyone in the store stopped in mid-sentence. The silence was icy. The little boy, thin even in his too-small sweater, was carrying a box of paper flowers, tied together with cheap ribbon. They looked like corsages. The child was an intrusion. His presence sliced through our shopping comfort like a sharp knife. In the hush, a clerk recovered her bearing and moved toward the boy to shoo him from the store. I swallowed hard, no longer feeling the least bit sophisticated. I didn't think I could bear the little guy's coming humiliation.

And then, my father saved us all.

All six foot four inches of Daddy were striding toward the boy, his deep, booming voice filling the store. "What have you got there, lad? My, what pretty flowers. I don't guess you'd let me buy one of those for my girl? You would? Well, thanks, son. Thanks, and Merry Christmas!"

The store let out its breath, the boy left with a full pocket and a smile, and I walked proudly down a Chattanooga street arm-in-arm with Daddy—wearing the tackiest purple flower you ever saw.

That flower, now carefully framed, hangs on our wall each holiday season. It brings back that wonderful day when my father reached out past proprieties and gave me the real Christmas. And it reminds me that Christmas still waits to be found again in unexpected places.

Father, You offer us Your best gift, wrapped in swaddling clothes. Thank You for loving us this much.　　　　　—Pam Kidd

21
SUN　**THE CANDLES OF CHRISTMAS**
　　　The Candle of Love

For God so loved the world, that he gave his only begotten Son. . . .　　　　　—John 3:16

This Sunday, we light the final candle in the Advent circle, the candle representing Love. My friend the old preacher defined *love* as "selfless concern for others." God showed us the meaning of that love on the first Christmas, when He sent us His only Son.

I have three sons. The last two were born late in December, so we twice had the special joy of a newborn baby in our home at Christmas. When Jonathan, the youngest, was six weeks old, he came down with meningitis. We rushed him to the hospital, where they did all kinds of tests, and ran tubes in and out of his tiny body. His condition was serious, and I was gripped by the fear of losing him.

My wife Joy and I took turns sitting by his stainless-steel crib, isolated from the other children in the ward so the infection would not spread. On the second evening, I was there late, all alone. Jon looked so weak and felt so warm that my fears overwhelmed me. I grabbed the bars of the crib and began to pray, "Oh, God, don't take Jon back now. I love him so much, and he doesn't even know me yet. How could You give him to me and then just take him back?"

And then, perhaps because it was so near Christmas, I had an overwhelming sense of God's presence with me. I seemed to see the Father standing at the edge of heaven, looking down at His infant Son coming into a world where He would be misunderstood, lied about and eventually killed. I knew that God understands fathers and their fears.

And now, every Christmas when I stand in church to sing the familiar carols and look down the row and see Jon standing there with his brothers, I marvel once again at the wonder of that love.

Father, fill me with a sense of the greatness of Your love for all people and help me to reflect that love in the lives of those who know me.
                                                    —Eric Fellman

22
MON

But Mary kept all these things, and pondered them in her heart.   —Luke 2:19

Parenting is a glorious but awesome responsibility. Often, it's long after the event that we find out how some of the things we do affect our children. And little things are sometimes the most important.

Our three children attended Friends Seminary, a Quaker grade school in New York City. Every year at Christmastime the school put on a pageant of the birth of Jesus. It was beautifully done, with costumed shepherds, angels, wise men and, of course, the Holy Family. Our daughter Margaret portrayed Mary in two of the pageants. And, naturally, I was there. What I didn't know was that in both years Margaret was worried that my busy schedule would force me to miss the pageants.

Years later, after Margaret graduated from college, a magazine asked her to write a story about her life with her famous father. Norman and I didn't see the story until it was printed. Imagine my sur-

prise when I read that one of the things that had meant the most to
Margaret when she was growing up was my attending those Christmas pageants. She was touched that despite my busy life and my
many other responsibilities, I was there when she wanted me, even
though she hadn't told me how important it was to her.

*Dear Lord, today let me plant seeds that will bear good fruit in the lives of
the young people You've made part of my life.*

—Ruth Stafford Peale

23

TUE   *Freely ye have received, freely give.*   —Matthew 10:8

It was Christmas week. Money was short, and my expenses were
high. I struggled to earn a few extra dollars by dressing small cellu-
loid dolls in hand-knitted outfits and placing them on consignment
at a neighborhood gift shop. I had an arrangement with Gladys, the
owner, to split the profit, which came to $2.25 for each doll sold. I
had delivered ten dolls to her over the previous weeks, which would
give me $22.50 for a few Christmas treats and a small table-top tree.
I pushed through the doors of the shop, praying that my dolls had
been sold.

"I've sold six," Gladys said as she rang open the cash register and
handed me $13.50. "Cheer up," she said as she saw my look of dis-
appointment. "We still have a couple of days left."

The tears welled up in my eyes. "There's a box of tissue in the restroom. You'll feel better if you freshen up a bit." Gladys put her arm
around my shoulders and walked me to the back of the store.

"I'm okay," I said, and smiled wanly. As I closed the restroom door
behind me and flicked on the light, I knew why Gladys had steered
me in. There, on the toilet tank, in a garland of holly, was a large jar
more than half-filled with dimes, quarters and dollar bills. It had a
huge red bow and a label that read:

> If you need, take.
> If you have, give.

I had a need, but I had a pride that didn't want to take. *Well,* I decided, *I can be one of those who takes now and hopes to give back with
extra later.* I took out ten dollars.

"Thank you, Gladys," I said, hugging her on my way out. "I'll put it back. I promise!"

She looked at me seriously. "There's no 'putting back.' Just pass it on. When you *have,* simply *give!*"

Through the years, I have passed on her blessing by keeping a "Gladys Jar" on the toilet tank in our bathroom. Sometimes it's nearly empty from visitors in need who have taken, but it's always replenished by those who generously give.

In the joyful spirit of giving and receiving, dear Lord, help me to share my blessings with those in need.   —Fay Angus

24
WED   THE CANDLES OF CHRISTMAS

In him was life; and the life was the light of men.   —John 1:4

In the center of the Advent wreath stands a single white candle. On Christmas Eve in my church, small candles are distributed to the whole congregation. A family is chosen to light the four candles of Hope, Peace, Joy and Love. They lift the four candles up from the circle of greens and use them to light the center candle, the Christ candle. As it is lit, the four outer candles are blown out and placed back in the circle.

Then, as the congregation sings "Silent Night," the minister takes the Christ candle and lights the candle held by one of the people in the first pew. While the song continues, the candlelight is shared and the overhead lights are dimmed as, person by person, the light of Christ is spread through the church.

Ever since I first experienced it as a child, this candlelight service has symbolized the Christian faith for me. The wonders of hope, peace, joy and love are brought together in the coming of Christ, the Savior. And yet His light is only available in the world if it is passed from each one of us to others. In this world, Jesus has no hands but our hands; no feet but our feet; no ears, eyes or mouth but ours. The wonder of Christmas, if it is to last all year, must live and grow in you and in me.

Lord, may the light of Your presence this Christmas Eve drive the darkness from every heart.   —Eric Fellman

25
THE CANDLES OF CHRISTMAS
The Candle of Christ

And his name shall be called Wonderful, Counselor, The mighty
God, The everlasting Father, The Prince of Peace.   —Isaiah 9:6

The symbol of the Advent wreath and candles is made complete in
our worship service for Christmas Day. As we enter the auditorium
on Christmas morning, only the single candle in the center of the
wreath, representing Christ, is lit. When the first carol, "Joy to the
World," is sung, an acolyte takes a candle lighter on the end of a long
pole and lights it from the center candle. Then he extinguishes that
candle and carries the light across the front of the platform to a tall
candleholder and candlestick on the left of the platform. After passing the light to this candle, representing the Lord's continuing presence with us, he sits down.

When the service is ended, after the final prayer, the acolyte returns to the large candle. He once again takes the light from the candle and then extinguishes it. Then he precedes the congregation on
their way out, leading the way into the week with the Light of Christ.
Then, on every Sunday until the next Advent season, an acolyte
comes forward at the beginning of each Sunday service and brings
the light back to its permanent place.

I am always moved by this simple ceremony. Christ came at Christmas and was the fulfillment of Hope, Peace, Joy and Love. He continues with us still, but He is not confined to our churches, He is in
us. His light comes in when we do, and goes out into the world with
us as we leave. His continuing gift of hope, peace, joy and love is delivered through His people—through you and through me.

Dear Jesus, may I be a joyful bearer of Your light into the world this Christ-
mas day and throughout the coming year.   —Eric Fellman

26
I am the voice of one crying in the wilderness, Make
straight the way of the Lord. . . .   —John 1:23

It was Christmas Day, and I was visiting the state psychiatric hospi-
tal as a representative of our local community mental health board.
The director updated me on the patients as we walked to the ward.
"We have a few violent criminals here right now," he said in

passing. I was startled. But we'd arrived at the Christmas party for the patients, and it was too late to ask questions.

During the Christmas carols, my eyes fixed on a large, tough-looking man sitting sullenly apart from the group. I wondered if he was a criminal. He certainly looked mean enough. I watched as he opened a package containing a purple scarf and saw the mistrust on his face turn to puzzlement. *Was he disappointed?* His second gift was a pair of purple gloves. Again a puzzled look passed across his face.

Later a nurse asked him, "Did you like your presents?"

I turned in time to see the wariness melt from his eyes. He fingered his scarf shyly and in a quiet voice replied, "This is the best Christmas I ever had."

I was dumbfounded. I knew nothing about his life, only that he'd been committed to a state psychiatric hospital and had no visitors. He'd eaten a bowl of ice cream and heard a few carols. An inexpensive scarf and a pair of gloves were his only presents. It seemed so little. Nonetheless, this was the best Christmas he'd ever had.

Knowing that made it the best Christmas I'd ever had, too. In the starkness of the hospital ward, I was given a glimpse of pure gratitude, a heart truly open to receiving. I think of the simplicity hiding within that fierce man each year as Advent begins.

Heavenly Father, may I receive the Christ Child in my heart with joy as Your most glorious gift.   —Julia Attaway

27
SAT   *The Lord is close to the brokenhearted and saves those who are crushed in spirit.*   —Psalm 34:18 (NIV)

I felt compelled to telephone my friend Nancy, but I hesitated. I had received her Christmas card with the sad news that she and her husband were divorcing. After nineteen years of marriage and four teenage children, he had left to start a new life of his own.

I stared at the phone. *How could I possibly comfort Nancy? What would I say?* Finally, I dialed her number, hoping that somehow just calling would let her know I cared.

Nancy shared the agony she was facing: the possibility of losing her house; finding a job; caring for her devastated children. "I had so many questions," Nancy said. "I begged God to guide me, to show me what to do, just as He had led Israel through the wilderness with pillars of cloud and fire. While I prayed, God brought to mind several people from church. 'Let them be pillars to you,' God seemed to say."

As Nancy poured out her dilemmas to her friends, some became pillars of cloud, shielding her from the scorching heat of despair. One took her out to dinner; another slipped a hundred dollars in her purse. Others became pillars of fire, aglow with God's wisdom. Gradually, answers began to unfold: Stay in the area until your son graduates from high school. Keep doing home day-care for now, but take classes to reactivate your teaching degree. Take some time for yourself at a nearby retreat center. Lean on us. Cry.

"And you're calling me today," Nancy said, "another pillar of strength."

I hung up the phone, amazed. God transformed my feeble effort to reach out to a friend into a pillar of support—and strengthened my own faith.

Dear Lord, thank You for the pillars of Your Presence in our lives.

—Mary Brown

28
SUN

And they shall call his name Immanuel, which being interpreted is, God with us. —Matthew 1:23

I sank into my chair at the Christmas service, absolutely drained from a week of helping to distribute food boxes to needy families in our community. On top of the usual physical and emotional strain of the season, I was terribly disappointed with someone who had promised to help me and then hadn't been there when most needed. I felt alone, abandoned and quite beyond the reach of Christmas.

The choir had just risen to sing when my attention was caught by the flash of a bright pink sweater. A parishioner named Carole had left her second-row seat and was now walking up the center aisle.

It took me a moment to realize that Carole was heading toward Hannah, a six-year-old acolyte who was seated by herself in the front row. The little girl was asleep, slumped precariously in her chair. Hannah's father was busy up on the stage and unaware that she was about to fall from her chair. And so Carole simply stepped forward and slipped into the seat next to the child. Hannah nestled down into Carole's arms as the choir sang, "God with us, alive in us, His name is called Immanuel."

A little girl slept, and someone had come unbidden, compelled by love. And despite my fatigue and my emotional burnout, Immanuel was again calling to me from the manger, ready to tuck me under His loving arm when my strength gave out.

Come, O come, Immanuel.   —Karen Barber

29
MON *Trust in the Lord with all thine heart; and lean not unto thine own understanding.*   —Proverbs 3:5

The vast warehouse was bone-chillingly cold, and I clutched my cup of coffee protectively. *I volunteered for this?* I asked myself. I had offered to help decorate floats for the Tournament of Roses Parade. Edith, a friend of mine from the church choir, was a chairperson for the *Lutheran Hour* float and, to cover expenses, had hired out volunteers to help the other float makers. Someone asked me if I was allergic to cottonseed, and before I could answer, I was whisked toward a float.

An older man in green sweatpants and a "Petal Pusher" sweatshirt knelt on a slab of plywood on the float, holding a paintbrush in one hand and a bucket of fuzzy gray stuff in the other. "My name is Jason," he said. "Are you here to help with the cottonseed?" I nodded and smiled.

At first, I wound up with more seeds stuck to my fingers than to the float, but Jason was patient. We worked side by side for a long time, talking. He had worked on floats for eight years, always for the *Lutheran Hour.* This year's theme, sports, was a good one, he thought, and did I know that the float we were working on represented fishing?

As I took the last handful of cotton, I sneezed. We were caught in a tiny snowstorm of gray fluff. Helping me pull a cluster of seeds from my hair, he asked, "Kjerstin, are you a Christian?"

"Yes, but it's hard sometimes."

"Why?"

"My problems start in Genesis. It just gets tougher from there."

Jason smiled and led me upstairs to a catwalk. As we looked down on the float we had been working on, I could see that a boat was taking shape.

"Jesus will stand on the rocks," Jason explained, "and men of all nations will cast nets over the side of the boat. Fishers of men, following their Father's footsteps. I think they had questions, too."

Father in heaven, all of Your works fit into Your wonderful design. Give me the patience to learn about it, bit by bit.   —Kjerstin Easton

30
TUE

And do not forget to do good and to share with others, for with such sacrifices God is pleased.

—Hebrews 13:16 (NIV)

The wonder of God's love, my husband George and I discovered, is often found at rest stops, those small green islands so clean and quiet after the roar of the highway. You meet so many nice people in that brief pause en route to your destination, people who become instant friends, stopping to admire your dogs, happy to share a map or their field glasses, or even to help you if you have car trouble.

And during holiday weekends, at most of these stops there is someone on duty to provide free coffee. One night as we came out of the building, we noticed the sign FREE COFFEE and a converted trailer where a few people were gathered. Although neither of us really wanted coffee, we decided, "Let's have some!" And there at the big open caravan, we found two middle-aged couples beaming behind a steaming urn.

"Who sponsors you?" I asked the pretty, gray-haired woman who handed me the cup.

"Us!" grinned her husband. "The four of us"—he introduced himself and his companions—"have been here every year for fifteen years and have never had more fun."

"What a nice, hospitable thing to do," I said.

"Well, actually it's more than that. It's to try to slow people down, and especially if they've been drinking, help sober them up." We all gathered closer to discuss the terrible toll of people killed on our highways during the holidays, and how good it feels to know you may have saved even a few by this simple, friendly act.

"We really enjoy doing it," they said. "It helps our marriages. We're closer as couples. And we meet so many wonderful people—like you!"

Dear God, bless those dear couples and make us more like them. They are truly ministering angels. Amen.   —Marjorie Holmes

31
WED

Blessed be the Lord, that hath given rest unto his people. . . .   —I Kings 8:56

Though Christmas 1997 is now history, the aftereffects have me still bouncing up and down like a man on a trampoline. And now it's time to welcome in another year, even though I haven't got all the loose ends of the previous one tied together.

What I'd like to do is call timeout, like a pair of Sardinian donkeys I once owned. My wife Shirley, our four kids and I used them as pack animals on an extended hiking trip. One day after a hot, arduous climb up a steep mountain, Pinocchio had had enough. He suddenly stopped in his tracks, slithered to the ground, rolled over on his side and closed his eyes. I thought for a moment he was dying. But when Figaro, his sidekick who mirrored Pinocchio's every move, did the same thing, I realized they were simply conducting a work stoppage—together. Unlike their equally exhausted master, they were smart enough to admit it and take action.

The experience reminded me of the story of a missionary couple going to their first post in remote Africa. In order to reach their station, they required the services of several native porters to carry their belongings. After one stretch that left everyone fatigued, the natives in unison put down their baggage and retired in the shade. Half an hour later they were still resting, and the missionaries became concerned. Unless they continued posthaste they would not reach their destination by nightfall.

"Shouldn't we move on?" the missionaries asked the head guide. "Not yet," he answered. "The porters believe they have traveled too far, too fast. Now they are waiting for their souls to catch up with their bodies."

Perhaps in the new year when you and I become harried by trying to do too much in too little time, we should follow the donkeys' example. And while we're trying to recover from our "jet lag," it might help to complement the restoration process with Bible reading and prayer. Not only will such a pause refresh us physically, it will give our souls a chance to catch up with our bodies.

> *Teach us, Lord, to use time wisely,*
> *So we make our efforts count,*
> *Help us keep our mental cool,*
> *Even when life's pressures mount.*

—Fred Bauer

Everyday Wonders

1 _____

2 _____

3 _____

4 _____

5 _____

6 _____

7 _____

8 _____

9 _____

10 _____

11 _____

12 _____

13 _____

14 _____

15 _____

16 _____

17 _____

18 _____

19 _____

20 _____

21 _____

22 _____

23 _____

24 _____

25 _____

26 _____

27 _____

28 _____

29 _____

30 _____

31 _____

Fellowship Corner

Here in the Fellowship Corner, you're invited to join the forty-six contributors to Daily Guideposts, 1997 *as they tell us how "The Wonder of God's Love" has been a part of their lives this past year. You may notice a few new faces among the familiar friendly ones, but like you, they're all part of the* Daily Guideposts *family.*

"As we celebrate the wonder of God's love," says FAY ANGUS of Sierra Madre, California, "this is the year John and I celebrate the wonder of our 40th wedding anniversary. 'Ours is a working arrangement,' he likes to tell me. 'I do all the work, and you make all the arrangements!' *Ha*! The fact of the matter is that we are a team, serving the Lord with joy and gladness. Engraved in our wedding rings is the commitment: 'One for the other and both for God.' These words, by the great missionary William Carey, continue to be the focus of the wonder of our love."

ANDREW ATTAWAY lives in Brooklyn, New York, with his wife Julia, daughter Elizabeth and their cat Kitty Cotta Sonatta. He came to Guideposts Books as an editor in 1995. "This last year has been particularly rich," Andrew says. "Elizabeth turned 2 last August. Watching her grow into the person God intends her to be has filled every day with wonder. And in becoming a part of the Guideposts family, I've been privileged to see God's love in action in the lives of our readers, our writers and my colleagues on the staff. It's been a source of great joy."

"Living in New York City has plenty of challenges for a new mother, and helping a child to see the wonder of God's love in a sea of people and concrete is one of them," says Andrew's wife JULIA ATTAWAY, a newcomer to *Daily Guideposts*. "One of my most important realizations came one day while I was on a crowded subway, seven months pregnant with Elizabeth. Looking up from my book, I suddenly thought, *Why, all these people were born!* Knowing that each person is an individual, crafted by God with love in a mother's womb, has helped me appreciate that the city is made up of human beings, not just impersonal masses of people." Julia and Andrew's 2-year-old daughter Elizabeth will soon become a big sister.

KAREN BARBER is a contributing editor to *Guideposts* magazine. She and her husband Gordon and their three sons Jeff, 18, Chris, 15, and John Daniel, 6, live in Augusta, Georgia. Karen has been grateful this year for God's unchangeable love. She says, "Jeff graduated from high school, Chris finished his freshman year, and John Daniel began elementary school. I was dreading Jeff's going off to college, when I walked into his empty room and there on the white board, under a complicated physics equation, was the entire alphabet written in wiggly handwriting complete with a backward *J*. I realized that those same simple ABC's were part of the complex physics equation as well. I knew then that although our family life may change, the love we continue to share is the one constant."

FRED BAUER of Princeton, New Jersey, says, "I find evidence of God's wondrous love in many places—a cloud-arching rainbow, a myrtle warbler's song, a Monet landscape, a Bill and Gloria Gaither hymn or a Christina Rossetti poem. But nothing reflects His transforming power like caring people: *Where is God's redeeming love/most visible, most prevalent?/In the smiling faces of/His children most benevolent.*" Some of the smile-makers in Fred's life this past year: his wife Shirley, who took early retirement after fifteen years as an elementary school librarian; his son Christopher, who with a team of twelve scaled America's highest peak, Mt. McKinley in Alaska; his son Daniel, who is completing work on a graduate degree in Civil War history at the University of Georgia; three grandchildren "whose exuberant hugs and kisses give height and depth to the wonder of God's love."

"Our lives have never been busier," says GINA BRIDGEMAN of Scottsdale, Arizona, "but we're having a lot of fun." The biggest change was the birth of Maria Angelina, now 2. Ross, now a 7-year-old second-grader, has shown himself to be a wonderful big brother. He likes to give Maria wagon rides around the backyard and read her stories. Gina's husband Paul recently designed the scenery for his 35th production for Grand Canyon University's theater department in Phoenix, and he taught a new class on Broadway musicals. Meanwhile, Gina led several "Holy Hilarity" playshops for the Fellowship of Merry Christians, helping Christians to explore and celebrate the joy of their faith. "That joy is a constant part of my faith," Gina says, "and while our lives are overflowing with joys, that's not where I most feel the wonder of God's love. It's more in the strength and comfort He gives during down times, and the reassurance that we'll come out on the other side of any darkness to the warm, loving light of His love."

Last year, MARY BROWN and her husband Alex of Lansing, Michigan, powerfully experienced God's love when their 8-year-old daughter Elizabeth came through a major car accident with only a bump on the forehead and one night's stay in the hospital for observation. "Besides protecting Elizabeth and the other children in the car pool (no one else was injured), God sustained us with the incredible compassion of the police, paramedics and hospital staff; people stopping at the accident to help; hospital volunteers occupying our 3-year-old son Mark with cocoa and coloring books; words of comfort from the Bible beside Elizabeth's hospital bed; and friends who prayed, cared for Mark, made our supper and welcomed us home the next day—safe and sound and profoundly grateful for God's loving care."

It was a year of blessings and changes for MARY LOU CARNEY and her family. Daughter Amy Jo married her high school sweetheart in a Thanksgiving weekend wedding. She wore her great-grandmother's cameo—the same one Mary Lou wore in her wedding twenty-six years ago. Husband Gary had his first bout with heart problems, and he and Mary Lou made several trips to the Mayo Clinic—all with good results. Son Brett came home from college to help run the family excavation business in Chesterton, Indiana. Mary Lou continues to edit *Guideposts for Kids*, and this year she saw her co-editor Wally the Turtle make his video debut in the *Guideposts Junction* series. "God's love has been such a blanket around us this year—softening the bumps and reminding us that we are, indeed, His closely held children."

"My wife Barbara and I have been flirting with moving to the farm in Texas," writes KENNETH CHAFIN of Louisville, Kentucky. "It's between Houston and Austin, a ninety-minute drive from where our children live. But the emotional energy required in deciding what to keep and what to give away as we move into a small house is quite large. Last November, on my 69th birthday, I began a journal, which has created in me a new sense of wonder at the way God has loved me and helped me through people along the way. One day I came into my office for a little while to sketch out plans for some engagements I had committed myself to. As I was leaving, a woman from an office down the hall asked me, 'Are they letting you go home early today?' Her question made me thankful that I'm at that wonderful time in my life when more of my energy can be spent on things I've always wanted to do."

MARK COLLINS, a first-time *Daily Guideposts* writer, lives in Pittsburgh, Pennsylvania, with his wife Sandee and daughters Faith, 5, and Hope, 4. Mark describes himself as a "reluctant" Christian. "I meet so many people who are so at peace with their faith, so strengthened and inspired. For me, it's a battle to be a Christian. I can't pretend it's otherwise." For solace, Mark plays a sport called dek-hockey, which is ice hockey without the skates. "I'm too old to play," he says, "but I'm too stubborn to stop. That'll be my epitaph—I'll have a phone affixed to the tombstone and the inscription 'God called, but Mark was too stubborn to answer.'" Mark is the author of a book of spiritual essays, *On the Road to Emmaus: Stories of Faith, Doubt, and Change* (Liguori). A second book of essays, *MWM ISO: Married White Male In Search Of*, is due out later this year.

HOLLIE DAVIS is currently a senior at West Virginia Wesleyan College in Buckhannon, West Virginia, but she spends much of her free time in Glenville with her father, stepmother, grandfather and her 18-year-old brother Kelly. Hollie is currently working on a double major in English literature and history, but she says, "I'm still undecided about my plans after college." When Hollie is not at home or in class, she spends her time outdoors, reading or sewing. "The wonder of God's love is that it is constant and has so much room for forgiveness. The wonder of the love is that it is unconditional."

"This has been a quiet but happy year for my husband Bob and me," writes DRUE DUKE of Sheffield, Alabama. "In the spring, a beautiful black cat showed up at our house, pitifully thin and terrified of everything. I was able to coax her to lap a bowl of warm milk, but I wasn't allowed to pet her. After a time, she'd rub against my ankles and purr, and eventually she accepted our love and became a part of the family. I was able to share in the Easter celebration at our church by writing the narration needed to tie beautiful on-hand music into a cantata for the morning worship service. En route to Huntsville to spend Christmas with our daughter Emily and our grandchildren, our car was rammed from the rear, crashed into another vehicle and was totally demolished. It was a real blessing that we sustained only a broken rib and painful whiplash. These things and countless others kept me deeply aware of the wonder of God's love."

KJERSTIN EASTON, a 1994 *Guideposts* Young Writers Competition winner, joins *Daily Guideposts* for the first time. Kjerstin lives with her parents Richard and Joyce, her brother Jay, two cats, one dog and a hamster in Yorba Linda, California. A freshman at the California Institute of Technology, she is studying electronics with an emphasis on robotics. Her hobbies include art, music and writing. "Two of the philosophies I live by," Kjerstin says, "are 'To thine own self be true' and 'This too shall pass away (with the help of our Lord).' These, combined with prayer, helped me get through some rough times as an exchange student in Germany last year. But then I was placed with a marvelous Christian host family who gave me a new appreciation of the wonder of God's love."

For ERIC FELLMAN of Pawling, New York, the wonder of God's love is most often revealed in the love shared between members of his immediate family, which includes his wife Joy and their three sons, Jason, 19, Nathan, 17, and Jonathan, 15. An awful lot of that love was gathered in one place last Christmas when sixteen Fellman brothers, sisters, cousins and grandparents stayed under one roof at a Utah skiing resort. "My best memory is of gathering together around the fireplace in the evening and telling family stories," Eric recalls. "I like to think of God loving us in just such an intimate, personal way."

It's been a year of greater church involvement for ROBIN WHITE GOODE and family. Robin, who lives in South Monsey, New York, is teaching a junior church class and she sang in the choir's Easter cantata. Daughter Jamie, who turns 5 this year and starts kindergarten in the fall, learned the whole cantata by heart (well, almost) just by attending rehearsals. Son David turns 7, and likes to bike, climb and do gymnastics. And husband Harley has become quite involved in their church's Promise Keepers group. "I've discovered the wonder of God's love in a new way through the powerful Easter story," Robin writes. "Although we have all 'forsaken him and fled' (Matthew 26:56), He still went to the Cross for us, because we so desperately needed a Savior."

The past year was a busy one for Pam and ARTHUR GORDON of Savannah, Georgia. In the spring, Pam went back to her native England to visit her sister Diana and their beloved Nannie, while Arthur stayed home and pretended—well, actually *did* work on a book designed to be a sequel to *A Touch of Wonder*, written more than two decades ago. Later on,

Van Varner, a fellow *Daily Guideposts* contributor and Guideposts editorial director, came down to Savannah from New York for a few days to lend a much-needed editorial hand. The finished product, called *Return to Wonder*, was offered to Guideposts readers about six months later. "I don't really like to write," Arthur says a bit glumly. "What I like is *having* written. Much more fun!"

For OSCAR GREENE of West Medford, Massachusetts, the year's happenings seemed to interrelate. He returned to the Coffee and Books monthly discussion at the public library, following a seven-year absence. He also led the session after the librarian fell ill. The Lenten season was busy, bringing a Wednesday evening soup supper and discussion period, followed on Sunday evenings by a lecture series at a local church. On Monday evenings, Oscar helps to conduct a Bible study. On his 77th birthday, Oscar motored to East Derry, New Hampshire, to serve as a sponsor for a young man's confirmation. Oscar and Ruby also quietly acknowledged their 54th wedding anniversary.

"The other night at dinner," says EDWARD GRINNAN of New York City, "I was complaining to my wife about how badly this year had gone. A couple we'd long been close to went through a divorce, a very good friend and mentor suffered a stroke, and one of our nephews was in a frightening car accident. The more I talked, the lower I felt. I pushed my unfinished plate aside, but Julee would have none of it. She pointed out that the divorcing couple has managed to stay on speaking terms, our friend who had the stroke is recovering nicely, and our nephew, despite totaling his new car, walked away with barely a scratch. I guess the wonder of God's love is that it is often as much or even more in evidence when things go wrong as when they go right."

"The past year has been good for my wife Carol and me," says RICK HAMLIN of New York City. "She has been busy selling her book about manners for children, *Elbows Off the Table* (she writes as Carol Wallace), and I was quite pleased to sell my book *Finding God on the A Train* (HarperCollins San

Francisco), which will be published this spring. My familiarity with the A train has increased, as I have recently been taking both boys, William, 9, and Timothy, 6, to school via the subway, the boys hovering as I read to them every morning (I hope the other passengers don't mind). When I feel disconnected and far from the wonder of God's love, I find letter writing the perfect help, preferably to someone I haven't spoken to in years, someone to whom I owe much gratitude. Then I can rediscover the wonder of God's love in those who have shown it to me."

MADGE HARRAH of Albuquerque, New Mexico, continues to write novels for young adult readers. Her latest novel, *My Brother, My Enemy* (Simon & Schuster), which will be published this spring, tells about a boy who gets involved in the Bacon Rebellion in Jamestown, Virginia, in 1676. Madge also speaks at writers' conferences and goes into schools to work with young authors. During the summer, she and her husband Larry spend time with their five grandchildren at their cabin in the Colorado mountains. She says, "As I look toward those majestic mountain peaks and brilliant blue skies, I think of Psalm 121, and I do indeed feel the wonder of God's nearness and love."

MARILYN MORGAN HELLEBERG of Kearney, Nebraska, is grateful for the combination of prayer and surgery that brought her freedom from back pain. Add cataract surgery in September and you've got an *almost* new senior citizen! A trip to visit a college friend in California, workshops in Denver and a family reunion created a busy but fulfilling year. Marilyn is enjoying having all her children and grandchildren in Kearney, now that Paul and his wife Cheryl and their six children have moved back from Colorado. Karen, in addition to being a mom and holding down a full-time job, has gone back to finish her college degree, giving Grandma the joy of baby-sitting three times a week. John, now a senior at the University of Nebraska, is looking toward graduate school . . . and teaching Mom how to use the Internet! "Becoming a Hospice volunteer has greatly enriched my life this year. The parting gifts that terminally ill people and their families give each other have made me deeply aware of God's stunning presence within human love."

"Earlier in the year, my responsibilities were getting me down," writes PHYLLIS HOBE of East Greenville, Pennsylvania. "Running my home, doing my work, caring for my father, looking after the animals in our family and becoming involved in community projects left me almost no time for myself. Finally, I took a break and visited a dear friend for a few days. But I needed four people to replace me! While the break did wonders for me, the most important part of it was coming home and realizing that I made a difference in the lives of those I love. Perhaps God was telling me that responsibilities can be blessings—if we learn to balance them with our own needs."

"The wonder of God's love struck me with new force this year when all four children were home for my milestone birthday in September," says MARJORIE HOLMES of Manassas, Virginia. "Never mind which one—I don't feel it, look it or act it! And they came again to be with me at Christmas: Mark from South Carolina, Mallory from California, Melanie only an hour away, and her sister Mickie who lives next door. And I marveled at the rich harvest of my life. So many books and articles that have affected other lives, and most recently a film contract for my trilogy of novels about the life of Jesus, starting with *Two from Galilee*. But the greatest wonder of God's love is to have these four grown children, every one of them healthy, attractive and successful, but above all, honest, decent and kind, and raising their own children by the same principles we taught them."

"This has been a year of firsts in many ways," says MARY RUTH HOWES of Jersey City, New Jersey. "For the first time in my life I have done a good part of my work at home. Though I don't miss the hassle of commuting on bumpy streets and jerky trains, I have missed the contact with colleagues. And for the first time I have retired! But I still have a number of freelance projects to occupy my time and keep me busy. One involved another first—completely retyping an edited manuscript, *Bringing Hidden Things to Light* by Lydia Istomina (Abingdon Press), to disk. Editing it was a most rewarding experience. In all the changes in my world, I am aware of God's loving goodness to me throughout my life. In the words of the hymn writer, 'I will praise Him for all that is past, And trust Him for all that's to come.' "

"I moved out on my own to an apartment near downtown Nashville, Tennessee." says BROCK KIDD. "It's exciting to have my own place in the world, but is has certainly taken some getting used to. Especially around dinnertime! Boiled spaghetti with canned sauce is a weak substitute for Mom's homemade spinach lasagna. As a rookie investment adviser, most of my time is spent 'paying my dues' in the office. I love what I'm doing, but it's very easy to become frustrated. Recently, when I experienced an unusually tough day, I got a phone call from my sister Keri. 'We're going to Seattle this weekend!' she said excitedly. My grandparents had been offered a free trip to Seattle, and they gave the trip to Keri and me. That Saturday, as we watched the sun setting over the Puget Sound, a cool breeze blew off the ocean. The smell of the sea was soothing, and I felt completely recharged. It didn't take much to realize God's love was with me and, as always, full of wonder."

PAM KIDD of Brentwood, Tennessee, writes, "Taped to the windowsill above my desk is a reminder, 'the wonder of God's love.' On the sill above that are photos of my children Brock and Keri, one of Harrison Dunn (my father who died in 1983), one of my husband David and me standing together with big grins on our faces, another of Bebe and Herb (my mother and stepfather). In each picture I can't help but see a perfect reflection of the intricate and far-reaching love of our heavenly Father! David and I celebrated our 25th anniversary this year. And what a grand celebration! We went to Puerto Rico, and it was a beautiful time. On the island of Vieques, the proprietor of the guest house where we stayed expressed great surprise when she learned we were celebrating our 25th. 'Everyone here thought you were on your honeymoon,' she said."

"Our year has been a steady stream of graduations," writes CAROL KNAPP of Big Lake, Alaska. "Kelly was class valedictorian and is loving King College in Tennessee. Brenda is about to graduate and will attend Cedarville College in Ohio. Tamara is graduating from Whitworth College in Washington, where she participated in a study trip to Israel. (She brought me the Sea of Galilee in a baby food jar.) Phil rededicated his life to Christ, and the Bible is now his favorite reading material. My husband Terry is making good use of the new shop he built. My interest in international understanding has led to work with AYUSA, an exchange student organization. I placed teens from Brazil, Japan, Mexico, Germany and the Netherlands in Big Lake! For me, the wonder of God's love is best described in something I wrote many years ago: 'He saved me from myself so I might rejoice in the very self that, apart from Him, I would have destroyed.' I both need and desire God's love in my life."

"This year my husband Lynn and I started living in an empty nest when Kendall, our youngest, went off to Westmont College in Santa Barbara, California," writes CAROL KUYKENDALL of Boulder, Colorado. "But I have found a serendipity in this new season of life: When the children are gone, you rediscover each other." To celebrate this milestone, Carol and Lynn spent two weeks in England this fall with another couple (see her August 18 devotional). "My favorite part was the Cotswolds, where we crisscrossed the tranquil countryside on footpaths. We spent days wandering through the green pastures filled with grazing sheep, which reminded me of the Bible's many descriptions of Jesus, the Good Shepherd, and His sheep. I'm surprised by the joy of this new season of life, especially after dreading it. Yet isn't that just like God? Out of the wonders of His love, He surprises us, He provides, He meets our needs."

"When I look at the past five years, I feel as if God has placed me in a wondrous protective bubble and transported me through life in His hands," says PATRICIA LORENZ of Oak Creek, Wisconsin. "In the fall of '92, with three children in college and a 12-year-old at home, I took a giant leap of faith and quit my job to stay home and write full-time. In '94, Jeanne and Julia graduated from college. In '95, Michael graduated and married Amy, his high school sweetheart. In '96, their baby Hannah was born. In the spring of '96, my first book, *Stuff That Matters for Single Parents*, was released by Servant Publications. And this year? Andrew, my youngest, is an active 17-year-old high school junior on the swim team, in the band and a member of the Civil Air Patrol. My second book, *A Hug a Day for Single Parents*, will be out sometime this year. So life around here is full of laughter, love and the wonder of God's protection for this single parent."

This past year held a career change for ROBERTA MESSNER of Sweet Run, West Virginia. She now works as the Patient Education Coordinator for the Veterans Affairs Medical Center in nearby Huntington. While Roberta suffers from almost continual pain from tumor growth, the wonder of God's love gives her comfort and strength when she needs it most. One day, as she browsed in a dusty antiques shop trying to distract herself from a particularly severe bout of pain, she noticed a picture of a weary woman bent over a plow in a field. Above it, someone had scrawled, "Can you find the angel in this picture?" "I turned that old picture every which way, squinting for any evidence of a divine presence. I found no angel, yet in my search I was filled with an overwhelming sense of peace and purpose. Despite the drain of constant pain, God is *always* working in my life. Even, and perhaps most especially, when I can't see Him."

KEITH MILLER and his wife Andrea, both writers, speakers and consultants, live in Austin, Texas. Keith's three married daughters and their husbands live in different parts of Texas, and each has two children—a boy and a girl—between the ages of 3 and 13. "I am delighted to be participating in *Daily Guideposts, 1997*," Keith writes. "I have always depended on my own devotional life to keep me within spitting distance of sanity, and the only devotional book I ever wrote, *Habitation of Dragons*, came out in Swedish and Spanish just as I was writing my devotionals for this year's *Daily Guideposts*. And I am writing a related book on the secret life of the soul. These days I sense a strong breeze of the Spirit bringing new life to God's people across America. And about that I am excited and grateful."

LINDA NEUKRUG and her husband Paul are still living in Walnut Creek, California. "I have seen many of our neighbors come and go in the decade or so that we've lived here, and I like the idea of being an 'old-timer' in my neighborhood." Linda continues to substitute teach, and has learned many lessons about dealing with children respectfully by reading a book called *Teacher and Child* by Haim Ginott. For a school project, Linda began tutoring English to a Russian woman in her seventies who has lived in the United States for three years. The project was supposed to last only seven weeks, but it was such an exciting experience for Linda that she is still doing it. As a result, she has discovered how many other people do volunteer work, from tutoring to working at soup kitchens to staffing suicide lines. "The wonder of God's love is shown every day by those who reach out with their very human hands and voices to share God's love in a tangible way."

"The reality of God's love was especially important to me this year," says RUTH STAFFORD PEALE of Pawling, New York. "A silly fall led to the replacement of my right hip and an extended period of recovery. The whole experience reminded me of how God's presence always seems much more powerful in the midst of difficulties. Often it seemed as if He were giving me a helping hand through the drudgery of exercises and rehabilitation. And the glow of His care stayed with me as I resumed the many activities with my family, travel and work at Guideposts."

"This past year our nest emptied after twenty-eight years," writes ROBERTA ROGERS of White Plains, Maryland, a newcomer to *Daily Guideposts*. "Tom moved to Denver and John to the Shenandoah Valley, each to begin a new career. Peter graduated from Daniel Webster College in Nashua,

New Hampshire, moved to Cape Cod and hopes for military flight school this year. David graduated from high school and entered Western Maryland College in Westminster. My husband Bill and I celebrated our 30th wedding anniversary. In recent months the wonder of God's Father-love has come to me in new ways. Slowly, I am seeing a lifelong habit of fearfulness dissolve into the freedom of life lived with the reality of His constant presence and peace. We have seen awesome examples of God's provision this year. He even found a wonderful way to get Bill sailing again."

DANIEL SCHANTZ is in his 29th year of teaching at Central Christian College in Moberly, Missouri. The college is growing, and this means increased hours and workload for him, but also an increase of joy. His wife Sharon lost her father, Edsil Dale, after long years of illness. A floodtide of cards and calls came as a tribute to his thirty-five years of teaching in Christian colleges. Granddaughter Hannah turned 4, and daughter Teresa announced her expectation of a child in the fall of '96. Dan and Sharon witnessed the protective love of God when a tornado rumbled down their street on the Fourth of July. The damage to their home was modest, and Dan enjoyed seeing the power of God up close. "I love storms, but I never thought I would be fortunate enough to live through a tornado. I thank God for His mercy in sparing lives and property, and in bringing the community of Moberly closer together in mutual sympathy."

"This year my husband Ernie and I rediscovered something," says SUSAN SCHEFFLEIN of Putnam Valley, New York. "Simple things nurture us most. I especially remember walking along the Potomac during a spring visit with my brother. How we laughed as the cherry trees showered a benediction of blossoms on our heads. How we snapped loads of pictures, hoping to capture that evanescent beauty. Family and friends, freshly baked bread, sunrises, snow on purple crocus, bird song, thoughtful acts of kindness—weaving back and forth across the loom of our lives, these simple, daily miracles reveal the wonder of God's love.

Through them God speaks to us everywhere. We have only to be still and listen."

"My husband Don and I experienced the wonder of God's love anew with the births of two more grandsons, Mark Schwab and Caleb Clancy," says PENNEY SCHWAB of Copeland, Kansas. "They join Ryan and David Schwab, who are 7 and 4. First smiles and first words speak powerfully of a wonderful, caring God." Penny's job as executive director of United Methodist Mexican-American Ministries testifies to the wonder of God's love, too. As people find healing and wholeness, they reach out to others—an expanding circle of love.

High points of the year for ELIZABETH (Tib) SHERRILL of Chappaqua, New York, were a trip to Israel with daughter Liz, and exploring Mexico's Copper Canyon with husband John. The year's most difficult time came with the news that the Sherrills' 45-year-old son John Scott, a country music writer in Nashville and father of three, had suffered a stroke. "The wonder of God's love was made daily visible to us," Tib says, "in the faces of the staff at Centennial Hospital, in prayers, letters and phone calls from friends and strangers, and in the devotion of his wife Raena, as John Scott recovers."

SHARI SMYTH of South Salem, New York, says, "I spent a lot of time this past year looking through my kitchen window to the pristine fields, the barn, the pond, feeling the powerful grip of nostalgia glue me to our house of eighteen years. We'd decided to sell. 'It's time,' my husband Whitney said gently. 'The children are grown. We don't need five bedrooms. We *do* need the money.' The first hour it was on the market it sold. This house, *our home.* 'I can't leave,' I cried. The phone rang. 'Hi, Mom,' said my 20-year-old son Jon, calling from Maine where he lives. 'We've sold the house,' I blubbered. Long pause. Then, 'That's good, Mom. Find a wonderful new place and don't look back,' he said softly. I'd gotten sound advice from the two men in my life. *It's time,* and *don't look back.* The love of my family and God will lead me to a wonderful new place."

"In the autumn, the trees outside my window were shedding their leaves, a natural fact, but one that left me sad," writes VAN VARNER of New York City. "It always has that effect, as though the world was dying. Then came my stroke, unexpected, sudden. I was in the hospital for a month, and for several months thereafter friends moved into my apartment to make sure that I was all right. I was all right basically, though my speech was slightly garbled, my right side weak. I set off for therapy three times a week and made a stab at conducting life as before, but gradually I came to see that it wasn't the same. And the winter outside was ferocious. The therapy sessions continued, the winter was the worst in memory, and as I began to doubt, spring finally arrived. What a wondrous thing. As life crept back into the trees, I saw myself as I was. It will take time. The world didn't die, and I am here to bask in it."

"This has been a good year for my family," says SCOTT WALKER of Waco, Texas. "This summer my wife Beth, my 13-year-old son Drew and I traveled for five weeks in the British Isles with eighty students from Baylor University. We studied the lives and writings of the British Romantic poets. It was a wonderful experience of watching my son 'come of age' and make many discoveries that he will remember all of his life. While we were gone, my younger children, Luke, 10, and Jodi, 7, spent five days at Disney World with their Aunt Ree. They also spent two weeks with each of their grandmothers. It was a wonderful summer for them. As I complete my third year at First Baptist Church of Waco, I am increasingly aware of the joy of being a pastor. The members of our church are a delight to lead, and they enrich my life in many ways."

DOLPHUS WEARY of Mendenhall, Mississippi, continues to spend about sixty percent of his time traveling on behalf of Mendenhall Ministries. He speaks across the country, encouraging the Body of Christ to love each other across racial, social and economic barriers, and challenging Christians to build bridges of reconciliation. Dolphus has also been busy working on his doctoral dissertation. This year, he and Rosie will celebrate twenty-seven years of marriage. Danita is in her first year of medical school; Reggie, 20, is a junior at Tougaloo College, majoring in business and accounting; 9-year-old Ryan is a fourth-grader at Genesis One Christian School. "When I see what God is doing in and through my family and my extended Mendenhall Ministries family, I'm amazed at how wonderful His love and grace is."

 BRIGITTE WEEKS of Port Washington, New York, writes, "For me and my whole family this has been a year of continual change. I've started living nearer the office during the week—more time to think and less to commute. I've been privileged to watch my son find a job he likes (but he moved in with me—quite an adjustment for us both), as well as see my daughter move toward graduation. The Guideposts Book Department has moved to a higher floor, where I can see the Empire State Building from my window! Professionally, the most exciting moments have come from contact with our *Daily Guideposts* readers via the World Wide Web. A truly wondrous sign of God's love is to be able to share this very special book with new people in new places, as well as meet old friends in a new world. Join us there if you get the chance: http://www.guideposts.org."

 MARION BOND WEST of Watkinsville, Georgia, writes, "My 87-year-old mother, whom my children and grandchildren affectionately call 'Gogee,' came to be with us this year when it was discovered that her cancer from eleven years ago had returned. My sons Jon and Jeremy encourage her to do what they call the 'Gogee Shuffle.' She laughs with them and does a sort of dainty, feminine version of Walter Brennan's joyful walk in *The Real McCoys*. God's wondrous love enables us all to laugh even in difficulty. Red Dog, a stray who found her way into our hearts and lives just before Mother arrived, often accompanies her outside and likes to sit right by Mother on the porch. Mother planned never to get involved with a dog again after all the strays I brought home as a child. But she and Red Dog have become an unlikely twosome."

BRENDA WILBEE of Bellingham, Washington, is an artist and author—and, as of this year, a mother-in-law! "My daughter Heather was married to Dallas Williams," she says. "But thank goodness I'm still just 'Mum' to Phil, a freshman at Seattle Pacific University, and Blake, a high school junior and rising drama star. This past year was one of God's wondrous love undisguised. Sometimes we don't see God's guiding hand until after the storm. This year, however, I clearly saw Him amidst the struggle. My health insurance was *not* canceled. I received a year's 'forgiveness' on my home mortgage. I was offered a much-needed job. The most wondrous of all? The many phone calls and letters from *Daily Guideposts* readers—reminding me over and over that God's love reaches us best through His people. Thank you!"

ISABEL WOLSELEY of Syracuse, New York, says, "Long ago I purchased a 'wordless book' and jotted a year on each page. I began with 1922, the date of my birth. Below the year, I write from five to twenty notes, the number depending upon the really significant events of that year's happenings: births, deaths, weddings, graduations, vacations. But also others, like 'mumps' on the 1948 page. 'Kelly (son) and family moved to Idaho.' 'Lisa (granddaughter) won regional swim meet.' Recently, I scanned all these pages and was impressed how the Lord's watchful care seemed to have hovered over me and every member of my family in every single listing. The other day I came across Psalm 112:7: 'He shall not be afraid of evil tidings: his heart is fixed, trusting in the Lord.' It's the Scripture verse I'm claiming this year to steady me when I read distressing headlines that could affect me and my family."

Authors, Titles and Subjects Index

Abraham (biblical character), 246, 250
Acceptance
  of difficulties, 249–50
  of forgiveness, 280–81
  of gifts with love, 85–86
  of God's will, 145
  of imperfections, 68–69
  of our limits, 131
"Achievement badges," 208
Achievements
  of everyday people, 125–26
Acknowledgment
  of others' feelings, 51
Advent
  1st Sunday in, 320–21
  2nd Sunday in, 330–31
  3rd Sunday in, 336–37
  4th Sunday in, 342–43
Advent meditation, 340–41
Advent wreath, 320
  see also *Candles of Christmas* series
Adversity
  strength out of, 249–50
Affirmations
  of faith, 254–55
  of marriage relationship, 304–05
Age
  see Birthdays; Old age
AIDS, 316–17
Alikeness, 142
All Saints' Day, 296
Alopecia areata, 245–46
Alzheimer's disease, 58–59, 80–81

Amateur radio operator, 232, 302–03, 333
Anderson Concerto for Typewriter and Ding Bell, 224–25
Anderson, LeRoy (composer), 224–25
Angels
  guardian, 127
  ministering, 350
  protection of, 69–70
  who hold us, 230–31
Angus, Fay
  selections by, 14–15, 78–79, 106, 128–29, 166–67, 193, 224–25, 239–40, 273–74, 344–45
Answered-prayer book, 65
Answers to prayer
  already present, 70–71
  continual, 65
  people as, 136–37
  slow epiphanies as, 12
  trusting in, 251–52
  unexpected, 183, 249–50
Anxiety
  dispelled by promise of God's presence, 128–29
  dissipated by stillness, 318–19
  surrendered to God, 279–80
  turning to God in times of, 187–88
  unnecessary burden of, 335–36
  walking with Christ through our, 52–53
Appendicitis, 188–89

Appreciation
  for home, 284
  of beauty, 99–100
  of one's spouse, 304–05
  of variety, 25
  showing, 154–55
Approval
  nurturing with, 124–25
Ascension Day, 129
Attaway, Andrew
  selections by, 29, 147–48,
    221–22, 290, 327–28
Attaway, Julia
  selections by, 24–25, 52–53,
    76–77, 112, 137, 156, 209,
    269–70, 297–98, 346–47
Attention
  in prayer, 175–76
Audition, 52
Augustine, St.
  on love, 106
Authenticity, 310

Babcock, Maltbie D.
  Words of Wonder by, 191
Babies
  in the night, 297–98
  joy of, 289–90
Back trouble, 82–90
Bad days, 45
Bakery cookies, 73
Ball playing, 183–84
Balloon animals, 131
Bananas, 46–47
Barber, Karen
  selections by, 109, 126–27,
    230–31, 285–86,
    348–49
Baseball cap, 141–42
Bauer, Fred
  selections by, 27–28, 53–54,

71–72, 116–17, 132–33,
    153–54, 201, 238–39, 307,
    350–51
Beauty
  appreciating, 99–100
  being true to oneself as, 17
  hidden, 223–24
  of snow, 336–37
Bed and breakfast, 101–02
Bedtime prayer, 55–56, 195–96,
    210–11
Beginnings
  comfort from, 291–92
Behavior
  infectiousness of, 41–42
Being oneself, 214–15
Being there for our loved ones,
    112, 193, 343–44
Being true to oneself, 17
Belief
  see Faith
Best, the
  bringing out, 36–37
  of the old, 168–69
  wanting, for family and friends,
    16
Bible, the
  see also Psalms
  angels in, 69–70
  children's need for, 314
  in our faith journey, 48–49
  living, 306–07
  living by, 10
  nourishing faith through, 49
  parables in, 290
  reminders of God's love in,
    247–48
  restoration through, 350–51
  sharing with others, 181
  strength found in, 310–11
  study of, 49, 116–17

Bible college, 308–09
Big C, the (Jesus Christ), 74–75
Biking, 110–11, 190–91, 258
Birds, 109–10, 186, 288–89, 334
Birthday present, 31
Birthdays
    attitude toward, 115
    celebrating, 222–23
Blackberry stains, 200
Blessers, 253
Blessing(s)
    see also God's blessings; God's gifts
    "little," 273
    of home, 284
    sharing our, 106–07, 344–45
    stars as a, 273–74
    suffering in silence as a, 110–11
Blindness, 199–200
Bluebells, 132–33
Bolger, Loretta (*Love Is. . .* series), 268
Books
    preciousness of, 192
"Borrowings," 56
Boundaries
    vs. freedom, 181–82
Boxes, 283–84
Bridgeman, Gina
    selections by, 16, 52, 97–98, 216, 242, 328–29
Brown, Mary
    selections by, 43–44, 77–78, 103–04, 193–94, 256–57, 276–77, 310–11, 347–48
Bumper stickers, 299–300
Bunyan, John (preacher and allegorist), 201
Butterflies, 225

Calm is contagious, 300
Camp ministry, 187
Campaign sign chairman, 298–99
Candlelight service, 345
Candles of Christmas series, 320–21, 330–31, 336–37, 342–43, 345, 346
Car accident, 145–46
Cardboard church boxes, 45–46
Caregivers
    encouraging, 50–51
Cares
    releasing, 103–04
Carillon, 186
Carney, Mary Lou
    Letters to Wally series by, 37–43
    selections by, 142–43, 161–62, 258, 291–92, 305–06, 339
Cars, 81, 114–15, 145–46, 163, 170–71
Carter, Jimmy (President), 49–50
Catholic Herald anniversary party, 102
Cats, 81, 107–08, 258–59, 312–13
Catskill Mountain camp, 208
Celebration
    of change, 222–23
    of togetherness, 115
Cemetery visit, 69
Chafin, Kenneth
    selections by, 22, 99–100, 175, 201–02, 240–41, 278, 332–33
Challenge
    of differences, 16
    of growth, 232, 282

Change
  being open to, 168–69
  celebrating, 222–23
  children and, 38–39, 57–58
  made by something small, 233
Chauffeur's rating, 133–34
Child rearing
  learning, 124–25
Children
  and setting a good example,
    41–42
  apologizing to, 13
  being there for, 343–44
  change and, 38–39, 57–58
  encouragers and, 36–37
  exuberance of, 79–80
  faith of, 48–49
  fear and, 40–41
  grief and, 42–43, 75–76, 77–78
  hope and, 296
  kindness and, 39–40
  need of, for God's word, 314
  our impact on, 30–31
  our spirits renewed through,
    173–74
  our trust in God's care of, 153
  problems of, 38–43
  self-esteem and, 301–02
  sensitivity to, 24–25
  teaching, about prayer, 55–56
  true giving and, 31
  witness of, 72
  wonder and, 173–74
Chinos, 200
Choices
  letting others make, 16
Choir practice, 70–71
Christ
  see Jesus Christ
Christlikeness
  how to demonstrate, 38–39

Christmas
  carols, 337–38
  gift, 341–42
  lights, 326, 331–32
  pageants, 343–44
  promise, 9
  songs, 340–41
  star, 338–39
  symbols, 337–38
  wonder of, 345, 346
Christmas Day, 346
Christmas Eve, 345
Church
  bulletins, 194–95
  without walls, 181
Churchgoing
  diverse congregations and,
    137–38
  fellowship in, 22–23
  growth of faith in, 90–91
  looking for God's guidance in,
    43–44
"Church lady" mother, 78–79
Circular barn, 203
Circular rainbow, 67–68
Closer to the Cross series, 82–90
College
  graduation, 155
  success at, 272
Collins, Mark
  selections by, 81, 125–26, 163,
    226, 261
Comfort
  see also God's comfort
  from beginnings, 291–92
  from hymns, 296–97
  gift of, 57
  of a mother's love, 118–19
  of a storm, 20–21, 210–11
  of God's love, 109–10,
    185–86

of good works, 348–49
safe places of, 248–49
"Commission verse," 10
Communication
    bridging gaps in, 29–30
    clear, 154–55
    prayer as, 257
    sharpening one's skills in, 232
Community United Methodist
    Church (Jackson Heights,
    New York), 138
Compassion
    see also God's compassion
    for our fellow man, 209–10
    in everyday life, 242
    in times of illness, 50–51
    showing genuine, 51
Computers, 118–19, 240–41,
    263–64
Confession, 55–56, 280–81
Consistency
    significance of, 284–85
Constancy
    see also God's constancy
    of love, 142–43
Contentment, 316
Conveyer belt, 103
Cookie drawer, 100–01
Corn snakes, 153–54
Corona, 67–68
Courage
    in the face of fear, 288–89
    of the handicapped, 17–18,
        143–44
    through God's presence,
        278–79
    to ask for help, 127
    to begin, 291–92
    to correct errors, 299–300
    to face down self-doubt, 272
    to help others, 326–27

to kneel with someone in front
    of Jesus, 76–77
to let go of fear, 84
to live the truth, 80–81
to speak out, 73
to take risks, 52
Cowper, William
    Words of Wonder by, 108
Crisis
    turning to God in times of,
        187–88
Criticism
    keeping, in perspective, 278
Cross, the
    praying at the foot of, 76–77
Crying
    comfort from, 248–49
    gift of, 75–76
Cupola, 173–74
Curly hair, 17
Cushman, Ralph Spaulding
    Words of Wonder by, 221

Davis, Hollie
    selections by, 69, 188–89,
        220–21, 283–84
Deadwood, 166–67
Death
    as a journey to God, 185–86
    children and, 42–43, 75–76, 77
    inevitability of, 104–05
Dentist, 28
Details
    becoming too absorbed in, 261
    making a difference with,
        101–02
Determination
    to succeed, 327–28
Devotional reading
    refreshing our spirits through,
        217–18

Differences
  appreciating, 25
  celebrating, 142–43
  challenge of, 16
  patience with, 332–33
  reaching out across, 303
Dignity
  maintaining, 130
Dirt biking, 258
Disaster drill, 333
Discipleship, 116–17
Dishwashing, 283
Diversity
  sensitivity to, 187
  thankfulness for, 137–38,
    261–62
Doctors, 136–37, 165
Doctor's office visit, 72
Dogs, 30–31, 181–82, 185–86,
  196, 211–12, 231–32, 277,
  312–13, 319–20, 330
Doing unto others, 41–42
Do-it-if-it-kills-me types, 128
Doll playing, 311–12
Dolphins, 213–14
Donkeys, 350–51
DoraMae (Love Is. . . series), 208
Doubt
  of oneself, 272
  prayer in times of, 88–89
Dreams that live on, 19–20
Drive to succeed, 157–58
Driving danger, 81
Dry heat, 217–18
Duke, Drue
  selections by, 56, 109–110,
    169–70, 212–13, 314,
    338–39
Duty
  placed before self-indulgence,
    182–83

Earth Day, 113
Easter Sunday, 89–90
Easton, Kjerstin
  selections by, 44–45, 90–91,
    154–55, 291, 349
Eating alone, 97
Eight-hundred-year-old church,
  291
E-mail, 118–19, 263–64
  see also Computers
Emergency, 274–75
Emerson, Ralph Waldo (writer)
  on human desire, 157–58
Empty nest
  celebrating, 222–23
  God's comfort in a, 20–21
Empty-pocket days, 66–67
Encouragement
  in the face of fear, 245–46
  through compassion, 51
  through fellowship, 43–44
  value of, 26–27
Encouragers
  of caregivers, 50–51
  through words, 10, 14–15,
    197–98, 307
  who bring out the best in us,
    36–37
  who take the time to boost
    others, 71–72
Endurance
  in the face of hardship, 218–19
England trip, 222–23
Envy
  vs. love, 36
Epiphany, 12
Epistles
  as treasures, 139–40
Everyday life
  achievements of, 125–26
  compassion in, 242

Example(s)
  of calmness, 300
  of Christlikeness, 38–39
  of prayer, 188–89
  of the homeless, 258–59,
      306–07
  of true giving, 31
  power of good, 268–69
  setting a good, 41–42
  teaching by, 228–29, 268–69
  that inspire, 19–20
  those who help others as,
      136–37
  to follow in old age, 54–55
Excellence
  significance of, 284–85
Exchange Sundays, 22–23
Exercise
  see also Walking
  stretching before, 211–12
Expectation
  faith as, 38
  hope as, 320–21
  living up to, 201–02
Exuberance of children, 79–80

Faith
  affirmations of, 254–55
  being rich in, 316
  childlike, 72
  during times of trouble, 201
  expectation as, 38
  experienced firsthand, 53–54
  good works and, 306–07,
      348–49
  growth in, 52–53, 90–91, 349
  in God's providence, 103–04,
      329
  in God's wisdom, 153–54
  in heaven, 129
  in one's friends, 202–03

  in the future, 39–40, 199–200
  in the unseen, 69–70
  in times of illness, 74–75
  instilling, in the young,
      219–20
  matured by problems, 196
  nourishing, through Bible
      study, 49
  of children, 48–49
  perseverance and, 268
  possibility balanced by,
      245–46
  prayer for, 88–89
  reaching for, 166–67
  serenity of, 238
  sharing one's, 111–12
Faithfulness
  in serving others, 238–39
Families
  as wonders, 216
  difficult times in the life of,
      285–86
  guidance from, 70–71
  patterns in, 192
  renewing bonds of love in,
      167–68
  reunions in, 183
  seeing clearly, 300–01
  thankfulness for, 319–20
Family Day of Prayer, 287, 315
Farming, 255–56
Father(s)
  and asking children's
      forgiveness, 13
  good example of, 228–29
  learning from, 163
  loving care of, 227–28
Father's Day, 163
Fear
  calmness in the face of, 300
  cast out by love, 269–70

Fear, cont.
children and, 40–41
dispelled by promise of God's
   presence, 128–29
encouragement in the face of,
   245–46
facing one's, 254–55, 288–89
freedom from, 80–81
letting go of, 84
love in answer to, 64
of the unknown, 244–45
prayer in times of, 40–41,
   97–98
procrastination due to,
   198–99
surrendered to God, 279–80
Feelings
acknowledging those of others,
   51
Fellman, Eric
Candles of Christmas series by,
   320–21, 330–31, 336–37,
   342–43, 345, 346
selections by, 45, 115–16,
   183–84, 217–18, 284–85
Fellowship
see also Guideposts Prayer
   Fellowship
amid diversity, 137–38
encouragement and new friends
   found through, 43–44
in churchgoing, 22–23
in retirement, 118
of Christians, 100–01, 181
of Christ's light, 345
through prayer, 315
Fence sitting, 214–15
"Festival of Trees," 340
Fiftieth birthday, 115
Fiftieth wedding anniversary,
   167–68

Filtering out the unimportant, 339
Fires, 223–24
Fishers of men, 349
Fishing, 330–31
Fiske, George Walter
Words of Wonder by, 279
Flag Day, 162
Flashlight, 160
Flat roof, 251–52
Flint, Annie Johnson
Words of Wonder by, 48
Floating, 208
Flowers, 132–33, 216–17
Focusing
on Jesus in prayer, 148
on the big picture, 339
Forgiveness
see also God's forgiveness
acceptance of, 280–81
asking for, 13
freeing nature of, 103
of oneself, 11–12
of those who have wronged us,
   8–9
our need for, 200
reaching for, 166–67
Fortieth wedding anniversary,
   239–40
Fourth of July, 182–83
"Fragile forest" (sign), 160–61
Francis of Assisi, St.
Words of Wonder by, 251
Free coffee, 350
"Free money," 145–146
Freedom
cost of, 147–48, 303–04
from embarrassment and fear,
   80–81
through forgiveness, 103
to be true to others and
   oneself, 214–15

to tell the truth, 152
vs. loving boundaries, 181–82
Friends
as guardian angels, 127
as "pillars" of support, 347–48
as the best medicine, 15–16
"being there" for, 193
carrying on good works of, 57
enemies as potential, 308–09
faith in, 202–03
fellowship among, 100–01
found in church, 43–44
gratitude for, 25–26
guidance from, 70–71
prayer for, 145, 146–47
steadfastness and, 309–10
thankfulness for new, 302–03
welcoming, 117
Friendship
as a gift, 118
cultivating, 115–16, 142
silence in, 193
taking a chance on, 241
with one's children's friends,
163–64
Future, the
dependent on today, 192, 287
faith in, 39–40, 199–200
focusing on, 11–12
looking toward with hope, 45
trust in God for, 334

Generosity, 242
Gentleness
practicing, 38–39
Gethsemane, 87
Gift(s)
see also God's gifts
accepted with love, 85–86
being there as a, 112
comfort as a, 57

from the heart, 31, 143–44
giving our, freely, 180
good example as a, 228–29
gratitude as a, 105
helping others to give, 216–17
hope as a, 21, 165, 296, 346
in unexpected places, 341–42
Jesus Christ as a, 338–39,
346–47
joy as a, 346
laughter as a, 229–30
life as a, 174, 209
love as a, 221–22, 273–74,
346
mercy as a, 195–96
of love, 226
of what we've been given, 316
of wisdom and friendship,
118
of wisdom in others' words,
184–85
oneself as a, 137
patience as a, 238
peace as a, 346
remembrance as a, 273–74
small, 224–25
tears as a, 75–76
thankfulness for, 317–18
that return to you, 156–57
time as a, 281–82
using our, to serve others,
333
Girl Scout, 142
Giving
children and, 31
freely to others, 45–46, 66–67
from the heart, 31, 143–44
help to the needy, 270–71
more than we're asked, 56
rewards of, 156–57
truly, 137

Giving, cont.
  unselfishly, 276–77
  vs. receiving, 326
  what we've been given, 180,
    316
  when we have, 344–45
GLAD, 305–06
"Gladys Jar," 344–45
"God moments," 213–14
God's blessing(s)
  enormity of, 143–44
God's care
  every day, 239–40
  for our loved ones, 153
  in life's storms, 20–21
  like a loving father's, 227–28
God's comfort
  in times of grief, 42–43
  in times of illness, 291–92
God's compassion
  our hope in, 45
God's constancy
  in the midst of change, 57–58,
    142–43
God's creation
  perfection of, 203
  renewal through, 191–92
  wonder of, 13–14, 99–100,
    213–14, 284–85
God's forgiveness
  for righteousness, 113
God's gifts
  being open to, 27–28
  passing them along, 212–13
  using, 118–19
  wonder of, 13–14
God's grace
  answers to our prayers
    through, 12
  working through our
    infirmities, 209

God's guidance
  for our direction in life, 144
  for our presidents, 49–50
  seeking and listening to, 43–44
God's hands
  our problems leashed to, 196
  putting ourselves in, through
    prayer, 215–16
  support from, 26–27
God's healing
  trusting in, 83
  waiting for, 82
God's help
  ever-present, 187–88
  expectation of, 38
  experienced firsthand, 53–54
  when communication is
    broken, 29–30
  when we are afraid, 40–41
God's kindness
  sharing, 50–51
God's kingdom
  building, 282
  in the fellowship of church,
    22–23
God's light
  available through us, 345, 346
  reflected in us, 310
God's love
  as our dearest "possession," 36
  comfort of, 185–86
  eternal nature of, 77–78
  even when we're unlovable,
    230–31
  forgiveness and, 8–9
  healing through, 47
  inclusivity of, 109–10
  loss turned into gain through,
    64
  protection of, 203
  purification through, 223–24

reminders of, 247–48
selflessness of, 342–43
trust in, 208
unconditional nature of,
    68–69
warming ourselves in, 23–24
which casts out fear, 97–98
wonder of, 89–90, 106, 350
God's mercy
    as our saving grace, 280–81
God's peace
    opening ourselves to, 193–94
    resting in, 218–19
God's plan
    acceptance of, 145
    confidence in, 158–59
    listening to, 312–13
    re-visioning, 288
    the unexpected as part of,
        138–39
    trusting, 313
God's power
    relying on, 220–21
    strengthing nature of, 260
God's presence
    constancy of, 9, 67–68
    courage from, 278–79
    felt in friends, 347–48
    healing, 82
    joy in, 330
    light of, in us, 345
    opening oneself to, 211–12
    peace found in, 330–31
    promise of, 128–29
    renewing ourselves in, 193–94
    strength found in, 84–85
    through prayer, 315
    trust in, 210–11
God's promises
    hope as belief in, 250–51
    of love, 247–48

of peace, 9
to provide, 276–77
trust in, 31–32
God's providence
    faith in, 103–04, 329
    for our children, 245–46
    for our every need, 66, 334
    inevitability of, 106–07
    of answers to prayers, 249–50
    of hope, 250–51
    of knowns in the unknown,
        244–45
    of safe places of comfort,
        248–49
    of tools along the way, 246–47
    over the seen and unseen in
        life, 277
    relying on, 126–27
    through His promises of love,
        247–48
    trust in, 22, 254–55, 276–77
God's spirit
    alive at Christmas, 337–38
God's strength
    in our times of need, 19
God's sufficiency
    to meet all our needs, 244–45
God's triune nature, 77–78
God's vision
    trust in, 183
God's voice
    all around us, 186
    listening for, 165–66, 174
    listening to, 312–13
    recognizing, 271–72
God's will
    acceptance of, 145
    discovering, 165–66
    readiness to do, 99
    thankfulness and, 189–90
    trust in, 86–87, 215–16

God's wisdom
faith in, 153–54
God's wonders
our families as, 216
praising, 161–62
God's word
see also Bible, the
faith through, 90–91
God's work
humility and, 96
Golf, 116–17, 175, 204
Good Friday, 87–88
Good Samaritan, 290
Good works
carrying on friends', 57
imitating those of others,
268–69
necessity of, 306–07
sharing our blessings in,
106–07
thankfulness for, 242
that inspire faith, 348–49
without fanfare, 229
Goode, Robin White
selections by, 31, 101–02, 142,
326–27
Gordon, Arthur
selections by, 13–14, 104–05,
159, 182–83, 261–62, 288,
310
Gossip (book), 259
Grace
see also God's grace
through prayer, 331–32
transformation through,
304–05
Grand Canyon, 191–92
Grandchildren
giving thanks for, 160
Grandmother Smith, 22
Grandparents

and learning from
grandchildren, 79–80
cherishing one's, 242–43
Grandparents Day, 242–43
Grateful Heart, The (book), 253
Gratitude
see also Thankfulness
for friends and life, 25–26
for our relationships, 134–35
for receiving, 344–45, 346–47
gift of, 105
Great catches, 183–84
Great Depression, the, 23–24, 56
Greene, Oscar
selections by, 23–24, 73, 118,
134–35, 157–8, 184–85,
214–15, 241, 272, 313
Grief
children and, 42–43, 75–76,
77–78
help for, 148
over loss, 30–31
teenagers and, 69
Grinnan, Edward
selections by, 15–16, 58–59,
75–76, 106–07, 145, 174,
187–88, 211–12, 254,
280–81, 316–17, 337–38
Growing older
see Birthdays; Old age
Growth
by learning from our mistakes,
159
challenge of, 232, 282
in friendship, 115–16
necessity of, 240–41
through new experiences,
172–73
through opportunities
problems present, 183–84
Guardian angels, 127

Guidance
see also God's guidance
from family and friends,
70–71
Guideposts Family Day of
Prayer, 287, 315
Guideposts Prayer Fellowship,
287, 315
Guilt
getting rid of, 166–67

Habit of prayer, 124
Haircuts, 66, 163–64, 252–53
Hale, Clara (Love Is. . . series),
296
Ham radio operator, 232,
302–03, 333
Hamlin, Rick
selections by, 19–20, 45–46,
70–71, 100–01, 140–41,
156–57, 181, 210–11,
271–72, 300–01
Handicapped, the
courage of, 17–18, 143–44
Happiness
in "little things," 273
with one's work, 238–39
"Happy Birthday to You" (song),
162
Harrah, Madge
selections by, 11–12, 98,
175–76, 183, 278–79,
299–300
Hat, 155
Hawaii vacation, 213–14
Haying, 255–56
"He Giveth More" (poem), 48
Healing
see also God's healing
by keeping silent, 252–53
through hugs, 190–91

through love, 47
through words, 14–15
Heaven
our hope of, 129, 212, 296–97
previewed by "God moments,"
213–14
Heirloom wristwatch, 168–69
Helleberg, Marilyn Morgan
Closer to the Cross series by,
82–90
selections by, 10–11, 46–47,
113–14, 128, 160, 192, 212,
253, 296–97, 331–32
Help
see also God's help
asking for, 98–99
dropping everything to
provide, 300–01
for neighbors, 274–75
for the needy, 212–13, 270–71,
290
from friends, 127
fulfillment in, 175
in times of grief, 148
simply being there as, 112
through prayer, 326–27
Hidden pain, 69
Hinckley, Jack (Love Is. . .
series), 96
Hoarding, 126–27
Hobe, Phyllis
selections by, 26–27, 80–81,
130, 262–63, 312–13
Hockenberry, John (TV
reporter), 17–18
Holbrook, Clyda (Love Is. . .
series), 64
Hollywood Bowl concert, 224–25
Holmes, Marjorie
selections by, 48–49, 223–24,
350

Holy Thursday, 86–87
Home
    thankfulness for, 284
Homeless, the
    example of, 258–59, 306–07
    help for, 156–57
Honesty
    in prayer, 55–56
    value of, 145–46
Honor
    sacred nature of, 182–83
Hope
    as a gift, 21
    as acting on the expectation of
        success, 320–21
    as belief in God's promises,
        250–51
    children and, 296
    Christ as fulfillment of, 346
    every day, 239–40
    focusing on, 197–98
    in times of illness, 165
    instilling in the young,
        219–20
    looking to tomorrow with, 45
    of heaven, 129, 212, 296–97
    signs of, 291
    warming oneself in, 23–24
Horseback riding, 154–55
Hospitality, 117
Hot-air balloons, 185–86
Housecleaning, 99
"How to Worship" (bookmark),
    43–44
Howes, Mary Ruth
    selections by, 54–55, 170,
        254–55, 308–09, 334
Hugs
    curing through, 190–91
Human touch
    power of, 135–36

Humility
    God's work and, 96
    our need for, 200
    putting others at ease through,
        102
    vs. pride, 141–42
    vs. righteousness, 113
Humor
    anxiety and, 335–36
    importance of, 102, 128
    in times of illness, 107–08,
        218–19
Husband and wife
    see also Marriage
    arguments between, 252–53
    celebrating differences
        between, 142–43
    cherishing each other, 226
    renewal between, 304–05
    tolerating differences between,
        25
Hymns
    American folk, 75
    comfort from, 296–97
    praising God through, 170

I CAN'T, 288–89
"I Have a Dream" (speech),
    19–20
"I Will Not Hurry" (poem), 221
Ice skating, 26–27
Ice storm, 20–21
"If only I had," 166–67
"I'll Be Home for Christmas"
    (song), 340
Illness
    children and, 24–25
    compassion in times of,
        50–51
    faith in times of, 74–75
    friends in times of, 15–16

gift of time in, 281–82
God's comfort in times of, 291–92
hope in times of, 165
human touch and, 135–36
humor in times of, 107–08, 218–19
prayer in times of, 19, 194–95
Immortality of our souls, 104–05
Imperfections
acceptance of, 68–69
Inexperience, 159
Inferiority complex, 109
Injustice
witnessing against, with serenity, 275–76
Insomnia
and listening for God's voice, 174
filled with prayer, 297–98
Intercessory prayer, 140–41, 146–47
Investments, 334–35
Irritability
countered by love, 106
Isaac (biblical character), 246

Jaguar owner, 170–71
Jehovah Jireh: God Will Provide series, 243–51
Jesus Christ
anointed with ointment, 85–86
as a gift, 338–39, 346–47
death of, 87–88
entry into Jerusalem of, 83
heals a possessed child, 329
in the garden of Gethsemane, 87
money changers in the temple and, 84
on the Sea of Galilee, 249–50

questioned by scribes and priests, 84–85
Jigsaw puzzle, 291–92
Johnson, Spencer (author), 328–29
Joseph, the carpenter, 320–21
Joy
as deep sense of well-being, 336–37
Christ as fulfillment of, 346
glimmers of, 225
in God's presence, 330
in the present, 328–29
of babies, 289–90
of giving, 326
of the simple, 283
openness to, in daily life, 27–28
prayer in times of, 44–45
"Just-in-case reserve," 212–13

Kidd, Brock
selections by, 22–23, 66–67, 143–44, 171–72, 197–98, 242–43, 298–99, 318–19
Kidd, Pam
selections by, 21, 65, 117, 136–37, 160–61, 185–86, 229, 251–52, 316, 341–42
Kindness
see also God's kindness
acts of, 66
as a step toward a better world, 39–40
good done through, 124–25
impact of our, 30–31
rewards of, 132–33
sharing, 50–51
showing, 258–59
Kitchen ceiling light, 49
Kitchen renovation, 261

Kitchen warmth, 23–24
Knapp, Carol
  selections by, 10, 68–69,
    145–46, 204, 260, 277,
    304–05, 340–41
Knitting, 138–39, 289–90
Kuykendall, Carol
  Jehovah Jireh: God Will Provide
    series by, 243–51
  selections by, 51, 110–11,
    189–90, 222–23, 288–89

Labor Day, 238
Lansing, B. (artist), 117
Laughter
  as medicine, 107–08
  at oneself, 102, 128
  found in work, 255–56
  gift of, 229–30
Laundromat, 159
Learning
  about childrearing, 124–25
  enrichment through, 240–41
  honor, 182–83
  how to be sick, 15–16
  through listening, 256–57
Legacy
  of love, 287
  of the stars, 273–74
Lent, 45–46
LeSourd, Len (*Love Is. . .* series),
  238
"Let Us Break Bread Together"
  (hymn), 37
Letters, 228–29
Letters to Wally series, 37–43
Life
  as a gift, 174, 209
  transitory nature of, 226,
    231–32
"Life's verse," 10

Limits
  accepting our, 131
"Linda" pen pals, 57
Line-jumper, 38–39
Lion and lamb, 230–31
Listening
  for God's voice, 165–66, 186
  learning through, 256–57
  to each other, 70–71
  to God's plan, 312–13
  to the counsel of others,
    184–85
Litter, 113
Little things
  importance of, 101–02, 343–44
  that make one happy, 273
Living expectantly, 316–17
Login name, 140–41
Looking
  at life differently, 233
  forward, 316–17
Lord's Prayer, 297–98
Lorenz, Patricia
  selections by, 49, 102, 127,
    163–64, 186, 213–14,
    252–53, 273, 301–02
LOVE, 331–32
Love
  see also God's love
  accepting gifts with, 85–86
  acts of, 258–59
  as a gift, 273–74
  as antidote to fear, 269–70
  as selfless concern for others,
    342–43
  between generations, 221–22
  Christ as fulfillment of, 346
  constancy of, 142–43
  despite wrongdoing, 152
  for one's fellow man, 162,
    201–02

forgiveness and, 8–9
gifts of, 226
good works out of, 348–39
in response to violence, 64
in unexpected places, 341–42
in unloving circumstances,
    106
increasing one's capacity for,
    113–14
legacy of, 287
rebirth of families and,
    167–68
taking to task out of, 169–70
treating others with, 154–55
trust and, 208
vs. envy, 36
Love Is . . . series, 8–9, 36, 64,
    96, 124–25, 152, 180, 208,
    238, 268, 296, 326
"Love wave," 64
"Lovingkindness Prayer,"
    113–14
Loyalty
    dogs and, 231–32

Magic carpet, 48–49
Mailtime, 139–40
Making a difference, 187
Malaprops, 209–10
Mam-ma, 242–43
Maple tree, 284–85
March, Frederick (actor), 275
Marriage
    see also Husband and wife
    affirmation of, 304–05
    gratitude for one's, 134–35
    names in, 29
    out-of-sorts days in, 29–30
    sharing in, 232
    taking a chance on, 52–53
Martin Luther King Day, 19–20

Marvel
    of each day, 281–82
Mary, the mother of Jesus,
    330–31
Maundy Thursday, 86–87
Medicine
    friends as the best, 15–16
    of laughter, 107–08
    stillness as, 318–19
Meditation
    enhanced by song themes,
        340–41
Memorial Day, 147–48
Memorial service, 260
Memories
    forgetting bad, 11–12
    of good deeds, 162
    of our servicemen, 340
Memory lapses, 58–59, 80–81
Mercy
    see also God's mercy
    as a gift, 195–96
    for those in need, 290
Messner, Roberta
    selections by, 28, 47, 66,
        131–32, 181–82, 216–17,
        263–64, 303–04, 340
Miller, Keith
    selections by, 55–56, 103,
        165–66, 195–96, 215–16
Mime-magician, 161–62
Miracles
    everyday, 78–79
    small, 138–39
Misadventures
    enjoying one's, 204
Mistakes
    asking forgiveness for one's, 13
    enjoying one's, 204
    forgiving oneself for, 11–12
    growth through our, 159

MOPS (Mothers of Preschoolers)
     International, 51
Morality
  placed before expediency,
     182–83
Motel robbery, 64
Mother Sherrill (*Love Is. . .*
     series), 124–25
Motherhood
  growing into, 124–25
Mother(s)
  comforting love of, 118–19
  impact of, 78–79
  many roles of, 131–32
  perseverance and, 268
Mother's Day, 131–32
Mountain biking, 190–91
Mourning dove, 109–10
Moving Violations (book), 17–18
MRI, 135–36
My Larger Education (book),
     214–15

Names
  in marriage, 29
  people behind the, 254
National Day of Prayer, 124
Nature
  wonders of, 191–92
Need(s)
  for forgiveness, 200
  responding to others',
     269–70
  sensitivity to others', 24–25
Needy
  help for the, 212–13, 290
Neighbor(s)
  helping one's, 274–75
  how to be a good, 262–63
  love for one's, 201–02
  serving one's, 333

Neukrug, Linda
  selections by, 12, 57, 73–74,
     99, 131, 172–73, 202–03,
     227, 259–60, 300
New, the
  adding the best of, 168–69
New experiences, 172–73
New generations, 173–74
New Testament
  see Bible, the
Newman, John Henry
  Words of Wonder by, 18
Nonexperts, 114–15
North Star, 148
Nursing, 137

Old, the
  keeping the best of, 168–69
Old age
  support systems in, 130
  volunteer work in, 282
  young spirits in, 54–55
One Foot in Heaven (movie),
     275
Openness
  necessity of, 214–15
  to new experiences, 172–73
  to nonexperts, 114–15
Opportunities
  problems viewed as, 183–84
  seizing, 198–99, 241, 283–84
  to be "just-in-case"
     representatives, 212–13
  to give, 156–57
  to love, 64
  to practice gentleness and
     patience, 38–39
  to share one's faith, 111–12
Ordinary, the
  seeking God in, 253
Out-of-sorts days, 29–30

Parenting
  our contract in, 155
  responsibility of, 343–44
Password invalid, 140–41
Past, the
  putting it behind us, 45
Patience
  as a gift, 238
  dogs and, 231–32
  in prayer, 313
  in problem-solving, 153–54
  practicing, 38–39
  with those with whom we
    differ, 332–33
Peace
  see also God's peace
  achieved through prayer,
    188–89
  Christ as fulfillment of, 346
  found in God's presence, 330–31
  in surrendering our worries to
    God, 279–80
  opening ourselves to, 193–94
  promise of, 9
Peale, Norman Vincent, 71–72
Peale, Ruth Stafford
  selections by, 31–32, 124,
    167–68, 275–76, 343–44
Pen pals, 57
Perfection
  illusion of, 109
  limits to, 131
  of God's creation, 203
Perseid meteor shower, 216
Perseverance
  mothers and, 268
  significance of, 284–85
Personal ministries, 111–12
Perspective
  changing one's, 233
  keeping things in, 278

Piggyback ride, 229–30
Pilgrim's Progress, The (book),
  201
Pillars
  Christians as, 209–10
  of support, 347–48
Pizza, 66–67
Plane flight, 129
Playtime while working, 229–30
Please Don't Feel Blue (book),
  21
Poor, the
  working with, 170–71
Positive thinking, 254–55
Possessions
  eye of the beholder and, 36
Possibilities
  balanced with faith, 245–46
  looking for, 283–84
Practice
  bolstering oneself with, 327–28
  in understanding, 133–34
  of prayer, 58–59
  of simplicity, 258
  prayer and, 227
Prairie crocus cups, 239–40
Praise
  every day, 239–40
  for God's wonders, 161–62
  in old age, 54–55
  prayer and, 44–45
  singing songs of, 170
Prayer
  answers to, 12, 65, 70–71,
    136–37, 183, 249–50,
    251–52
  as communication, 257
  as reunion with God, 58–59
  at the foot of the Cross,
    76–77
  attentive, 175–76

Prayer, cont.
  bedtime, 55–56, 195–96,
    210–11
  constant, 189–90
  daily tasks turned into, 194–95
  enhanced by song themes,
    340–41
  examples of, 188–89
  Family Day of, 287, 315
  focusing on Jesus in, 148
  for acceptance, 145
  for faith, 88–89
  for friends, 145, 146–47
  for our enemies, 286–87
  for our presidents, 49–50
  for the needs of others, 97,
    326–27
  for those we dislike, 156
  giving thanks in, 195–96, 316
  habit of, 124
  honesty in, 55–56
  in times of fear, 40–41, 97–98
  in times of illness, 19, 194–95
  in times of insomnia, 297–98
  in times of thanks, praise and
    joy, 44–45
  intercessory, 140–41, 146–47
  knitting a, 289–90
  learning God's will through,
    215–16
  Lord's Prayer, 297–98
  "Lovingkindness Prayer,"
    113–14
  meditation before, 211–12
  National Day of, 124
  patience in, 313
  practice and, 227
  refreshing our spirits through,
    217–18
  requests for, on E-mail,
    263–64
  restoration through, 350–51
  shining Christ's light through,
    160
  slow epiphanies through, 12
  staying on the right path
    through, 160–61
  strength found in, 19, 310–11
  teaching children about, 55–56
  that God's will be done, 86–87
  that knits us to friends, 309–10
  to increase one's capacity for
    love, 113–14
  touch of joy through, 225
  transforming nature of, 331–32
Prayer Fellowship, 287, 315
Precious Present, The (book),
  328–29
Present, the
  cherishing, 328–29
  living in, 198–99
Presidents' Day, 49–50
Pride
  as an obstacle, 96
  pitfalls of, 171–72
  quarrels out of, 141–42
Priorities
  setting our, 27–28
Privacy
  vs. being a good neighbor,
    262–63
Problems
  leashed to God's hand, 196
  of children, 38–43
  turning to God in the face of,
    187–88
  viewed as opportunities,
    183–84
Problem-solving, 114–15
Procrastination
  due to fear, 198–99
  how to short-circuit, 73–74

Psalms
    see also Bible, the
    Psalm 71, 54–55

Quoist, Michel
    Words of Wonder by, 308

Radnor Lake Natural Area,
    160–61
Rag bag, 158–59
Rainbow, 67–68
Rainy Monday (painting), 117
Read, Miss (author), 259
Reading
    as relaxation, 259–60
    last chapters first, 22
Reality
    focusing on the good side of,
        288
Reaping what one sows, 334–35
Rebukes
    out of love, 169–70
Receiving
    gratitude for, 344–45, 346–47
Reconcilers, 303
Record holders, 242
Regrets
    getting rid of, 166–67
Rehearsal dinner, 127
Relationships
    see also Families; Father(s);
        Grandparents; Husband
        and wife; Marriage;
        Mother(s)
    nurturing, 175–76
    sensitivity in, 196–97
Remembrance
    as a gift, 273–74
Renewal
    of families, 167–68
    of mind, 304–05

our, in God's presence,
    193–94
through children, 173–74
through God's creation,
    191–92
Resentment
    freeing oneself from, 103,
        166–67, 180
Rest stops, 350
Resurrection, the, 89–90
    heralds of, 291
Retirement
    fellowship in, 118
    volunteer work in, 282
    work in, 175
Reunion(s)
    in families, 183
    missed, 68–69
    prayer as a, with God, 58–59
Re-visioning, 288
Revolutionary War sites, 53–54
Righteousness
    vs. humility, 113
Riley, Dick (Love Is. . . series),
    180
Ripken, Cal, Jr. (baseball player),
    242
Risk-taking, 52, 71–72
Rixey, Eppa (baseball player),
    125–26
Rockwell, Norman (illustrator),
    288
Rogers, Roberta
    selections by, 29–30, 146–47,
        199–200, 232, 279–80,
        302–03, 333
Role model(s)
    being a, despite fear, 300
    who show the way, 136–37
Roller coaster, 198–99
Root beer floats, 301–02

Roses, 216–17
Rossetti, Christina
  Words of Wonder by, 338
Round barns, 203
Running etiquette, 257

Sacrifice
  as price of freedom, 303–04
Safety
  stretching past one's, 52
  trusting in God for our, 87–88,
    199–200
  trusting in God for our
    children's, 31–32, 153
Saint, Dora (author), 259
Salt and pepper shakers, 230–31
Samaritan, 290
Sargent, Taft (coal miner), 316
Savage, Minot J.
  Words of Wonder by, 134
"Sawing wood," 197–98
Schantz, Daniel
  selections by, 25, 79–80,
    114–15, 133–34, 168–69,
    196–97, 255–56, 274–75,
    317–18, 334–35
Schefflein, Susan
  selections by, 17, 113, 148,
    173–74, 203, 287, 309–10
School pictures, 248–49
Schwab, Penney
  selections by, 36–37, 137–38,
    191–92, 209–10, 268–69
Scotland, 270–71
Seasonal affective disorder
  (SAD), 305–06
Secondhand furniture store,
  334–35
Security
  in God, 311–12
Seeing the essence of people, 254

Segregation, 303
Self-acceptance, 68–69
Self-consciousness, 17
Self-doubt, 272
Self-esteem
  building, in children, 301–02
Self-forgiveness, 11–12
Selflessness of love, 342–43
Self-pity, 110–11
Sense of humor
  importance of, 102, 128
  in times of illness, 107–08,
    218–19
Sensitivity
  in relationships, 196–97
  to diversity, 187
  to others' feelings, 51
  to others' needs, 24–25
Serenity
  witnessing against injustice
    with, 275–76
Series Seven licensing exam,
  171–72
Serving others
  as a reason for being, 136–37
  better, 157–58
  instead of oneself, 298–99
  life centered on, 212
  preparation for, 116–17
  quietly, 242
  sensitivity in, 24–25
  wherever we are, 238–39
  wholeheartedly, 28
  with whatever we have, 46–47,
    333
Shade trees, 287
"Shall We Gather at the River"
  (hymn), 297
Sharing
  fellowship with others, 181
  friendship, 118

in marriage, 232
kindness, 50–51
laughter, 229–30
more than we're asked, 56
one's faith, 111–12
our blessings, 106–07,
    344–45
our thankfulness, 105
our troubles, 52–53
rewards of, 132–33
the Bible, 314
Shepherds, the, 336–37
Sherrill, Elizabeth
    Love Is . . . series by, 8–9, 36,
    64, 96, 124–25, 152, 180,
    208, 238, 268, 296, 326
Shooting for the moon, 71–72
Silence
    friendship in, 193
    healing through, 252–53
Simon, Neil (playwright)
    on risk-taking, 52
Simple, the
    joys of, 283
Simplicity
    practice of, 258
Singles ads, 304–05
Sister Irene (Love Is. . . series),
    36
Sixteenth-birthday dinner, 44–45
Sleeplessness
    and listening for God's voice,
    174
    filled with prayer, 297–98
Sleepy Hollow Golf Course,
    204
Sleet, 20–21
Slough of Despond, 201
"Slow epiphanies," 12
Smiles
    importance of, 30–31

Smyth, Shari
    selections by, 20–21, 115,
    141–42, 162, 196, 225,
    286–87, 311–12, 330
Snakes, 153–54
Snow, 277, 336–37
"Song of the Creatures" (poem),
    251
Song themes for Christmas,
    340–41
Sorrow
    for wrongdoing, 280–81
Sowing and reaping, 334–35
Speaking out
    about what is right, 73
    in witness, 72
Spending time with the Lord,
    271–72
Spiders, 300
Spilled orange juice, 130
Spontaneity
    in prayer, 175–76
Sprained shoulder, 110–11
Spring beauty, 99–100
St. Moritz, 31–32
St. Patrick's Day, 77–78
Standley, Roy (Love Is. . . series),
    152
Star of Christmas, 338–39
Stars
    legacy of, 273–74
Statues
    Christians as, 209–10
Steadfastness
    to prayer, 309–10
Steindl-Rast, David (author), 253
Stewardship, 143–44, 276–77
Stillness
    as medicine, 318–19
Storm
    comfort of a, 20–21, 210–11

Storm, cont.
second chances in a, 46–47
warnings, 196–97
Strangers
welcoming, 117, 302–03
Strength
see also God's strength
found in prayer and the Bible,
19, 310–11
from good works, 348–49
in times of trouble, 249–50,
260
our faith in God as, 329
Stretching
value of, 211–12
Stroke, 25–26
Stubbornness, 316–17
Stumbling, 220–21
Success
drive to, 157–58
felt in risk-taking, 52
Summer camp, 208
Sunday school teacher, 169–70
Sunglasses, 233
Sunshine
being, for others, 305–06
Super Bowl Sunday, 28
Support
of friends, 347–48
systems for, in old age, 130
Surfing, 220–21
Surplus yarn, 138–39
Surrendering ourselves to God,
246–47
Swimming
instruction, 208, 227
pool, 128–29
Swindle, Harold and Ruby (Love
Is. . . series), 326
Switzerland, 31–32, 167
Symbols of Christmas, 337–38

Sympathy
practice of, 133–34

Taking charge, 246–47
Tape recorder, 327–28
Tasks
turned into prayers, 194–95
Tax time, 106–07
Teachers
veterans as, 303–04
who inspire trust, 98–99
Teaching
and making friends, 308–09
by good example, 228–29,
268–69
children about prayer, 55–56
evaluation, 278
honor, 182–83
with love, 154–55
Tears
gift of, 75–76
Teasdale, Sara
Words of Wonder by, 164
Technical writer, 313
Technology
mastering new, 240–41
thankfulness for, 263–64
Teenagers
grief and, 69
self-consciousness of, 17
their security in God, 311–12
trusting in their safety,
31–32
valuing, 285–86
ten Boom, Corrie (Love Is. . .
series), 8–9
Tenaciousness, 316–17
Tennis, 116–17
Thankfulness
see also Gratitude
for answered prayers, 65

for diversity, 137–38, 261–62
for families, 319–20
for gift of mercy, 195–96
for God's gifts, 212–13
for home, 284
for love between generations, 221–22
for new friends, 302–03
for new technology, 263–64
for second chances, 46–47
for seeing family members clearly, 300–01
for today, 328–29
for wonder, 160
in all circumstances, 189–90
necessity of expressing, 317–18
prayer in times of, 44–45
sharing our, 105
to bless as, 253
Thanksgiving Day, 317–18
"Thanksgiving" (poem), 308
Throwaways
beauty in, 223–24
Thrush Green (books), 259–60
Time
gift of, 281–82
management of, 103–04
Timeout, 350–51
Tithing, 276–77
"Titus Woman," 51
Today
as determinant of the future, 192, 287
enjoying, 328–29
Togetherness, 77–78, 115
Tomorrow
dependent on today's actions, 192, 287
focusing on, 11–12
looking toward with hope, 45

making it better, 39–40
trust in God for, 334
Tornado, 274–75
Touch
power of, 135–36
Tournament of Roses Parade, 349
"Tract Lady," 111–12
Transfiguration
our hope of, 212
Treasure
moments of wonder as, 10–11
the Epistles as, 139–40
Trento, Italy, 193–94
Trust
absolute, 208
how to establish, 98–99
Trust in God
about the fruits of our labor, 187
for answers to our prayers, 251–52
for everything, 306–07
for faith, 349
for healing, 83
for our children's safety, 31–32, 153
for our direction in life, 22, 144
for our purpose in life, 158–59
for our safety, 87–88, 199–200
for the future, 334
for true freedom, 181–82
in His faithfulness, 202–03
in His plan, 313
in His presence, 210–11
in His vision, 183
in His will, 86–87, 215–16
in the face of problems, 153–54

Trust in God, cont.
  in times of illness, 245–46
  instead of oneself, 171–72
  to find path to success, 272
Truth
  freeing nature of, 80–81,
    152
Truthfulness
  necessity of, 214–15
TV remote controls, 25

Understanding
  practice of, 133–34
Unexpected, the
  Christmas and, 341–42
  God's plan and, 138–39
Uniqueness
  of each of us, 47, 241
United Nations Day, 286–87
Unknown, the
  fear of, 244–45
Using time wisely, 350–51
U-turns, 299–300

Valentine's Day, 47
Value
  of encouragement, 26–27
  of honesty, 145–46
  of stretching, 211–12
  of throwaways, 223–24
Variety
  appreciating, 25
Varner, Van
  selections by, 25–26, 69–70,
    97, 200, 231–32, 284
Verisimilitude, 310
Veterans
  as teachers, 303–04
  in the holiday season, 340
Veterans Day, 303–04
Vietnam, 329

Virginia bluebells, 132–33
Volcano replica, 278–79

Wakefulness
  and listening for God's voice,
    174
  filled with prayer, 297–98
Walker, Scott
  selections by, 30–31, 49–50,
    105, 129, 153, 190–91,
    228–29, 258–59, 283,
    306–07
Walking, 160–61, 193, 229
Walking sticks, 222–23
Wally the Turtle, 37–43
Washington, Booker T. (writer),
    214–15
Washington, George (General),
    53–54
Weary, Dolphus
  selections by, 13, 72, 111–12,
    144, 170–71, 187, 219–20,
    282, 303
Weddings, 142–43, 226
Weekend getaway, 189–90
Weeks, Brigitte
  selections by, 17–18, 118–19,
    138–39, 155, 233, 289–90,
    315
Welcoming
  friends, 117
  strangers, 302–03
Well-being
  joy as a sense of, 336–37
West, Marion Bond
  selections by, 19, 50–51,
    74–75, 107–08, 135–36,
    165, 194–95, 218–19, 257,
    281–82, 319–20
Wheelchair journeys, 17–18
Widowers, 134–35

Wig, 66

Wilbee, Brenda
  selections by, 57–58, 198–99,
    229–30, 270–71, 335–36

Wisdom
  heard in the words of others,
    184–85
  to correct errors, 299–300

Witnessing
  against injustice, 275–76
  by children, 72

Wolseley, Isabel
  selections by, 9, 67–68,
    139–40, 158–59, 227–28,
    329

Women's Board of Domestic
    Missions of the Reformed
    Church in America, 275–76

"Wonder" (poem), 279

Wonder(s)
  see also God's wonders
  children and, 173–74
  of Christmas, 345, 346
  of God's creation, 13–14,
    99–100, 213–14, 284–85
  of God's love, 89–90, 106, 350
  of Nature, 191–92
  thankfulness for, 160
  treasuring moments of, 10–11

Woodcarver, 238–39

"Word encourager," 10

Words
  see also God's word
  healing through, 14–15
  significance of, 30–31

Words of Wonder series, 18, 48,
    75, 108, 134, 164, 191, 221,
    251, 279, 308, 338

Work
  see also God's work
  being happy with one's, 238–29
  fun found in, 255–56
  interrupted by playtime,
    229–30
  with young people, 219–20

World Communion Sunday,
    271–72

World War II, 147–48, 162, 340

Worries
  surrendered to God, 279–80

Worry piles, 103–04

Wright, Orville and Wilbur
    (aviation pioneers), 339

Wrongdoing
  love despite, 152
  sorrow for, 280–81

"You can do it!," 307

Youth
  working with, 219–20